MW00323032

MYSTERIOUS TRAVELERS

Great Comics Artists Series
M. Thomas Inge, General Editor

MYSTERIOUS TRAVELERS

STEVE DITKO

AND THE SEARCH FOR A
NEW LIBERAL IDENTITY

ZACK KRUSE

University Press of Mississippi / Jackson

The University Press of Mississippi is the scholarly publishing agency of
the Mississippi Institutions of Higher Learning: Alcorn State University,
Delta State University, Jackson State University, Mississippi State University,
Mississippi University for Women, Mississippi Valley State University,
University of Mississippi, and University of Southern Mississippi.

www.upress.state.ms.us

The University Press of Mississippi is a member
of the Association of University Presses.

First printing 2021
∞

Library of Congress Cataloging-in-Publication Data

Names: Kruse, Zack, author.
Title: Mysterious travelers : Steve Ditko and the search for a new liberal
identity / Zack Kruse.
Other titles: Great comics artists.
Description: Jackson : University Press of Mississippi, 2021. | Series:
Great comics artists series | Includes bibliographical references and index.
Identifiers: LCCN 2020042479 (print) | LCCN 2020042480 (ebook) | ISBN
9781496830531 (hardback) | ISBN 9781496830548 (trade paperback) | ISBN
9781496830555 (epub) | ISBN 9781496830562 (epub) | ISBN 9781496830579
(pdf) | ISBN 9781496830586 (pdf)
Subjects: LCSH: Ditko, Steve—Criticism and interpretation. | Comic books,
strips, etc. —History and criticism. | Comic books, strips, etc. —United States.
Classification: LCC PN6727.D58 Z748 2021 (print) | LCC PN6727.D58 (ebook)
| DDC 741.5/973—dc23
LC record available at https://lccn.loc.gov/2020042479
LC ebook record available at https://lccn.loc.gov/2020042480

British Library Cataloging-in-Publication Data available

CONTENTS

PREFACE

"All Lives Change"

Somewhere in the back of my head—the part that's farther back, where you can only faintly make out your inner voice—I heard myself say that what I was about to do was wrong. I heard myself asking whether or not I was crossing a line, and whether this was a transgression I would forgive someone else for committing. There are almost no publicly available photographs of him, aside from a 1959 photo shoot in his studio. He hasn't sat for anything that resembles an interview since 1968. Comics industry friends and acquaintances who have met him in the past warned me against visiting his office—typically based on rumors they'd heard from second-, third-, and *n*th-hand sources. But how could I resist? No other artist, in any medium, has had as profound an effect on me as he has. From the time I first encountered his work, as a fifth-grader in the early 1990s, I was immediately struck by how different it was from everything else I was reading. I recognized the characters, of course, but his versions of them seemed alien and beautifully grotesque in a way that insisted their heroism was defined *without* reference to Charles Atlas. His comics moved me then; later in my life, they challenged and confounded me; today they are objects of scrutiny, from which I think we gain greater insight into the evolution of the American political consciousness. So I did it. I knocked on Steve Ditko's door. He answered.

In July 2017, I was on a research trip to New York City, preparing for this very project, and I decided to stop by Ditko's office. I had his address from letters we had previously exchanged, and I had worked with Ditko and Robin Snyder (Ditko's longtime editor and copublisher) during my career in comics retail in the early 2000s. Considering Ditko's advanced age—eighty-nine at the time—I knew that if I was going to do this, I had better do it right then. I wandered up to his office building midmorning, and when I got off the elevator, there was his door, with a large silver sign embossed with "S. Ditko" in bold, black letters, exactly like all the other signs in the narrow hallway. I knocked and stepped back, not knowing what to expect. Through the door, I heard the sound of a telephone ringing. It was an older phone, with the familiar hammer-and-bell ring of my childhood. The phone continued to ring; no one answered it. No one answered the door, either. Feeling deflated, thinking I had missed him or that he simply refused to come to the door, I turned back to the elevator. Then I heard the loud clack of the deadbolt. I spun around, and there he was. Whoever or whatever he expected, I can't say, but my presence did not please him. And he was right to feel that way. I was imposing on him and on his time.

"Whadda ya want?" he said, rolling his eyes so deeply and with such great irritation that his whole body rolled with them. The man owed me absolutely nothing, and I didn't presume he would remember me from the letters we had exchanged or the books I had sold for him and Snyder. I introduced myself, told him that discovering his work had changed my life, that it had set me on a course that had brought me to this very moment.

"Yeah, well, all lives change," he said.

"That's true," I answered, "but your work, specifically, changed mine."

From there he seemed to acquiesce to my presence and indulged me with a brief, pleasant exchange. I got to say thank you, and we never once talked about the past. I'll cherish that experience forever. Steve Ditko was kind to me; he was generous with his time; he listened; he responded; he offered me more than he had any reason to. I hope that he would have seen the value of this exploration of his work and might even have been inclined to engage in the debate.

I think he would.

MYSTERIOUS TRAVELERS

1

"FROM OUT OF THE DEPTHS!"

Rethinking the Work of Steve Ditko

"Hidden in a cave, beneath the burning sands of New Mexico," a green behe-moth in tattered purple pants smashes his fists against blue-gray rock. His head throbbing, he agonizes as the change overcomes his body. He screams out, "I want to remain as I am! I want to be . . . *the Hulk*!" But no matter how much the Hulk tries to suppress the cooler-headed Bruce Banner, he can't keep Banner inside. The transformation completes, and Banner forces the Hulk back inside his mind. A short while later, Banner ponders whether he is capable of perceiving reality any longer, and which of his two identities is his true self. Bruce Banner, or the Hulk? (fig. 1.1). Later in the story, Banner has the startling realization that he only becomes the Hulk when he is at his most psychologically strained and vulnerable, "when the pressure becomes unbearable."[1] After this epiphany, the Hulk's story was no longer *just* about blistering action or the youth movement against the establishment, as shown through the conflict between the Hulk and the American military. The story of the Hulk became, in this moment, about a battle within the mind between the rational and the irrational and the power of the mind to manifest itself in physical form. The life of Bruce Banner became about the search for emo-tional balance and rational control over the sometimes irrational mind.

Plotted and conceived by Marvel Comics stable artist Steve Ditko, this story appeared in *Tales to Astonish* #60 (1964). It was a watershed moment in the history of the Hulk. Before 1964, the Hulk was a bit of a mess, and there was no clear sense of *why* Bruce Banner transformed into his raging alter ego. Sometimes it happened at night; other times, it happened because Banner forced the transformation by blasting himself with gamma rays. The Hulk was created by Jack Kirby, but it was Ditko who refined the character, offer-ing readers what would become one of the Hulk's defining characteristics: he

Figure 1.1. The Hulk faces an internal struggle as he fights to remain in his brutish form against the more rational mind of Bruce Banner. Dialogue edited by Stan Lee; Steve Ditko pencils; George Roussos (as George Bell) inks; Sam Rosen letters. "The Incredible Hulk," *Tales to Astonish* #60 (October 1964). © Marvel Comics.

is a manifestation of Banner's psychic state. A preoccupation with one's own interior space and the specter of losing control, *becoming* the darker thoughts and anxieties, was not unique to Ditko's work on the Hulk. The compulsion to explore the mind and the challenge of exorcising its demons were a central theme of the comics Steve Ditko produced over his sixty-five-year career.

Alongside peers like Jack Kirby and Wallace Wood, Steve Ditko helped to redefine the superhero genre at Marvel Comics, where Ditko cocreated one of the most widely recognizable characters in the world: Spider-Man. At Marvel, Ditko also created Dr. Strange, and along with course corrections on the Hulk, he tweaked characters like Iron Man, designing the red-and-gold armor that defined the character's aesthetic. In addition to key character developments, Ditko also invented the corner boxes that became a hallmark of Marvel comics covers for decades. At Charlton Comics in the 1960s, Ditko cocreated Captain Atom with the writer Joe Gill,[2] and on his own, Ditko reinvented the Blue Beetle and created the Question, all characters later purchased by DC Comics and featured prominently throughout the 1980s and beyond. At DC Comics, Ditko created the Creeper, the Hawk and the Dove, Shade the Changing Man, and many others. These creations barely scratch the surface of Ditko's contributions to the comics medium, but they are characters who have had lasting appeal with readers and have been licensed across other media, from cartoons to movies to toys and more.

Yet for many readers and critics, Steve Ditko is an enigmatic figure whose work presents a difficult challenge. Even a cursory glance at his comics demands that the reader recognize the political nature of popular art, from its conception and creation to its production and distribution. Ditko then takes it a step further, needling his intellectual opponents by insisting that his work needs no justification and is an end in itself. For him, popular art need not make any concessions to its audience or other market pressures. While many focus on—and are troubled by—Ditko's incorporation of Ayn Rand's Objectivism into his work, a closer reading suggests a more complex worldview.[3]

Although the influence of Rand, the Russian-born novelist and self-styled philosopher, is indisputable, Ditko has never claimed (at least in print) to adhere to any one set of political or philosophic ideals. Instead he appears to merge several different political, philosophical, and popular ideologies of varying coherence into a singular artistic and intellectual voice. Further, his distinct perspective predated and continued beyond any identifiable influence of Objectivism in his work. Ditko never hung out a shingle advertising himself as a philosopher or theorist, but his comics and essays situate him within a tradition of other thinkers who worked out systems for analyzing the world and human relationships through fiction. Although Ditko's work places him within a particular tradition, my aim in this book is not to insist that his work was a touchstone for political action but to propose that it *reflects* an important transition in American thought. Ditko's philosophy is most accessible through his comics, and he typically limited explicit commentary about his career and philosophy to essays, most of which appeared in small-press and self-published works. The somewhat limited availability of these texts seems to have encouraged some readers to take it upon themselves to interpolate their imaginations of comics history and Ditko's politics.

In fairness to readers who have made such interpolations, often attempting to read Ditko exclusively through the lens of Objectivism, Ditko did give them some reason to do so. His work visually and rhetorically referenced Objectivist thought. However, when thinking of Ditko characters who *specifically* reference Objectivism, one is limited to the rather infamous cases of the Question and Mr. A. The Question's alter ego, Vic Sage, has a physical appearance that matches *The Fountainhead*'s Howard Roark, from his gaunt features to his flaming red hair, and speaks in a manner obviously reminiscent of any number of Rand's heroes. Mr. A's name refers to the notion of "A is A," a direct application of Rand's interpretation of Aristotle's Law of Identity. Moreover, in Ken Viola's 1987 documentary *Masters of Comic Book Art*, Ditko provides a voice-over explaining the *philosophy of Mr. A* as being indebted to the thinking of Ayn Rand. So a foundation does exist for limiting Ditko to such readings, but influence and interest in a particular thinker do not necessarily make one a disciple, and neither does basing a *character* on the philosophy of a particular thinker. While never disavowing Rand, Ditko also went to some lengths to distance his philosophy from Rand's and never publicly claimed to be an Objectivist. Like any other student of philosophy, Ditko operates within a network of thinkers and ideas. That being said, in no way should Ditko be let off the hook for the elements of Objectivism he embraced. I have attempted to point out many of those links in the following chapters, but reducing him to a mouthpiece for Rand does not reflect the whole of his thinking, nor does it help demonstrate how his complicated thinking makes sense of some shifts in contemporary liberal politics.

Misreading Ditko

To date, academic work examining Ditko's contributions is virtually non-existent, which only appears to intensify common misreadings and misunderstandings about Ditko and his career. What limited critical output exists fixates on Ditko's interest in Objectivism, which, while important, constitutes a smaller part of his overall contributions to the comics medium. In 2008, the comics historian Blake Bell, who also edits reprint volumes of Ditko's work for Fantagraphics, released a biography of the artist, *Strange and Stranger*. In that book, Bell attempts to provide a background for Ditko and place his work within a useful historical framework, and the book succeeds in situating Ditko within a larger historical and cultural context. However, Ditko challenged major claims that Bell makes both in the book and in various interviews, such as the highly plausible assertion that Ditko left Marvel because of issues related to creator rights and royalties.[4] Bell's claims do appear to be substantiated by ones made by the comics historian Robert Beerbohm in 2012 (noting a personal conversation with Ditko in 1969 that Ditko later requested not be made public in Beerbohm's copublication *Fanzation*),[5] and in 2019 the comics writer and historian Mark Evanier claimed to have had a similar conversation with Ditko in 1970.[6] Contra Bell, Beerbohm, and Evanier, Ditko refuted claims that he left the company because of owed royalties and instead points to his working relationship with Marvel editor Stan Lee, which Ditko makes clear in his 2015 essay "Why I Quit S-M, Marvel."[7] Doug Wolk's Eisner Award–winning *Reading Comics* from 2008 features a chapter on Ditko that traffics in all sorts of unusual claims that range from gross misreadings, like the assertion that Ditko's work on Dr. Strange was about drug culture, to gross misinformation, like the falsehood that Ditko retired in 2000 and that he only did a few series for Charlton Comics (Ditko worked consistently for the company from 1953 until it folded in 1986).[8]

Troublingly, critical discussions about Steve Ditko often regurgitate these kinds of misunderstandings and misinformation, and even a cursory overview of his writing would better inform, if not resolve, most of these issues. Although informative and well-intentioned, Jonathan Ross's 2007 BBC documentary *In Search of Steve Ditko* perpetuates many of these easily resolvable misapprehensions and apocryphal stories that have little historical grounding. At one point in Ross's documentary, the author and comics writer Neil

Gaiman shares an oft-repeated myth that one of the reasons Ditko quit Marvel in 1966 was because of a dispute with Stan Lee over the secret identity of Spider-Man's nemesis the Green Goblin.

At the time, it had not yet been revealed in the comic that the Goblin's secret identity was Norman Osborn, the father of Peter Parker's best friend, Harry. According to lore, and repeated by Gaiman in the documentary, Stan Lee came up with this idea, and Ditko vehemently disagreed, arguing that it would be more realistic if the Goblin was a completely unknown person in the series, a stranger to Peter Parker and his family. Ditko says that this claim is categorically false. It was he, and only he, who devised the Green Goblin's character arc.

In a 2009 essay for Robin Snyder's comics history newsletter *The Comics*, Ditko, in his distinctive prose,[9] wrote: "I knew from Day One, from the first [Green Goblin] story, who the [Green Goblin] would be. I absolutely knew because I planted him in J. Jonah Jameson's businessman's club, it was where JJJ and the GG could be seen together. I planted them together in other stories where the GG would not appear in costume, action." Ditko wanted Peter Parker's personal life and trouble with his boss at the *Daily Bugle*, J. Jonah Jameson, to intersect with the difficulties he was facing as Spider-Man. So Ditko placed Norman Osborn in the same social circles, highlighting how similar personalities are drawn to one another. And as for the Goblin being the father of Peter's best friend, Ditko emphasizes that he "planted the GG's son (same distinctive hairstyle) in the college issues for more dramatic involvement and storyline consequences. . . . So how could there be any doubt, dispute, about who the GG had to turn out to be when unmasked?"[10]

The gulfs of difference between what many of Ditko's readers believe about his contributions versus what he says about them, and between an assumed version of comic book history perpetrated by a small but powerful number of voices versus Ditko's recollection of events, are indicative of several things. First, they point to a version of comic book history that raises the same kinds of questions that Jack Kirby and others did in their post-Marvel comics and interviews about how credit was doled out and mythologized at Marvel. The second—and I consider this more fully later in the chapter—is that Ditko supports his version of events with clear visual evidence from the stories he plotted and produced with limited input from his editor. To this second point, it is made abundantly clear that the best way to understand how Ditko shaped his stories and character arcs is to closely read and examine the visual elements of each story, tracking their presentation, history, and development, as opposed to defaulting to popular impressions or selective memories.

This is not to say that Ditko's essays resolve all critiques of his work or his accounting of events, bar critical interventions, or suggest that authorial intent should be given primacy. While I believe Ditko's creative claims are convincing, at least when stacked against competing accounts, my aim in this book is not to settle such disputes. When historical misunderstandings and philosophic misapprehensions foreground critical approaches to an author's work, the result, no matter how well intended, not only perpetuates misinformation but inhibits fellow scholars. Thus, in a case such as Ditko's, rife as it is with misinformation and lore, it is particularly worthwhile to take the author's account—as well as how the author views his contributions to collaborative work—into consideration before drawing critical conclusions regarding that author's philosophy or history.

In the case of Steve Ditko, these issues take the form of relying on unfounded assumptions about his relationship to Objectivism and whether Objectivism is the primary (if not sole) force in what fans and critics believe about Ditko's financial existence,[11] his artistic output, and the fiction of his reclusiveness. My primary concern is that reducing Ditko's work to "Objectivism" becomes a shorthand for both those who seek to discredit Ditko's work and those who claim it as evidence for Objectivism's sociocultural value. I certainly do not expect such a claim to be taken at face value. Several recent examples of this shorthand occur in comics studies.

The political science scholar Claudia Franziska Brühwiler's "'A Is A': Spider-Man, Ayn Rand, and What Man Ought to Be" presents a brief history of Ditko's relationship with Objectivism, but her essay's underlying premise is that Objectivism is the sole governing force in Ditko's life and made him a recluse, the latter of which is an odd claim, as it simultaneously assumes a familiarity with Ditko's personal life along with the unusual notion that Objectivist epistemology insists on introversion. Brühwiler, who specializes in studying the work of Rand and libertarianism in literature, presents a view of Ditko that ultimately depends on the challenged history in Bell's *Strange and Stranger*. She makes several minor errors regarding the names of Ditko's characters (referring to the alter ego of Mr. A as "Rex Greiner" instead of Rex Graine), the order of events (she erroneously claims Mr. A was created in 1969), and other small inaccuracies.[12] Although the minutiae are not particularly damning on their own, they diminish her argument in the aggregate. Still, Brühwiler's critiques of Rand are compelling, and her mapping of Rand's influence throughout comics history, beyond Ditko, is noteworthy, but neither of these highlights does much to further the conversation around Ditko or his contributions.

"Popular Culture, Ideology, and the Comics Industry: Steve Ditko's Objectivist Spider-Man," by Antonio Pineda and Jesús Jiménez-Varea, offers a much more compelling perspective on Ditko's application of Objectivist metaphysics to his run on *The Amazing Spider-Man*. However, the article still cites dubious accounts from Stan Lee about the creation of Spider-Man[13] and the hows and whys of the dissolution of the relationship between Lee and Ditko,[14] all of which have been disputed by Ditko, Jack Kirby, and others for some time. Like the Brühwiler article, these problematic historical assertions do not completely undo Pineda and Jiménez-Varea's critique. They do, unfortunately, demonstrate an uncritical, even if common, approach to historicizing Ditko's comics. Moreover, the article seems to completely ignore the large body of superhero work that Ditko developed after leaving Marvel by implying Ditko resented and had a distaste for superheroes with special powers,[15] a notion that falls apart under any scrutiny.

If we set the problematic historical elements aside, Pineda and Jiménez-Varea cite several instances of how the actions of Peter Parker and plot resolutions reflect the kind of heroic ethics demanded by Objectivism and how they lead to the "triumph of the hero." Convincing as these moments are, the authors' argument ultimately boils down to reducing Ditko's work to an exercise in applying Objectivism to superhero comics.[16] It is hard to argue that this is the precise perspective of either of the authors, but by largely neglecting or misreading Ditko's perspective on the development of his heroes and plotlines, the authors perpetuate a popular conception of Ditko's work instead of developing a more critical one.

The journalist and cultural critic Andrew Hultkrans devotes a chapter to Ditko in *Give Our Regards to the Atom Smashers! Writers on Comics*, edited by Sean Howe. Hultkrans immediately betrays his assumptions about Ditko from the outset, continually identifying how "repellent [he] find[s] Ditko's cultish devotion to the pseudo-philosophy of Ayn Rand."[17] While maintaining his sharp-edged approach, Hultkrans goes on to develop a sensible historical perspective for Ditko's work, and like the other critics noted here, he makes distinct connections between Ditko's work on Spider-Man and Objectivism. Beyond that, Hultkrans falls in line with others who want to reduce the corpus of Ditko's post-1962 work to a parroting of Ayn Rand. Yet in his brief consideration of Dr. Strange—the initial creation of whom Ditko had all but complete creative control over—and how the character operates, Hultkrans observes that these narratives are "utterly incompatible with Objectivism."[18]

Depending on one's understanding of Objectivism, one may be inclined to agree with Hultkrans on that specific point, but in the end, he treats what he supposes to be the incompatibility between Dr. Strange and Objectivism as an oddity, rather than giving it serious consideration. Furthermore, Hultkrans neglects other post-Marvel works, like the horror and suspense stories Ditko produced for *Eerie*, *Creepy*, and various titles at Charlton Comics, as well as the numerous other comics Ditko released in the decades after his initial stretch at Marvel. All these comics employ similar visual and narrative elements to those found in Ditko's Dr. Strange stories. This omission by Hultkrans is problematic, as it ignores a significant portion of Ditko's output in the 1960s and 1970s, a period when, according to Hultkrans, Ditko had allegedly been producing "hectoring Objectivist" work.[19] One certainly could not

demand that Hultkrans, or anyone else, provide an in-depth analysis of Ditko's oeuvre before drawing useful critical conclusions. However, Hultkrans,
like the other historians and critics considered here, has reduced Ditko's work
to Objectivist tracts similar to the Christian fundamentalist screeds and moralizing of a Jack Chick publication. Clear exceptions to that reduction are
then treated as abnormalities instead of reflecting a more complex worldview.

In my scholarship, I, too, have fallen prey to this kind of thinking. "Steve
Ditko: Violence and Romanticism in the Silver Age" was my first published
academic work, and it discussed thematic and narrative links between Spider-
Man and Blue Beetle, as well as the Question, Mr. A, and "the right to kill,"
a concept that Ditko pioneered in superhero comics in the 1960s. When I
wrote the article, I was wrapping up my master's degree and was eager to get
my scholarship into circulation; but looking back, I see that I overempha-
sized the role that Objectivism played in those narratives. As a result, I either
neglected to discuss or just missed some of the subtlety that drove the subjects of my article. The Objectivism was right there on the surface; I had a lot
of familiarity with Rand's work, and—not at all to my credit—I jettisoned any
prior doubt and accepted the preexisting narrative about Ditko's philosophic
beliefs. Like the other scholars discussed in this chapter, it's not that I think
lensing Ditko's work through Rand for that piece was necessarily an invalid
means of interpretation; it was, however, a grossly incomplete approach. I
have revised and tried to recuperate the basic arguments of that article in
chapters 5 and 6. Additionally, I am guilty of overemphasizing Ditko's intellectual contributions with concepts like "dark karma," and in my 2017 article
for *Inks*, I do not do nearly enough to address the contributions of regular
Charlton writer Carl Memling and how his scripts, along with others in the
horror and weird genres, lay the groundwork for identifying dark karma as a
reflection of popular discourse in American life. I have attempted to correct
this significant issue in chapter 3.

It is not comics critics alone who have anchored themselves to the notion
that Objectivism is the singularly defining element of Steve Ditko's work.
Objectivist scholars and proponents seeking to identify Ayn Rand's cultural
impact, presumably demonstrating that her work is seen as merit-worthy in
popular media, also employ this approach. The *Journal of Ayn Rand Studies*
ran such articles in 2003 and 2004. In the first, "Replies to Chris Matthew
Sciabarra's Fall 2002 Article: Fancy Meeting Rand Here," Robert M. Price seeks
not to analyze Ditko's work but rather to catalog some of Ditko's post-Marvel
superheroes and then link them to Rand's Objectivism. An avid comics fan,
Price is not a comics scholar by trade but a well-known Lovecraft critic and
theologian. In "The Illustrated Rand," Chris Sciabarra links Ditko to Rand as
part of his effort to identify recent references to Rand in academe and popular
culture as "nothing less than Rand's cultural ascendancy as an iconic figure."[20]

Sciabarra provides a much more in-depth treatment of Ditko than Price and identifies clear evidence of Rand's influence on Ditko's creative output, going so far as to refer to Ditko as "the gold standard by which to measure Rand's impact."[21] Just as with Hultkrans, Pineda and Jiménez-Varea, Brühwiler, and myself, the connections to Rand that Price and Sciabarra rely on are a small number of easily classifiable characters—characters that fit within the journal's particular worldview. Price and Sciabarra are undermining the narrative and philosophic impact of Steve Ditko's output by, again, reducing it to a simple exercise in Objectivist metaphysics.

It's no wonder that Ditko often referred to interpretative approaches to his work as "engaging in fictions and fantasies."

Reading Ditko with Ditko in Mind

Of course, calling these other critical approaches into question should not be construed as a claim that Ditko did not actively engage with Objectivism. He did. Shortly after his death in June 2018, the Atlas Society, the Objectivist nonprofit organization, published a brief commentary on Ditko's work, identifying the artist as a longtime and generous financial supporter of the organization.[22] The piece also noted the Atlas Society's efforts to recruit Ditko to work on a comic book adaptation of Ayn Rand's *Anthem*, an offer Ditko politely refused. According to onetime Ditko editor Mort Todd, Ditko was offered a similar opportunity at Marvel to adapt *Atlas Shrugged*, with the project being inked by veteran artist John Severin: a dream artistic team-up. Ditko refused this offer as well.[23]

The Atlas Society is one of the two parties involved in a schism within Objectivism in 1990 over whether Rand's philosophy was an open or closed system, with the society's founder, David Kelley, insisting on the former. In Kelley's—and thus the Atlas Society's—conception, Objectivism can and should be held up to the same scrutiny and revision as any other philosophy that wishes to remain vibrant and relevant after its initiator's passing. For Kelley, this kind of "open Objectivism" can be pursued without diminishing its initial impact. The society has also actively worked with a figure important to this study: Nathaniel Branden. Branden, the former associate and lover of Ayn Rand, helped to shape much of Objectivist thought in its early conception through his contributions to Objectivist newsletters and as the cofounder, with Rand, of the Nathaniel Branden Institute, which folded after Branden's infamous split with Rand.

Ditko, it would seem, adopted a similarly open, if not revisionist, approach, and in the 2013 essay "Anti-Ditko 'Fans,'" he bitingly calls into question commonly held beliefs about his relationship to Rand and Objectivism, and the "*implication*" that he "completely understood and agreed with, accepted, everything she wrote."[24] One can discern something more difficult in Ditko's work than merely a parroting of received wisdom from Ayn Rand. In saying that we need to take a step back and check our own personal and political baggage, my inquiry into Ditko's work does not dismiss those earlier historians and critics. In many ways, the limitations of those earlier readings of Ditko's work have paved the way for positioning Ditko within ongoing philosophic and political conversations and have helped to demonstrate how comic books can facilitate and initiate public philosophic discourse.

One of the ways I approach this repositioning of Ditko's work and philosophy is by considering what Andrei Molotiu—an art historian, comics scholar, and producer of abstract comics—has referred to as the "melodically arranged" sequences and the formal elements of Ditko's work,[25] interrogating what they reveal about the narratives and ideologies that Ditko presents to his readers.

Molotiu considers the rhythms and pacing within the framework of what he has termed "sequential dynamism," which consists of the compositional elements "internal to each panel and the layout, that . . . propels the reader's eye . . . and that imparts a sense of . . . visual rhythms."[26] Of additional importance is Molotiu's notion of "iconostasis," which he defines as "the perception of the layout of a comics page as a unified composition."[27] In his analysis of Ditko's work on *The Amazing Spider-Man*, Molotiu makes a compelling case for applying his terminology. He further demonstrates that his approach results in a "complex interweaving" of formal and visual elements and "the story's representational, and even thematic, aspects."[28] Molotiu's enlightening approach to the formal elements of Ditko's output has helped to inform my interpretations and how I situate the comics considered in this study.

Although not at all interested in Steve Ditko, Paul Karasik and Mark Newgarden's *How to Read Nancy*—which breaks down *one* of Ernie Bushmiller's *Nancy* comic strips into all its visual-narrative components—also performs some heavy lifting in conceptualizing and interpreting the formal elements of comic book pages. *How to Read Nancy* does not claim to put forward any "Grand Unified Theory of Comics," but it does provide a practical insight into comics composition as it contextualizes each of the significant formal elements, revealing the machinations of comics art that allow the medium to "communicate swiftly and efficiently and with all the working parts laid bare."[29] Those formal elements, as the comics scholar Pascal Lefèvre argues, "are anything but a neutral container of content in the comics medium; form shapes content, form suggests interpretations and feelings. Without considering formal aspects (such as graphic style, *mise en scène*, page lay-out, plot composition) any discussion of the content or themes of a work is, in fact, pointless."[30] While I do not scrutinize panel by panel each of the stories I consider here, much of the interpretive work in the following chapters depends on how the visual elements of each story communicate a distinct philosophic outlook.

Moreover, in this book, I take account of Ditko's approach to artistic creation. Through both his essays and comics, Ditko has put forward something of a politics of artistic creation. In his 2002 essay "At Some Point,"[31] he calls into question the term "creator" and its adjuncts as it pertains to the production of comic books and the matter of how credit is apportioned for the end product. For Ditko, "creator" is a prestige term often claimed by editors, writers, and artists, but one that neglects the important roles played by inkers, colorists, letterers, and the myriad other hands and voices that contribute to comics production. Ditko asserts that each of these participants claims to have contributed "something that did not exist before," but Ditko is not so sure that is always the case. While those contributions have tremendous importance, he questions whether it is sensible to identify those later contributions as points of origin or meaning making. Without a clear standard for what constitutes "creation," the value of such a word is dubious for Ditko. "Creator," then, is an imprecise way of explaining a project and doling out credit. This complicates matters considerably, especially for a study like this one that associates a specific set of philosophic and political ideas with a single author, who is often collaborating with other artists, and who is overseen by an editor. This is further complicated by an industry where, as Ditko believes, the desired prestige of calling oneself a creator can overstate the actual intellectual contributions being made. Because of what he sees as the "questionable meaning" of the word "creator," Ditko takes the time to more fully shape his perspective in the essay "ART!?," also from 2002.[32]

As is the case in a number of his essays, "ART!?" takes up the challenge of first trying to lay out an operational definition of the key terms in play and calls into question what Ditko perceives to be problematic assumptions about what constitutes art, under what circumstances an object becomes "art," and who is rightly dubbed an "expert" on such matters. Ditko seems to concede that there are not hard-and-fast answers to questions such as who is responsible for the content of the comic book page. "In theory," Ditko says, "it should be the artist." He explains:

> A proper comic story/art panel must have a purposeful, visual coherence, visual unity, and visual integrity. . . . All of the panel elements clearly fit. . . . The harmonious arrangement of the panel . . . is like a clock and the parts that make it up. The parts must be designed, produced and properly organized for the clock to run and continue showing the correct time.[33]

This requires a deft hand, a careful eye, and a clear sense of narrative cohesion. While Ditko is confident that such a combination of features is most sensibly traced to the artist—like himself, Wallace Wood, or Jack Kirby—he is clear that this is not always a practical reality, since comics often pass through many hands before being received by the public. In a manner that surely is about the public perception that editors, particularly Stan Lee, are the sole creative force behind any given comic book, Ditko laments:

> The operating principle is that once the artist's work is turned in, then the "real" panel/page "creative" thought and work begins. The "real comic art creation" takes place after an artist has brought something into physical, visual existence. "Real comic art creation" is not done by the artist but by any handler who follows him.[34]

Aside from taking a jab at Stan Lee's claims for the creation and creative contributions through the dialogue he added and edited, Ditko argues that this approach is wildly different from a division of labor wherein the writer has constructed a full script with specific panel breakdowns. In Ditko's conception, unless the artist is working from a full script, that initial artist, the penciler, is bringing "the creation" into existence. As such, that artist is no mere illustrator. The artist is, rather, the generator of all the major narrative components, and thus the driving force behind the comic.

During his time at Marvel between 1955 and 1966, Ditko identifies divisions of labor as gray and murky at best. At Marvel, "the artist [did not] work from a full script or from any script. *No Script.*"[35] He explains that there was occasionally a synopsis, but such documents were never standardized, if they were received at all. Ditko does not articulate it in this way, but his point is clear: at Marvel, the artist was the writer, with the only real constraint being the length of the story. For Ditko, this meant at least penciling the pages and turning in a "panel script": a thumbnail breakdown of the page describing the action and suggested dialogue. Then the editor—who, in Lee's case, is also credited as the "writer"—included dialogue modified at his or her discretion. For Ditko, this practice is distressing, as it leaves "almost no chance" for narrative cohesion, especially if the editor makes character and dialogue choices not necessarily in step with how the artist has developed the story. Even if the panel art, as produced by the penciler, maintains its narrative integrity, the input of later contributors—be they editors, dialogists, inkers, or colorists— may distort the narrative. Ditko still insists that, without these other elements, the comic page is incomplete.

I agree with Ditko that, for good or ill, all the contributors to the comics page contribute to its ability to be a sensibly understood shape and form. However, I think the most important thing to recognize here is what undergirds his explanation: at Marvel, he was working as both a writer and an artist. Once Ditko's completed pages were turned in, they made their way to Stan Lee, who added dialogue based on Ditko's panel scripts and occasionally farmed out the inking to other artists employed by the company. For Ditko, this was often, if not always, a corrupting element to his stories as he conceived them. I understand Ditko's point as a cue to judiciously separate his visual narratives from the dialogue Lee provided, and even, in some cases, to separate Ditko's original pencils from the final inked and colored pages.

I recognize the nostalgic fan-impulse to clutch the mythmaking of the Merry Marvel Marching Society and the desire to treat the magic that bubbled out of the Kirby-Ditko-Lee cauldron at Marvel in the 1960s as the product of some alchemical reaction that could only be produced when these three were added in the proper ratios. But it is clear that, to get at the core of what was influential as well as what was philosophically and politically important about Ditko's work, we need to cast those comforting but historically dubious impulses aside. According to Ditko, beginning in the early 1960s, he and Lee were not even on speaking terms.

Lee, in his infamous hagiographic interview with the *New York Herald Tribune* in 1966, as much as admitted that he had no idea what Ditko was doing before he received a stack of completed story pages, and also publicly acknowledged that Ditko began insisting on inking his own work.[36] I accept Ditko's contentions about the nature and perception of the finished comic book page, and I agree that the addition of Lee's captions and dialogue—and, sometimes, Lee's choice to bring in a separate inker—has often distorted the visual narrative and even character identity. I discuss a peculiar instance of this in chapter 4. In separating these elements and zeroing in on Ditko's work, I aim not to eliminate the contributions of Lee and others to the stories examined here but to place Ditko's work, on its own terms, under the microscope.

A Different Kind of Liberalism

By taking into account the visual-philosophic motifs that Ditko has laid bare, and by considering how those formal elements make sense of the representational and thematic elements Ditko explores throughout the whole of his creative and polemical output, this book places Steve Ditko within historical and theoretical conversations about American political discourse and more specifically the emergence of neoliberalism in the twentieth century. My claim throughout the book is *not* that Steve Ditko necessarily influenced political actors through the philosophic explorations presented in his comics and essays. Instead I maintain that Ditko's work reflects a dynamic shift in the American liberal conscience, rooted in popular philosophic and metaphysical thought. Using Ditko's oeuvre as a *lens* for identifying a major sociopolitical transition that is rooted in an exaltation of the self, one associated with esoteric and occult thought in the interwar and post–World War II period, provides an opportunity to understand how an important segment of American political thought helped buttress neoliberalism and the libertarian movement.

Deeply concerned with issues of interiority and the self, Ditko's work helps demonstrate the rise of such political thought and action in several interesting ways, not the least of which is his particular and selective application of Objectivism. Cultivating his epistemological sense of the world, Ditko's interest in Rand is typically understood as appearing in his work from the 1960s onward, particularly with characters like the Question and Mr. A; however, his commitment to ethical and metaphysical issues predates this period. In brief, what is at stake for comics scholarship in this project is the development of an intellectual history of Steve Ditko, positioning his work and philosophic perspective as a means for understanding some varietals of twentieth-century American political consciousness and the evolution of that consciousness.

In place of conceiving Ditko's politics exclusively through the lens of Objectivism, or presuming that such a philosophy and politics first become visible with his superhero work at Marvel in the 1960s, I instead begin with Ditko's entry into the comics industry in 1953 to help identify and trace a clear philosophic and political outlook that remains consistent throughout his career and only later picks up Objectivist, neoliberal, and libertarian thought along the way. Doing so reveals, first, that Ditko's work was never fully shackled by Objectivism and, second, that his approach has a much more complicated relationship with mystical thinking than Objectivism would admit.

As such, Ditko's convoluted—but intellectually and ethically consistent— approach gives us insight into a strand of American political and religious thought that invites a sense of compatibility among conservative and libertarian political values along with religious, often Christian, ones. This kind of thinking, in one sense, may be understood as the "religious Right," but in another sense it provides insight into the cultural cache of contemporary mystic thinking like that provided in Norman Vincent Peale's *The Power of Positive Thinking* (1952) or the so-called "prosperity gospel" associated with early practitioners of New Thought like the Christian Socialist Wallace Wattles, author of *The Science of Getting Rich* (1910), as well as with later religious figures such as Joel Osteen or the success of occultic New Age books like Rhonda Byrne's *The Secret* (2006).

Unquestionably, Ditko would reject and denounce the kind of wish-thinking offered by either Osteen or *The Secret*, but scrutiny of his work reveals an intellectual approach to the self and interiority that aligns with a mind-over-matter, occultic approach to existence similar to the ideas of those controversial figures. Even more intriguingly, this approach, while easily identifiable in Ditko's work, can also be observed in some of the most prominent individualist thinkers of the mid- and late twentieth century, particularly in Objectivism, as conceived by Ayn Rand and her onetime intellectual heir Nathaniel Branden.

For many readers, taking seriously supposedly fringe movements like New Thought, self-help books like those produced by Carnegie and Peale, and thinkers like Rand who regularly cultivated controversy will present a challenge.[37] What this study asks is that we check our intellectual baggage, either for or against those thinkers and movements, at the door. Instead of scrutinizing these ideas for confirmation of an a priori political ideal, ask whether significant segments of the public took these ideas seriously and how they were developed and popularized. Beyond this study, consider the broader consequences of these ideas in popular media and American political life. In thinking through the political landscape after the 2016 presidential election, the lyrics of David Byrne come to mind: "And you may ask yourself, 'Well, how did I get here?'" Even if one takes the view of a more cynical Byrne verse and says, "My God! What have I done?," this is all the more reason to interrogate these thinkers and ideas to form a more complete understanding of late twentieth-century thought.

Moreover, recognizing the historical and cultural significance of political figures like former Federal Reserve chairman Alan Greenspan—who presided from the Reagan administration until 2006—demands an understanding of Rand, for whom Greenspan provided essays that appeared in books like *Capitalism: The Unknown Ideal* (1966). Acknowledging the importance of Ronald Reagan brings with it the baggage of Reagan's interest in mystic thought, and his quoting of the New Thought occultist Manly P. Hall in speeches and essays.[38] The intrigue surrounding the presidency of Donald Trump has made more explicit Trump's application of Norman Vincent Peale as being central to how he carries himself.[39] These ideas, however seemingly fringe, have had a significant impact on American political life, and ignoring or dismissing them does not strike me as a viable option.

To be clear, Ditko never explicitly associated himself with any one political figure, party, or singular idea. Rather, while acknowledging his intellectual debt to Rand, Ditko always presented his ideas and philosophy as his own: over time, he mixed and collected what he thought were the best ideas about the self, ethics, and philosophy and distilled them into a worldview that underwrote his interaction with the world. He believed that this was true for most people. In a 2016 essay appearing at the back of *Out of This World*, a compilation of new and reproduced Ditko stories, he wrote, "*Everyone* acts on *his philosophy* however well-known or understood." In the same essay, he addresses critics who have negatively linked him to Rand, defensively suggesting that those critics are out of their depth, having likely never read Rand. But before that, he is careful to place distance between himself and Objectivism and lashes out at critics

who choose to remain philosophically dumb and act as philosophically enlightened [and] continue to express their incompetence with their linking their anti-Ditko story and art and A. Rand's Objectivism philosophy.

> Yet, few CBFs [comic book fans] have actually read the articles I have written
> and the comic books I have written, drawn and published.[40]

This issue is an important one for Ditko. Setting aside the clear frustration
with people who he seems to think are misreading him (if they are reading
him at all), the takeaway here is that Ditko insists that no one-to-one cor-
respondence exists between his comics and Objectivist thought. Further, in
both his comics and essays, the artist has made clear that he is engaging in
some other kind of thought not tethered to Objectivism.

A reader of history and philosophy, Ditko constructed his worldview by
borrowing from a variety of thinkers and ideologies where he saw fit. Linking him to the ideological construct I identify in this study is intended not to
pigeonhole Ditko but to demonstrate how his work reflects a broad, consequential popular approach to ideology. Put differently, my purpose is not to
obliterate ideological readings of Ditko but to recalibrate the conversation to
consider Ditko's work as presenting a more nuanced view of the world and
the mind than previous criticism has allowed. In recovering Ditko's less-read
and less-discussed works, or even introducing them to new readers, this study
achieves those ends.

Ditko's approach to philosophy represents a sort of religion-after-religion
that is focused on the self and the power of volition in determining one's worth
to one's self and, thereby, to society at large. Although Ditko rejected any association with mysticism as a serious worldview,[41] his work provides insight into
a kind of *mystic liberalism* that emerges in the mid-twentieth century. A corollary to neoliberalism, which represents a resurgence of nineteenth-century
economic thought and laissez-faire capitalism, mystic liberalism merges neoliberal ideals with a revival of nineteenth-century occult and mystic thought
as it relates to the formation of the individual. Along with its sociopolitical
implications, a term like "mystic liberalism" carries some etymological baggage, and accordingly, I am working within a specific set of referents.

Occult historians, like Mitch Horowitz and Gary Lachman, have invoked
a "liberal" political trajectory for occult and esoteric traditions in America,
as a counterpoint to other histories, like those of Nicholas Goodrick-Clarke,
that have linked occult and esoteric ideas with the Far Right. In the context of
that conversation, "liberal" is more easily understood as describing leftist and
progressive political ideologies. I am not necessarily deploying "liberal" in the
same way. "Liberal" is, in the most generous sense, a contested term with an
almost equally contested history. Recent studies, like Helena Rosenblatt's *The
Lost History of Liberalism*, propose a "word history of liberalism,"[42] developing a genealogy that roots the term in French and German thought that goes
on to "illuminate how liberals defined themselves and what they meant when
they spoke about liberalism."[43] I apply a similar methodology to Steve Ditko

as I examine how his writings inform and complicate the philosophy that appears in his works.

Additionally, in her considerations of liberalism and the question of character, Rosenblatt notes the criticism of French liberalism by the diplomat and historian Alexis de Tocqueville in *Recollections: The French Revolution of 1848*, and his concern about the impact of socialism as a strange and dangerous "malady of men's minds."[44] The underlying problem with socialism, as Rosenblatt frames it, was a moral one, but in Tocqueville's text it also seems apparent that what is at stake is a weakened mental constitution giving way to the emotional incoherence of a mob, which was taken advantage of by socialist conspirators.[45]

Rosenblatt effectively argues for the value and importance of recalibrating conversations about liberalism, particularly as her work provides an opportunity to note the connection between the importance of a strong mental constitution, antisocialism, moral behavior, and antiemotionalism that is found in the work of Steve Ditko. However, I still find value in considering what Rosenblatt identifies as the Enlightenment's—and thus thinkers like John Locke—carrying forward the importance of liberality.[46] Moreover, contemporary American libertarians often qualify themselves as the "true" liberals, typically by gesturing toward the Enlightenment. To that end, I am using "liberal" in the sense that C. B. Macpherson identified in his reevaluation of liberal individualism, *The Theory of Possessive Individualism* (1962). Contra Rosenblatt's later study, Macpherson writes that liberalism is, in part, rooted in the seventeenth century and the Lockean assertion of "the free rational individual as the criterion of the good society."[47] While Macpherson lays important groundwork for how I deploy "liberalism," there are important complicating factors along the way. Among those complications is the relationship of liberalism to capitalism and how it was revised by the Austrian and Chicago economic schools. Further, many of those revisions happen outside scholarly discourse, as individualist writers like Rand link the criterion of the good society—in conjunction with the laissez-faire capitalist theory of the Austrian economist Ludwig von Mises and the Chicago economist Milton Friedman—to the belief in, and the practice of, capitalism.[48]

I also depend on several different historical approaches to occult and esoteric thought. When it comes to my application of "mysticism," I am employing the usage provided by Arthur Versluis, a scholar of Western esotericism, in *Magic and Mysticism* (2007). Versluis explains that "mystical traditions . . . explicitly reject worldly aims in favor of *inner* or spiritual illumination."[49] Versluis's definition is also useful in thinking through other major concepts and movements in this book, like New Thought. John Haller's *The History of New Thought* (2012) identifies New Thought as a movement that believes "the mental world was the only true reality and the material world its creation," which is to say that it is by exploring the inner world that "the individual find[s] lasting health and happiness."⁵⁰ Haller also links mid-twentieth-century practitioners of New Thought mind power, including Carnegie and Peale, to a move toward "terms such as *capitalism, profit,* and *rugged individualism* as they replaced well-used concepts of *public virtue* and *self-reliance*" in an American liberal vocabulary that embraced the prosperity gospel.⁵¹ Haller further notes that "material wealth became its own just reward" for New Thought's prosperity,⁵² a turn that is synchronistic with Rand's rise in popularity throughout the mid-twentieth century.

Merging these applications of liberalism and mysticism results in a kind of thinking where the individual human imagination can now discern the machinations of the cosmos and harness its powers. In other words, through such discernment, the individual makes an object of the cosmos. To be clear, this is not the same as Rudolf Steiner's anthroposophy, a nineteenth-century esoteric philosophy, which also insists that there exists an objective spiritual world that is graspable through independent, disciplined, rational inquiry and individual experience. In Steiner's anthroposophy, the spiritual world exists as a separate plane that evolves along with the earthly one. In mystic liberalism, the cosmos that must be explored and made object exists not without but within. Thus, through an apparently rational, reasoned exploration, the individual extrapolates from the cosmos an unambiguous, universal ethical code of conduct. In place of attempting to reach and interact with another plane of existence, the mystic liberal is seeking control over, and the improvement of, their present one. Mystic liberalism is a kind of occult scientism whereby a sense of ultimate truth and knowledge is not gifted by an ethereal authority; rather, it is a secret revealed and earned inside each unique human conscience.

Mystic Liberalism's Metaphysical Cosmology

Ditko's mystic liberalism offers two distinct cosmological precepts that undergird his philosophy: dark karma and cosmic intraspace. Respectively, these precepts function to demonstrate how rational justice should be meted out and how individuals may reach a point of self-actualization by plumbing the depths of their consciences and exorcising the demons within. Visually, these concepts appear immediately in Ditko's work in the 1950s (chap. 3) and are especially prevalent in his horror, weird, and suspense stories. These concepts—particularly cosmic intraspace—are not limited to these narrative modes. They also appear in superhero comics with characters like Dr. Strange in the early 1960s (chap. 4) and are rearticulated with street-level, hardboiled heroes like Mr. A (chap. 6) and later creations like Static in the 1970s and 1980s (chap. 7). Again, what is at stake in identifying Ditko's mystic liberalism and its precepts is not so much ascribing some kind of intentionality to Ditko's intellectual-artistic approach but rather using Ditko's work as a lens for understanding what would become a powerful segment of American life and thought from the mid-twentieth century onward.

More precisely, what mystic liberalism offers is a new way of conceiving the intellectual and ethical framework that many libertarians and members of the American Right of the twentieth century depend on to produce and reproduce "individuals." Additionally, whereas neoliberalism works to satisfy questions about *inter*personal economic political activity, mystic liberalism interests itself in *intra*personal political activity. The entanglement of mystic thought and liberalism is perhaps most compellingly observed by Max Stirner in *The Ego and His Own* (1845), but the expansion of that network to include the occult and individualism appears to be a more specific product of the twentieth century and is immediately recognizable in popular art and discourse. Defining and identifying mystic liberalism provides a means for recanalizing how we interpret art and media of the mid-twentieth century.

Steve Ditko's creative and polemical output offers an insight into this concept that—because it is simultaneously philosophical, literary, and visual—provides a clear sense of how to construct a practical understanding of mystic liberalism and how to identify and draw critical conclusions about its effects as it appears across media. Although a more complete realization of mystic liberalism and its applications in the ongoing conversations about the role of liberalism in American literature and culture will appear in chapter 2, it is worth at least briefly developing here a sense of how we can observe two of its major tenets, dark karma and cosmic intraspace, as visual and narrative motifs in Ditko's aesthetic.

When conceptualizing something like dark karma, I should note that Ditko is not alone in the mid-twentieth century in (mis)appropriating the Hindu and Buddhist conception of karma, so much so that, in the popular American lexicon, the term has become a shorthand for receiving one's comeuppance, good or bad. In many cases, the word "karma" has lost any substantial meaning at all. In *Karma Cola* (1979), the documentarian and author Gita Mehta notes, "As options proliferate all over the globe [for karma], the ability to understand the nature of necessity appears to be diminishing and bondage means something else again. So the terminology has accommodated itself to the needs of those who use it."[53] Mehta is writing in the context of the so-called New Age movement of the 1960s and beyond, but this appropriation of Eastern religious and mystic thought by the West runs deeper than the Beatles hanging out with Ravi Shankar and Maharishi Mahesh Yogi.

The occult historian Mitch Horowitz asserts in *Occult America* (2009) that, on account of the formation of the Theosophical Society in 1875, cofounders Henry Steel Olcott and H. P. Blavatsky became "the single most significant Western figure[s] in the modern religious history of the East,"[54] certainly where the introduction of karma into Western discourse is concerned. Blavatsky's *Isis Unveiled* (1877), Horowitz shows, "popularized the word *occultism* and made the concept a matter of passionate interest among artists, authors, and spiritual seekers of the Western world."[55] Blavatsky writes about karma in many of her works, and in *Isis Unveiled* she first describes it as "the power which controls the universe, prompting it to activity, merit and demerit."[56] Blavatsky then points to karma as working conjointly with one's "mental state" as being the cause of individual, personal conditions, suggesting that if one is miserable or content, then it is of one's own doing. Further, one may gain contentment by doing things such as unifying the mind and body into a single self through greater contemplation.[57] In later works, like *The Key to Theosophy*, Blavatsky expands her sense of karma as being merciless, going so far as to suggest that there can be no ultimate forgiveness from God and that karma works as the means for punishing misdeeds, thus setting the universe aright.[58]

Although Ditko never makes any explicit written reference to it, a Blavatskian sense of karma is still useful in making sense of how a concept like justice operates in the Ditkovian imaginary. Ditko offers his sense of karma in *Mr. A* #1 (1973); in his configuration, karma relies on two basic principles: it is merciless toward evil, and it may only be understood by its observable effects. For Ditko, "evil" is a choice to "act against [one's] own life" by rejecting "good," and justice is not a restoration of the victim but rather a punishment of the victimizer—there is no mercy and "no escape for would-be destroyers of any good."[59] To this latter point, a dark karmic justice may be a supernatural occurrence, it may appear to be a mere coincidence or accident, or it may be the *fictional* hero deliberately ending the life of a criminal. This last instance is where Ditko develops his most philosophically complete concept: "the right to kill," which depends on the assumption that "any man who claims the right to another's efforts or life automatically renounces the concept of rights and their protection of his right to his own legitimate efforts and life."[60]

While *Mr. A* #1 offers a useful illustration of how dark karma operates, it is important to note that this is not a call for the literal extermination of "destroyers of any good." Rather, it's an intellectual exercise that permits allegorical representations of the abstract notions of "good" and "evil" as Ditko places them in conflict with each other. Put differently, the right to live and possess property depends on one's continued adherence to a set of ethical principles that bar individuals from imposing their will on others. To make this plain for readers, Ditko uses the death and killing of characters who violate those principles. Chapter 6 offers a detailed exploration of the complexities of "the right to kill" as a concept.

Deploying Mystic Liberalism

Ditko's "right to kill," in an exceedingly superficial sense, presents a challenge to cultural expectations and the editorial practices that many publishers adopted during the buildup to, and in the wake of, the formation of the Comics Code Authority. The Code, introduced in 1954 by the Comics Magazine Association of America, was a set of self-censorship guidelines developed under the guise of protecting the comics industry from government censorship. Though adhering to the Code was voluntary, failing to meet the Code's demands meant a loss of distribution outlets, jeopardizing publishers' ability to sell comics at all.

Although lethal violence was not specifically prohibited by the Code, "scenes of excessive violence," along with "brutal torture [and] excessive and unnecessary knife and gunplay," were. Moreover, major publishers, like DC Comics, had in-house guidelines that prohibited superheroes from deliberately taking human life.[61] In other words, the circumstances were such that Ditko would not, and likely could not, have fully realized his narratives as he would have seen fit, and his interest in reintroducing explicit, lethal violence to superhero comics is indicative of the intellectual approach he had been providing readers all along. Specifically articulated in the first issue of *Mr. A*, "the right to kill" was previously employed by the Question in *Blue Beetle* #4 (1967). In a backup feature to that issue, the Question ends the lives of two criminals by kicking them into a sewer to drown.

The Question's actions directly violated the Comics Code, and while adhering to the Comics Code hamstrung the killings Ditko portrayed in *Blue Beetle* #4, the meaning was made clear to readers through Ditko's visuals. Further, in later essays like ". . .The Right to Kill!" and comic strips like "Social Justice," Ditko directly responds to the kind of cultural criticism that resulted in the Code. However, for Ditko, neither of these instances is a singular product of the Code; rather, they are representative of the philosophic, intellectual approach that Ditko brought to his work. The Code simply provided the target for his preexisting notions. In other words, "the right to kill" always existed in his comics; responding to the Code was the opportunity to fully articulate that "right." Using the "right to kill" is first defended by instances of dark karma, and later, individual human agents gain access to the "right" by learning about this dark karmic order through an exploration of cosmic intraspace.

Just as there is a right to kill, so the right to live is inherent in the Ditkovian and mystic liberal imaginary, but individual personhood is not guaranteed. One might exist, in other words, as a formless mass of flesh with a mind made of mush—a scenario that is realized both literally and figuratively in Ditko's work. In the literal sense, the Mindless Ones, a teeming horde of shapeless, humanoid lumps, inhabit the outer reaches of Dormammu's Dark Dimension in *Doctor Strange*, constantly threatening the ordered—albeit evil—domain under Dormammu's control. More often, however, these characters appear in the figurative sense, and often as the victims of dark karma. Among many others, a specific example of this occurs in the story "Deep Ruby!," which first appeared in *Eerie* #6 (1966) and was a collaboration between Ditko and writer-editor Archie Goodwin.

A seemingly straightforward supernatural horror story in the vein of pre-Code horror comics or *The Twilight Zone*, "Deep Ruby!" tells the story of Lester Darrow, a jeweler, and how he came to be in a physically and mentally shambolic state—"a leering, lurching example of how low humanity could sink."[62] Although Lester cannot account for how much time has passed since his life changed so dramatically, he can recall how this apparent transformation took place. One night, Lester is approached by a revolting back-alley degenerate who shows him a strange-looking red gem, the likes of which the jeweler has never seen before. Looking at the gem, Lester is consumed with an irrational lust for the object. As he stares ever more deeply into the gem, his greed increases, and by unknown means, he is transported and trapped inside the object.

Once within the gem, Lester tumbles through a nightmarish, Dalí-esque landscape—reminiscent of those traversed by Dr. Strange—where he is attacked and carried off by demonic-looking figures who attempt to feed Lester to a giant, disembodied, fang-toothed mouth (fig. 1.2). When Lester pleads for the demons to explain why this is happening to him, one responds that the color of the gem is created by human blood, and Lester is to be the next sacrifice that would sustain the gem's color. At this moment, Lester miraculously breaks free of the demons' grasp and makes a run for it, only to find that he is still trapped within the gem. Speaking through the barrier of the gem to the man who had tempted and trapped him there, Lester agrees to pay any price, just so long as he can be free. The man agrees, but in typical O. Henry fashion, after Lester is freed, it is he who is now doomed to take up the role of the back-alley degenerate. Lester is then left haunting alleyways, searching for someone else to tempt and trap within the gem so that he might be free again.

What a story like "Deep Ruby!" presents, in Ditko's mystic liberalism, is an instance of a living human being failing to actualize as a complete, productive individual. Encountering a challenge to his ethics and his sense of rationality, Lester is plunged into a cosmic intraspace—a symbolic, interior realm where he must face the demons that would tempt him away from individual personhood and thus a dignified existence. Failing to deny his impulsive greed and accepting the gem from the derelict, Lester is reduced to the same driveling, shambolic state as the man he took the gem from, rendering him a grotesque, subhuman figure. Lester forfeits his mind to whims and thereby forfeits his personhood. This seems plain enough from the change in Lester's figure between the opening and final panels of the story, but the inclusion

Figure 1.2. Lester Darrow is escorted into a gaping maw by the inhabitants of the ruby. Written by Archie Goodwin; art by Steve Ditko; letters by Ben Oda. "Deep Ruby!" *Eerie* #6 (November 1966). © New Comic Company.

of the cosmic intraspace inside the gem adds an important symbolic layer. Within the infinite interior of the gem, the reader gets a glimpse of Lester's mind—the place where he must overcome his irrational impulses.

The tangled passageways that Lester plummets through and the demons he encounters stand in for the challenges one must face and overcome on the road to rationality and individual actualization. Because Lester cannot ward off the demons of greed and steer his way clear, he is left to beg the derelict holding the gem for help. This begging for help from others only deepens Lester's problems because, at this point, he has surrendered more than his mind to irrationality; he has surrendered his agency to another. In Ditko's work, cosmic intraspaces function as areas where his characters are forced to plumb the depths of their psyches, facing their impulses and shortcomings, where they must *choose* to fight and exorcise those demons or succumb to them. The consequence for relenting to the ghosts and demons that haunt individual minds is nothing less than a rejection of life.

Many of Ditko's horror and weird suspense stories adopt a similar narrative structure; however, not all his explorations of cosmic intraspace end as bleakly as "Deep Ruby!" The story "From Out of the Depths," first printed in *This Magazine Is Haunted* #14 (1957),[63] presents one such case where engaging with cosmic intraspace and its denizens results in triumph and hope.

Narrated by the series' horror host, Dr. Haunt Wonder, "From Out of the Depths" tells the story of Juan, a "Mexican peon," who owns "a dried up sandy waste that was once black fertile earth" along the coast of the Gulf of Mexico.[64] At the outset, Juan, his family, and his farm are in dire straits; meanwhile, unbeknownst to Juan, a shapeless creature whose appearance is "so different from anything we know that it is beyond comprehension" lurks outside his door. Significantly, the creature has emerged from the darkened depths of the Gulf and is creeping toward Juan's home. Meanwhile Juan sits at his table, contemplating what to do about his failing farm so that he can save himself and his family; Dr. Wonder assures the reader that Juan is a man plagued with worry.

As the reader learns of Juan's troubled thoughts and fears from the narrator, Juan looks out his window, hoping for a sign of rain, noting "how helpless man is against nature." Juan is wishing for a better life without taking personal action, either literally or within his conscious mind. However, when he sees the creature from the depths shambling toward his home, Juan moves to defend his property and his life against this threat from inside the Gulf. In a rather obvious manner, the creature represents all of Juan's internal struggles: his worry about the survival of his family, his frustration with nature. Making this even more obvious in the narrative, as he steps outside and encounters the creature, he resists his fears and worries and attacks the unknown thing, seeing it as an "alien . . . symbol of all his troubles, something tangible he can strike back at."[65] As soon as he overcomes his fear and strikes the shapeless monster, it immediately dissolves, dissipating into the sky, where it forms clouds and rains on Juan's once barren farmland (fig. 1.3).

In one sense, "From Out of the Depths" might convincingly be reduced to a tale of man's ability to overcome and dominate nature for his survival. In another, more compelling, sense, it is not nature that Juan overcomes but rather his own fears, worries, and self-doubt. Like Juan's troubles, the creature emerges from an internal space, and that it has any recognizable features at all, Dr. Wonder insists, is a product of our "imagination that causes [us] to see things that are not there."[66] When Juan tangles with the creature, it makes a "soundless shriek" that only Juan can hear, causing him to cringe and recoil in fear.[67] Further, that the creature evaporates into mist once Juan demonstrates the courage and fortitude to stand up to his fears is even more telling: it is not the external world or nature that poses the greatest threat to Juan and his family but his fears from the depths of his psyche, which have manifested themselves as the amoeba-like creature from the depths of the Gulf.

Wishing his troubles and fears away and blaming the uncontrollable forces of nature only heaped more misery on Juan; only when he took individual action was he able to triumph. Unlike Lester Darrow, who is dominated by his greed and lust for the unearned in "Deep Ruby!," Juan is able

Figure 1.3. Juan faces the darkened symbol of all his troubles and fears as it emerges from the murky depths of the sea. No confirmed writer credit (but likely Joe Gill); art by Steve Ditko; unknown letterer. "From Out of the Depths," *This Magazine Is Haunted* #14 (December 1957).

to master his shortcomings and earn the opportunity for a productive life. Regardless of the outcome in each story, what Ditko's cosmic intraspace presents to his characters is an opportunity to take control of their existence by mastering the space within themselves through a sense of rationality. This kind of exercise runs parallel with the mystic notion of Blavatsky and others that one achieves success and contentment in one's life by unifying the mind and body through contemplation. Failure to achieve success and contentment, therefore, is a failure of contemplation and the inability to master one's own interior spaces.

Mystic liberalism and its corollaries to the work of Steve Ditko, as applied to the two stories just discussed, act as more than a specific reading of the artist's work. Because Ditko worked in the popular culture industry, reaching audiences at a mass—even global—scale, and did so for nearly seventy years, it is worth considering how these concepts apply broadly to American culture, especially at the time when Ditko was at his most productive, from 1953 to the mid-1980s. If mystic liberalism helps us to understand the intellectual and artistic trajectory of Ditko's work, we might then be able to use Ditko's work as a lens for understanding how this unique political outlook developed and was challenged in the American political consciousness of the same period. Although such a consideration has broad implications across popular media and political thought, *Mysterious Travelers* will focus specifically on comics and the dialogue that occurs within the medium's narrative history as it debates Ditko's worldview and its potential consequences.

Comics are useful in exploring how a creator's philosophy affected American culture and politics precisely because comics are a medium that, through the means of their production and distribution, has been able to reach mass audiences in ways relatively inaccessible to the works of great philosophers, economists, and political theorists of the same period or before. With a few notable exceptions, comics were not produced by trained philosophers and academics, and they have largely carried on their political conversations away from the intellectual and political elite. But that has never rendered comics impotent in political discourse.

Embracing their platform, comics became a vehicle for decrying societal ills, like racism and anti-Semitism, as in the comics produced by EC in the 1950s; comics were a means for Jack Kirby to air his grievances about the working conditions of the comic book artist, specifically working for Stan Lee at Marvel, through characters like Funky Flashman in *Mister Miracle*; comics were a site of the counterculture and antiwar movement of the 1960s through comics like *Blazing Combat* and the underground works of Spain Rodriguez, Gilbert Shelton, Trina Robbins, and Robert Crumb; comics were a means for the cosmopolitan culture of the early Los Angeles punk scene to be considered in the Hernandez brothers' *Love and Rockets*; comics were the medium Steve Ditko used to offer readers a philosophic—often didactic—alternative to the counterculture; and comics were the means by which Alan Moore and Dave Gibbons responded to Ditko's worldview in *Watchmen*. That comics have always been political is obvious, but recognizing the level of political engagement they are involved in is important for conceptualizing how mass markets were exposed to political and philosophic ideas and debates. Although these examples are limited and brief, they do demonstrate a history of comics persistently engaging with—and unabashedly attempting to persuade—their audiences about political and social issues. Many, if not most, of those readers were children and adolescents still developing their understanding of how to navigate the world around them. Like many readers of this book, I was one such child and adolescent.

Engaging with Ditko

I can't quite recall how I was first exposed to superhero comic books, but the first comic I remember owning was *Batman* #402 from 1986. My parents would have bought it for me off a grocery store spinner rack, and I remember stowing it with my other book and record sets—which featured characters like He-Man, the Super Friends, and Spider-Man. The cover of that issue of *Batman* featured the titular character choking another person dressed as Batman. Right there on the cover! Batman choking another Batman! And in big, bold text: "There's nothing so savage—as a man destroying himself!" Without intentionally overstating it, I had something of an existential crisis. My worldview was completely rattled, and my four-year-old brain ran wild with the concept presented on this cover. "How could Batman fight *Batman*?!" I wondered, and for what seemed like hours, I sat there on my bedroom floor, staring at that cover, marveling at the possibilities. How could a man, much less a *batman*, fight himself? Little did I know that Steve Ditko had long been grappling with strikingly similar issues in the decades before this issue. From that moment forward, I was hooked, and my parents' and grandparents' acquiescence to my habit allowed me access not just to comics but to my sense of self as well.

It was in 1992, the thirtieth anniversary of the creation of Spider-Man, that I first recall encountering Steve Ditko's work. In the early 1990s, Marvel launched a series in the vein of their *Masterworks* line of collected editions called *Marvel Milestone Editions*, single issues that reprinted some of the company's most famous and important comics. It was a great place for a burgeoning collector to get a taste of the kinds of comics that had come before. They even featured a silver border around the cover to match the *Marvel Masterworks* line, priming consumers to follow up with those more expensive collected editions. The series also had the effect of more formally introducing the likes of Jack Kirby and Steve Ditko to young readers. It was here where I first encountered Ditko in reprints of *Amazing Fantasy* #15 and *The Amazing Spider-Man* #1. I had never seen anything like them before, and they captivated me.

The way Ditko's characters contorted and moved, his focus on the hands as a means of human expression, the way his characters emoted and created drama on the page, the way his layouts dictated the tone and pace of the narrative, along with any number of other idiosyncratic elements, were things that I obsessed over for years, decades. When I first read *The Amazing Spider-Man* #33 as a kid, I was moved to tears because it was the first time I felt like I *understood* Peter Parker—that his heroism was defined not by his superpowers or costume but by his heart and mind. This was a profound revelation for my young mind and, as I would realize much later, a product of Ditko's particular psychological approach to characters.

As I grew older, I gained access to something I imagined to be disposable income, as well as the ability to travel to faraway comic book conventions, and I began to pursue Ditko's work wherever I could find and afford it. After my childhood investments in Spider-Man, Dr. Strange, and Speedball, I found Ditko's Charlton and DC superheroes, like Blue Beetle, Captain Atom, the Question, the Hawk and the Dove, and weird heroes like the Creeper and Shade the Changing Man. At first I bought those issues solely because of Ditko's name, but when I read them, I found myself perplexed by their contents—especially with characters like the Question and Hawk and Dove, because of their obvious political and philosophic investments. I didn't quite have the vocabulary to articulate it at the time, but through those works, I first understood that comics had political and rhetorical aims for their readers.

From there, I began to indulge myself with Ditko's horror and science fiction titles, as well as his later contribution to titles like *Rom*, brief stints on *Chuck Norris and the Karate Commandos*, and short-lived series like *The Destructor*. Around the same time I was digging through back-issue boxes looking for those titles, I came across characters like Static and eventually found a copy of *Mr. A* #1, which I snatched up for the paltry sum of nine dollars. As I read through these comics, it wasn't just Ditko's philosophy and politics that I confronted; I began to realize how his thinking manifested on the page *visually* through his layouts and how he rendered the contents of each panel.

By this time, I had long known about the conflicts between Ditko and Stan Lee, outlined earlier, as well as the conflicts that Jack Kirby had with Lee, so encountering a page where Ditko's art did not quite match the dialogue that was edited or supplied after his pages were complete did not come as a great shock to me. But in *The Destructor* #4 (1975), dialogued by Gerry Conway and edited by Larry Lieber, I became most keenly aware of how Ditko's politics appeared visually and were uncompromised enough to disrupt the flow of the narrative.

In that issue, Jay Hunter, the series' protagonist, has been captured by a group of unusual-looking people with superpowers living in a hidden underground city called the Secret Citadel. The leader of the group, Kronus, explains to Hunter how the city came to be and how its citizens were grotesquely mutated and given superhuman abilities. As part of his tale, Kronus tells of how his parents confronted the multimillionaire who financed the building of the Secret Citadel, Abraham Caldwell, a man whom Kronus describes as *"evil incarnate"* (fig. 1.4).[68] Kronus explains that Caldwell built a shoddy nuclear power plant to fuel the city, and because of his negligence, the power plant failed catastrophically, mutating the generation of children born in the Secret Citadel. Enraged by what has happened, Kronus's parents, who are academics, confronted and beat Caldwell to death before surrendering to the authorities. That's the story as Kronus tells it and as Conway scripts it. Ditko's art tells a very different story.

Instead of a dystopian setting, the Secret Citadel is a highly sophisticated, futuristic-looking city, complete with flying cars and Kirby-esque machines. It's clean, sleek looking, and functioning. Abraham Caldwell has an erect posture, and in spite of the words written for him by Conway, along with their particular points of emphasis, Caldwell has a calm, rational, and polished demeanor. Caldwell is clearly a man in control of himself, and depending on one's perspective, the millionaire industrialist even appears heroic. Meanwhile, Kronus's parents and their academic friends are rendered as slouching, disheveled, and overweight grotesques, wracked with emotion and anger at the "evil" Caldwell, and their attack on Caldwell and his aides is depicted as frenzied, irrational, and overwrought. While Conway's dialogue makes the attack sound, at worst, born of righteous anger, Ditko's art shows the attack to

Figure 1.4. Ditko's art contravenes Conway's script, reinforcing Ditko's own worldview instead of capitulating to the politics of the dialogue provided. Written by Gerry Conway, penciled by Steve Ditko; inked by Al Milgrom; letters by John Duffy. "Doomsday—Minus One," *The Destructor* #4 (August 1975). © SP Media Group.

be the product of an irrational mob mentality, born of a hatred of what Ayn Rand imagined to be "men of the mind."

In February 2018, via Twitter, I asked Gerry Conway whether he had any recollection of this collaboration and the stark differences between his script and Ditko's finished art. He responded briefly, writing, "Probably. Ditko is an Ayn Rand absolutist. I'm a squishy libtard." Setting aside the political commentary, Conway says he liked working with Ditko, and it seems clear that Ditko going off in his own direction with the visual elements of the narrative did not come as a surprise to Conway. That Conway has an air of expectation about the changes made in *The Destructor* speaks directly to Ditko's steadfastness in making his ideals part of his work. Further, in a later tweet in the same conversation, Conway added that, when he worked with Ditko, Ditko worked from full scripts, but the two of them only ever met in person once. That Ditko was working from full scripts by Conway but still decided to tell a different story from the script, again, reinforces the primary importance of reading the formal elements of any of Ditko's work—be it a collaborative or more singular effort—when teasing out an ideological message.

Atlas Comics, the publisher of *The Destructor*, folded after this issue was released, and the final installments of the story were never printed, so it is difficult to speculate on how things shook out for Jay Hunter, Kronus, and the dwellers of the Secret Citadel. However, a potential reading of this issue is that Kronus is an unreliable source of information, and later in the issue Kronus does prove himself to be of complicated motivations, if not villainous. Even so, if one chooses to read Kronus as complex or unreliable, such a reading does not cancel out the visual depictions of the Secret Citadel's financier, the mob that murdered him, or the political implications of those depictions. Abraham Caldwell hardly falls in line with the grotesque features of Ditko's other villains, whereas Kronus's parents fit the physical depiction of any number of Ditko villains, from their posture to their twisted faces and wide, bulging eyes. Whether it was a decision by Ditko or by Conway to contravene the other is less important than the fact that Ditko's politics are presented visually. From this point, as well as nearly countless others, we can extrapolate a way to interpret Ditko's visual rhetoric and place it within the context of a larger political philosophy. It is that larger political philosophy that I explore here as a means for positioning Ditko's work as an entry point to broader cultural and theoretical conversation.

Whatever the outcome of a book like *Mysterious Travelers* is, and whatever way it is received and interpreted, Ditko was right about at least one thing: all lives do change. The following chapters are intended to demonstrate how—tucked away in a Manhattan office building, behind a heavy metal door in a narrow, austere-looking hallway—the work of a particular creative voice provides insight into one of the myriad ways American political life changed during the twentieth century. Beginning with Ditko's earliest horror and suspense stories, moving into his superhero comics of the 1960s and 1970s, transitioning into his creator-owned work of 1960s into the 1980s, this book explores the development of Ditko's political philosophy, how it can be conceived through mystic liberalism, some of the broader implications of Ditko's philosophy, and how other politically active voices in comics responded to such a worldview. Tracking this intellectual history will help us gain a better understanding of an unusual, but powerful, strand of the American political consciousness that develops alongside the neoliberalism of the mid-twentieth century and how that peculiar strand of mystic liberalism informed popular discourse and popular media for decades to come.

2

BEYOND WHAT WE ARE TOLD IS FACT

Mystic Liberalism and Closing the Gap between "Is" and "Ought"

The new age began in part as a reaction against authority in favor of individualism and the right to test belief by personal experience. By acquiring the right to think for himself in religious matters, man also gained freedom to live according to his convictions. . . . Thus inward guidance led the way to another and more spiritual phase of liberalism.
—Horatio Dresser

During a heated argument about whether or not he should investigate the murder of a colleague, Stac Rae—alias Static, a research scientist who possesses a powerful suit that enhances his physical abilities—argues with a cool intensity that "truth has no exceptions," and he sees "no dichotomy between *is* and *ought*."[1] This scene from Steve Ditko's *Static* gets right to the core of what drives mystic liberal thought: eliminating the difference between the world that could be and the world that currently exists. Mystic liberalism is the convergence between a spiritual search underwritten by a gospel of healthy-mindedness and the postwar politics of neoliberalism and its individualist and capitalist ideals. In *The History of New Thought* (2012), the New Thought historian John Haller notes a pull within the New Thought movement toward "a more secular ideology of success and prosperity."[2] I agree with his general observation about New Thought, and it underwrites the substantial political component of this transition to a more secular mind power movement. The folding in of that political component reveals a distinct approach to considering how political reality was shaped in twentieth-century America, perhaps best exemplified in the 1980 election of Ronald Reagan.

Mitch Horowitz draws specific attention to how Reagan infused New Thought and mind power language into the declaration of his candidacy in 1979, where Reagan confidently proclaimed, "If there is one thing we are sure of, it is . . . that nothing is impossible, and that man is capable of improving his circumstances beyond what we are told is fact."[3] What this chapter sets out to establish is, first, the intellectual and political overlap that prohibits mystic liberalism from being easily reducible to either popular configurations of liberal politics or New Thought mysticism, and, second, a set of parameters for identifying mystic liberalism in its applications as a mode of political critique.

Assuming Control over One's Own Circumstances

Embedded within Reagan's call for the improvement of Americans' circumstances is the suggestion that Americans were not already living up to their potential. That, somewhere along the way, there had been a failure. For Reagan, this failure comes not from within but from without: government restrains individuals, and the way to improve one's lot is to remove oneself from the clutches of outside control in favor of an inward-looking, individuated approach to government and to life. Politically, mystic liberalism is deeply indebted to the notion that failure is always an option. Failure builds character. Failure demands that we reassess and revise. Failure facilitates change. Books like Norman Vincent Peale's 1952 best seller *The Power of Positive Thinking*—a book that, in its current printing, boasts a staggering five million copies sold—is filled with stories of individual redemption where someone, usually a businessman of some sort, had been struggling or had failed in some substantive way. After placing their trust in Peale's counsel and adopting his positive thinking approach, their troubles are resolved and their future looks brighter. Peale supports his methods with anecdotes about other independent practitioners of positive thinking who have the ability to suggest "positive ideas concerning [a] proposition until a new set of attitudes gives them a new concept of the facts."[4] Reagan echoes this exact sentiment in his 1979 candidacy speech. On a personal scale, the failures of an external reality can be transformed through active belief in Peale's calls to "assume control over your circumstances."[5]

Without direct reference to Peale, Steve Ditko offers his own approach to assuming personal responsibility and control in *witzend* #6 (1969), where the artist identifies who and what he thought were some of the world's great failures in a piece called "The Avenging World." As it was initially presented to readers, "The Avenging World" appeared in two parts across issues #6 and #7 of *witzend* and was later compiled and revised for a new publication in 1973 and revised again for republication in 2002. A mixture of comics, collage, and political cartooning, "The Avenging World" identifies how failures of certain mind-sets, particularly passive neutrality, led to what Ditko saw as the world's worst social and political ills, including fascism and Soviet communism.

Witzend was an independent comics publication where "grizzled veterans, raw beginners, and off the wall kids could meet, collaborate, and bounce ideas and sensibilities off each other's heads."[6] Unofficially, it was the publication of the Wallace Wood Studio. Wood was a veteran of the famous Eisner and Iger Studio, where he worked on backgrounds for *The Spirit* in the 1940s. In the 1950s, he helped shape EC Comics with his science fiction comics, worked on a number of Harvey Kurtzman's war comics, and helped establish *Mad*. In the 1960s, just before the launch of *witzend*, Wood produced a memorable run on Marvel's *Daredevil* and created *T.H.U.N.D.E.R Agents* for Tower Comics. Until his passing in 1981, Wood reached comics readers through a wide variety of genres and styles and had a number of key collaborations with Steve Ditko, including *The Destructor* story mentioned in chapter 1. Through *witzend*, Wood provided a space where new talent, ideas, and approaches to comics could find an audience, and it was a platform where a single issue would showcase up-and-coming cartoonists like Art Spiegelman alongside veterans like Ditko, Reed Crandall, and Harvey Kurtzman.[7] *Witzend* was designed to be a publication devoted to "innovators of popular art, for the benefit of the limited but ardent audience who appreciate their efforts."[8]

Ditko took seriously that mission of innovation without the constraints of commercial publishing, and in the pages of "The Avenging World," he offered a visually arresting polemic that addressed what he saw as the fundamental conflict in the human condition: life and anti-life. The piece opens on an anthropomorphized globe; a human body with an oversized globe for a head, covered in bandages, stands on crutches, his arm in a sling. Set against a background of collaged newspaper clippings that note the political and social turmoil happening around the globe, a narration box insists that "the state of the world is just the *demonstrative, proveable effect* of the degree to which man has refused to allow himself to know what is right and to act in the manner proper for man." Man, here, is defined in perceivably Aristotelian terms as "a rational being." The bruised and battered globe then angrily informs readers that what is at stake is a failure to think and behave rationally. "The state I'm in was *caused* and there's a lot of people working hard, *knowingly and unknowingly* to make sure my condition gets worse," exclaims the globe. Negative thoughts and ideologies, consciously and subconsciously held, are at the root of the problem and, according to the globe, always lead to "more misery."[9] Significantly, the notion that these negative thoughts are the root of both individual and worldwide problems—failures—is very much in line with the worldview propagated by Peale in *The Power of Positive Thinking*, and like Peale, Ditko identifies the primary barrier to improvement as passivity. In Ditko's configuration, this passivity is personified in the Neutralist.

For Ditko, neutrality is an evasion of consciousness that permits injustices to happen, and the more aggressive the Neutralist's agnosticism is, the more detrimental it is to active, productive minds. For Ditko, the Neutralist—portrayed as cartoonishly blind with dark glasses—cannot see the difference between a political system in which "man's rights come from the state, society, god, by vote," and one in which each individual, by virtue of their existence, possesses "the inalienable right to life, liberty, and the pursuit of happiness."[10] This political binary runs parallel to the kind of liberalism claimed by American libertarians, and was also first printed in the September 1969 issue of *Reason*—a political magazine dedicated to the libertarian movement. Ditko further contemplates such politics in another collage made up of contemporary headlines. In this collage, the Neutralist— dressed as a police officer, whistling and twirling his baton—stands among a number of writhing, anguished, and dying bodies, whose interiors are partial newspaper headlines like "Hanoi Charges," "Disorder Area in Berkeley [missing text] under Disaster Curfew," and "Romania Studies Expanded Forces." All of these point to the problem of the state and statist intervention, and with the exception of the implicit criticism of American action in Vietnam, the rhetoric Ditko employs is not dissimilar to that which Reagan capitalized on in his 1980 campaign (fig. 2.1).

The story that follows takes on common libertarian concerns of taxation, where a blue-collar laborer has his hard-earned wages stripped from him and given to another character, illustrated as a sort of vagabond, who refuses to work and support himself. As a representation of "the ruling power," the Neutralist decides to divide the blue-collar worker's wages evenly between the wage earner and the derelict in the name of "true equality for all, based on the feelings and needs of the majority." The Neutralist continues that "we all have to sacrifice something, but this way, no one loses everything, and besides, who's to judge what's right or wrong?"[11] This is but one example of how the choice between life and anti-life functions in Ditko's comics; here, the anti-life choice is to use political power and state-sanctioned force to redistribute wages.

Employing this kind of reductio ad absurdum argument about economic policy is problematic at best, but it offers a useful indicator for a late twentieth-century liberal imagination of government intervention in individual economic life, fitting neatly within the Randian and libertarian axiom, borrowed from Lysander Spooner, that "government, like a highwayman, says to a man: *Your money, or your life.* And many, if not most, taxes are paid under the compulsion of that threat."[12] How Ditko adds to the conversation is by locating the source of this problem—the equivocating of the Neutralist and its resultant evils—in individual acts of thought and choice, and where choosing not to decide is a deliberate act of evasion.

Figure 2.1. The Neutralist blindly ignores the chaos and violence—along with political and ethical crises—perpetuated by what Ditko presents as the statist elements of the American Left and Right. Art by Steve Ditko. First printed in *witzend* #6 (Spring 1969) and *Reason* vol. 2, #1 (September 1969). © Steve Ditko.

Ditko makes plain again that this is a matter of conscious thought in the closing moments of part 2 of "The Avenging World" from *witzend* #7. The penultimate page, which precedes a coda presented by Mr. A, features another newspaper collage, except this time the distraught globe is filled with headlines that link terms like "racism," "fear," "terrorism," "violence," "crime," "riot," "bandits," and "war" with more complete headlines like "Jeering Rebels," "Soviet Rape of Baltic Nations a Counterpart of Nazi Genocide," "Pope Hits Catholic Critics," and "Anti-Cop Violence Feared." Beneath the globe is a white and black card—with the white on the left and the black on the right—standing in for Ditko's notion of the choice between life and anti-life. An avatar for those positions inhabits each section of the card, and between them is a slouching, gray, and black-speckled figure, holding the hand of the avatar for anti-life while the avatar for life stands off to the left, erect and alone, exemplifying that the evils of the world are often ready to tempt and lure away the rational mind toward evil and irrational thoughts and actions—actions that result in the negative terms that populate the inside of the globe.

The globe makes this precise point while emphasizing the role of the negative mind in creating distressing political and social circumstances: "Behind the cause of every disastrous headline . . . *you will find a man who first made a mess of his mind* by corrupting rationality with irrationality," and "no man can build a meaningful, lasting structure by corrupting the foundation of his effort,"[13] with that corruption being the result of irrational thoughts. Whereas Peale and other mind power advocates, along with political allies like Reagan, advocate the ostensible positive effects of applied mind power and thinking, Ditko reveals personal and political threats created by negative thoughts and a type of equivocation that refuses to choose or acknowledge the consequences of one's choices.

In later printings of "The Avenging World," through a series of caricatures, Ditko identifies others, besides the Neutralist, who are responsible for the world's social and political ills, including the religious, enlightened spiritual gurus, bleeding-heart humanitarians, the "political power-luster," and so-called "pragmatic businessmen," all of whom refuse to see themselves for who they really are or to identify the magnitude of their own intellectual and moral failings. Among these targets is also the "skeptical intellectual," who, while wearing a mortarboard and clutching a disorderly clump of books and scrolls, declares, "*Nobody* can *know anything for certain!* There are *no* absolutes, *no* truths. . . . Our senses *deceive* us."[14] This last caricature is significant, as it sets Ditko's philosophic approach in opposition to that of an academic, intellectual elite and defines Ditko's perspective as one based not on theoretical precepts as much as on an experiential reality that, despite his opposition to spiritual gurus, aligns him with the felt and perceived reality of mystic and occult thought, particularly as it pertains to the mind power movement. Popularizers like Peale depended not so much on academically quantifiable data as on reasoned, qualifiable experiences. Ditko's suggestion of the merging of the rational with the experiential is well suited to mystic liberal thought as it developed over time.

Coping, Adapting, and Imagining a New World

The cultivation of mystic liberalism is not a story of an intellectual elite and their challenges to established philosophies and institutions; rather, it is about how the masses process their historical moment, how they re-create religion after religion failed, and how they create space for themselves in the liberal marketplace after capitalism is revised. The story I want to tell about mystic liberalism is less concerned with questions of being. Instead I am interested in the question of becoming. Who will people be when they deal with the fallout of these great failures? How will they re-create themselves? How can an *ought* be transformed into an *is*?

In the early years of the twentieth century, one of the sites of that becoming was Johnstown, Pennsylvania, location of the leading steel producers in the country. The industry's demand for labor attracted thousands of immigrants in search of work and an opportunity to improve their circumstances in their home countries or to create a new life in America. In Johnstown, many of these immigrant laborers came from East Central Europe—thousands of them, in fact. But life in Johnstown was often volatile for these immigrant laborers as work at the Cambria Steel Company, the city's major mining and steel operation, ebbed and flowed; and for many, the crippling effects of the Great Depression and the St. Patrick's Day flood of 1936 exacerbated their struggles. Survival and self-reinvention in the face of continual uncertainty, punctuated by often-brutal economic and social circumstances, were the order of the day for many immigrant and first-generation American families in Johnstown. In the introduction to her ethnographic study of the Johnstown immigrants, *For Bread with Butter*, Ewa Morawska describes the situation in Johnstown as one of continual coping and adaptation: the "peasant-immigrants and their children [had] to solve problems and realize cultural goals and expectations in a restricted environment."[15] Among those surviving, coping, adapting families were the Ditkos.

Census records indicate that the Ditkos emigrated to the United States around 1900 from the Austro-Hungarian Empire, with post–World War I records referring to their country of origin as the newly defined and independent Czechoslovakia. Their son, Stephen, would later father the artist Steve Ditko. The older Stephen was born in 1901 as an American citizen and remained in Pennsylvania, finding work in Johnstown as a master carpenter at a steel mill. And while the recently arrived Ditkos and their American-born children were adapting to the tumultuous industrial landscape of

Johnstown with other East Central Europeans, it was the third generation of Ditkos in America who would eventually articulate a way to "solve problems and realize cultural goals and expectations in a restricted environment" by means of intellectual and artistic labor, "to invent ways to bring the environment into closer conformity to their purposes."[16] In November 1927, Anna and Stephen Ditko welcomed their second child, Stephen J. Ditko. Very little has been written about the younger Steve Ditko's early life, and my aim here is not to construct a biography but to provide a useful backdrop for a different way of imagining the world from which he emerged. Before the younger Steve enlisted in the US Army after World War II in 1945, and before he moved to New York City to study under and work with the comics luminary Jerry Robinson at what would eventually become the School of Visual Arts, before he cocreated Spider-Man and created Dr. Strange, he lived in a community constrained by the circumstances imposed by class and ethnicity.

To relieve the pressure of these binding forces, families and individual members of Johnstown's immigrant community took on a paradoxical existence that demanded participation in the larger marketplace as a means of achieving the goals that brought them to America while simultaneously congealing themselves into smaller, more isolated in-groups defined by familial, ethnic, and cultural affiliations.[17] Many, particularly those of the second generation, were then left with the frustrating chore of trying to navigate the liminal space between the American cultural myths and assumptions about the ubiquity of opportunity for individual achievement, on the one hand, and their lived experiences with the institutional enforcement of class and ethnic boundaries at school and work, on the other.[18] Explaining how this played out for Johnstown's second-generation immigrants, Morawska writes:

> As everywhere else in Pennsylvania, Johnstown was swept up in the school reform and Americanization movement, and the immigrant children at the beginning of the century were taught the natural superiority of American civilization and its fundamental values of freedom, equality, and personal achievement. [Morawska's] second generation informants remembered well being told as children in the classroom "America is the best country on earth"; "America is the land of opportunity for all"; "You can become what you want"; and "Don't be a coal miner." Equally ingrained in the memory of those who attended public schools in Johnstown was another recollection—of recurrent feelings of embarrassment and inferiority to the "American" children, caused by difficulty with the English language (in the early grades), "foreign" dress, and "unpronounceable" names.[19]

This kind of palpable inconsistency between the dominant cultural ideology of equal opportunity and the kind of particularism that was experienced continued well through the interwar period, creating a clear sense that although immigrants and their children were free to look up and around them, they were tightly bound to their physical and cultural place.[20]

Within that bounded existence, immigrant workers and their children were forced to look inward, both to themselves and to their own racially and ethnically segregated communities, for support through the development of mutual aid coalitions, societies, clubs, and church parishes, building their own schools and newspapers. They constructed what Morawska calls an "internal framework" to cope with the challenges and restrictions of coming to America. And while some intermingling certainly occurred between immigrant communities in Johnstown,[21] these separate, if not fully individuated, frameworks for each segment of the immigrant community of Johnstown helped recently arrived East Central Europeans move purposefully toward achieving the goals that had brought them to America in the first place.[22]

Put differently, for the immigrant community to survive, its members had to reinvent themselves, both as individuals and as a people. The apparent solution was not to look outward toward the paternalism extended by the politically powerful Cambria Steel Company, along with its irregular labor opportunities and union busting,[23] nor was the solution to look to America or Americans, whose particularist attitudes fueled the segregation of Johnstown.[24] To adapt, to re-create themselves in America, the members of these communities had to recognize that the promises of their new country were mostly just that. If these promises would ever materialize for themselves or their children, they would come at a great cost, as they consistently faced concurrent threats from financial instability and strained living conditions, which were only maintained by insecure, hard labor.[25]

The efforts toward survival and self-reinvention became a multigenerational task, and a morally and spiritually focused, parochial education for second- and third-generation immigrants—one that reinforced the practical values attained through hands-on hard work that trumped formal education. For many, this was an entirely rational approach, as the labor of coming generations would only generate more income that would sustain the family and, perhaps, improve their station.[26] And while, in a rather straightforward way, this appears to be a sign of social differentiation, it has the unintended consequence of signaling a kind of philosophic, as opposed to wholly pragmatic, outlook that relies on lived experience and rational decision-making similar to something like natural philosophy, which gained popularity in the Romantic and German tradition through thinkers like Goethe, as a means of linking the sensible, natural world and spiritual existence.[27]

It would seem unlikely that peasant immigrants would have a deep familiarity with the precepts and evolution of natural philosophy as Western thought moved toward the natural sciences. However, the milieu in which they existed before coming to America, and the pragmatism of focusing on labor and its tangible outcomes, does seem to signal a focus on the "matter" portion of Cartesian dualism and a view that matter can be produced by the labor of one's mind. As it pertains to the development of mind power and New Thought, Haller identifies a blending of Descartes's "mind/body dualism . . . to the body/soul spirituality of Jesuit Priest and philosopher Pierre Teilhard de Chardin,"[28] in which New Thought thrived, offering a mind-over-body approach to a development of the self and a prosperous life.[29]

Part of this New Thought solution to the problem of Cartesian dualism was to imagine a nexus of the body and soul[30] that would permit an understanding of the mind as a generative force that acted in concert with the material world and "complemented rather than competed with reductionist" materialism.[31] In large part, this suturing together of the natural and spiritual worlds allows the quantifiable world of the body to become an extension of the qualifiable experiences of the mind. Haller refers to this suturing as an existence "beyond mechanics and geometry, serv[ing] as the instrument of God's purposes,"[32] and it reflects an insistence that the inner, spiritual life determined the practical, measurable world. This view of the body—and what is reaped from the practical world—as a direct product of the labor of the mind fits within the paradigm that Morawska sets out for the Johnstown immigrants. Moreover, the kind of practical rationality expressed by these immigrant communities, paired with their predominantly parochial education, is also reflective of Enlightenment liberalism, particularly the kind of rationalism associated with Locke's sense of natural law.

In this sense of natural law, Locke posits that, through reason, we can understand that no one has the power to "take away the Life or Property of another,"[33] and property is generally understood as the "Lives, Liberties and Estates,"[34] and those estates are "made out from" the dominion granted to Adam by God in Genesis; the "Children of Men . . . could make . . . distinct titles to several parcels [of the land] for their private uses."[35] Those distinct titles, then, are produced by the "*Labour* of [one's] Body, and the *Work* of [one's] Hands,"[36] which belong uniquely to the user of that labor and those hands. That is, a life can be built. Importantly for understanding both Locke and his importance to mystic liberalism, Locke held natural law "as an Eternal Rule to all Men," which is "unwritten, and so nowhere to be found but *in the minds* of men."[37] As such, the natural law that guided its practitioners is understood innately or through carefully practiced reason and rational introspection.

The actions of Johnstown immigrants are further linked to Lockean liberalism with their focus on attaining property by means of their labor and practical actions. To be sure, there is not a one-to-one correlation between the kinds of property available to the Johnstown immigrants—home ownership, for example—and Locke's imagination of property as being the product of creating utility from a given piece of land. However, the approaches to property are not entirely divorced, and according to Morawska, many Johnstown immigrants, using their peasant backgrounds, used their newly acquired property for gardens and other practical concerns.[38] The drive to acquire property was a major component of the self-reinvention of these communities, in no small part because of the personal achievement and financial security property symbolized. For these communities, it was clear that the most reliable way to overcome uncertain social and economic circumstances and earn property-holding status was through stubborn determination and practical actions, grounded by a moral and spiritual education.

Albeit unintentional, the kind of uncertainty encountered in Johnstown as it ran alongside the often-unfulfilled promises of America emerges as a kind of hybrid worldview. As opposed to a philosophic outlook born of a formal, intellectual, academic approach to observations about physical and metaphysical existence, the kind of thinking that we can glean from Johnstown depends on the lived experiences of its inhabitants: a more praxeologic method, or a kind of practical ratiocination.[39] Moreover, although the commitment to community and mutual aid that became part and parcel of the survival of Johnstown's immigrants would seem to run counter to later formations of liberal individualism found in mass culture, the volitional nature of these kinds of safety nets and their establishment outside the corporate and governmental institutions speak to a reliance on personal, familial social networks as opposed to a government-funded welfare system that conservative and libertarian thinkers would accuse of depending on the use of force, as opposed to choice.[40]

It is within this intellectually complex communal liberalism that Steve Ditko spent his youth—a nuanced existence that demanded at once individual success and communal support, practical action and spiritual motivation, to be American and not American, to be committed to one's labor and unable to capitalize on it, to need societal support and learn to operate without it.

Illuminated Politics and Impending Cultural Change

The disappointments and failures of the promises of American life for immigrants ran concurrent with other perceived failures during the period after World War I. Just as the promises of achievement and success in America fell dramatically short, so too did the promises of adventure and heroism for the generation that went off to fight in the trenches and face the no-man's-lands in France. Setting aside the complications this would have presented to first- and second-generation immigrants originating from Central Powers countries, like many of those in Johnstown, the Great War represented a larger failure than that of any set of social circumstances. It represented the failure of authoritative institutions, the failure of religion, the failure of God.

Moreover, challenges to established religious institutions would not have been new to people of East Central European descent, nor would such challenges be to many Americans, who seemingly existed in a perpetual state of spiritual revision from the word go. The myriad approaches to religious and mystical thought throughout the West ranged from extremely traditional, conservative perspectives that wanted to re-entrench centralized authority to the extremely liberal perspectives that sought not just freedom of thought and belief but a freedom of action that, for some, would border on licentiousness. The American Northeast, with its Burned-Over District and Psychic Highway, was a major site of spiritual change, both radical and conservative.[41] Similar to the ways in which America has imagined itself as a great experiment in republican politics, so too has it served as a haven and laboratory for religious experimentation. Whether one takes these perspectives, these religions-after-religion, as fantasies or as acceptable truths is significantly less important than the effects these beliefs can have once they become institutionalized as part of the values and social groups of a particular culture. Ultimately, as Nicholas Goodrick-Clarke puts it, these fantasies become an "important symptom of impending cultural changes and political action."[42]

While the Industrial Revolution attracted immigrants from Central Europe to places like Johnstown—offering the potential for a transformed, if not better, existence—earlier generations of Central Europeans had produced waves of occultists and mystic thinkers who were often forced to abandon their homelands as they searched for their own transformative experiences and new lives, often leading them to the Americas. The occult diaspora is an important component of those East Coast religious movements noted earlier, but through organizations like the Freemasons, it is also inextricably linked to the political foundations of American government, influencing private and public existence. Writers on the occult, like Mitch Horowitz, Gary Lachman, James Webb, and Nicholas Goodrick-Clarke, have constructed convincing histories of the occult and how these myriad systems of belief commingled and evolved over centuries, typically tying their origins to the early modern era and its challenges to Catholic hegemony in Europe, as well as the period's political and cultural pressures. What is at stake is that these are and were sincerely held ideas that informed political actions for a range of communities.

Further, these modern accounts of occult history also work diligently to link occult and esoteric beliefs to political reform, an entanglement that Webb sees most directly as a product of post–World War I anxieties leading to what he calls an "illuminated politics." For Webb, to be "illuminated" is to be of a "reality that transcends the materialist point of view and the emergence of the rejected—both ideas and men—into unaccustomed positions of prominence."[43] In other words, an illuminated politics emerges, in part, because of the challenges presented by a social and political underclass, and, Webb continues, the occult "embodies basic attitudes toward both universal and historical conditions."[44] Although both Lachman and Horowitz mount persuasive challenges to Webb's narrow historicizing,[45] both also seem to embrace Webb's sense of an "illuminated politics" as an effective means for understanding the relationship between the occult and the political maneuvering of the West, along with the twentieth-century Western occult revival during the interwar period and beyond. Although I do not seek to position this book as anything resembling a complete occult history, I do seek to employ a broader, established occult history to explain a particular operation of an illuminated politics.

Histories of the occult, like those just noted, often contain dual yields: they provide insight into how such beliefs motivated a politically powerful elite while also noting how those same conceptions of reality were often grounded in historical moments and populations that demanded social change because practitioners either were, or believed themselves to be, powerless. The quest for a kind of illuminated politics, in that case, is, as Goodrick-Clarke insists, an indicator of pending societal change resulting in the consolidation or redistribution of political power, be it in a liberal context like the French Revolution or with the rise of fascism in Weimar Germany. Even if it is uncomfortable to acknowledge, the common ground in the establishment of an illuminated politics is societal and economic uncertainty. That uncertainty can have any number of potential causes, but as the authors noted earlier have convincingly maintained, this uncertainty was met with opposition from a more politically powerful establishment, be it the church or the state. This led to micro and macro rebellions or escape to destinations that, ostensibly, were more spiritually egalitarian, like the United States.

To put it more directly, I am forming an argument dependent on a multilayered syncretism that, at one level, holds that the kind of spiritual seekers who were attracted to the United States in its early years were drawn there because they saw an opportunity to practice and experiment with new forms of belief, self-directed forms of discovery. In an adjoining moment, many people, like those who populated Johnstown, Pennsylvania, migrated because they were also seekers, looking for an improved social and economic existence. That both of these communities emerge from a place that was, as all the historians noted earlier acknowledge, a locus of transformative esoteric thought is too coincidental to overlook.

These syncretic complexities are expanded not only by the diversity of religious experimentation already happening in the United States, but also by the uncertainty experienced by the Lost Generation after World War I. Moreover, these postwar uncertainties and anxieties manifested in popular and political forms, reinforcing and perpetuating themselves among the masses, largely through what was later known as modernism as its literary modes were made available to mass audiences through publishers of pulp novels.[46] But, as should be clear, not everyone was so nihilistic as many of the modernists, and there were many who began looking for *something* rather than learning to accept that there was *nothing*.

Like the immigrants who came to America and turned inward toward their isolated communities for salvation and growth, America, and the West at large, was also asked to turn inward when trying to recuperate from the perceived failures of God and the state. For these seekers, the question was one of regeneration. Part of that quest meant looking to generations past and how they attempted to resolve these concerns. One of the ultimate consequences was the cultivation of a class of organic intellectuals who did not rely on traditional modes of knowledge production or the contemporary intelligentsia.[47]

One of the most significant figures to emerge from the smelter of the occult factories in America was the Russian-born immigrant Helena Petrovna Blavatsky, more famously known as Madame Blavatsky in the fin de siècle milieu. Although Blavatsky had never really disappeared from the public consciousness in the way many other ideanauts of her ilk had, it was through her that the term "occult" became part of the public lexicon, and her ideas were less related to the establishment of doctrinal authority than they were about the individual search for enlightenment, a particularly useful notion for people looking for something other than the perceptibly hollow liturgical promises of established religion.

Blavatsky arrived in America in the early 1870s with the intent to challenge Spiritualism by, in part, revealing its limitations. Blavatsky's aim was not to debunk the claims of Spiritualism, as Harry Houdini would make his mission in later years. Rather, although Blavatsky admired Andrew Jackson Davis, the movement's founder, she wanted to illuminate a path toward a higher truth. Of course, Blavatsky did not claim that her role as shepherd was her own invention; it was revealed to her by a secret order of masters of ancient wisdom, the "Mahatmas," who had achieved a kind of *inner* purity. On this fateful mission to America, Blavatsky met Henry Steel Olcott, a former Civil War officer who was invested in Spiritualism.

After their partnering, Blavatsky and Olcott went on to develop Blavatsky's magnum opus, *Isis Unveiled*, an expansive text that covered a variety of occult subjects, revealing to readers that there were secret teachings unknown to both mainstream religion and scientific materialism. This hidden doctrine would provide a kind of cosmological unity that was available to all by gaining access to a divine wisdom. Blavatsky and Olcott organized their suppliants in this quest for wisdom into the Theosophical Society, but as Horowitz points out, Theosophy "was not a religion itself but rather aimed to plumb the *inner depths* of religion."[48]

For Horowitz and others, Blavatsky opened the Western mind to a modern notion of the man of wisdom.[49] This, of course, is different from the Nietzschean notion of the wise man atop the mountain, as in *Thus Spoke*

Zarathustra. Rather than the wise man coming down from the mountain to examine and impart his wisdom to the people, in the Blavatskian configuration, it is up to individual seekers to find the wise man. Of course, this is not to say that there were not other men of wisdom in the Western tradition who must be sought; one might point to mythic figures like Christ or Merlin or even Nietzsche's muse, Zarathustra.

What Horowitz argues is that Blavatsky reignites a contemporary interest in such figures, and this interest is, in part, made more modern and compelling because Blavatsky's Mahatmas are accessible now, as opposed to being unreachable figures of an ancient past. One need only to search, and through that search, the spiritual pilgrim could do more than drink from the same deep waters as the man of ancient wisdom. That pilgrim could drink *with* him. If one could not physically connect with such a person, then there was at least the possibility to directly connect through some psychic, invisible means. At the least, the searcher could connect through a tradition that was emanating from something contemporary. Whether any of these possibilities were literally actualized by anyone is significantly less important than the romantic notion that they *could* have been for the individual true believer.

That Blavatsky reintroduces what Horowitz calls "the intercessor, the adept, the master, the figure of wisdom, the invisible helper" is significant to the evolution of the American popular and political consciousness. This intercessor comes from a mysterious, unknown place, imparts wisdom or knowledge, or perhaps rights a wrong, and disappears from the scene—a sort of occult vigilante. One might be inclined to point to other intercessory figures who appeared earlier in American literature, as in George Lippard's "Ring, Grandfather, Ring,"[50] or in more sinister intercessors as in Nathaniel Hawthorne's "My Kinsman, Major Molineux," and I would agree. What both of these examples appear to point to is a preexisting interest in mystical influence in the founding of America and its liberal ideals—in a romantic and cautionary sense, respectively. While such literature may have primed the pump, it was the efforts of Blavatsky and the Theosophical Society that provided a particular occult shape for this intercessory figure, making such an archetype available to mass culture for popular appropriation and reinterpretation.

Another major popular component of Blavatsky's Theosophy is her understanding of the machinations of karma, which in many ways operates like the intercessory function of the Masters of the Ancient Wisdom. In her essays on the nature of reincarnation and karma in *The Key to Theosophy*, Blavatsky offers the following notion of karma:

> It [is] the *Ultimate Law* of the Universe, the source, origin, and fount of all other laws which exist throughout Nature. . . . *Karma* is that unseen and unknown law *which adjusts wisely, intelligently and equitably* each effect to

its cause, tracing the latter back to its producer. Though itself *unknowable*, its action is perceivable.[51]

Blavatsky's claim here that karma can be understood by its observable effects gives karma the appearance of a machinelike apparatus for sorting out good and evil, the metaphysical existence of which is provable through observation. This kind of scientizing of karma—that, like gravity or evolution, it can be observed and measured through its products and effects—will be important to bear in mind later, but for my immediate purposes, note that karma, like the hero-vigilante or the wise intercessor, comes from an unknown, mysterious place, acts on behalf of a sort of infinite, cosmic wisdom, and disappears until its powers are needed again.

But, of course, Theosophy did not have exclusive jurisdiction over access to cosmic wisdom or the gifts of prosperity and health that it grants. During the scientizing of the mid-nineteenth century, matters ranging from illness to nature to economics to human behavior could all be mechanized and scrutinized so as not just to draw observational conclusions about the past but to make testable predictions of the future, harnessing the power of these predictions for the betterment of humankind. Within this cultural current, questions begin to surface about what else could be scientized for societal or individual benefit. Could one mechanize and tap into the supernatural—Christian or otherwise—or could one develop a protocol for creating happiness or wealth? Was there a formula for transforming one's dreams into tangible reality? These questions were answered in the affirmative by what would eventually be called New Thought, a system of belief that had its origins in Christian Socialism and was, by the mid-twentieth century, fully co-opted by neoliberalism. With its origins in Christian Socialism and its promise of making one's wishes come true if one just believes hard enough, it is not difficult to see why New Thought would be compatible and, indeed, embraced by a country—one with an already established mythology about individual achievement—in the throes of cultural and economic upheaval in the nineteenth century. This embrace would provide the footholds for New Thought to become reinvigorated in the global crises of consciousness and economics that followed World War I.

In many ways, New Thought is like most religions and religious movements: it is open to interpretation; its genealogy up to the present is tangled and sprawling;[52] and it works as a sort of Velcro ideology that can attach itself to lots of other ideologies. As a result, New Thought is difficult to contain and is often commonly understood through its antecedents and cousins in mesmerism, Christian Science, and the more commonly—if vaguely—used "power of positive thinking," among others. In its essence, New Thought imagines "the subconscious as an extension of Divine power,"[53] postulating that humans, through concerted, positive thought, can alter their physiology to improve their health, create and maintain happiness, create improved social interactions, and create wealth. Rooted in mystical and occult thought, typically blended with Christianity, New Thought has had a robust, porous spiritual network that allowed its ideas to disseminate widely, undercutting the kind of hierarchy found in organized religion. But despite these religious roots, it was New Thought's secular iterations that produced some of its most recognizably influential texts.

Two of the most widely read secular texts to come from New Thought were Dale Carnegie's *How to Win Friends and Influence People* (1936) and Dr. Norman Vincent Peale's *The Power of Positive Thinking* (1952). Whether Peale's or Carnegie's readers knew they were imbibing thinly veiled mysticism or not, New Thought's emphasis on success that comes from a can-do attitude made a terrific religion for the congregations of corporate America. Maintaining an appropriate amount of self-esteem became paramount, and believing that one could achieve greatness through the power of thought meant not that one could, but that one *would*. But the midcentury focus on self-esteem, success, and personal independence produced some competition for the superficially secular strands of New Thought, yielding one of the most popular, influential, and controversial philosophies of the twentieth century: Objectivism.

Within the same milieu of sustained interest in the occult and New Thought positive thinking came an interesting bit of syncretism: just as it was a Russian-born immigrant, Madame Blavatsky, who introduced the vocabulary of the occult to the modern Western lexicon, so it was another Russian-born immigrant, Ayn Rand, who reshaped the imagination of capitalism for a popular audience through her philosophy of Objectivism. Like Blavatsky, Rand grounded her beliefs by cultivating a close inner circle of followers. She gained popular appeal by disseminating her ideas through mass-market book publication, and novels like *Anthem* (1938), *The Fountainhead* (1943), and her magnum opus, *Atlas Shrugged* (1957), as well as nonfiction essay collections such as *The Virtue of Selfishness* (1964) and *Capitalism: The Unknown Ideal* (1966), which feature work by Rand, Nathaniel Branden, and Alan Greenspan, had a major cultural impact and remain in print today from major mass-market publishers.

Rand's philosophic approach was a response to what she held as the failures of collectivism—with which she lumped religion—especially as she experienced it during the Russian Revolution. Further, like Blavatsky's attempt to revive perceived ancient wisdom, Rand attempted to rehabilitate the image of capitalism in an era of New Deal progressivism while also working to revitalize interest in her own version of Aristotelianism, Aristotle having fallen out of favor with some contemporary philosophers.[54] And like the assurances of a new age that New Thoughtism propagated, Rand and her onetime associate and lover, Nathaniel Branden, attempted to build a philosophy for the "new intellectual," resisting the academic and intellectual elites who dismissed their ideology.[55]

Harnessing a Benevolent Universe

Objectivism, as constructed by Rand, holds itself as an optimistic view of life that celebrates human achievement, exalts reason and rationality, and values the individual over the collective. In explaining this idealistic view, Rand writes, "My philosophy, in essence, is the concept of man as a heroic being, with his own happiness as the moral purpose of his life, with productive achievement as his noblest activity, and reason as his only absolute." And like the esotericists and mystics of before, Rand cites her own lived experience as some of the greatest evidence for the effectiveness and worth of this belief system, claiming that she has "held the same philosophy I now hold, for as far back as I can remember. . . . I have never had to change any of my fundamentals."[56] If it worked for her, then it can work for anyone who sufficiently devotes themself to a nonsacrificial pursuit of reason and personal happiness. The heroes of Rand's novels, and her ideals, travel down just such a path, neither giving nor receiving what Rand would identify as the undeserved. Objectivist heroes were men and women of achievement: in *The Fountainhead* they are artists and builders like Howard Roark, and in *Atlas Shrugged* the heroes are captains of industry, but they can also be, like Rand, creators of ideas—and whatever their talent, they are producers who are pitted against society's looters, those who lust after the unearned and wish to devalue human achievement.

As with my earlier considerations of occult and esoteric thought, the intellectual and philosophic merits of Objectivism are not quite what is at stake for me, and there is much to be scrutinized within the idealistic framework Rand established. So while Objectivism will not be able to escape critique here, that precise evaluation is not my principal interest. Moreover, there already exist numerous serious examinations of Rand and Objectivism from a range of perspectives.[57] Instead I want to be able to reasonably identify the philosophy, as it self-describes, and from there consider a particular application of it within popular culture.

Without a doubt, the syncretic work being done here will ruffle the feathers of some ardent Objectivists, but again, this book is a consideration of effect rather than intent. Further, a precedent has already been set for attempting to merge Objectivism with different kinds of (often mystical) thought.[58] Admittedly, some of that blending of Objectivism with seemingly antithetical ideas exists on the fringes of the cultural conversation surrounding Rand, but others exist in highly visible ways in popular culture. Indeed, the appropriation of Rand occurs across a wide range of belief systems, from ostensibly Christian politicians[59] to the Church of Satan, the latter insisting that although Rand's philosophy and Satanism are unique from each other, "Satanism drew from Objectivism as even Rand drew others."[60] Horowitz, too, comfortably blends an interest in the Church of Satan, Madame Blavatsky, New Thought, and Objectivism as part of his own work.

The obvious difficulty here is that for Rand and Objectivists, mystic and esoteric thought is incompatible with an objective, natural view of reality. But moments in Objectivist thought contravene this position, pointing to a more complex view. For example, according to the Atlas Society, "Objectivism holds that we live in a 'benevolent universe'" that would afford us the opportunity to "achieve happiness and exaltation." And though Objectivism rejects the notion that either reality, as it exists, or a deity is watching over human action, nature can be commanded, "and this is what makes the universe essentially benevolent: It is propitious to beings like us."[61] So although Objectivists pride themselves on their reason and rationality—believing they have banished the ghosts of previous philosophy and religion—something about this ideology remains haunted.

The notion of a "benevolent universe" alone implies some kind of exterior force that guides nature along; even if it does not concern itself with human affairs, at least a minimal form of agency is implied. Would a truly objective reality not begin from the null hypothesis, with no behavior or perception inferred other than ambivalence? Objectivism's dedication to laissez-faire capitalism and Adam Smith's "invisible hand" is another area that raises questions about the infusion of mystic thought;[62] so, too, does the acceptance of transubstantiation that occurs with Locke's notion of property that materializes through labor; and the infusion of Nathaniel Branden's conception of self-esteem also points to a kind of "science of the mind" capitalizing on the work of Wallace Wattles, though quite differently motivated.[63] What all these sources have in common with occult and esoteric thought, like Theosophy and New Thought, is that they rely on the "conviction that divine mysteries existed not at a top rung of the cosmic ladder but within the settings of ordinary life."[64] The notion of "self-esteem" was incorporated into Objectivism by Rand and, particularly, Nathaniel Branden, who, after his excommunication from Rand's Objectivist movement, made a career as a pop psychologist, writing over a dozen books on self-esteem.

Taking all of this into consideration, Objectivism's claims to a kind of material rationality appear to be a shell game where the concretes, the intellectual absolutes that Objectivist thought extols, are always under one of the other shells. One can make a case that, at its core, Objectivist epistemology depends on the same kind of mystical thought that, as the question suggests, was part and parcel of the religious thinking that Objectivism claims to render obsolete, including the occult thought attributable to later movements like New Thought and Theosophy.

As has been pointed out, those overlaps would be and are still vehemently denied by Objectivists, and terms like "mysticism" are demonized in their lexicography. Earlier individualist philosophers like Max Stirner associated concepts like ethics, reason, the family, and morality with the shackles of mystical thought imposed by religion and the state.[65] To skirt such criticism, Rand and her ilk needed also to demonize previous philosophers like Stirner by labeling them "counterfeit individualists," accusing them of being unprincipled hedonists and whim[66] worshippers.[67] Stirner is seldom mentioned or deeply interrogated in the collections of early Objectivist thought by Rand and others, and the brief criticism noted here does little to address Stirner's critiques and the question of the ultimate origins of notions like "ethics." However, through the work of Steve Ditko, we can gain insight into this apparently contradictory mode of thinking propagated by Objectivism, as well as the genealogical transition from the more openly mystical and religious individualist movements of the nineteenth century and the early twentieth in the United States into the allegedly more materialistic neoliberal and libertarian political thought of the post–World War II period.

Unfortunately for Objectivism, the dodging of the mystical issue is not quite satisfactory, and to that end, it is worth at least briefly considering Stirner's position on matters of the self, and his concern with the ghosts of the mind, the mystical prisons, that have the potential to trap the individual egoist.[68] Stirner categorizes the very sacredness of truths, whether they be allegedly secular or explicitly spiritual, as ghosts of the mind. These ghosts include but are not limited to "laws," "rights," "morality," "family," "love," "religion," and even "science" and "reason" themselves. Stirner writes:

> *Concepts* are to decide everywhere, concepts to regulate life, concepts to *rule*. This is the religious world . . . bringing method into nonsense and completing the conceptual precepts into a rounded, firmly-based dogmatic. Everything is sung according to concepts, and the real man, I, am compelled to live according to these conceptual laws. . . .
>
> Liberalism simply brought other concepts on the carpet; human instead of divine, political instead of ecclesiastical, "scientific" instead of doctrinal, or, more generally, real concepts and eternal laws instead of "crude dogmas" and precepts.[69]

In the most generous scenario, acceptance of such concepts should be treated as volitional, with the recognition that they are artificial constructs. In the ideal situation, Stirner argues, they should be exorcised from one's mind, and only once that happens can one legitimately consider oneself free. To Stirner, if one cannot eliminate these specters of mystical thinking, then freedom is never really possible, and without such an exorcism, a full comprehension of the self is nearly impossible.

In his essay "Counterfeit Individualism," Nathaniel Branden accuses Stirner of proffering an individualism based on "doing whatever one wishes, regardless of the rights of others," and insists that Objectivist individualism "is at once an ethical-political concept and an ethical-psychological one."[70] This is all well and good, but it ducks Stirner's major questions: *Where do "rights" and "ethics" originate? Who or what is the prime mover there? And whatever the answer, does abdicating one's mind to those ethical principles or those notions of rights differ in any significant way from deferring to a god or the state? Is one still not dominated by mystic forces that are allegedly beyond one's comprehension?* The answer for Stirner is obvious, but this raises questions about what exactly is the supposedly counterintuitive relationship between Objectivism and mystical thought.

To address this point, considering Theosophy as well as the New Thought movement is helpful.[71] However, it is first worth unpacking Objectivism's vehement rejection of anything that it considers to be "mysticism." According to the *Ayn Rand Lexicon*, "mysticism" is understood as "the acceptance of allegations without evidence or proof, either apart from or *against* the evidence of one's senses and one's reason. Mysticism is the claim to some non-sensory, non-rational, non-definable, non-identifiable means of knowledge, such as 'instinct,' 'intuition,' 'revelation,' or any form of 'just knowing.'"[72] The immediate issue here, as Stirner would point out, is how the fields of ethics, politics, and reason evade this definition of mysticism. Stirner's position is that they do not, and Objectivism's attempt to scientize metaphysical concepts, making them in some way tangible and thus justifying their dominion over human psychology and action, helps to make Stirner's case for him. One significant way in which this happens is through Rand's attempt to treat ethics "as a science" to discover and define a reasonable code by which to live.[73]

Rand's attempt to scientize ethics is reminiscent of earlier attempts by occultists and mystics to make spiritual and religious matters not just discernible to, but measurable by, the human mind. For H. P. Blavatsky, a clear instance of this is her consideration of karma. The metaphysical existence of karma, and its machinelike apparatus for sorting out good and evil, is provable through observation. This notion runs parallel to Rand's insistence that ethics is an "objective necessity" for sorting out values (i.e., good and evil), which preexist as a "metaphysical fact."[74] In both cases, the existence of good and evil is, as Rand explains, an "unalterable condition of man's existence."[75] Although Blavatsky and Rand differ on whether or not the prime mover in this situation is knowable (Blavatsky says no, and Rand does not attempt to explain where good and evil originate beyond repeating her conception of "reason"), in both cases, "good and evil," "karma," and "ethics" return us to Stirner's contention that these are mystic entrapments that haunt any attempt at an individuated existence.

If significant questions remain about the layering of mysticism and liberal individualism or whether believers in either made a conscious connection between the two, then the emergence of the New Thought movement should put those concerns to rest. In *A History of the New Thought Movement* (1919), Horatio Dresser, a leader of the movement and son of its founder, provides a history of the movement itself, as well as introducing the concept of the "new age" more than a half century before it became a proper noun in the 1970s. For Dresser, "the history of the New Thought is for the most part the record of one of several contemporaneous movements in favor of the inner life and the individual," and it is set in opposition to what he considers the "subjectivism of the nineteenth century."[76]

Dresser positions New Thought as the central component of the new age, which he defines as being a response to the horrors of World War I, and asserts that "the new age began in part as a reaction against authority in favor of individualism and the right to test belief by personal experience,"[77] further asserting that "to be liberal is to be of the new age."[78] For Dresser, what was needed for the new age was "a spiritual science,"[79] one that assisted in interpreting Christian scripture and also psychological healing and better living, all achieved through individual introspection and action positioning each person as their own "priest and physician."[80] Further, Dresser insists, "If we fail in life, our own attitude is at fault."[81] Without getting too far ahead of myself, this is precisely the kind of thinking that Steve Ditko employs in his introduction to *Avenging World*, writing that "nations, races, and groups don't cause problems, individuals cause problems. The world isn't in a mess, people are a mess," and cleaning up the world's problems begins with "'man,' with a single person—with oneself!"[82]

In Dresser's explanation of the lineage of New Thought, he prefigures the kind of thinking that would appear from Ayn Rand and Nathaniel Branden when he writes:

Man is by divine purpose, by birth, and his true human inheritance, free. He must come forth and "claim by his freedom," the true freedom of his inner or spiritual nature. He should take his cue from the ideal, not from the actualities of his natural existence. He should rely on himself, develop his inner powers, believe in his own experiences and intuitions.[83]

Compare the previous passage to the following from Rand's "The Objectivist Ethics":

Nothing is given to man on earth except a potential and the material on which to actualize it. The potential is a superlative machine: his consciousness; but it is a machine without a spark plug, a machine of which his own will has to be the spark plug, the self-starter and the driver; *he* has to discover how to use it and *he* has to keep it in constant action. The material is the whole universe, with no limits set to the knowledge he can acquire and to the enjoyment of life he can achieve. But everything he needs or desires has to be learned, discovered and produced by *him*—by his own choice, by his own effort, by his own mind.[84]

While Rand, of course, jettisons any explicitly mystic language, both Dresser and Rand demand an acknowledgment of man as a being born both free and with access to unlimited potential that can be achieved only by means of his "inner powers" and his continual engagement with them. A suspension of that engagement means, for Dresser, a forfeiture of his freedom, and, for Rand, an abandonment of rationality, terms that are all but interchangeable in the Objectivist mind-set.

The overlap of New Thought and Objectivism continues with the introduction of "self-esteem" into Objectivist thought by Nathaniel Branden. For Objectivism, self-esteem can only be earned by performance: actualization of one's abilities without apology. Indeed, this idea pairs nicely with the New Thought movement and its advocacy for reliance on oneself to "develop [one's] inner powers, believe in [one's] own experiences and intuitions." Branden takes this several steps further by arguing that a lack of self-esteem is the root cause of nearly all societal and psychological ills, including but not limited to drug addiction, domestic violence, alcoholism, and all varieties of crime. All of these extend from the absence of self-esteem, and the suspicious link between this way of thinking and the specious reasoning of Horatio Dresser's notion that "if we fail in life, our own attitude is at fault," is nearly impossible to overlook.[85]

The links between Branden—with his push for "self-esteem"—Objectivists, and occult and mystic thought do not stop there. Branden, a previously self-identified Marxist converted to capitalism by Rand, championed the cause of self-esteem, and after his excommunication from Rand's Objectivist circles in 1968, he spent the 1970s through the 1990s as a self-styled self-help, pop-psychology guru, writing a dozen or so books on self-esteem, beginning with *The Psychology of Self-Esteem* in 1969. During Branden's time with Rand, and the lifespan of the Nathaniel Branden Institute (NBI), Branden operated NBI in a manner indistinguishable from other cultlike self-help seminars,[86] raking in thousands on thousands of dollars.[87] Perhaps tellingly, in *The Ayn Rand Cult*, Jeff Walker compares the relationship between Rand and Branden to Christian Science's Mary Baker Eddy and her follower Ebenezer Foster,[88] Christian Science being a precursor to New Thought. Walker's history provides further insight, linking Branden with the New Age psychologist Roger Callahan, the developer of so-called Thought Field Therapy, along with Lee Shulman and his book *Subliminal: The New Channel to Personal Power*.[89] Moreover, Branden is an advocate of hypnotism,[90] a practice with deep roots in occult and mystic thought going back to its origins with mesmerism and Andrew Jackson Davis.[91]

While there remains an all but zero percent chance that the likes of Ayn Rand or those who inherited the Ayn Rand Institute would acknowledge any overlap that Objectivism and its offspring have with the occult and mystic thought that directly preceded it, it seems clear that the principles of those earlier thought forms are mirrored in Objectivism. Not only would Rand have vigorously denied the claims made here, but we can trace moments where she made other such denials regarding the influence that Nietzsche had on her development as a thinker and even her own familial history with Judaism. Rand denied both influences at every opportunity,[92] but as later critics and historians like Jeff Walker and Brian Doherty have pointed out, the overlaps with, and influence of, Nietzschean philosophy form an inescapable component of Objectivism. In *The Ayn Rand Cult*, Walker also makes the case that Objectivism is essentially rooted in Judaism and the Jewish experience, but, of course, Rand would move quickly to deny any linkage of her philosophy with anyone but herself, much less the collective experience of her religious and ethnic heritage.[93] So the potential denial from Rand or her acolytes faces significant opposition when stacked up against the textual, cultural, and historical evidence to the contrary. Further, if one accepts the claims of the likes of Jeff Walker and Michael Shermer that Randian Objectivism operated (and continues to operate) as a cult, existing principally to venerate its inerrant and omniscient leader, then one need only take objections with a grain of salt, in the same way that biblical critics, Christian mystics, and early individualists of the nineteenth century understood the infallibility of the church.

The question remains: is it possible to rectify the mystical problem in Objectivist thought? I don't believe it is, certainly not in a way that would bust all the ghosts lurking within the philosophy. Objectivism seems to be guilty of the same sin it accuses mystics of: the philosophy wants it both ways. Objectivism wants a wholly rational, machinelike universe, with preexisting ethical codes and value systems that can be discerned by the human mind and experience, and also one that is free from mysticism and the "ghosts of the mind." The shell game Objectivism is playing, which continually puts such an existence just one move away, is not sustainable either as a thought exercise or as a coherent philosophy. This seems more than evident based on the philosophic arguments mounted by Stirner, as well as the documented history of Objectivism, and the situation is only made worse when Objectivism is easily compared (not contrasted) with competing occult and mystic thought also popular during the twentieth century. Objectivism was not polluted at some point; it was corrupted from the start and never convincingly established itself as being even internally consistent. Indeed, particularly with its arguably cultlike existence, Objectivism ultimately operates as another kind of religion, one ironically similar to those that it tried to delegitimize, making it a useful set of values for an illuminated politics interested in economic liberalism.

If the circumstances of Theosophy, New Thought, and Objectivism are components of a particular kind of illuminated politics, how can we narrow Webb's initial notion down to a specific set of operations that can be observed as a part of American political discourse in the twentieth century? Part of what drives Webb's illuminated politics is not just the crisis of consciousness of the post–World War I period but that, in the simplest terms, such a crisis demands that people decide "whether things are going to get better or not, and what [they] can do about [their] life's situation." In other words, if a person disapproves of the circumstances of their existence, what can that person do to produce a better one? In Webb's formulation, this can take place at the societal level, leading to the leveling of institutions or the embrace of force as an effective means of change, or it can also work on the level of self-improvement of the individual. Acknowledging that this question arises frequently throughout history and philosophy, Webb insists that the crisis of World War I led to a revision of the human being as one "palpably imperfect and self-destructive," leading to the rise of fascism and Nazi Germany.[94] Webb makes a compelling case here that, in spite of the objections of later writers on the occult, does help to make sense of the kind of cultural and intellectual milieu that would produce such horrific results. The obvious limitation of this perspective is that it does not account for how the postwar crisis of consciousness attempted to resolve itself elsewhere.

The kind of illuminated politics at play in the United States vacillates between gestures toward conservative traditionalism and progressivism, but in the interwar and post–World War II periods, the dominant forces are perhaps better understood as a kind of mystic liberalism. In the same way that Webb's illuminated politics emerge from "the rejected—both ideas and men—into unaccustomed positions of prominence," mystic liberalism, too, is rooted in ideas that had previously failed and were either outright rejected or revised to a point where they were no longer recognizable as their previous forms. Whether the practitioners of mystic liberalism were actually a rejected class is a more complicated issue. In the sense that many of the components of this belief system are rooted in progressive esoteric and religious movements and the experiences of immigrant and laboring classes, yes, these are people who lived on the margins of mainstream American culture. However, as mystic liberalism refined its operations and adopted the precepts and methodology of New Thought, it conscripted operatives from a wide range of social and economic classes who were united by an ideology that benefited these individuals unevenly.

By syncretizing New Thoughtism with reconfigured notions of capitalism and individualism, particularly those found in the writings of Ayn Rand

and, later, Nathaniel Branden, mystic liberalism works as a corollary to libertarianism and neoliberalism. I use "neoliberalism" to indicate a social and economic theory that posits that an unfettered, or at least less regulated, free market will foster the conditions for better income distribution and economic growth while encouraging the social and technological advances that will make these economic circumstances possible. This view also holds that state intervention in the market will either cripple or eliminate the possibility of such growth and development. As I have emphasized throughout, if we accept the general notion that neoliberalism represents a resurgence of nineteenth-century economic thought and laissez-faire capitalism,[95] mystic liberalism posits a revival of late nineteenth-century occult and mystic thought as it relates to the formation of the individual through a decentralized, personal quest for the self. Further, through that search, and by maintaining positive thoughts—a sense of self-esteem—one can materialize a better, more socially and financially prosperous existence.

Like neoliberalism, this insistence on shifting away from the constrictions of institutionalized knowledge production—and therefore self-production—harkens back to classical liberal ideology, which, as considered by early proponents like Locke and later ones like Mill, rejects absolute authority as a means for granting existence, either literal or by means of social class. The state, religion, lineage—none of these things should be the deterministic forces in the production of the individual (an individual being an entity who has a preexisting right to property, life, and liberty, and, for the mystic liberal, individualized cosmic understanding). This mode of thought is distinct from relying on the state or organized religion to be the distributor of these ideas as privileges.

Mystic liberalism works as an addendum to this idea, pointing to a means through which individuals might identify where those preexisting rights originate by making the cosmos object. In the face of scientific and atheistic challenges to anything resembling a divine order and origin for human existence, mystic liberalism responds by making the machinations of some kind of cosmological order object. By systematizing mystic ideas like karma, god, or—as someone like Max Stirner might suggest—ethics, mystic liberals allow themselves to maintain the ideals of classical liberalism and provide a tangible, reasoned order that supports their political actions. In this regard, mystic liberalism takes things a step further by providing specific means for reproducing individuals; by plumbing the depths of their psyches, reading specific texts, and rationalizing and ordering certain abstract concepts, adherents of this kind of thinking gain special abilities to heal themselves, know the cosmos, gain and preserve wealth and independence, and rationalize the origins of preexisting rights outlined in a more classically liberal approach.

Free from the Wills of Others

While the production of mystic liberalism works within ongoing conversations about liberalism, individualism, and the self, this ideology is not necessarily a response to intellectual shifts in academia or among intellectual elites. Rather, mystic liberalism is a movement that has practitioners who either claimed or actually had a more modest intellectual pedigree. Because they were not among the elite, it would seem that their occasional poaching and repackaging of philosophic, ancient, or non-Western ideas within an experiential context that conforms to their preexisting belief system helps make these ideas palatable to their believers. Put differently, mystic liberals are responding to their cultural milieu, formulating an ideology that, by its largely experiential nature, is a reactive search for tangible results by the masses, as opposed to the critical examination of admittedly abstract notions by academic philosophers.

For mystic liberals, ultimate truth and knowledge are not granted, gifted from an outside authority, but are discovered, earned by excavating each unique human conscience. Once the secrets and means to objectifying the cosmos have been established, then they become easily transmittable to other people who may discover the same secrets for themselves, and then those people can choose to embrace or reject those secrets. This element of personal choice is also important because access to the machinations of the cosmos is only available through an internal search; only by interrogating the conscience or consciousness can these secrets be revealed and confirmed. They cannot necessarily be granted by some ecclesiastical authority. Spiritual leaders can only make the apparatus of illumination available, and from there, illumination is autodidactically acquired, making everything comprehensible for those who are willing to do the work. Although the notion of self-producing individuals in a liberal political economy is not a new idea, the emphasis on mystic thought—in some cases a belief in the literal power of positive thinking—is an important distinction with peculiar results in the interwar and post–World War II era.

While the word "individualism" does not appear to surface in English until almost 1800, and its contemporary usage does not come along until the late 1820s,[96] it is only in the mid-nineteenth century that the term becomes commonly used in print.[97] However, liberalism, as an outgrowth of post-Enlightenment attitudes, sets Western thought on the path to its early usage by Alexis de Tocqueville[98] and John Stuart Mill,[99] and twentieth-century approaches to classical Enlightenment liberalism have worked to demonstrate that connection, if not conflate the terms. In many cases, this conflating of terms and usages is convincing, as in the case of C. B. Macpherson's theory of possessive individualism.[100] For my purposes, what is useful about possessive individualism is that it makes a convincing case for how liberalism functions in the service of the production of humans.

For Macpherson's formulation of possessive individualism, "what makes a man human is freedom from the dependence on the wills of others,"[101] and the distinction made in this proposition—who is and is not a person—is essential to the question of how fully formed individuals navigate a liberal space. This, along with Macpherson's six other propositions for possessive individualism,[102] gives a clear sense of the political and economic circumstances that allow individuals to operate free of obligation to society. What it does not do is provide the apparatus for achieving that freedom and, therefore, the (re)production of individuals. So while possessive individualism is useful after the fact, the intervention made by mystic liberalism provides a mechanism for creating some of the individuals that occupy the space defined by Macpherson.

But classical liberals were interested in mechanisms for production as well, and in the case of Locke, the production and gaining of property can only result from one's labor. Mystic liberalism does not reject labor as the means for creating and gaining property. Instead it expands the notion of labor to a labor of the self. One's physical labor, one's art, is, for many mystic liberals, like Steve Ditko, a driving force in creating meaning, but one should also toil away at self-understanding, thereby creating oneself. One way to do that is to explore what I refer to as cosmic intraspace—plumbing the depths of the mind and battling ghosts and specters therein (I explore this idea in more depth in later chapters). Further, if there is a god or cosmological order, cosmic intraspace allows one to insist that god or order is not beyond one's ability to comprehend, control, and reconstitute, either by gaining access to ancient wisdom or through the power of positive thinking.

While, ultimately, this is only an introduction to mystic liberalism, what I hope to have demonstrated in this brief space is the function of this particular variety of liberalism in the American ideoscape of the twentieth century, and the search for tangible answers in response to the perceived and actual failures of God, the state, and capitalism during the first half of the twentieth century, as well as confronting the illusory aspects of the American dream. Mystic liberalism attempts to rectify the complexities of these competing notions, acting as a kind of religion-after-religion, one that relies not on the distant promises of a rewarding afterlife filled with warbling but on the more immediate promise of a better here and now achieved by one's own actions. A deeper excavation of this notion would probe the implications for institutions like religion and government and how they transformed as a result, but mystic liberalism is, first and foremost, an ideology by and for the masses to help them cope with the rapid changes brought on by the twentieth century and a desire to escape a sense of obligation to the institutions that had lost relevance, even if their core tenets had not.

With that in mind, an efficient means of understanding mystic liberalism is to consider how it was made available to, and perpetuated by, the masses, namely, through popular art. The comic book industry, the early labor for which was almost entirely made up of the children of immigrants and people living on the margins of society, is one such medium for disseminating mystic liberal ideology. A member of the second generation of comic book artists to enter the industry, it was Steve Ditko who would emerge as the one to most effectively present these concepts to his readers. At first he achieved this almost exclusively visually, and later as a polemicist.

An Unlikely Bridge Builder

Ditko would not have labeled himself a mystic liberal. In fact, it would be highly unlikely that he would acknowledge allegiance to the labels associated with any one set of political, philosophical, or spiritual ideals. Moreover, Ditko has identified himself as being more than skeptical of people who would identify themselves as harbingers of singular truths that contradict his sense of a rationally operating natural world, decipherable through Aristotelian logic. Among the caricatures of "negative minds" noted early on in this chapter, another figure that Ditko takes to task in later editions of "The Avenging World" is that of the Mystic.

The Mystic, as Ditko portrays such a person, is not understood in the same way in which I am using the word, as presented by Versluis, Horowitz, and others interested in esoteric traditions. Rather, Ditko's Mystic refers to religion. The Mystic is dressed in an outfit cobbled together from Christian symbols, a wizard's cloak (complete with moons and stars), and talismans with vague references to witchcraft and voodoo. Flanking the Mystic are God and Satan, the former demanding obedience to his "HOLY TRUTH!," even if that truth is "undefinable" and "unknowable." God dares the reader to "PROVE IT IS NOT!" absolute truth. On the other side of the Mystic is Satan, who promises any hedonistic pleasure so long as the believer will agree to an "EASY PAYMENT PLAN." As the Mystic listens to both voices, he vacantly stares at the reader, clutching a Christian Bible and a staff adorned with tags reading things like "humility," "mindless," and "guilt." At his feet lies a small cauldron of money, ostensibly bilked from believers of both God and Satan alike.[103] All of this points specifically to a lampooning of organized religion and the authority it holds over its believers, either in an acceptance of the supernatural power of God or in the rejection of God in favor of another kind of mindlessness in the hedonism offered by Satan. For Ditko, both are a con intended not to liberate souls or minds but to liberate believers' money from their wallets (fig. 2.2).

This distinction in how Ditko defines mystics is an important one. Less about the dangers of any specific religion, the cartoon is a warning against

Figure 2.2. The befuddled Mystic is confounded by god and devil alike. Art and text by Steve Ditko. *Avenging World* (2002). © Steve Ditko.

the dangers of surrendering the autonomy of one's own mind and labor to an invisible authority. In this case, that authority can offer no observable, measurable results—only the weight of an unnamed guilt and threats of eternal damnation. This version of mystic thought, while in line with Randian notions, runs counter to the usage of mysticism identified in chapter 1: a call for "inner spiritual illumination" and a deep contemplation of one's own experiences of, and interactions with, the world.[104]

Ditko's initial interactions with the world happened in Johnstown, Pennsylvania, a city where, throughout the early part of the twentieth century, surviving, coping, and adapting were the order of the day. In the same social context, where the realities of survival butted up against bootstrap American dreams, there also existed belief systems that offered the masses, and those living on the margins, access to the tools that would bring them out of their situation and into something better. They were offered intellectual mechanisms for actualizing better or at least more fulfilling lives. Of those triangulated here, we know for certain that Steve Ditko was, at minimum, drawn to and influenced by Ayn Rand's Objectivism. In spite of the distance he placed between himself and Rand, his open acknowledgment that he applied some of her ideas is well documented in works he published through independent outlets and copublished with Snyder. He has not publicly admitted to an interest in the occult in the same way, but close scrutiny of his work speaks to its influence.[105]

It is difficult to say what specifically brought Ditko to an interest in Objectivism. And with the exception of George B. de Huszar's *The Intellectuals: A Controversial Portrait* (1960), I was not able to uncover any documentation where Ditko reported on precisely what influential books he read and when he read them.[106] Further, we have no external, verifiable accounts that provide convincing insight into what or when that moment was. Stan Lee has claimed that it was he who first introduced Ditko to Rand, and this version of events goes unchallenged in Blake Bell's unauthorized Ditko biography *Strange and Stranger*.[107] However, anyone even mildly familiar with Lee's self-aggrandizing and hagiographic approach to his own life knows to take this account with more than a grain of salt: maybe it's true; most likely it's not, or its credibility is at least strained. If one were forced to speculate, it may be that Ditko was first exposed to Rand through *The Fountainhead*, like many of his generation, or perhaps he saw the novel's film adaptation, or perhaps he attended an NBI seminar in New York (which we have unconfirmed, anecdotal evidence of), or, more likely, a combination of those things. At this point we simply don't have the documentary evidence to say precisely when it happened.

What can be argued with certainty is that explicitly Objectivist themes first began to appear in *The Amazing Spider-Man*, where, in issue #21, an Objectivist letter writer complains about (and likely misreads) the depiction of J. Jonah Jameson in issue #10. Ditko was plotting the comic, as he did with all his collaborations with Stan Lee, and a Randian approach to the hero is inscribed all over both Spider-Man and the "Master of the Mystic Arts," Dr. Strange, during this period in the early 1960s in a way that does not appear in Ditko's earlier work. By the time Ditko left Marvel and was producing new superhero work for Charlton Comics in 1966, Objectivism had become one of the components of his work, and new characters, like the Question, not only parrot Randian vocabulary but even look like Rand's heroes: Vic Sage, the Question's alter ego, is a dead ringer for Howard Roark, right down to the gaunt facial structure and red hair, again suggesting that *The Fountainhead* was an influential text for Ditko.

Before the early 1960s, Ditko's work does not seem to specifically engage with Objectivist thought in any discernible ways. However, it does demonstrate a clear interest in karmic retribution and interiority, which I explore more thoroughly in the coming chapters as "dark karma" and "cosmic intra-space," respectively. Like Objectivism itself, these terms pair well with both Blavatsky's karma and New Thought's internal search for self-empowerment.

In place of an outright conversion to Objectivism, like Nathaniel Branden's, it seems more that Ditko took his existing imagination of justice, the self, and psychological development and layered Objectivism over the top of it all. Because Objectivism became the top layer, and the one most readily perceivable by his readers, it became understood as the defining element of his work—also making questions about conversion possible—when, in reality, he had simply added new words to his existing lexicon. So if the question is "Is Steve Ditko an Objectivist?," the answer is no.

Although he has identified his clear interest in Rand's philosophy, he has been careful never to unambiguously identify himself as an Objectivist. In an April 2008 letter to copublisher and editor Robin Snyder, Ditko ponders how fans and critics will respond to his new work, *The Avenging Mind*, and then firmly distances himself from Rand and Objectivism. Ditko first wonders if his cultural and comics industry criticisms will be "considered 'rants,' 'eccentric,' 'hectoring' [an obvious reference to the Hultkrans piece discussed in chap. 1], 'crackpot Randish dogma,' 'street corner ranting,' 'unbalanced,' etc.? And where have I actually put, used, Rand's name or labelled Objectivism in my comics?"[108] In a September 2017 letter to Snyder, Ditko further laments fans identifying his characters with conservative politics. Referring to readers who accuse the Question of having "'right-wing beliefs,'" Ditko insists, "I did not give him right-wing beliefs so this must be [the reader's] confession."[109] The separation between Ditko's own philosophy and the philosophy and actions of his characters is an important distinction to make. On the other hand, although Ditko in no way considered himself an Objectivist, it is clear that a substantial portion of his philosophy is, on some significant level, informed by Objectivism. In that way, perhaps unsurprisingly, Ditko's interest in Rand is similar to Rand's interest in Aristotle: Rand acknowledges the value and importance of Aristotle to her own work but is specifically not an Aristotelian. She, like Ditko, claims her own set of ethical and philosophic standards, and Aristotle functions as a thin edge of the wedge to lure people to her way of thinking.[110]

To that end, I argue that Ditko is better understood as a mystic liberal, not because this is a category he would adopt or approve of himself, but because of the broader conversations in which his work is more comfortably situated. In pivoting away from a closed-system reading where each of his works *must* be contained by Objectivism or right-wing American politics, an application of mystic liberalism invites a more open approach where critiques of Ditko's work are held up to scrutiny against a more complex worldview. Operating as an organic intellectual, Ditko's autodidactic interest in the changing world as it was influenced by Western art and philosophy also produced work that displays no anxiety about engaging with or employing mystic thought, like the kind found in New Thought, as a means of making philosophic arguments through his art. When Dr. Strange travels into some kind of interior, cosmic intraspace, he does so as part of a journey to find himself. Likewise, Peter Parker's internal monologue carries a similar weight; Peter combs the landscape of his mind to find his sense of self, which he arguably does by issue #33 of *The Amazing Spider-Man*.

Regardless of any perceived or actual lack of internal or logical consistency within Objectivist individualism, Steve Ditko's work does maintain a coherent voice that bridges the gap between the occult and mystical thought that permeated Dresser's post–World War I "new age"—an emerging liberal-individualist imaginary that would be adopted as part of the neoliberal and libertarian movements of the twentieth century, most succinctly understood as what I have identified as mystic liberalism. The consistent, defining thread here is that Rand, Blavatsky, practitioners of New Thought, and other occultists and mystics all argue that whatever invisible forces may exist in the human experience—good and evil, karma, God, the invisible hand—are all accessible to the human mind. They are machines that can be observed, dismantled, examined, reconstructed, and put to use as part of one's day-to-day existence, not as external forces but as an internal, individual quest to actualize one's own potential.

And as Ditko, Rand, Blavatsky, believers in New Thought, and certainly the neoliberals of the late twentieth century would assure us, a failure to succeed, to make sense of these machines, to actualize our own potential, is our own fault. Mystic liberalism, as we will see it demonstrated by Steve Ditko, allows its practitioners to apply the lessons learned by the immigrants in Johnstown. Survival and progress mean adaptation and coping with hardship, and those changes can only be made, and success achieved, by turning inward: turning each *ought* into an *is*.

3

OVERWHELMED BY A CLOAK OF DARKNESS

Dark Karma and Cosmic Intraspace in Early Ditko Comics

By the 1950s, Carnegie, Peale, and Rand had obliquely triangulated a popular, secular interface for mystic liberalism, but, of course, this was not the only site of a subtle, substantial shift in popular culture. This mystic liberal interface became available to an even wider audience when it appeared in one of the most popular media of the decade: comic books. The early 1950s were a time of rapid and radical change in the comic book industry, culminating in the creation and implementation of the Comics Code Authority in 1954. The year before the Code took hold of the industry, a young Steve Ditko published his first comics work after moving to New York. In that brief, pre-Code window, working most prolifically in the weird and horror genres, Ditko advanced what would become the narrative and aesthetic trademarks of his career. Ditko developed these visual trademarks while working with a number of writers whose names have largely been lost to history.

In trying to better understand the working relationships between Ditko and whatever uncredited writers he worked with, I consulted with the comics historian Robin Snyder, who specializes in cataloging creator credits. After I contacted Snyder, who was also Ditko's longtime publishing partner, it became clear that there is good reason to believe that Ditko never actually knew or interacted with most of the writers whose scripts he brought to life. According to Snyder, "The layout and design, characterization, and so forth" were most likely "the product of Ditko's imagination."[1] However, that does not preclude Ditko from being intellectually or artistically moved by his collaborators, however absent or distant. For example, the first story I consider in this chapter, "Day of Reckoning," was written by Carl Memling—who wrote many horror and suspense stories for Charlton—and is perhaps best described as typical of his output at Charlton. "Day of Reckoning," as illustrated by Ditko, features narrative elements found in many of Memling's stories, regardless of which artist was interpreting and illustrating them.

For a study of the work and ideas presented by Steve Ditko, the consistency of plot points in Memling scripts is less significant than the two following points. First, these themes were already part of the larger milieu of comics and popular media, and their manipulation by Ditko is in line with his treatment of other preexisting tropes. Second, they are an entry point for Ditko to begin experimenting with such ideas *visually* in his own later comics work, putting a finer point on their philosophic potential. Moreover, I should also note that many of the specific narrative elements highlighted in this chapter might easily be found in other horror and suspense comics of the 1950s—both before Ditko and independent of his influence. As such, we would be mistaken to presume that Ditko had total, original creative agency over the deployment of either dark karma or cosmic intraspace; hints at, and variations of, these ideas can be found in a number of other comics, and certainly throughout the work of Carl Memling. What is significant is that as Ditko begins working with the elements found in these early stories, they lay the groundwork for an artistic and philosophic trajectory that transcends this period in his career, gradually taking on a life of their own in his oeuvre. This trajectory supports Snyder's assertion about Ditko's relationship with many of his early collaborators, but early on, it seems fair to acknowledge that Ditko was likely playing with prefabricated ideas before taking more of the reins in his freelance work.[2] As Ditko developed his visual approach, he defied many of the norms of the science fiction and horror genres, and his work during this period might best be classified as a kind of comic book "weird fiction."

Citing H. P. Lovecraft, the writers Ann and Jeff VanderMeer identify "weird fiction"[3] as a narrative form that "represent[s] the pursuit of some indefinable and perhaps maddeningly unreachable understanding of the world beyond the mundane," and as marked by "a 'certain atmosphere of breathless and unexplainable dread' or 'malign and particular suspension or defeat of . . . fixed laws of Nature.'"[4] Working very much in this vein, Steve Ditko developed cosmological forces of dark karma and cosmic intraspace that lie at the root of a mystic liberal outlook and were the philosophic tenets and narrative conventions that dominated his creative output throughout his lifetime and into his posthumously published works. Focusing primarily on dark karma, this chapter more fully introduces and defines both concepts as well as demonstrates how early in Ditko's career these notions took hold and cooperated to create a consistent narrative voice. Although it is the force of dark karma that dominates Ditko's early work, the introduction of cosmic intraspace and the related notion that psychological terror, struggle, and triumph are distinctly internal matters complicate Ditko's work in a unique way within the weird fiction tradition. This complication not only separates Ditko from the seemingly less introspectively oriented work of many of his predecessors and contemporaries but also demonstrates Ditko's career-long interest in the individual and the belief that the dangers that threaten both the individual and individualism come not from without but from within. Like the blending of mystic thought with popular, secular sensibilities for other mystic liberals, the motifs of dark karma and cosmic intraspace would eventually merge with Ditko's interest in Objectivism. Recognizing these tropes in work that predates his interest in Objectivism is critical to developing a coherent reading of Ditko's reflection of American political and philosophic discourse.

Offering more than a close reading of a sample of historically significant comics, my inquiries in this chapter also help to prime Ditko's work to fit within the historical and theoretical conversations about American political discourse that this book takes on. Ditko weaves together a number of occultic, philosophic, and political threads to develop an ideological formation that provides a distinct sense of the ethical and political parameters in which American individuals could and should operate in the middle years of the twentieth century. The introduction of my key terms "dark karma" and "cosmic intraspace" helps establish a vocabulary that will assist in demonstrating the broader implications and applications of the themes embedded within Ditko's work.

Such an application need not be limited to Ditko's output; rather, dark karma and cosmic intraspace are observable in the comic books and popular fiction that followed Ditko, positioning the creator as a lens for understanding the evolution of the American political consciousness in the twentieth century. The most radical of the cultural parameters Ditko introduces in these early works is the granting of "the right to kill": the licensing of the hero-vigilante to dispatch the criminally and morally corrupt as he chooses.[5] Such stories were not new to the twentieth century, nor were they limited to narratives exclusively interested in radical individualism, but one of the key points of separation between Ditko's notion of "the right to kill" and its prototypes in dime novels and pulps is a more active employment of a Westernized sense of karma. A benefit of this development is that the inclusion of a karmic element in determining the narrative fates of ne'er-do-wells creates a space where the disparate political leanings of writers and artists converge.

The distinct understanding of karma that informs dark karma and the right to kill was popularized by H. P. Blavatsky in the late nineteenth century and still had a hold on the American consciousness in the post–World War I and interwar periods.[6] Blavatsky played a key role in making karma part of the American lexicon, and according to the occult historian Mitch Horowitz, Blavatsky's first major work, *Isis Unveiled*, "popularized the word *occultism* and made the concept a matter of passionate interest among artists, authors, and spiritual seekers of the Western world—more than it had been any time since [the] Renaissance."[7] After attracting the American public's fascination and introducing them to her particular sense of Buddhism and Hinduism, Blavatsky explained her sense of karma as being both distributive—thus satisfying leftists, like later popularizers of Theosophy such as Annie Besant—and merciless, which would have satisfied some on both the left and the right. Emerging at the same time as Blavatsky's occult teachings were the radical individualist philosophies that were later associated with neoliberalism and libertarianism.[8] It was this new construction of the American individual, eventually led by the writings of Ayn Rand, that provided additional moral and ethical support for those individuals to act as karmic agents of justice, eradicating criminal and otherwise undesirable elements from American society. These networks of thought would not only reveal themselves in the comic books, pulp fiction, and popular media of the mid-twentieth century but also became key areas of contention in the 1980s as contemporary cultural producers began responding to and challenging their predecessors.

In comic books, narratives featuring karmic agents appear prominently in Ditko's work, and he uses these narrative motifs to justify intellectually the use of extreme violence in the crime, weird, horror, and superhero genres. That Ditko also introduced such agents within the pages of superhero comics proved a significant development in the history of the genre; it was Ditko who returned the right to kill to superheroes in the Comics Code era in *Blue Beetle* #4 (1967) before more fully realizing the concept in a 1973 issue of *Mr. A*.[9] This maneuver directly prefigured the gritty, more violent comics that would dominate the 1980s and 1990s, thus significantly informing the narrative trajectory of the medium during that period. In reconceptualizing how Ditko arrived at that pivotal moment, where superheroes reassume jurisdiction over life and death, it is important to note that the notion of the right to kill was not new for Ditko in the 1960s but was the extension of an ongoing project that began with his earliest work and appears in his motifs of dark karma and cosmic intraspace. I provide a more detailed analysis of "the right" in chapter 6, to show how the two motifs constitutive to its eventual emergence developed early on in Ditko's work; in this chapter, I focus primarily on stories Ditko produced for Charlton Comics' anthology series *The Thing*.

Weird Tales of Suspense, Horror, and Comeuppance!

Before moving to New York and beginning his career in comics, Steve Ditko was an avid comics reader and had already worked hard to develop his distinctive style.[10] Ditko was a product of comics' Golden Age,[11] and during the time he was doing most of his reading, the comic book industry was under increasing scrutiny from parent-teacher organizations and other guardians of culture. This increasing scrutiny was partly due to a sense of nostalgia for the newspaper "funnies" before the comic book, as a format, became a significant form of escape for young readers. However, it was not nostalgia alone that made parents distrustful. The brutally violent crime comics that followed and mimicked Lev Gleason Publishing's *Crime Does Not Pay* contributed to the increasing concern, and by 1948, the National Education Association, along with parents' groups, was already calling for the federal government to regulate the comics industry.[12] It was during this same period that Bill Gaines took over EC Comics from his father, Max. Upon taking over the company, Bill Gaines became determined to create a new trend in comics and immediately jumped on the crime comics wave that followed the success of *Crime Does Not Pay*, and by 1950 Gaines had begun producing horror titles. Under Bill Gaines, EC embraced the horror genre and weird fiction elements found in Lovecraftian and post-Lovecraftian pulp stories, merging them with biting social commentary on war, anti-Semitism, racism, and lynching, among other social and political concerns. Gaines's radical departure from his father's lineup of kids' comics and Bible stories was successful, and like the wave of crime comics that followed *Crime Does Not Pay*, the success of Gaines's horror comics began a new trend in the comics industry. By 1954 more than forty different horror comics titles were being printed every month by a variety of publishers.[13]

Many of Gaines's imitators were able to find financial success by adopting the horror and weird fiction genres, and they provided a platform on which many young artists could cut their teeth. Among those young artists was Steve Ditko, whose first published work appeared in the romance title *Daring Love* #1 in 1953. Ditko worked in nearly every available comics genre for a range of publishers, but he seemed to be most at home with Charlton Comics, working on their weird fiction, science fiction, and horror titles. Like most comics publishers, Charlton was more interested in sales than anything else and frequently changed its product line to match current trends. In addition, the company paid some of the lowest page rates in the industry.[14] However, for young and adventurous creators like Ditko, the lack of pay was offset by the amount of creative freedom afforded to writers and artists.

Indeed, the editorial latitude offered at Charlton was a significant factor in Ditko's loyalty to the company, presenting as it did an opportunity for Ditko both to cut loose and to work with the stories that inspired him most. Ditko was keenly aware of the cultural and industry-wide importance of the comics produced at EC, and in a 1959 letter to Mike Britt, Ditko wrote: "Today's efforts are a far-cry from those Golden Years of comics—before the code and when EC was setting the standards."[15] This kind of reflexive awareness is worth noting, as it emphasizes not just the influential role that Gaines's EC had on the later key creators but also the role that EC had in helping Ditko set narrative standards in his own weird fiction and horror tales. While the EC stable often used weird and psychological horror to deliver distinct sociopolitical messages,[16] Ditko's work grappled with psychological torment and had distinct philosophic undertones that explored issues of morality, individuality, personhood, and interiority.

Part of Ditko's early foray into the horror genre was a four-issue sequence of *The Thing*, a comic that Charlton billed as "Weird tales of suspense and horror!"[17] Ditko's run on the series lasted from issues #12 through #15 (he left the series after contracting tuberculosis and returning home to Pennsylvania to recover). These stories, along with a few others, mark the end of Ditko's work before the implementation of the Comics Code; they differ stylistically from his later efforts, and they represent a period in the artist's career during which he is neither restrained by the Code nor influenced by the Objectivism that would become inextricably linked to his work in the late 1960s. While the stories contained in these issues of *The Thing* are not the didactic, philosophic allegories of Ditko's later work, Ditko's visuals for these stories do reveal deep ontological concerns about how abstract concepts, particularly justice, manifest in concrete forms.

In nearly every case, Ditko's art seems to give justice its own kind of agency, rendering it as a dark karmic force that exists only to punish, not to reward. Furthermore, the dark karma that permeates Ditko's early horror work not only fails to reward but also rarely restores innocent victims; instead it acts as a manifestation of a corrupt cosmos that consumes its own wicked inhabitants. Of course, the kind of karma on display here does not have a one-to-one relationship with karma as it is understood in Buddhist or Hindu contexts. While his later creation of Dr. Strange directly links Ditko to a knowledge of and interest in the occult and Eastern mysticism, we have no reason to conjecture that Ditko was personally interested in Eastern religions or philosophy during the time he worked on *The Thing*. Rather, the forces found here seem more closely linked to the Western conceptualization of karma popularized by Madame Blavatsky and her Theosophist movement.[18]

Whether Ditko was a reader of Blavatsky or closely acquainted with other Theosophists remains unclear as a historical matter, but even if he was not, that Blavatsky's imagination of karma permeated the culture of Ditko's youth is enough to have had some influence on how he developed the narrative motifs examined here. Moreover, Theosophy appears to have a significant influence on the creation of characters like Dr. Strange, whose master, the Ancient One, seems to reference Theosophy's "Masters of the Ancient Wisdom."[19]

In her essays on the nature of reincarnation and karma, Blavatsky offers her Theosophic notion of karma, writing in *The Key to Theosophy* (2016):

It [is] the *Ultimate Law* of the Universe, the source, origin, and fount of all other laws which exist throughout Nature. Karma is the unerring law which adjusts effect to cause, on the physical, mental and spiritual planes of being. As no cause remains without its due effect from greatest to least, from a Cosmic disturbance down to the movement of your hand, and as like produces like, *Karma* is that unseen and unknown law *which adjusts wisely, intelligently and equitably* each effect to its cause, tracing the latter back to its producer. Though itself *unknowable*, its action is perceivable.[20]

Blavatsky expands on this understanding by explaining the distributive properties of karma and how, because every human being is connected, at least at the spiritual level, we all collectively suffer or rejoice at the hand of karma.[21] Consequently, one can imagine a universe structured by both cosmic punishment and reward, and therefore when a sin is eradicated, the whole of humanity is lifted. However, the collective, distributive nature of karma does not preclude either individual punishments for misdeeds or individual agents of karma. For Blavatsky, one can understand karma only through its observable effects—not its originator—and no one can clearly identify the means or motives of that prime mover.

Of equal importance, according to Blavatsky, there can be no ultimate forgiveness of wrongdoing from God. The results of a crime, be it individual or collectively enacted, cannot be obliterated. Instead a crime creates a ripple effect that runs throughout the universe, and there must always be a reckoning: that ripple must run ashore. The cosmos must be put back in balance, and this balance, of course, is achieved through the machinations of karma, which "may be instantaneous, [though the] effects are eternal."[22] With this merciless cosmic understanding in mind, and because there is apparently no way to deny *how* or even *that* karmic justice is meted out, this paradigm has plenty of room for individual agents of cosmic-karmic justice to punish criminal actors with extreme prejudice, without even requiring the motive of revenge to justify their actions. Rather, they are acting on behalf of karma, of an imagined sense of cosmic justice.

The dark karma that Steve Ditko offers his readers is an addendum to Blavatsky's conception and depends on karma's mercilessness. Ditko presents his readers an *individuated* suffering that results from sin; however, in stories where society or its instruments sin (such as, for example, through corrupt government or police action), it is then the whole of society that collectively suffers. This collective suffering specifically occurs in the story "Doom in the Air."[23] A sheriff allows an accused criminal to be lynched and buried alive without a trial. Later, the US government uses the land where the man was buried to test nuclear weapons. A bomb is dropped on the area, and the radiation reanimates the murdered man. After his resurrection, he begins a reign of terror that specifically targets his tormentors, but because he is radioactive, he uncontrollably poisons and murders everyone in his path, guilty and innocent alike (fig. 3.1). Thus the significant deviation here between Ditko's dark karma and a more Blavatskian notion of karma is that Ditko's stories are principally interested in punishment for, and the cosmic consumption of, evil, not a restorative balancing of the scales.

Nevertheless, the two approaches to karma converge again when Blavatsky notes that "as a general rule, and within certain limits which define the age to which we belong, the law of Karma cannot be hastened or retarded in its fulfillment."[24] Indeed, Ditko's approach is identical. His dark karma is a cosmic force that, once set into motion, must be sated. One of the clearer instances of Ditko's dark karma at work appears in "Day of Reckoning," scripted by Carl Memling.[25] The tale takes place in a shipyard in the late eighteenth or early nineteenth century and tells of the demise and revenge of Jabez Grimm, a "tight-fisted skinflint" who refuses to pay his shipbuilders what they are owed, thus "cheating [them] out of [their] rightful wages."[26] Such themes of greed contrasted with the notion of "a day's work for a day's pay" persist in Ditko's narratives.[27] By immediately identifying Jabez Grimm as an abusive, dishonest employer who keeps his shipbuilders wallowing "in the bitterest poverty,"[28] Ditko suggests that the cycle of violence that will ensue is deserved. While this narrative maneuver may relieve the reader of any discomfort in witnessing the coming torture of Jabez Grimm, it also reveals that Jabez Grimm is both a product and a perpetuator of a corrupt order who must be punished. One has to wonder how such punishment can take shape without bloodying the hands of the innocent. Dark karma provides a palatable solution for that problem.

After being cheated by Grimm, three shipbuilders conspire to get their revenge on him by first assaulting and kidnapping him. In a key moment in the story, after the assault, the three men decide to rob Grimm—taking more than their earned and deserved wages. After the robbery, the men further seal their fate by torturing Jabez Grimm, tying him up, sewing his mouth shut, and then sealing him inside the hull of a newly constructed ship, where he eventually starves to death (fig. 3.2). Had they taken only what Grimm owed them, the assault—and perhaps even the torture—*might* be counted as a kind of vigilante justice and thus a restoration of order. Instead, because they turned to theft—thereby revealing their own corrupt nature—the three men cannot remain agents of a dark karmic force; they must also be consumed by it. It is Ditko's visual insistence on the consumption of evil—bad actors being sucked, dragged, or pulled into some darkened place—that distinguishes dark karma from its narrative cousins at EC, where evil characters receive their comeuppance in manners of all varieties. "Day of Reckoning" provides a useful template for how to identify the visual operations of dark karma.

Figure 3.1. The consequence of the evils of nuclear war and a crooked justice system begins a tour of major American cities to inflict on them the horrors of an unjust state. Written by Carl Memling; art by Steve Ditko; letters by Charlotte Jetter. "Doom in the Air," *The Thing* #14 (June 1954).

After murdering and robbing Jabez Grimm, the three shipbuilders go about their days without much thought until, one by one, they are mysteriously killed—each grisly death accompanied by a haunting, distant laughter. Of course, the ghost of Jabez Grimm is terrorizing the three shipbuilders, and the murders are progressively more violent—drowning, crushed by a ship's mast, and near decapitation. When viewed in the light of the dark karmic forces that govern Ditko's narrative, these deaths are necessary to maintain some kind of cosmic consistency whereby a corrupted world consumes its own wicked inhabitants. This notion of consumption is supported by two of the three deaths, where in each case the victim enters into and is thereby consumed by dark, interior spaces before meeting his demise. When the ghost of Jabez Grimm takes his revenge on the first shipbuilder, the man gets his leg caught in the chain of an anchor that has dropped on its own, and the man is pulled into the sea, where he is drowned (fig. 3.3). The third shipbuilder to die hears the strange, distant laughter of Grimm's ghost and enters into the darkened hull of a ship, where he is murdered off panel (fig. 3.4). Even in the second case, where the man is crushed by the ship's mast, he is frozen in place, unable to jump or move—trapped by the shadow of the falling mast (fig. 3.5).

Figure 3.2. With his lips stitched together, the tortured Jabez Grimm is sealed inside the ship that will be his tomb. Written by Carl Memling; art by Steve Ditko; letters by Charlotte Jetter. "Day of Reckoning," *The Thing* #15 (July–August 1954).

Figure 3.3. One of Jabez Grimm's murderers is yanked into the sea. Written by Carl Memling; art by Steve Ditko; letters by Charlotte Jetter. "Day of Reckoning," *The Thing* #15 (July–August 1954).

Figure 3.4. Another of Jabez Grimm's murderers is lured into a darkened space where he meets a mysterious but horrible end. Written by Carl Memling; art by Steve Ditko; letters by Charlotte Jetter. "Day of Reckoning," *The Thing* #15 (July–August 1954).

Figure 3.5. Frozen by terror and the shadow of the falling mast, another of Jabez Grimm's murderers is consumed. Written by Carl Memling; art by Steve Ditko; letters by Charlotte Jetter. "Day of Reckoning," *The Thing* #15 (July–August 1954).

In all three cases, the victims are pulled into a physically darkened place they cannot escape from before being destroyed, and in their individual deaths, we can read the perpetuation of a dark order where no real justice is done.

The murder of Jabez Grimm is never solved—or even noticed by the public—and the murderous shipbuilders might have seemed to be free to go about their lives until the supernatural intervention of Grimm's ghost. Moreover, all three of the shipbuilders' deaths are treated as accidents or mysterious happenstances, with no effort made to solve the crimes. The implication is that no additional human justice need be done because the dark karmic order of the universe is capable of identifying and preventing evil as it occurs; as such, it is up to cosmic and supernatural forces to cleanse the world of its malevolent residents. This cleansing occurs as a result of the world drawing evildoers *into* itself. The bleak outlook that Ditko offers his readers here is not unique to these stories; the tropes and motifs that he develops here recur throughout his work, across genres.

As noted early in this chapter, "Day of Reckoning" presents an interesting problem for linking the notion of dark karma in this story to Ditko. Key to this complication is that many of Memling's scripts for *The Thing*, as well as for other publishers, employ some of the *exact* same plot elements as are found in "Day of Reckoning." A particularly sharp example of this comes from *The Thing* #8 (1953), which includes the story "A Grave Situation," written by Memling and drawn by John Belfi. Briefly, the story is about a treasure hunter who betrays his partners and is then murdered by those partners because of his betrayal. The murderers wrap their victim in chains and toss him into the sea to drown (fig. 3.6). With his dying words, the treasure hunter curses his former partners, and, sure enough, one by one they all die in mysterious accidents. One drowns after the killers' boat capsizes (fig. 3.7), another is accidentally hung by a swinging rope on the ship that rescues them, and a third is crushed by a falling ship's mast—too paralyzed with fear to move out of the way (fig. 3.8). While I try to remain generous to Memling and the working conditions that might necessitate this kind of repetition, he was clearly recycling plots. Based on the plot repetition alone, this pattern is disruptive for theorizing dark karma as something distinct to Ditko's work early in his career.

However, I think that Ditko distinguishes his approach to these plot elements and includes a specific aesthetic that will be witnessed in later stories. The claustrophobia and the sense of being swallowed—literally and figuratively—by darkness so readily visible in Ditko's panels are not at all apparent in Belfi's version of the story. Specifically, consider the drownings in figures 3.6 and 3.7 as they compare to the drowned victim from "Day of Reckoning" in figure 3.3. In the former, one man is tossed into the sea, where he gurgles his way toward the bottom, and another slips off a boat into the water. In the latter, drawn by Ditko, the victim is *pulled into* the sea and engulfed by

Figure 3.6. Similar to the circumstances of the later story "Day of Reckoning," Memling writes a revenge drowning for artist John Belfi. Written by Carl Memling; art by John Belfi. "A Grave Situation," *The Thing* #8 (April 1953).

Figure 3.7. Unlike Ditko's drowning in "Day of Reckoning," Belfi's art emphasizes the plot device element of the drowning, in contrast to Ditko's consuming waters. Written by Carl Memling; art by John Belfi. "A Grave Situation," *The Thing* #8 (April 1953).

it. This seems to me an important distinction in how these deaths are portrayed and how they are understood: I argue that Ditko visually emphasizes the deliberative nature of the death by extrahuman forces in a way not found in Belfi's version of the story. Similarly, when comparing the victims crushed by falling masts, both are trapped in the shadow of the mast as the darkness covers their bodies, but in the Ditko version (fig. 3.5), the victim is shown, like the drowned one, as having been swallowed, concealed by the cause of his death. This is not true of the Belfi story (fig. 3.8). As I note in the opening of this chapter, it is not that I believe Ditko is the sole originator of the dark karmic forces that permeate these stories, but his visual stamp is unmistakable when compared to other artists working in the same moment, within the same zeitgeist, and from essentially the same script. It is understandable— even expected—that other writers and artists in comics have similar interests, narrative and philosophic—especially as many worked their way through comics studios, as Ditko did, first with Jerry Robinson and then in Joe Simon and Jack Kirby's studio. However, the visual flourishes Ditko adds to each of these early stories for *The Thing* provide a particular narrative flavor that is observable throughout his career.

As a brief example of how this swallowing up of evil appears in other genres and later work, take "Kill Vic Sage!," a Question backup feature that appeared in *Blue Beetle* #4 in 1967.[29] By this time, Ditko had read Ayn Rand's Objectivist novels and had begun applying his own brand of Rand's philosophy to his work. Intriguingly, Ditko appears to have woven his previous

Figure 3.8. Although both Belfi's and Ditko's victims are paralyzed with fear from the falling mast, Belfi's character is the victim of a mysterious accident, whereas Ditko's is swallowed by some dark karmic agent. Written by Carl Memling; art by John Belfi. "A Grave Situation," *The Thing* #8 (April 1953).

interest in a dark karmic order with the alleged hyperrationality of Objectivism, and "Kill Vic Sage!" offers an excellent example of the merging of these two intellectual prospects. At the end of the story, the Question has kicked two violent criminals into the rushing waters of a sewer, refusing to save them from drowning, assuring them that their inevitable deaths are a fate they have earned.[30] As for the shipbuilders in "Day of Reckoning," there is no legal justice for these criminals, no restoration of order (only a removal of evil), and like the shipbuilders, the Question's victims are swallowed by the dark, dingy tunnels and darker waters of the sewer—the corrupt world consuming its own vile inhabitants.

While the majority of his early weird fiction and horror stories are invested in visually demonstrating the world as a corrupt and perverse place, a place where the only chance for salvation lies in the wholesale extermination of evil, Ditko does *occasionally* offer clemency to, but not restoration of, moral innocents. One such instance of the clemency afforded by dark karma appears in the story "Library of Horror," a story that also provides early insight into how dark karma entangles with cosmic intraspace.[31] "Library of Horror" achieves such an entangling by confining the motivations for evil and the punishment by dark karmic forces within interior, often claustrophobic, spaces.

First printed in *The Thing* #13 in April 1954, this story introduces readers to the struggling author Ken Rolland, who craves greatness and is "willing to kill for it."[32] In addition to confronting the story's visual elements, the reader also encounters several key motifs that surface throughout Steve Ditko's career: dark karma, greed, and lust for the unearned. Ken Rolland works for a pulp magazine publishing weird fiction, and one night after receiving some harsh criticism from his editor, Rolland takes to the darkened city streets to clear his mind and find some inspiration. While out wandering the city, Rolland comes upon a strange-looking bookshop that seems to be beckoning him inside. Once he reaches the shop's front door, he is greeted by a haggard and shriveled shopkeeper who informs Rolland that he is always looking for "special customers" like him and that the store is a library of horror novels and ancient mystical texts.[33] However, if Rolland wants access to the store's inventory, the price is a human soul. The shopkeeper promises Rolland the ability to "*enter* the world beyond" so that he can write about the experience he has in that unknown space.[34]

In addition to the challenging narrative that Ditko's art presents,[35] the story is also an early instance where he begins to develop his sense of pacing through complex and dense panel layouts designed to create a sense of claustrophobic anxiety. Within those dense layouts, Ditko uses an exceptional amount of detail to close the interior space of each panel, with depictions of cluttered bookshelves and narrow alleyways, as well as cosmic intraspaces full of tangled, tentacled negative space (figs. 3.9, 3.10, 3.11). Ditko's narrative and visual tactics, along with his formal use of negative space and Zip-A-Tone, pushed the printing capabilities of the notoriously cheap Charlton press to their limit; however, they exemplify the cosmic, claustrophobic terror that would become a defining feature of Ditko's horror work throughout his career.

Desperate and greedy for success that he is unwilling to earn by means of his own mind and labor (a classic sign of moral weakness in Ditko's work), Rolland agrees to bring the old shopkeeper a soul. By bringing the shopkeeper bodies, dead or alive, Rolland gains access to the horror library and its bizarre collection of ancient tomes and books of the dead, all of which, he believes, will help him to write the kinds of stories that will bring him fame and fortune. Rolland's access to these forbidden grimoires demonstrates, in one sense, his desire to reach beyond into the unknown and retrieve some kind of self-serving power. In a Lovecraftian sense, studying such books is an invitation to be destroyed by an ancient and terrible force from beyond human understanding—an unknowable horde of denizens from without. Ditko offers an alternative, where the great and terrible secret of these texts lies not in the outside world but in a world within: within the texts themselves, and within the mind of the reader.

Figure 3.9. Ken Rolland enters a cluttered library in an early example of the kind of claustrophobic settings that would become a hallmark of Ditko's work. Art by Steve Ditko; writer unknown, if not Ditko; letters by Charlotte Jetter. "Library of Horror," *The Thing* #13 (April 1954).

Agreeing to the shopkeeper's demand to bring him a dead body, Rolland stalks a "dirty, littered alleyway" and comes across a "derelict," whom he promptly strangles before delivering the corpse to the shopkeeper.[36] Key to this scene is not just that Rolland is so consumed by his lust for fame that he is willing to commit murder, but that his victim is described in such base terms. It is not a human being that Rolland murders, or even a homeless person, but a *derelict* living in a filthy alley. While Rolland is most certainly the villain in this case, one observes Ditko's dark karma once again at work: the expunging of another undesirable figure from the world.

After bringing his first victim to the shopkeeper, Rolland is granted permission to peruse the library. Shortly after he begins reading, Rolland is literally pulled into a book, sending him to a world beyond his own through a tangled nightmare passage. This tentacle-like hallway leads Rolland to a cavern where sees a host of demonic figures devouring the soul of the murdered derelict. Taking advantage of the scene, Rolland writes down everything he sees, and when he returns to the ordinary world, he puts his notes in narrative form, selling the story and achieving great success. Tempted by the fame and attention from that story, Rolland murders again and again, delivering each victim to the shopkeeper, with every victim granting the author continued access to the world beyond and an infinite supply of narrative material that he was not able to conceive on his own. It is not clear that all of Rolland's victims after the first were similarly dehumanized, but without details surrounding their characters, it is the first victim, the derelict, that gives the reader the clearest insight into Ditko's worldview.

What separates "Library of Horror" from the kind of dark karma that runs through the remainder of Ditko's contributions to *The Thing* is that this

Figure 3.10. Ken Rolland chokes the life out of a derelict in a dingy, narrow alleyway. Art by Steve Ditko; writer unknown, if not Ditko; letters by Charlotte Jetter. "Library of Horror," *The Thing* #13 (April 1954).

Figure 3.11. Rolland plummets inward into the cosmic, demonic space hidden inside the book. Tangled, tentacled internal landscapes like this one would appear throughout Ditko's later work, in a variety of genres. Art by Steve Ditko; writer unknown, if not Ditko; letters by Charlotte Jetter. "Library of Horror," *The Thing* #13 (April 1954).

story features both an innocent victim and the restoration of that victim by means of a literal resurrection. We find no other instance of this kind of restorative justice in Ditko's pre–Comics Code horror stories. In fact, many stories, like "Doom in the Air" (also written by Memling), involve mass murder with no cap for the body count and no defeat of evil. In another instance, "Inheritance" features an ending where the man trying to stop an evil curse from taking hold is murdered and the curse is unleashed on mankind.[37] Both of these examples appear in *The Thing* #14 and demonstrate that, during this period in Ditko's oeuvre, when tipping dark karmic scales, it is typically in favor of a corrupt, evil order inflicting itself on the world. That Ditko deviates from his usual narrative in this instance is useful in this reading, as—perhaps counterintuitively—it also reinforces the notion of dark karma defined here.

If dark karma's imperative is to employ evil forces not to defeat but to consume other evil forces in a seemingly endless cycle, without specifically rewarding good for its deeds, then "Library of Horror" has utility in establishing this term as a key development in the evolution of Steve Ditko's artistic-narrative voice. The trajectory set forth for Ken Rolland helps establish this utility. After committing an unspecified number of murders to deliver souls to the demons of the shopkeeper's world beyond, Rolland eventually leverages his success as an author into wealth and something resembling a normal life. As a part of that normal life, Rolland gets married and stops delivering souls to the old shopkeeper, thus losing access to his muse in the world beyond. Predictably, after Rolland stops murdering people, his money dries up, and he finds himself unable to write well enough to match his previous success. Again, readers face a villain whose major sin is a desire for the unearned, and whose greed will lead to his eventual comeuppance. In the case of Ken Rolland, he again stalks the dark and foggy streets of his city, searching for a victim to deliver to the shopkeeper for one more glance into the cavernous, demonic world beyond, and he finds just such a victim. However, this time Rolland is so wracked with guilt over what he is about to do that he refuses to look at the person's face—again suggesting that there was some methodology to his previous murders and that successive victims were akin to the derelict he first sacrificed. Rolland strangles his victim, a woman, to death and delivers her to the shopkeeper, who sends Rolland on one more trip to the world beyond. In perfect O. Henry fashion, Rolland descends into the nether realm to witness the demons feasting on the soul of his victim, only to discover it was actually his wife he unwittingly murdered. Certainly, Ditko has pulled this narrative maneuver right from the EC Comics playbook, but setting up Rolland as someone who lusts after unearned success and is willing to murder for it goes a long way in establishing the narrative and philosophic conventions that would define Ditko's later work.

After realizing that his victim was actually his wife, Marion, Rolland rushes in to rescue her, and the two narrowly escape from the demonic realm. This escape brings Marion back to life, but unfortunately for Rolland, escaping from the demons means they will have to be satisfied in another way. The shopkeeper allows Marion, an innocent, to live, and in her place it is Ken Rolland who must be sacrificed to the demons and their hunger for human souls. Rolland refuses to submit to the shopkeeper's demand, pulls a gun, and attempts to shoot the shopkeeper. This desperate attempt fails, as the bullets do not affect the shopkeeper, who then reveals his true identity: Death. The story's final panel sees "Ken Rolland scream[ing] out his last, [as] the cloak of darkness overwhelmed him to take him back to the beyond."[38] Within the space of just these last few panels, Ditko has concretized several key aspects of dark karma, set a standard for the pathos that will continue throughout the body of his work, and woven into those two elements the cosmic intraspaces that would become emblematic of his creative vision.

Of course, the dark karmic elements are most clearly established through the fate of Ken Rolland; however, that the shopkeeper is revealed to be Death in human form is telling. By rendering Death as a collector of souls to be fed to demons, the story again reminds the reader of the dark karmic forces that haunt the corrupt human world insofar as Death is both an evil force (insisting on murder and human sacrifice) and also one that acts to remove morally suspect people from existence. To further establish the corrupt nature of the world and of Death, eater of dark souls, Death does not seem to differentiate between evil people and innocent ones, but when confronted with the choice between devouring an innocent (Marion) and a villain (Rolland), Death chooses the villain. That Death makes this choice is intriguing from a narrative standpoint because, after her resurrection, Rolland's murdered wife is granted her life and freedom but receives no other restitution. There is no real justice done for Marion: she still suffered strangulation at the hands of her husband, she still has no financial prospects after Rolland squandered their funds, and she is utterly abandoned after witnessing Death take Rolland away screaming. There is no additional punishment for Marion, but there is no justice either—thus establishing that the world is a corrupt and unjust place that imposes itself on the innocent. The only reprieve for the innocent is that the dark karmic forces of the world are perpetually in motion, literally and figuratively consuming the world's evil actors.

In addition to this advancement of Ditko's karmic perspective, "Library of Horror" provides readers another early glimpse into Ditko's dark vision for cosmic intraspace. Although it is a theme that would permeate almost the entirety of his oeuvre, Ditko's interest in cosmic intraspace is rooted in the weird horror and suspense stories he produced at Charlton in 1954, and "Library of Horror" is a transitional work that integrates the Lovecraftian landscapes associated with his sense of cosmic intraspace with lurking dark karmic forces. The kind of psychic and physical space that Ditko renders is unique because of its investment in personal interiority as opposed to the cosmic outer space of many of his peers. In place of the threats, hopes, and infinite beings stationed beyond humanity's ability to see or reach outward toward, Ditko's cosmic intraspace is constantly looking inward: in books, in pocket dimensions, in claustrophobic spaces containing infinite dread, or in the human consciousness. Of course, cosmic intraspace is not limited to these few examples, but they are easily identifiable in any number of weird, suspense, and horror stories where Steve Ditko has left his narrative mark, and they are peculiar to his own narrative, philosophic, and pathological sensibilities.

As an immediate example, one may be inclined to compare the weird and dreadful cosmic intraspace of Steve Ditko's work in a Dr. Strange story to the optimistic and operatic vision of the cosmic found in the superhero work of Jack Kirby, or even in Kirby's horror and suspense stories.[39] Indeed, Ditko's interest in cosmic intraspace similarly adopts different modes and has applicability across genres. While a character like Ken Rolland is subjected to the dark cosmic intraspace that devours the souls of the damned, Dr. Strange encounters Eternity—a character who is literally the whole of the cosmos contained within a humanoid shape.[40] So, too, does Spider-Man, Peter Parker, confront his own intellectual and emotional challenges as part of an internal monologue that results in radical shifts in his behavior and attitudes.[41]

Ditko's early interest in dark, cosmic, supernatural spaces existing within the ostensible boundaries of the earth is not limited to these stories, and in "Die Laughing," which also appeared in *The Thing* #13, Ditko offers readers yet another glimpse of the kind of cosmic intraspace and claustrophobia that would define his aesthetic.[42] The plot of "Die Laughing" involves college fraternity brothers (a frequently problematic group of individuals in Ditko comics) and the hazing of incoming pledges. The ringleader of the hazing activities, Rex Chandler, is particularly interested in physically and psychologically tormenting the pledges with his seemingly never-ending series of practical jokes. Rex's final test for the pledges is for them to tour a haunted house from top to bottom, and behind a bizarre-looking locked door on the top floor, Rex claims to have an especially terrifying prank prepared. Reluctantly, the pledges agree to enter the haunted house, and one by one, each pledge disappears, leaving no hint as to what could have happened to them by the time they reached Rex's final prank. After hearing nothing from the pledges, Rex jokes that maybe they died laughing, and decides to go into the house and drag the pledges out.[43]

Like the pledges before him, Rex never returns, and the remaining fraternity brothers decide to investigate the house. By the time they reach the top floor, the boys discover a large metal door that presumably conceals Rex's final prank. When they open the door, they find Rex on his knees, his hair bleached completely white and any sense of youth or robustness ripped away from him, leaving a decrepit shell of Rex's former self. Rex can't articulate what he saw in the darkness that left him in this miserable state, and the pledges are never found or heard from again. Later, after a more thorough search of the house still reveals no sign of the pledges, Rex dies of "extreme shock," and the authorities burn the house down, as the narrator reports that the pledges "have never been seen again! What strange and horrible fate *engulfed* them will probably never be known."[44]

The plot elements alone refer the reader back to Ditko's dark karma, and while Rex's "crimes" are apparent, the sins of the pledges seem to be their willingness to surrender their own independent minds and actions in exchange for acceptance from their fraternity brothers. Noting again that Ditko was ostensibly not acquainted with the writing of Ayn Rand at the time this story was published, this kind of plotting certainly prefigures that interest, and it is an attitude that will be revisited in the earliest Spider-Man stories in 1962 and 1963, which also seems to predate Ditko's investment in Rand's philosophy. However, the key here is the story's visual characteristics. Ditko crams the page with tight-fitting panels, and most of the panel interiors are set at odd angles or are close shots of one or more characters in the foreground. Cluttered, dark negative space and a

Figure 3.12. Terrified fraternity brothers enter a haunted house as part of their hazing, where they are confronted with a jagged, claustrophobic space, similar to the ones found in "Library of Horror." Art by Steve Ditko; writer unknown, if not Ditko. "Die Laughing," *The Thing* #13 (April 1954).

multitude of sharp edges and jutting angles often surround the panels that have only one character in the foreground (figs. 3.12, 3.13, 3.14). These visual elements create a sense of claustrophobia, which heightens the terror on the page, but they also work to demonstrate the infinite dread of tightly closed spaces, running in an equal and opposite direction from the exterior cosmic dread conjured up in

Figure 3.13. Although he does not render it with as much detail as in other panels, Ditko emphasizes the eeriness of the house by stripping its clutter down to jagged shapes and negative space cut through with wisps of fog. Art by Steve Ditko; writer unknown, if not Ditko. "Die Laughing," *The Thing* #13 (April 1954).

the works of H. P. Lovecraft. In the case of Lovecraft, the reader is often left with a sense of smallness and inadequacy in the face of an unending and expanding universe, but Ditko's narratives reveal the horror of being crushed by a cosmos that is perpetually closing in, with nowhere to escape.

That the horrors of "Die Laughing" all take place unseen within the enclosed structure of the house is also telling—especially when considering the ways in which Ditko's cosmic intraspace manifests. While the kinds of tangled intraspaces that appear in "Library of Horror" are representative of the more visually striking expression of Ditko's cosmos, "Die Laughing" offers a particular insight into his interest in claustrophobia and, just as important, his assertion that the unknown materializes from within, not from without. Specific to this case, the unknown horror that rips away Rex's youth—and eventually his life—is contained within the symbolic darkness of the house and the literal darkness as it is represented on the comic page. The unknown also lurks behind the closed door on the house's upper level, again demonstrating that such cosmic spaces can only be accessed through portals, like the book in "Library of Horror," and how each death in "Day of Reckoning" takes place either inside of something (a boat, the sea) or in the darkness of a shadow. These narrative choices, combined with dark karma, blend together to create a distinct narrative voice and help position Ditko as an artist who is making literary maneuvers in his work, as opposed to purely commercial or financial ones.

To be sure, Steve Ditko was not working in a vacuum and would not want to claim that he was unique in bringing about change to the comics industry. However, Ditko's use of narrative concepts such as dark karma and cosmic intraspace to justify the use of extreme violence in comic book narratives intellectually—even in the superhero genre—represents a significant contribution to the comics medium in the United States. What these very early contributions by Ditko demonstrate is more than a primitive version of an artistic style.[45] They represent the introduction of a narrative and philosophic

Figure 3.14. As the fraternity brothers move ever deeper into the labyrinth of the house, they are confined to the staircase, which spirals toward the dread that awaits and draws the boys in. Art by Steve Ditko; writer unknown, if not Ditko. "Die Laughing," *The Thing* #13 (April 1954).

perspective that Ditko refined over a sixty-five-year period. Furthermore, even though Ditko's philosophic perspective adjusted with his experiences and encounters with other writers, the early appearance and persistence of dark karma and cosmic intraspace provide evidence of Ditko's intellectual consistency. This kind of intellectual consistency is exceptionally useful in shaping a clear understanding not just of the artist's oeuvre but of how his contributions influenced his contemporaries.

4

"'TWAS STEVE'S IDEA"

A Secret Racial History and a Search for the Self with Dr. Strange

Dr. Strange is East Asian. Was Asian. Is still kind of Asian? It's hard to say, except that it wasn't, and then it was (fig. 4.1).

In 2016, the controversy surrounding the Dr. Strange film adaptation was the whitewashing and political erasure of Tibet in the film by casting Tilda Swinton as the Ancient One, a character depicted in the Dr. Strange comics as an elderly Tibetan man. This would be troubling enough, but no one seemed concerned about the casting of Benedict Cumberbatch in the film.[1] And why would they? Dr. Strange had been depicted as unquestionably Western and white ever since Steve Ditko left the character in 1966. Of course, my focus in this book is on the development and dissemination of mystic liberalism, but ignoring the issue of race in Dr. Strange stories, particularly as envisioned by Steve Ditko, leaves any analysis of the character incomplete. My intent with the following brief consideration of race in Dr. Strange is not to develop sustained argumentative claims about the racial attitudes of the people working in the Marvel offices in the 1960s.

The critical examinations of matters of race and representation in comics are important, stand independent of the intention and attitudes of creators, and require thoughtful examination. Recent comics scholarship, like Qiana Whitted's *EC Comics: Race, Shock, and Social Protest*, has also cast a powerful critical eye on the publications that were working through the problems and complexities of race and ethnicity in mid-twentieth-century America. The comics Whitted studies challenge commonly held notions that comics had previously eschewed issues of social justice. In addition to complicating the legacy of EC Comics, Whitted's book makes plain that issues of race and social justice were important ones for future colleagues of Steve Ditko, like

Figure 4.1. Dr. Strange makes his first appearance in his East Asian identity. Dialogue edited by Stan Lee; Steve Ditko art; Terry Szenics letters. "Dr. Strange: Master of Black Magic!" *Strange Tales* #110 (July 1963). © Marvel Comics.

Wallace Wood, who first published Ditko's Mr. A in *witzend* and collaborated with Ditko on a number of projects as an inker.

Whitted is also careful to point out that depictions of race in comics are visual constructions, and characters in EC's social justice comics—as well as their proxies in EC's readership—are often taken to task over this imagination of racial identity. Whitted exemplifies these problematics with the story ". . . In Gratitude," where the parents of a white American soldier believe that the friend he wrote home about was also white because they read their son's "'raceless' prose as unquestionably white."[2] A similar problem seems to occur with Dr. Strange, where the "raceless prose," in the most generous scenario, has confused readers about the character's racial and ethnic identity. Lending further support to this idea, Whitted notes the art historian W. J. T. Mitchell, who, in *Picture Theory: Essays on Visual and Verbal Representation*, writes:

> The assumption is that "blackness" is a transparently readable sign of racial identity, a perfectly sutured image/text. Race is what can be seen (and therefore named) in skin color, facial features, hair, etc. Whiteness, by contrast, is invisible, unmarked; it has no racial identity, but is equated with normal subjectivity and humanity from which "race" is a visible deviation. . . . That is why forms of resistance to these stereotypes so often take the form of disruptions at the level of representation, perception, and semiosis.[3]

A similar problem seems to have arisen with Dr. Strange's East Asian heritage. Whitted, in her consideration of the African American characters of EC's comics, illuminates a subversive message that is "visible" in the multi-level disruptions of stereotype where characters' words (or relative silence) are seemingly "at odds with [their] skin color, embod[ying] the deeply flawed assumptions of blackness as a 'perfectly sutured image/text.'"[4] It is not at all the case that Asian and African American experiences and critiques thereof are interchangeable, but some confluence emerges in what Whitted and Mitchell highlight as the problem of whiteness and the troubling assumption of its racelessness in prose and perception and, further, the assumption that nonwhite characters are identifiable almost exclusively by their visual depiction and some kind of vocalized affectation. Indeed, this is the very problem with typical readings of Dr. Strange as a white character.

Apart from Whitted, a number of other critical texts have taken on the issues of race and representation in American comics, particularly pertaining to African Americans,[5] and a number of recent comic books and graphic novels have addressed the issue of Asian American representation. The cartoonist Gene Luen Yang's *American Born Chinese*, for example, is a powerful and important meditation on racism, representation, and Asian American life. Similarly, the journalist Jeff Yang has compiled the comics anthologies *Secret Identities* (2009) and *Shattered* (2012), which feature comics from Asian American cartoonists. Jeff Yang's volumes adopt the conventions of traditional comics genres to disrupt pervasive stereotypes and, like Gene Luen Yang, give voice to the lived experiences of Asian Americans. A sustained inquiry into Asian representation in American comics is vitally important to comics studies, particularly as it relates to how that representation has occurred over time and a historical consideration of publishing practices. Without such a study, at the time of this writing, we do not have substantial enough evidence to make significant, supportable claims about how the attitudes of specific people in the Marvel offices affected the production of Dr. Strange or how he has been presented in the decades after Steve Ditko's departure from the character.

What the existing evidence does support is that Ditko intentionally designed the visuals, plotted, and wrote the first Dr. Strange story with an East Asian man in mind. I am most confident about this assertion because I put the question of Strange's race to Ditko in a 2014 letter, to which he responded: "The answer is seen in the first published Dr. Strange story." That's all he said. Some may gain the mistaken impression that Ditko's response is not direct enough to eliminate any debate about the character's origins, but I don't think that's the case at all. Rather, it is clear to me that the character's intended, original race was unambiguous to Ditko. In Ditko's rendering, Doctor Strange is tall and lank, his hair is thick and dark, he has heavy-lidded and narrow eyes, angular eyebrows, and his skin tone is a light beige. All East Asian characters do not have an exclusive set of phenotypical traits, of course, but these design choices are in line with the depiction of other, earlier, East Asian characters that seem to inform the way the cast of Doctor Strange's stories were illustrated, including characters like Ming the Merciless from *Flash Gordon* and Stuff the Chinatown Kid, the sidekick from DC Comics' *Vigilante* stories of the 1940s.[6]

Along the lines of Mitchell's problematizing of the image-text suturing in depictions of race, any ambiguity surrounding Strange's race came well after Ditko's invention of the character and his first appearance in *Strange Tales* #110 (1963). What a response like the one I received also illustrates is Ditko's commitment to the idea that his work stands on its own, separate from himself, and any intention and related meaning are made clear by him, through the work, both visually and narratively. I take Ditko seriously on this point, and debates about authorial intent notwithstanding, this is important to take into consideration because it leads to the conclusion that building a sound reading of Ditko's work means first deciphering and contextualizing the visual elements he presents.

Moreover, not only is Dr. Strange depicted as East Asian, but Ditko, in *Down Memory Lane*, a 2019 collection of letters exchanged between Ditko and Robin Snyder, offers clues that invite an even narrower identification of the character—like other cast members in the series—as being specifically from Tibet. In a lament about fan and critical speculation surrounding his source material and inspiration, Ditko first dispels the commonly held notion that the infamous window in Dr. Strange's Sanctum Sanctorum (fig. 4.2) "'must have come from [Will] Eisner's Spirit [comic strip],' had to be done from something read or seen by the expert inquirer and not [Ditko's] own National Geographic files on Tibet."[7] Even if one is reluctant to assume that Dr. Strange is specifically Tibetan, that Ditko was drawing specifically on this imagery points, at minimum, to a character shaped by Ditko's interpretation of Far Eastern imagery and culture to create a character who is not just enthusiastic about those traditions but is *of* those very traditions, be they real or imagined.

What is also clear is that the decision to render Dr. Strange as East Asian, or at least of Asian descent, is an important and progressive one. That Asian characters had previously appeared in heroic roles in American comic books and pulp fiction is not contested: Green Hornet worked with Kato, Crimson Avenger with Wing, and Blackhawk with Chop-Chop; Stuff saddled up with Vigilante; and spy characters like Jimmy Woo had peppered the superhero landscape from the 1930s onward. But these characters were typically relegated to sidekick status alongside their white counterparts, and though Jimmy Woo played more of a leading role in his appearances in *Yellow Claw*, he disappeared after *Yellow Claw* ended, and was busted down to supporting cast when he reemerged in Jim Steranko's *Nick Fury, Agent of S.H.I.E.L.D* in

Figure 4.2. An external view of Dr. Strange's Sanctum Sanctorum in Greenwich Village. The symbol in the window has been part of the decor of Dr. Strange's mansion since *Strange Tales* #110. Dialogue edited by Stan Lee; Steve Ditko art; Artie Simek letters. "Let There Be Victory!" *Strange Tales* #141 (February 1966). © Marvel Comics.

1967.[8] What each of these instances demonstrates is that, although there was East Asian representation in comics by a number of publishers, the industry had an ongoing problematic relationship with those characters and how they were presented to readers.

An important example of that troubling relationship comes from Marvel's anthology comic *Amazing Adventures* #1 (1961). That issue features the introduction of Dr. Droom in a story edited by Stan Lee (who also credits himself as the writer), with pencils by Jack Kirby and inks by Steve Ditko.[9] The character would go on to appear in five more issues of *Amazing Adventures* before the series was retitled *Amazing Adult Fantasy* with issue #7. In a manner that the Ditko fanzine publisher Rob Imes links to the radio-cum-film character Chandu the Magician,[10] Anthony Droom, a white, Western doctor, visits the mystic East, where he is called on by a Tibetan lama for medical assistance. Impressed with Droom, the lama replaces an aged mystic master with Droom to carry on the everlasting battle of good versus evil. In a kind of body switch that would remind contemporary readers of Jordan Peele's horror film *Get Out* (2017), the white Droom is transformed into an Asian man after receiving his powers. The troubling and explicit implication of this kind of plot device is not only that white characters have the ability to perform other racial identities but that those identities can be commodified for and parceled out to white characters who are portrayed as being more worthy of them.[11]

Where Ditko separates himself from his contemporaries on matters of representation is that Dr. Strange was the lead character with a largely Asian supporting cast. Whatever problematic elements are evident in his early stories, the matter-of-fact tone with which the character and his race were initially presented avoided some of the more exploitive elements that populated other contemporary comics featuring heroes of color. Although he certainly plays into long-standing tropes and stereotypes about Eastern mysticism—an important component of mystic liberalism's association with Theosophy—Ditko does not offer any special pleading for Dr. Strange's race or ethnicity, nor does he embrace racist dialogue affectations to signal Strange's race. In fact, Dr. Strange's Anglicized first name, Stephen, was an invention of Stan Lee's and was not introduced until *Strange Tales* #115, which presents the character's origin. Incidentally, this also came at a point when Stan Lee had taken more of an interest and stake in the character's development.

Without coincidence, Lee inserts an origin story that is an obvious reworking of Dr. Droom's origin, bringing along racial complications similar to those Lee had credited himself with scripting for Dr. Droom in *Amazing Adventures*. In fact, Lee's origin for Dr. Strange draws directly from the Dr. Droom origin, but it inverts the race switching, masking Ditko's Asian Dr. Strange with the white Stephen Strange: a doctor who travels to the mystic East and is then enlisted by an ancient master. All of this is cribbed from Lee-Kirby-Ditko Dr. Droom stories, and none of it is obvious from, or foregrounded in, the first two Ditko stories. It seems apparent that this kind of unoriginal editorial input was part of Lee's inability to see the character through. But Lee had started to exert some editorial and creative influence just before this.

In the issue preceding the origin, *Strange Tales* #114, Lee, as editor, assigned George Roussos (working as George Bell)[12] to ink Ditko's pencils, and in that first instance Roussos remains reasonably faithful to Ditko's pencils, at least in terms of Dr. Strange's physical and racial makeup. However, after Lee's origin story, according to Ditko, Lee attempted to take more of an interest in the plots, which involved aliens (*Strange Tales* #118), a haunted house (*Strange Tales* #120), and a guest appearance from the Thor villain Loki (*Strange Tales* #123). It was also during this period that Lee assigned George Roussos back to *Strange Tales* and the character began to take on more distinctly Anglo features. Ditko cast suspicion on Lee's choice to assign Roussos in his 2008 essay "He Giveth and He Taketh Away," asking, "And did Lee ever say why he suddenly gave Dr. Strange to Geo. Bell (George Roussos) to ink?"[13]

Ditko stops well short of saying that Lee wanted to control Strange's physical appearance, but the implication is clear, especially when one considers Ditko's initial rendering of the character and observes that the character readopted his Asian characteristics after Ditko reassumed fuller narrative control with *Strange Tales* #126. Ditko claims that it was after Lee's repeated failures to grasp the character's potential, in the stories leading up to *Strange Tales* #126, reflecting the kind of inconsistency that Ditko is so adamantly opposed to, that he insisted the character be returned to his creative control, with himself credited as plotter, penciler, and inker. Lee agreed because, as Ditko puts it, Lee "was ready to drop Dr. Strange because of his difficulties [in developing the character] and [Ditko] told him that [he] should be inking and could do Dr. Strange because [he] saw Dr. Strange's potentials."[14] After the transition back to Ditko had gone into effect in *Strange Tales* #126, Dr. Strange's presentation is more in keeping with Ditko's consistent effort to make obvious his characters'—internal and external—identity, including Dr. Strange's racial makeup.

It is entirely possible, but unlikely, that Lee did not know Dr. Strange was designed as an East Asian character, which may account for his apparent inability to see the character's potential. This is possible because Lee was not involved in the character's initial conception. For many readers, this might come as a surprise, because the credits for the first Dr. Strange story, as printed in 1963, do not properly attribute the whole of the story to Ditko. Rather, Stan Lee is credited as the writer, though in reality Lee was merely the editor. Lee had no input in the initial plotting, scripting, or penciled pages. Dr. Strange, as Lee once said dismissively, "'twas Steve's idea."[15] Ditko "brought in to Lee a five-page, penciled story with a page/panel script of [his] idea of a new, different kind of character for variety in Marvel Comics. [His] character wound up being named Dr. Strange because he would appear in *Strange Tales*."[16]

Naming characters in this way was not particularly innovative and had its roots in the horror host characters who first appeared in comics in 1942 with *Crime Does Not Pay*'s Mr. Crime.[17] Not only does the character's name hew to the tradition of the horror hosts of the past—like those Ditko worked on at Charlton, such as the Mysterious Traveler in *Tales of the Mysterious Traveler*—but nothing in the Lee-edited dialogue or narration boxes specifically states the character's race. This leaves the reader with only Ditko's art to decipher the character's heritage. It is the rendering of Dr. Strange's facial features that clarifies his East Asian background, and the depiction of the character—particularly in the costuming and the Cloak of Levitation—draws obvious influence from Alex Raymond's Ming the Merciless from *Flash Gordon*.[18]

In spite of the problematic ways such features had been exaggerated in the comic books and strips of earlier years, the lack of exaggeration by Ditko, the coloring of the character, and the lack of racist dialogue affectations temper specific, racially charged overtones that Dr. Strange might otherwise have borne. Instead Ditko presents the character with a certain dignity that—like the kinds of heroes Ditko has created throughout his career—needs no justification for his existence. What you see, in a somewhat literal sense, is what you get. Although it is well intended, this kind of color-blind approach does indicate a certain amount of white privilege on Ditko's part to suggest that a nonwhite character could be defined in a manner that supersedes race or that such characters could avoid double consciousness. However, problematic as such an erasure is, it does reflect the ostensibly more progressive perspective of the civil rights movement in the 1950s and 1960s in its call for individual judgment to be based on the content of one's character. It is also a far cry from earlier and contemporary modes of Asian representation in comics.

That the issue of race is muddled for Dr. Strange is more telling of the kind of misreading that happened, intentionally or not, after other creative voices became involved with the character, especially after Ditko left Marvel in 1966 and other artists and writers took over the development of the character's mythology. For Ditko, such changes from "others and outsiders"[19] corrupted his artistic vision for his characters at Marvel, and he went out of his way to say he had social issues in mind, not just in his letter to me but in essays like the one noted earlier. Whether it was the "gimmick" of Spider-Man's costume concealing his race and ethnicity so that readers could identify with him (alongside the fear it created in criminals) or Dr. Strange's race, according to Ditko, "There was no 'we.'"[20] And these were not accidents. These were his deliberate choices.

Of course, Ditko was not the first comic book artist to create a character of color, but in terms of the superhero genre, Ditko's approach is an important one that could have set a tone for greater inclusivity in the production of superhero comics if editorial and collaborative decision-making had not altered Dr. Strange's initial trajectory. After all, Strange predates Jack Kirby's creation of the Black Panther—who is typically cited as the first hero of color in mainstream comics—by more than three years, but even Black Panther did not star in his own title until *Jungle Action* in 1973.

Meanwhile, Dr. Strange was a feature player in *Strange Tales* until the series was ultimately dedicated to only his adventures and retitled *Dr. Strange* before its cancellation in 1969. Strange eventually returned to regular publication in 1971 in *Marvel Feature*, and then with *Marvel Premier* in 1972, and a Dr. Strange solo book titled *Dr. Strange: Master of the Mystic Arts*, which ran until 1987. He again received a new title in 1988: *Dr. Strange: Sorcerer Supreme*, which lasted ninety issues and was canceled in 1996. Excluding a less-than-two-year gap from 1969 to 1971, Dr. Strange had nearly thirty-five years of consistent publication. Had the whitewashing of Strange not occurred, no other character of color—particularly one leading or coleading a title—would have had as sustained a publication history at either Marvel or DC.[21] For a publisher like Marvel, whose editorial pages often touted the company's interest in being a bulwark against racism, the choice to recast Strange as white disrupts that image, suggesting a secret racial history for its characters where creative intent butted up against corporate and editorial influence.

Again, without some kind of documentation, or even an anecdote, we have no way to definitively say precisely who initiated the whitewashing of Dr. Strange, or if it was a deliberate move, or, no matter how much it strains credulity, if it was an accidental misreading of Ditko's work. Hints are certainly visible here and there, but no explicit evidence or commentary has yet been revealed. What does appear certain is that the *initial* creation was Ditko's alone, and essays like "He Giveth and He Taketh Away" make plain that any potential corruptions of the character's initial intent did not come from his hand or mind. It is also obvious that Ditko believes the character's intended racial makeup is clear from the first published story, and it is only with the character's origin story that obvious Anglicized elements are added. Readers may draw whatever conclusions they wish from the evidence gathered here, but what remains true is that after Ditko left the character and Marvel in 1966, outside of notable, recent exceptions by Chris Bachalo and Marcos Martín, Dr. Strange has exclusively been depicted as white up to and including the casting of Peter Hooten in a 1978 made-for-TV movie and, of course, Benedict Cumberbatch in the 2016 film adaptation by Marvel/Disney.

Between Darkness and Dawn

Whereas racial inclusivity is not a clear or exclusive element of mystic liberalism, Dr. Strange offers one of the most profound explorations of cosmic intra-space and its relationship to the development of the individual. While other, more secular explorations of the cosmic interior that each individual contains are readily apparent in characters like Spider-Man, Blue Beetle, the Question, Mr. A, and others, it is Dr. Strange who offers the most direct, literal exploration of that space. This occurs with Strange as he explores his own identity and ascends from the tutelage of his master, the Ancient One, to becoming Sorcerer Supreme through his own incursions into myriad interior worlds. These interior worlds include the minds of others and dimensions beyond, where he must beat back the hordes of mindlessness and even his own evil opposite on his path to self-actualization and enlightenment. Along that journey, Dr. Strange encounters more than just those who fail as liberals by embracing a lust for power over others. He comes face-to-face with a literal, if not idealized, interpretation of cosmic intraspace when he meets the character of Eternity—an entire sentient universe encapsulated in humanoid form. If there is a character who embodies the qualitative effects of mind power in the shaping of one's own identity and universe, it is Dr. Strange.

In the mystic liberal imaginary, mind power is paramount in establishing individual identity. If people can't control their emotions, if they can't create the foundation for their own innate response to the world, then they run the risk of becoming awash in a sea of gray personlessness. What Ditko's Dr. Strange stories, as a series, offer is more than Dalí-esque landscapes. Through the embrace of those surrealist interior spaces, Ditko develops one of the most complete narratives about cosmic intraspace and the importance of *interior* over *exterior* space—exterior space like the operatic visions of contemporaries such as Jack Kirby (fig. 4.3). Instead of taking up an interest in the origins of the universe through timeless Celestials, living planets, Source Walls, or even a clash between New Gods, Ditko examines what it is to face an obsession with perceivable anti-life, one that predates Kirby's—much later— use of the term. What is at stake for Ditko—and, indeed, the mystic liberal more generally—is the establishment of an iconoclastic self that refuses not just the collective but the collectivist and, therefore, evil impulses of the demi- urgic force of the *world*. In the Ditkovian sense, to be an individual is not to be of the world but to be separate from it, and that separation is artistically established through Dr. Strange and his incursions into the interior spaces that would demand either his subservience or his compliancy.

Dr. Strange faces not just challenges of supremacy by Baron Mordo or the dominance of multiple realms by Dormammu; he faces the challenge of his own inadequacies as a master of the mystic arts and his own internal struggles. But even so, when he is first introduced, he is not a man without substantial talents. He has the ability both to explore his own intraspace and to examine the psychic struggles of others. In the very first Dr. Strange story, the fully formed but still examining Dr. Strange agrees to help a man haunted by a mysterious figure in his dreams. À la Freud, Jung, or even Nathaniel Branden, Dr. Strange agrees to investigate this troublesome, mysterious figure in the man's dreams. Dr. Strange discovers that a villain named Nightmare, a Ditko creation, is the cause of the man's troubles. By facing Nightmare alone, Dr. Strange is, like the psychoanalyst or the all-seeing mesmerist, able to see into the man's dreams and confront the evil within this unnamed supplicant.

Within the span of five short pages, Dr. Strange is able to expel Night- mare from the man's psyche in a way not dissimilar to the means by which a psychotherapist may be able to eliminate the ghosts of a patient's past by confronting and treating this specter as legitimate, then expelling it from the patient's subconscious. Aside from the ghost-busting elements of Ditko's nar- rative, what is also important is the embrace of these phantomistic elements of

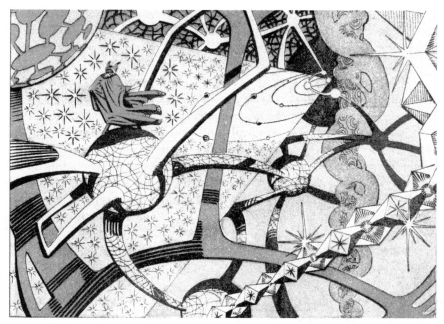

Figure 4.3. Dr. Strange looks out onto the vistas of cosmic intraspace in Eternity's realm. Steve Ditko art. "If Eternity Should Fail!" *Strange Tales* #138 (November 1965). © Marvel Comics.

the human experience as real and in need of attention. In no way does Ditko deny that negative, or even immoral or amoral, experiences play a part in any given individual experience. Unlike Ayn Rand or a Christian fundamentalist, Ditko does not treat such thoughts or experiences as failures; rather, he treats them as challenges that must be overcome for the individual to fully develop. Put differently, through a character like Dr. Strange, one learns that to become a heroic individual, to embrace oneself, to be comfortable with the heroic destiny embedded within each of us, one must first acknowledge and confront the weaknesses within and challenge the mindless hordes that threaten us all with their reasonless, unchecked emotion.

Dr. Strange's adventures to the cosmic intraspace—whether they be dreamscapes or dark dimensions—result in Strange confronting the demons that haunt the subconscious (Nightmare), the temptations of power and greed (Dormammu), or one's own evil opposite (Demon), and Strange's modus operandi is to explore these internal realms and expose these phantoms, both for himself and for those who seek his assistance. Dr. Strange is at once a psychonaut and a therapist. For him to fully realize his own potential as a student of the Ancient One and the mystic arts themselves, he must do more than expose and embrace the ghosts of the mind, à la Carl Jung. He must subdue and expel those ghosts, exerting the cleansing authority of his own mind and will. However, before he can take these strides toward greater consciousness and control over his own being, Dr. Strange often finds himself literally subdued and bound, typically manacled and gagged, so as to prevent him from casting any spells against his foes.[22]

For Strange to escape these situations, he cannot count on physical strength; rather, he relies on his ability to project himself in an astral form, leaving his physical body behind and allowing his consciousness to drift into myriad planes of existence, corporeal or otherwise. It is the power of Strange's mind that is paramount; his corporeal body is merely a fragile vessel for that greater entity. In large part, one of the major functions of the symbolism that appears throughout the early Dr. Strange adventures is the exploration of the relationship between mind and body. And, without fail, it is the mind that is paramount and must be perfected. This is a key component of the mystic liberal imaginary, as it emphasizes the importance of mental, intellectual labor.

Neither Ditko's essays nor his comics spend much time considering economic liberalism, much less neoliberalism, as it appears alongside, and in conjunction with, the mystic variety (although Ditko certainly wrote about the virtues of capitalism with some aplomb). So the connections among reaching greater consciousness, a labor of the self, and the achievement of greater wealth or corporate maneuvering are not actually at stake for Ditko as much as the production of whole individuals, principally of the philosophic and artistic variety. This is worth noting if for no other reason than it is a narrative motif that occurs throughout Ditko's long career, and while there are certainly instances, like that of Jabez Grimm in "Day of Reckoning," that concern themselves with pay commensurate with a day's labor, the emphasis is not on equitability between management and labor but on the importance of contracts and payment for services rendered. Rather, like the Lockean configuration of the creation of property, the creation of the individual—and the establishment of value for that person—treats productive, intellectual labor as an act of creation.

Through an excavation of one's own cosmic intraspace, and a willingness to expose and confront the ghosts, demons, and perils of the subconscious, an individual is formed and set on a path of dignified suffering toward, in Ditko's particular case, a heroic ideal. In the case of other mystic liberals, like H. P. Blavatsky, this kind of internal search may lead to an understanding of universal brotherhood and the connection of all races across time and space.[23] For mystic liberal practitioners of New Thought, it may actually mean upward mobility in a corporate neoliberal environment, as in the cases of Dale Carnegie and Norman Vincent Peale, or, as in the case of Neville Goddard, that the human imagination is God, the creator of all things. The confederate nature of mystic liberalism allows for a tremendous plurality of approaches that all focus on the importance of plumbing the depths of one's own consciousness to render oneself whole and make sense of the external world and one's own connection to, or separation from, that world.

Although Ditko's approach has much in common with Goddard's, his character's path of self-creation—perhaps unexpectedly—mirrors Max Stirner's advancement of the egoist. Stirner, as I pointed out in chapter 2, was a critic of Enlightenment liberalism and the ghosts that haunt it—the state, the church, the family—but as should also be clear by this point, one of the primary functions of mystic liberalism is to harmonize otherwise oblique or even paradoxical relationships in service of the creation of individuals, capital wealth, power, and so on. And this is true of each of the major components of mystic liberalism: Theosophy, New Thought, and Objectivism all draw on arcane, forgotten, or rejected ideas and beliefs; manipulate them in a way that services each movement's own ends; and implement those revisions as truisms.

It is at least partially within such a context that Ditko's heroic ideal operates in a manner similar to Stirner's egoist. For Stirner, the true egoist poses a frightening threat to society, and either society must banish such a person to the outer recesses of society's perceived reality, or if the egoist is treated as an existing person, then they must be denigrated as a sinner or labeled in some other excommunicative manner. To be sure, a major separation between Ditko and Stirner is that Stirner rejects the notion of moral, ethical goodness and evil, regarding them as shackles no more or less powerful than the trappings of any other societal institution. Where Ditko and Stirner converge is with the reception of the egoist, the ideal human. Such a person "exists only as a bogie or phantasm" in the minds of the masses.[24]

In rather obvious ways, the phantasmagorical nature of the heroic ideal Ditko portrays and that of Stirner's egoist is also present in pulp heroes like the Shadow, the Spider, and the Avenger, each of whom is temporally and theoretically in line with the development of mystic liberal ideology. On top of all of this, Ditko, like other purveyors of mystic liberalism, draws on and repurposes the narratives of the past in the service of a particular ideology. In Dr. Strange, the egoist is the phantasmagorical outsider who haunts people who behave irrationally or unjustly through his ability to access their literal, internal consciousness and expose them as the frauds they are, at which point those frauds are forced to confront the fact that whatever misfortune has befallen them is a result of the identity they generated for themselves with(in) their own mind.

A clear instance of this occurs in the story from *Strange Tales* #110 discussed earlier. The story opens as a typically Ditko noirish drama, where, on a stormy night in a city, in the liminal space "between darkness and dawn," a man fitfully writhes in bed. He awakens crying out after a nightmare, and he nervously resolves to find the mysterious Dr. Strange, whose name is only "spoken in whispers," to help free him from whatever is tormenting his sleeping mind.[25] From the outset, Dr. Strange is established as a mysterious, apparitional figure whose existence can only be discovered by circuitous means or by traveling in the right esoteric circles, the same obscure means that one might associate with the occult practices prescribed by Madame Blavatsky, to find a hero who, also like Blavatsky, has ethereal, psychic access to a master of ancient wisdom in the Ancient One. It is in that muddled space between the darkness and the dawn where the proclaimed master of the black arts does his work, disentangling the darkness from the light, exposing the shadows cast by evil thoughts and deeds and exorcising them.

In the daylight hours, the unnamed client appears at the door of Dr. Strange's Greenwich Village manor. The client begs Strange for his help, and the good doctor agrees to find the answers by doing nothing less than entering the client's dreams that very night. The client returns home to prepare for Strange's visit, and in the interim, Dr. Strange enters a trance that allows his astral spirit to leave his body and travel to "a hidden temple somewhere in the remote vastness of Asia," where he consults with the Ancient One, "from whom all of his powers stem." The Ancient One does not provide Strange with any particular advice other than a warning that danger approaches. The Ancient One also offers Strange a grim reminder of his own mortality, and a reminder that one day Strange will have to replace him.

That evening, Dr. Strange goes to the client's home and, by way of astral projection, leaves his physical body and enters the client's dream. Once inside the dream, Strange immediately encounters the figure haunting the client: a Marley-esque, cloaked apparition, bound by chains. When Strange interrogates him as to why he torments the client, the cloaked figure responds only that the client knows why and that he is a symbol of the evil the client has done. The figure also tells Dr. Strange to ask the client about a Mr. Crang, whom the client later confesses to have ruined in business. During the encounter with the symbol for the client's torment, Dr. Strange also encounters Nightmare, a ghastly figure that commands much of the internal nightmare dimension Strange has trespassed into.

Nightmare, whom Strange identifies as his "ancient foe," attacks the hero to exact the price for one such as Strange entering a hostile dimension—per "the rules of sorcery," Nightmare declares. At the same moment, the client wakes to the knowledge that Dr. Strange knows his terrible secret and decides to murder the doctor. Dr. Strange, now facing life-threatening danger in both the internal and external worlds that he simultaneously inhabits, calls on the Ancient One to assist him. He is eventually able to escape the twin perils, forcing the client to confess his sins and set himself on a more honest, upright path that one day will allow him to sleep again.

Aside from the allusions to Blavatskian occult relationships between master and apprentice, the ability to astral project and explore the limitless planes of existence is also corollary to the abilities that other Theosophists, like Charles Webster Leadbeater, claimed for themselves.[26] But for positioning an artist and writer like Steve Ditko within the scope of mystic liberalism, the most significant moments in the story come with the explicitly symbolic appearance of the client's own lingering guilt, that one's dreams (and, in this case, nightmares) exist in an internal nightmare dimension, how one's own thoughts and deeds manifest both psychically and within the material world, and, finally, the therapeutic effects of confronting one's own failures. To this last point, the client says that he regrets coming to Dr. Strange for help because he has had to confront his own crimes, but it is precisely this recognition that Strange says will lead the client to salvation. It's not just what the client did that was wrong; it's that his conscious and subconscious thoughts were generative elements of his outward existence, and only by seeking the assistance of an adept—one who functions as a therapist, in this case—can the client move forward and regain access to a saner existence.

The therapy angle to this story is significant if for no other reason than it marks an additional, more secular link to mystic liberalism. Of course, it would be absurd to posit that psychology and the practice of psychotherapy are necessarily implicated in mystic liberalism; they are not. Rather, the link I am pointing to comes from a number of approaches to these practices by mystic liberals, and how these sources all indicate that—just as it occurs with Dr. Strange's client—it is the power of one's conscious and subconscious mind that creates one's reality, be it one of joy or misery. Such thinking is foundational to the work of Nathaniel Branden in his writing on the importance of self-esteem and his contributions to Objectivism.

During his time with Rand, Branden headed the Nathaniel Branden Institute (NBI), which operated from 1958 to 1968, the closure of which coincided with Branden's excommunication from the Objectivist movement by Ayn Rand. NBI was located in New York City, and it has been reported anecdotally that Ditko frequented NBI in its heyday, where he heard Rand lecture and allegedly met with her on several occasions.[27] Although I'm squeamish about unsubstantiated anecdotes regarding Ditko's whereabouts and interactions more than a half century ago, the clear influence of Rand's and Branden's work on Ditko and the proximity of NBI to Ditko in New York certainly make this a reasonable possibility, and I am tentatively willing to accept it.

That being said, Ditko's proximity (or not) to NBI, Rand, and Branden is ultimately secondary to what his comics reveal and how they reflect the mystic liberal ideology that was propagated at NBI and practiced by Branden as a therapist. Branden's therapeutic approach focused primarily on the role of self-esteem in the development of individuals, and his books demonstrate a conviction that self-esteem is at once a fundamental human need and a greater force than a self-worth defined by external achievements. To

Branden, "Self-esteem is the experience that we appropriate to life and the requirements of life." In this configuration, self-esteem is not an automatic disposition and cannot be delivered by an outside force; rather, individuals must labor over and earn self-esteem and thus possess it.[28] It would not be too great of a stretch to link the laboring over, earning, and possession of self-esteem to the Lockean imagination of how property is produced and retained.

As discussed in chapter 2, these ideas work as an obvious corollary to the mind power of New Thought movements; in fact, they are practically indistinguishable. Being "appropriate to life" falls within Branden's sense of what defines better living: rising to the occasion of life's challenges, rationality, and, most important, the attraction of good fortune. This latter benefit comes straight out of the mind power, New Thought playbook and is probably most readily recognizable through its abuse in books and films like *The Secret*. In *The Six Pillars of Self-Esteem* (1994), Branden goes so far as to invoke the Law of Attraction, which is the notion that one's thoughts reflect their life's experiences. Pleasure or pain, wealth or poverty, sickness or health, all occur as a result of one's mental state. The mind is a generative force of one's own existence, and like attracts like. Positive thoughts bring good fortune, and negative thoughts or feelings create negative experiences.

The Law of Attraction has its roots in the mind cure philosophy of Phineas Quimby, but the term was coined by H. P. Blavatsky in *Isis Unveiled*. It was then later adopted by New Thought, a movement influenced by Blavatsky, through the work of Prentice Mulford and Ralph Waldo Trine; and by way of New Thought, it was then secularized and popularized in the service of self-help and neoliberal capitalism in the late 1930s by Napoleon Hill in *Think and Grow Rich*. Branden makes only a minor cosmetic change to this notion by substituting the term "self-esteem" for mind power or the power of positive thinking. Branden writes, "The level of our self-esteem has profound consequences for every aspect of our existence." Writing specifically about interpersonal relationships, he continues: "The reason is that *like is drawn to like*, health is attracted to health."[29] The opposite, of course, is also true. For Objectivism, positive self-esteem is only earned by actualizing one's abilities without apology. Indeed, this pairs nicely with the New Thought movement and its advocacy of reliance on oneself to "develop [one's] inner powers, believe in [one's] own experiences and intuitions." As noted in chapter 2, Branden positions himself squarely within the mind power tradition by linking the absence of positive thinking and self-esteem to nearly every conceivable social and personal ill.[30]

Relatedly, the roles of self-esteem and the Law of Attraction inform the stakes of Dr. Strange's encounter with his client in *Strange Tales* #110. The client's own chiseling thoughts are what led to his corrupt actions, and those actions, in just the way Branden insists, circle back on the client's subconscious state and his dreams, rendering him a tangled emotional wreck. Moreover, not only did the client's inadequate self-esteem underwrite his crimes and psychological turmoil, but this mixture of circumstances is also what drew to him both the Marley-esque apparition in his dreams and the evil Nightmare. For Branden, positive self-esteem is, "in effect, *the immune system of the consciousness*."[31] When that immune system is jeopardized, self-esteem and consciousness itself are endangered, attracting negative, destructive forces like those encountered by Dr. Strange's client. "I didn't suspect my dreams were caused by the many men I'd ruined in business," the client glumly confesses after the nature of his dreams is revealed to him.

The solution to this problem, where one cannot or will not identify the cause of one's psychological turmoil, as Ditko's story instructs, is to enlist the help of a therapist—in this case, a "Master of Black Magic" who can access the cosmic intraspace of another by mystic means and then expose and combat the evil forces within. To be sure, the client himself is not capable of doing battle with the ruler of the Nightmare dimension, thus requiring Dr. Strange's professional help. More important, however, is that Dr. Strange forces the client to confront his own misdeeds, and by acknowledging and confessing, the client has an opportunity to rebuild his life and cultivate a more positive, ethical sense of self. Failure to do so would only perpetuate his misery, and as Dr. Strange warns, acknowledging and cleansing his inner demons "will be the only way [he] can ever sleep again."[32]

A Test of Will

But not everyone's conscience is as susceptible to change as Dr. Strange's first client. Many of the demonic figures that Dr. Strange encounters on his psychonautic adventures into the seemingly limitless realms of the interior have an insatiable lust for power, especially when it comes to power over others and the exterior, mundane world. One such being is Dormammu, ruler of the Dark Dimension. The character's name is first mentioned by Strange's archrival, Baron Mordo, in *Strange Tales* #111, but he first appears in a two-part story in *Strange Tales* #126 and #127 in 1964, after Ditko reassumed more control over Dr. Strange's stories. Unable to leave his post in the Dark Dimension, Dormammu still has designs on power and conquest over the exterior universe, specifically Earth, which is protected by the Ancient One and his protégé, Dr. Strange. Because Dormammu must remain within the confines of his own dimension, he sends a messenger in spirit form to the Ancient One in an attempt to lure him into the Dark Dimension so that Dormammu may dispatch the Ancient One and begin his conquest. After receiving the messenger, the Ancient One summons Dr. Strange and informs him of the looming danger. Because the Ancient One is "too aged—too weary—to stop him," Dr.

Strange volunteers to confront Dormammu in the Dark Dimension, a place "fraught with strange dangers," and defend the earth against a being whose "power is beyond description."[33]

Accepting his apprentice's decision to face Dormammu, the Ancient One sends Strange to the world of the dread one, and when the mists clear, Strange arrives in a surrealist landscape, typical of Ditko's work, where he immediately faces a colossal, "unspeakable menace" guarding the doorway into the Dark Dimension. The behemoth guarding the door immediately levels an attack against Dr. Strange, and tellingly, the assault is not physical but instead takes the form of a mystic ray that targets Strange's mind—"a test of *will*."[34] It comes as no surprise that Dr. Strange's will—the power of his mind—overcomes the behemoth's mystic ray. Symbolically, however, this test is a significant moment in delivering a mystic liberal message: before one can confront the dark, supposedly insurmountable forces within, one must demonstrate the psychic fortitude to take on such a challenge. Just before entering the Dark Dimension, Dr. Strange exclaims that he is "committed to the battle of [his] *life!*,"[35] but in the Ditkovian and mystic liberal senses, the battle is not just *of* his life but *for* it.

As I discuss in chapter 6, later Ditko characters like Mr. A argue that the battle for, ownership over, and creation of one's own life and personhood are determined by one's ability to overcome darker, irrational urges. Throughout Ditko's run on the character, Dr. Strange makes just such a journey as he faces the demons and evils of these interior realms in his quest to become worthy of replacing the Ancient One as Sorcerer Supreme, thus fully actualizing himself and his heroic potential. So it is what Dr. Strange encounters in the Dark Dimension that fully commits him to the battle *for* the realization of his life, as symbolized by the greatness of the charge that awaits him as the future Sorcerer Supreme.

After passing the initial test of will, Strange enters the Dark Dimension and is immediately observed and scoffed at by Dormammu. In Ditko's design, Dormammu has a cascade of flames and mist and only the vaguest indication of a head atop a fully formed body, and this design is revealing about the character's identity and nature. While his body is complete and menacing, that his head lacks a distinct shape is representative of his incompleteness as a rational being. Part of the lesson with this visual representation is that power—be it physical, imperial, or magical—is not the measure of one's value or even wholeness as a person. It is the mind and its form—and therefore its physical manifestation—that demonstrate value and worthiness. This lack of rationality, this weakness, is even more obvious to the reader when the dread one's servants, not as a challenge to Dormammu's authority but as a matter of exercising caution, suggest that the human Strange may be stronger than expected. For this perceived insult, Dormammu attacks and imprisons his minions for their insolence in daring to question his judgment.

Meanwhile, Dr. Strange continues to demonstrate his rationalism as he runs a gauntlet of emblematized challenges on his path to face Dormammu, each one demonstrating both that diving deeper into one's cosmic interior is a dangerous business and that the means of conquest in that space are wit and will. The first stage of Dormammu's gauntlet is a faceless, diminutive humanoid shape that emerges from a pocket of space within the Dark Dimension, and whenever Strange blasts him with mystic energy, the creature grows larger. In the second stage, Dr. Strange is "seized by the dwellers below" after being sucked into a floating two-dimensional object that serves as a portal to another world within the Dark Dimension.[36] The dwellers below that pulled Dr. Strange down are visualized as a mass of mechanized, humanoid shapes, perhaps automatons, who do not speak and attempt to tangle Strange in some sort of webbing or mesh. Dr. Strange's actions and spells have no effect on these automata, and they are only warded off by a powerful blast from his enchanted amulet.[37]

Escaping the dimension of the dwellers below, Strange immediately encounters a handful of Dormammu's nameless lieutenants, one of whom traps Strange in a nearly impenetrable cloud of mystic energy. At first, Strange struggles against the restraining force of mystic energy, and as against the previous attackers, his spells are useless against it—he must again rely on his enchanted amulet. He first cuts a small hole in the containing energy to blast his enemy and then manages to burst the pocket around him, standing in a pose that implies the pocket is burst by energy emitted from Dr. Strange's body (fig. 4.4). The other attackers, realizing that Dr. Strange is their superior, escape through their own interdimensional portals.

Finally, as Strange moves forward for his showdown with Dormammu, he is accosted by a mysterious woman who has observed all his trials against the dwellers of the Dark Dimension. In later appearances and stories, this woman would come to be known as Clea, but for now, she is a nameless inhabitant of the Dark Dimension, who offers Strange a dire warning before his encounter with Dormammu. Fraught with worry, Clea implores Strange to retreat before the dread one destroys him. Of course, Dr. Strange refuses and marches on toward the showdown.

This sequence of trials illustrates the stations of self-creation envisioned by Ditko's brand of mystic liberalism. My language here is deliberately evocative of the Stations of the Cross, the imagery of Jesus on the day of his crucifixion, a seminal event in establishing his godhood in Christian mythology. Each of Dr. Strange's battles with the inhabitants of the Dark Dimension is a symbolic test that any prospective individual must pass by exploring his or her own cosmic interior. The first battle, where Strange faces the diminutive, faceless creature who grows with each successive attack, is an early indicator that brute force and physical action are not necessarily effective means of either

Figure 4.4. Encapsulated by a cloud of mystic energy, Dr. Strange struggles before relying on his cunning and using his enchanted amulet. Dialogue edited by Stan Lee; Steve Ditko art; Stan Goldberg colors; Artie Simek letters. "The Domain of the Dread Dormammu!" *Strange Tales* #126 (November 1964). © Marvel Comics.

overcoming or becoming. Rather, wit, cunning, and the creative and destructive powers of the mind should be put to their fullest use.

When faced with the challenge of the creature who grows when Strange applies the physical force of his spells, he faces the circumstances that Ella Wheeler Wilcox attempts to account for in her writing on obstacles in *The Heart of New Thought*: "Do not stop to excuse any delinquency or half-heartedness or defeat by the plea of circumstance or environment. The great nature [of the mind] makes its own environment and dominates circumstance. It all depends on the amount of force in your own soul."[38] I would not argue that Ditko had this precise passage or thought in mind, but aside from being essential to New Thought, it is certainly in keeping with the imagery in his work and the resolution of Dr. Strange's encounter here. When less-focused energy fails him, Strange relies on the force within his soul and the knowledge he has gained to dominate his opponent.

This reliance on the force of the soul carries Dr. Strange through his next two battles as well. When he is pulled down into his fight with "the dwellers below," his soul is again placed at hazard as he squares off against the mechanized mass, none bearing a distinct identity, their machinelike appearance embodying the conformity and programmability of those who have abdicated their sense of identity to an outside authority. In this specific case, that authority is Dormammu, but the implication is much broader. Dr. Strange proves his independence from such (un)thinking by escaping the dwellers below, whose very name carries the burden of a collectivized identity.

Similarly, as Dr. Strange has to escape the influence and control of conformity to the collective, he also has to rend himself free of containment and control by any one person, and this happens in the third phase of the gauntlet that Strange runs. When he is encapsulated in a pocket of energy by one of Dormammu's lieutenants, he is, on one level, challenging the authority that any one person may claim over another, revealing that such power dynamics must be resisted and defeated by wit and cunning. At another level, after Strange bursts the cloud of energy around him, he also demonstrates that he is equal, if not entirely superior, to these others, and he says as much.[39] By proving himself an equal, Dr. Strange closes out an important sequence in the labor of creating an individual self: at all three points, he demonstrates his ability to separate himself from others, proving that he is the master of his own identity, actions, and fate. But for Dr. Strange, and mystic liberalism, there is one more test to pass before one is able to confront the darkness within and ascend to complete individuation.

The fourth and final stage of the gauntlet Strange runs in his exploration of the Dark Dimension is the threat of self-doubt. In his efforts to challenge the evil urges that threaten life and the external world, Dr. Strange's encounter with Clea is the last battle he must win before encountering Dormammu. Narratively, this brings Strange full circle from the initial test of will that he had to pass to gain access to the Dark Dimension; now he faces yet another test of will, but this time he is confronted with the futility of his actions against a more powerful being of negative energy. When Clea first appears, all the reader knows about her is that she has long inhabited the Dark Dimension and lived under Dormammu's iron rule. Understandably, she is skeptical of any challenges to his authority, and because she is so beleaguered by her existence, she has given up any hope that Dormammu's power can be limited, much less defeated. Clea's concern is earnest and forceful. "You cannot suspect how *powerful* he is! You throw away your life by facing him!" she warns.[40] Clea is experientially challenged when it comes to seeing the outcomes for those who dare defy Dormammu's authority.

To that end, Clea does not pose a physical threat to Dr. Strange or his mission, but her words, actions, and fretting symbolize a kind of reluctance and fear that must be overcome. Although Clea is in no way villainous, that she inhabits the Dark Dimension and tries to prevent Dr. Strange from moving on in his quest is telling, but her character is more complex than being an obstacle for Strange. Just as she represents the doubts and consternation that one must eliminate in taking the risk of formulating a self, so she also represents the inherent good that resides within these darker places and how that goodness can be repressed and worn down until it no longer has the strength or will to fight. Eventually Dr. Strange grants Clea protection after she helps him defeat Dormammu, but she elects to stay in the Dark Dimension after Strange offers her safe passage to Earth. This is again telling of the complexity not just of Clea's character but of the Dark Dimension itself, because even though she is outwardly plagued by doubt, she cannot help but believe in the strength of Strange's inherent goodness. In the same way that her doubts were an obstacle for Dr. Strange to overcome, Dormammu and the residents of the Dark Dimension must contend with her embodiment of doubt as they try to exert their own evil will.

Steadfast in his resolve, Dr. Strange acknowledges Clea's kindness in her warnings and then moves past her to face Dormammu, but just before the battle begins, Clea pleads with Strange once more, this time to renege on his challenge to Dormammu, not for his own sake but for the sake of both Earth and the Dark Dimension. To prove her point, Clea opens a portal to the outer reaches of the Dark Dimension, showing Dr. Strange a danger greater than the controlled evil of Dormammu: the Mindless Ones. These brutish inhabitants of the Dark Dimension are "primitive, savage, totally devoid of love or kindness, or any type of intelligence! They live only to *fight* . . . and to destroy!"[41] But as with any of the Ditko and Lee collaborations, it is the visual representation of these characters that is most informative. The Mindless Ones are a destructive horde that threatens to wreak havoc on Dormammu's dread domain. Individually, they are lumbering, craggy, slouching, gray creatures lacking any distinct shape, who indiscriminately attack anything they can, including one another, with their lumpy fists and beams that they blast from the cyclopic slats of their eyes.

The Mindless Ones are an important component of the cosmic intraspace of the Dark Dimension because, like the earlier tests of Dr. Strange's will and the power of his mind, these creatures, too, pose a threat to rationality and the security of one's own moral, ethical identity. An evil being like Dormammu might be reasoned with, but the Mindless Ones cannot. Although Dormammu lusts for power and control over others, the Mindless Ones lust only for the destruction of others. And as the reader and Dr. Strange learn from Clea, it is

Dormammu's power that keeps the Mindless Ones at bay by means of a mystic shield he has erected around the inner core of the Dark Dimension.

The symbolic stakes of this scenario are tremendous and are important for both Ditko's work and mystic liberalism more broadly. The incredible evil power of Dormammu and the dastardly cunning of Baron Mordo present significant dangers to the world defended by Dr. Strange, but the Mindless Ones are perhaps the greatest threat in Ditko's Dr. Strange stories. The Mindless Ones represent the unmitigated drive of the mob, the collective that has abdicated any sense of reason or rationality, and, most importantly, self. They seek not to achieve but to destroy. It should come as no surprise that this theme runs throughout Ditko's work, and the visual motif of the mob is ever present. In Ditko's Dr. Strange stories, to resist the mobs of the mundane, external world, one must first learn how to resist them in the cosmic intraspace of the mind.

Confounding the Negative Temptations Within

As should be clear by this point, the Dark Dimension is a representational space: it is the place in the mind that contains powerful temptations as they relate to ethics, morality, and the creation of an individual identity. Throughout this two-part story, we have seen Dr. Strange square off against conformity to and control by others. The Mindless Ones do not seek control; they have no values, no principles, and, to put it right on the nose, *no minds*. In the Ditkovian configuration of mystic liberalism, the Mindless Ones' attacks on the Dark Dimension operate in a manner similar to what Ayn Rand might consider "an attempt to *disintegrate* man's consciousness," and for her, "disintegration is the preface to the death of the human mind," leading to the "retrogression of an adult mind to the state of a mewling infant."[42] Rand articulated her sense of "disintegration" almost a decade after the publication of the Dr. Strange stories in question, but the idea remains useful and prescient here because it helps to articulate precisely the threat Ditko's Mindless Ones present to the mind space of the Dark Dimension.

What is also telling about the Mindless Ones' presence in Dormammu's domain is that while these lumbering oafs threaten the external world, their point of origin lies in the segment of the mind populated by the other perceived weaknesses and evils already discussed. By having already accepted and exploited the collectivized principles that Dr. Strange had to ward off in defense and development of a reasoning individual identity, Dormammu has opened himself up to the perpetual attacks that take so much of his energy and focus. Conversely, Dr. Strange has no such lack of focus or diminished power, because he has overcome those earlier collectivized principles that Dormammu has embraced.

But just because Dr. Strange has overcome the principles that are the engine of Dormammu's Dark Dimension does not mean that the threat of the dread one also disappears. In fact, it complicates the relationship between Strange and Dormammu in interesting and profound ways. After Clea reveals the truth about Dormammu's role in keeping the Mindless Ones at bay, Dr. Strange faces something of a crisis: Dormammu must be kept in check and stopped, but for now, he serves as a necessary barrier between humanity and the Mindless Ones. For Ditko, the stakes are at once psychological and political: how can the individual, rational mind come to terms with and defeat the evil of fascistic despotism without succumbing to the mob rule of collectivism?

For Dr. Strange, there is not a clean defeat of either, and the consequence is an ongoing battle against such thoughts and ideologies that must continually be both acknowledged and overcome. Resolving that he cannot abandon his oath to the Ancient One—and, indeed, his commitment to self-creation—Dr. Strange presses on toward his challenge to Dormammu. When he arrives in Dormammu's chamber, he sees that Clea has been captured, and Dormammu has linked her fate to Dr. Strange's. As the mystic battle between the two rages, Strange quickly learns that Dormammu's power is greater than his own, and he can see no clear path to victory. Upon this realization, he again struggles with doubt, and, all but explicitly acknowledging the Law of Attraction, Dr. Strange steels himself, thinking, "I must not allow my mind to dwell on thoughts of defeat!"[43]

As Dr. Strange fights on, what neither he nor Dormammu realizes is that because of the effort Dormammu is exerting, the mystic barrier holding back the Mindless Ones has begun to weaken. Perhaps this weakening results from the power of Dr. Strange's positive thinking, or perhaps it demonstrates the inherent weakness in Dormammu's ability because of his own motivations or negative thoughts. If the story fits into anything resembling the blended ideology of mystic liberalism, then it is both. As the Mindless Ones begin to break through the barrier, Dormammu must turn his attention away from Dr. Strange, instead focusing on expelling the Mindless Ones and reforming the barrier. What happens next reinforces the relative power of thought and motivation in beating back the destructive horde. As Dormammu struggles to regain control and reestablish the barrier, Dr. Strange, recognizing the horrific threat the Mindless Ones pose to the inhabitants of the Dark Dimension and Earth, decides to help Dormammu. The combined effort of the two foes proves to be more than enough, but that Dr. Strange helped him enrages Dormammu, because it places him in Strange's debt. It is at this point that Dr. Strange has something of an epiphany.

After Dormammu swears his debt to Dr. Strange, Strange decides to "go easy" on him and makes only two demands: first, that Clea—in this story, an avatar of caution, worry, and doubt—have no harm done to her; and second, that Dormammu vows never to invade Earth. Dr. Strange is willing to make this deal because he recognizes that Dormammu follows some kind of personal code, even if it is an evil one by Strange's standards. Like the other obstacles Dr. Strange encountered in the Dark Dimension, Dormammu is defeated only by the power of Strange's mind and reason. The physical battle between the two played out to, in the most generous terms, a stalemate. That Dr. Strange acknowledges Dormammu's code is less to demonstrate the villain's humanity than it is to show that, even if an evil cannot be eradicated, the dark urges that exist in the cosmic intraspace of the mind can be kept in check by means of reason and rationality.

This is the epiphany that Dr. Strange claims and offers to readers: when exposing and confronting the darker elements of the mind, completely vanquishing those forces is not necessarily feasible. Rather, one must first acknowledge and negotiate with those darker elements, and only then can one establish their identity and control over them—an exertion of the power of the mind. The negotiation presented in this tale is similar to the resolution of the first Dr. Strange story: the client must learn to accept, confront, and overcome his own negative thoughts and their manifestations. The major difference between Dr. Strange and his client in that first story is that Strange is able to confound the negative temptations within, and he is able to do so by maintaining his resolve and positivity.

That Clea elects to remain in the Dark Dimension is an indication of the necessity of entertaining caution and doubt when facing the negative urges of the mind, but self-doubt is ultimately an obstacle to self-actualization in the mystic liberal sense. Clea's status as an inhabitant of the Dark Dimension, of course, does not mean she is an entirely negative figure. Throughout all her appearances in Ditko's work on the series, she is portrayed as inherently good—a demonstration that the behaviors and thoughts that populate the Dark Dimension exist on a sliding scale. Dr. Strange also acknowledges this spectrum when he ponders the dimension's innocents. This complication is less a condemnation of Clea's timidity and self-doubt than it is a warning against how power-lusting forces, like Dormammu, can terrorize and traumatize good people into a state of subservience. In Clea's case, it cleaves her to a cruel and unrelenting dimension where she must struggle against her abuser and the internal conflict created by that abuse.

Upon Dr. Strange's return from the Dark Dimension, the Ancient One rewards him with a new magical cloak and a more powerful amulet; indeed, these are the costume elements that would become some of the most readily identifiable visual elements of the character. Not without coincidence, the new amulet, the Eye of Agamotto, looks precisely like a real amulet: the Eye of the Buddha, which is a circular amulet with an eye in the center, surrounded by Snail Martyrs. The Eye of Agamotto is almost identical in its design and lends additional evidence that Ditko had, at the barest minimum, invested time in researching mystic texts and likely spent some time in curio shops (fig. 4.5). After bestowing these items, the Ancient One also explicitly informs Dr. Strange that not only is Strange worthy of these sacred occult tools, but Strange will be the one who replaces him. As Strange walks away, the Ancient One considers "the awesome weight of the responsibility, and the unimaginable loneliness" that Dr. Strange will have to bear once he accepts the mantle.[44] The isolation and loneliness of enlightenment form a tragic theme that runs throughout Ditko's superhero work, but it is also the price that Ditko's heroes willingly pay for self-creation and continual betterment.

An Embodiment of the Universal Mind

While Dr. Strange remains on a continual quest for self-discovery, creation, and perfection, he encounters greater and greater dangers with each dimension of cosmic intraspace he visits. At one point, he even confronts a demonic doppelgänger who attempts to assume Strange's identity before the doctor thwarts him.[45] In this latter stage of Dr. Strange's search, the Ancient One's weakened state is at its most dire, and he is only able to whisper one word: "Eternity." Strange takes this as a clue that only the secret of Eternity will be able to save the Ancient One. With nothing more than the Ancient One's fevered mutterings to go on, Dr. Strange begins to search for the meaning of "Eternity." Strange is unable to find any answers in the ancient occult tomes or from any of the masters of ancient wisdom he entreats. The secrets he seeks, metaphorically, are the secrets of the ultimate self that he has sought all along, and the literal embodiment of that self, which brings with it cosmological truths and the ability to thwart any inward, nagging evils and doubts.

Meanwhile, Dormammu continues to lurk in the background, attempting to circumvent his agreement with Dr. Strange by tempting, employing, and controlling the power-hungry Baron Mordo. Because Mordo lacks the ethical and intellectual constitution to resist the temptation of the evils within, he makes an excellent proxy for Dormammu to work against Dr. Strange. Mordo's excellence, however, has more to do with his role in Ditko's melodrama as an avatar for the incomplete self, or what Ayn Rand might refer to as a "second-hander," insofar as "his ambitions are motivated by other men. He's not really struggling even for material wealth, but for the second-hander's delusion—prestige."[46] Unlike Dr. Strange, Mordo's sense of self is motivated by his secondhand nature: he seeks only the power and prestige in supplanting the Ancient One, and when he turns his will over to Dormammu, his self-esteem is a product of whatever Dormammu bestows on him.

While Dormammu's continual failures *could* be excused as simplistic narrative moralizing, they also demonstrate the power of the Law of Attraction

Figure 4.5. Dr. Strange receives the Eye of Agamotto for his defeat of Dormammu. On the right is an image of the Eye of the Buddha talisman found in curio shops. The Eye of the Buddha image is from Cat Yronwode's Lucky Mojo Curio Company. Yronwode worked with Ditko at Eclipse Comics in the 1980s. Dialogue edited by Stan Lee; Steve Ditko art; Stan Goldberg colors; Sam Rosen letters. "Duel with the Dread Dormammu!" *Strange Tales* #127 (December 1964). © Marvel Comics.

and its relationship to self-esteem. As Rand—and Branden with his more obvious mystic influence—would suggest, the second-hander creates his own failures and misery by attracting not just the similarly minded but also those who seek power and influence over others. According to Rand, the second-hander admires dictators—in the way Mordo is drawn to and draws on the internal evil of Dormammu. As a result of Mordo's failing, he has "got to force [his] miserable little [personality] on every single person [he] meet[s]," embracing and attempting to emulate the tyrants he so admires. Characters like Mordo possess no sense of self, no sense of independence, because, as Rand argues, these characteristics "do not exist *within* [the second-hander]."[47] What Mordo wants is power without responsibility.[48]

As willing as Dormammu is to lend that power to Baron Mordo in service of his own search for power, neither he nor Mordo is able to defeat Dr. Strange, and along the way, Dormammu learns that Strange is seeking the secrets of Eternity. Seeing Eternity as the greatest threat to his own existence, Dormammu determines to wrest those secrets from Dr. Strange by threatening the life of the incapacitated Ancient One. In Dormammu's tyrannical lust for power and control over others, he extols precisely the evils that Ditko would have learned from his encounters with Randian thinking: the greatest danger to Dormammu is a fully formed self, an independent mind.

In her essay "The Soul of the Individualist," Rand describes despotic second-handers as being "made to destroy the ego, themselves and others," with the aim of either destroying creators or harnessing them, which she saw as synonymous.[49] The literal creative force of the mind that is central to New Thought, and Ditko's philosophic interest in the role of creativity, in the artistic sense, become tangled here, demonstrating how New Thought mysticism and the alleged rationalism of Randian individualism merge in the service of mystic liberalism, and Dormammu represents a threat to those blended ideologies. Embodying precisely the self-destroying force that Rand describes, Dormammu simultaneously attempts to harness the knowledge that Dr. Strange gains in his search for Eternity, eliminate Dr. Strange by proxy, and then do the same to Eternity—all of which eventually lead to Dormammu's defeat and the loss of his own power.

The knowledge that the dread one wants to extract from Dr. Strange was hard won by the sorcerer. Mitch Horowitz spends much of *Occult America* cataloging some of the most important occultists and mystics in American history, and in each of the cases he explores, one or both of the following occurs: the mystic embarks on a personal, internal, psychological search for revealed knowledge not commonly found in existing religious texts, or the mystic has secret knowledge bestowed on him or her by a master of occult and ancient wisdom. In the latter case, for example, Blavatsky both was the pupil of her Masters of the Ancient Wisdom and served as the master to her own inner circle. To that end, Horowitz spends considerable time in both *Occult America* and *One Simple Idea* examining how, throughout the history of the mind power movement that generated New Thought, one sees a consistent pattern of new, self-proclaimed masters emerging, either rebelling against their own masters or, like Blavatsky and Dr. Strange, sharing, promoting, and expanding the wisdom they earned and received from their own teachers. Earning wisdom was active and experiential and not gained by relying on passive, rote memorization or the expediency of didactic lessons; not coincidentally, this process of earning wisdom runs opposite to Rand's second-handers.

With that history in mind, one should not be surprised that Dr. Strange could not gain knowledge of Eternity by skimming ancient texts or by simply asking other learned mystics to tell him who or what Eternity was. Rather, although the Ancient One opens the gates for him, Strange must labor over the knowledge and experience Eternity to understand what it is. After gaining these experiences, he can then apply what he learns to cure the Ancient One's weakened state and stave off the onslaught of the second-handers Mordo and Dormammu. To access the Ancient One's wisdom, Dr. Strange calls upon the Eye of Agamotto to open a third eye in his forehead, which allows him to attempt to penetrate the Ancient One's mind. But because, as is seen throughout his earlier search, he cannot simply extract and harness the Ancient One's wisdom, he encounters a series of traps deployed by the Ancient One's subconscious mind: barriers to protect the Ancient One's own labored-over knowledge. Proving his worthiness to his master, Dr. Strange gains access to the Ancient One's own internal cosmos by allowing himself to trust and be trusted by the Ancient One. The master assures Strange that his efforts to defeat Dormammu and Baron Mordo have "put [his] inner mind at rest," and then he grants Dr. Strange access to "the secret of how to contact Eternity."[50]

Armed with the secret knowledge earned from the Ancient One, Dr. Strange removes himself to a distant jut of craggy rock and repeats an elaborate incantation that causes the Eye of Agamotto to leave his chest and grow to an enormous size, and where the eye had been, a portal opens into the world of Eternity. Once Strange has entered this new dimension, he drifts through a twisted, knotted cosmos full of layered and intersecting planes and long corridors, all visually revealing the elaborate networks of ideas and differences that make up any individual cosmic intraspace. Having mastered numerous other dimensions and internal realms, Dr. Strange is able to easily navigate the complexity of this space, moving toward the brightest star in the cosmos, which is actually another doorway that resembles the Eye of Agamotto. Once Strange crosses that threshold, he feels psychically drawn toward a bright light at the end of a long, darkened hall. Reaching the end of the hall, Strange discovers it is actually a tiny universe emitting the light, and before his very eyes, the universe expands, growing into a humanoid form. This is Eternity (fig. 4.6).

A humanoid shape, filled with a visible universe, Eternity is a being of immeasurable power. Visually, Eternity represents the ultimate self and the creative force of the fully realized mind, literally creating himself using the power of his mind while simultaneously revealing that mind. Eternity is the living embodiment of cosmic intraspace, and Ditko unsurprisingly makes the visual choice to represent Eternity as a living cosmos, symbolizing both the mind's infinite power and its capacity for creation. After telepathically evaluating Dr. Strange and noting his worthiness, Eternity refuses to bestow any new powers on Strange and reiterates the point made throughout Ditko's run on *Strange Tales*: physical "power is not the only answer"; wisdom is the key to defeating Dormammu and Mordo. Eternity then dismisses Dr. Strange, insisting he has more pressing, world-shaking matters to attend to.[51]

One might mistakenly dismiss Eternity's revealing that the power was within Strange all along as a bit *Wizard of Oz*–esque, but the mind power message is unmistakable (and this is true of *The Wizard of Oz* as well), and Eternity, along with his message to Dr. Strange, is an embodiment of the New Thought concept of the "universal mind." For the New Thought author Ernest Holmes, the universal mind "is the potential ultimate of all things,"[52] and for fellow New Thoughter Charles Haanel, it is

infinite and omnipotent, has unlimited resources at its command, and when one remember[s] that it is also omnipresent, we cannot escape the conclusion

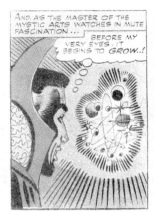

Figure 4.6. At last, Dr. Strange comes face-to-face with Eternity, the living embodiment of cosmic intraspace. Dialogue edited by Stan Lee; Steve Ditko art; Sam Rosen letters. "If Eternity Should Fail!" *Strange Tales* #138 (November 1965). © Marvel Comics.

that we must be an expression or manifestation of that Mind. A recognition and understanding of the resources of the subconscious mind will indicate that the only difference between the subconscious and the Universal is one of degree.[53]

If Dr. Strange went in search of Eternity to retrieve and earn the right to gain the being's power to save the Ancient One and battle Dormammu, then Eternity's message that Strange already has the power to defeat his enemies is precisely Haanel's definition of the universal mind: wisdom. The resources of the mind are all that Strange needs, and that he has reached and is worthy of the embodiment of the universal mind, Eternity, is all the power he could ever hope to obtain. Dr. Strange, through the power of his own mind, has access to the infinite and may dispose of that power as his (sub)conscious allows; the source of all power is the cosmos within. And it is within the subconscious where Eternity remains, as Strange's precise memory of the being fades when he returns to the external, earthly realm.

Believing Eternity's message to be a kind of cipher, Dr. Strange returns to the earthly plane, only to find that the Ancient One has been kidnapped by Mordo and Dormammu, and at once Strange is hurled into combat with the two. The fight takes place over the next three issues of *Strange Tales*, where, just as before, Strange must rely on his cunning and wit to overcome the treachery of Dormammu and his earthly proxy. Dr. Strange outmaneuvers the dread one by playing to Dormammu's vanity, and after defeating Dormammu in combat, Dr. Strange banishes him back his own dimension, forbidding him to ever again turn his power against Earth. Similar to his prior victory, Dr. Strange has won a symbolic battle against the darker elements of the mind, but he cannot eliminate those forces totally; they must always be contended with and pressed ever further backward. To make this point plain, Dormammu, in his defeat, still has a trick up his sleeve: claiming that he can never truly lose, he imprisons and threatens the life of the innocent Clea, who mustered the courage to help Dr. Strange in the fight. Before he can follow after her, Dr. Strange is warned against such an errand by the Ancient One, who reminds Strange that Clea—the avatar of doubt—is bait, a mental trap set for Dr. Strange. The Ancient One assures his apprentice that no harm will come to Clea so long as Dr. Strange remains free.

With Dormammu in retreat, Dr. Strange sets out on new challenges that continue to test his mental power, both his mystic acumen and his ability to stay resolute in the face of solitude. But the nagging presence of Dormammu and Strange's ethical commitment to rescue Clea carry with him, eventually leading to a cataclysmic showdown between the avatars of the second-hander and the self when Dormammu and Eternity clash in Ditko's last Dr. Strange story in *Strange Tales* #146.

Titled "The End—at Last!," the chapter opens in the Dark Domain, where Dormammu is raging and soliloquizing about his plans to destroy first Dr. Strange and then Eternity so that he may "reign over all that is."[54] Dormammu enacts his plans by first traversing the dimensions to that of Eternity, where he attempts to trap and contain the universal mind by catching him off guard. But Dormammu's spells are not enough to prevent Eternity from summoning Dr. Strange and warning him of Dormammu's pending attack. Strange reenters the Dark Dimension through the Eye of Agamotto, where he immediately confronts Dormammu so as to free Eternity from Dormammu's spell. Once more, Strange is only able to succeed by relying on his wit, and he is able to release Eternity from Dormammu's trap, from which Eternity explodes into the fray.

By liberating Eternity, Dr. Strange, in an oblique way, has unlocked the power of his own subconscious mind against the aggressive forces of darkness represented by Dormammu's self-denying ethos. After Eternity is freed, the embodied cosmos first tries to reason with Dormammu, but these efforts are in vain. After all, Dormammu is living unreason, and the ruler of the Dark Dimension immediately moves to attack Eternity, even as the cosmic giant still attempts to warn him of this folly. Rather than choreographing an elaborate fisticuffs between the two, as he had done when Dr. Strange battled Dormammu and Mordo, Ditko presents the clash in just two splash pages. Over those two pages, Dormammu leaps toward and is absorbed by Eternity in the first page, and a tremendous explosion from within Eternity's body occurs in the second (fig. 4.7). This artistic choice is significant for at least the reasons that it demonstrates the immense power of the two beings and shows that Eternity, particularly, is capable of both consuming and expelling the negative thoughts and principles Dormammu represents.

Figure 4.7. In their final epic clash, Dormammu is swallowed by the cosmic intraspace of Eternity. Dialogue by Dennis O'Neil; Steve Ditko art; Artie Simek letters. "The End—at Last!" *Strange Tales* #146 (July 1966). © Marvel Comics.

The explosion generated by the clash of these two diametrically opposed forces—and their existential incompatibility—reveals the kind of binary philosophic approach to human nature and action that would appear in Ditko's later comics with characters like the Question and Mr. A. And although the narration boxes leave ambiguous the fate of Eternity after the explosion, Ditko's visuals make the outcome more certain, as the universe inside of Eternity blasts outward, filling the timeless void where the battle is taking place. That void represents the blank slate of the mind—as each of the dimensions explored throughout Ditko's Dr. Strange represents individual minds or facets thereof. While Dormammu believes that Eternity has perished as a result of the blast, what he fails to recognize is that Eternity has consumed the empty space and all within it. As the elements of Eternity absorb the void, the reader is further alerted to the dangers of trying to exist in the space between the self and the anti-self, as Dormammu attempted by trying to dominate Eternity. This warning comes in a sequence of six panels on the page immediately following Eternity's explosion and consumption, and a large panel on the next page.

In that progression, Dormammu is hurled outward and finds himself between two meteors, one cold and black, the other a bright ball of fire—as opposite as Eternity and Dormammu, self and anti-self, mind and anti-mind, life and anti-life. For Ditko, there can be no middle ground between the two, not even for one as powerful as Dormammu. When the two meteors collide, a massive blast occurs, and the darkened object crumbles and falls away as the bright, burning comet continues on (fig. 4.8). Similar clashes happen over the remaining panels, each time the colder object being destroyed as Dr. Strange is pulled into a separate plane by the restored Ancient One.

When Strange and the Ancient One reunite, the master informs the pupil that Dormammu's physical body has been destroyed, rendering him a *mindless* disembodied spirit, and although it is the Lee-edited dialogue that explicitly states Dormammu's mindless state, the careful reader of Ditko's visual narrative has known all along that Dormammu never had much of a mind in the first place. The same dialogue reveals that the fate of Eternity is uncertain, but again, Ditko's visuals tell a different story, leaving just enough mystery to be provocative. After this bit of exposition, Dr. Strange then uses his power to liberate "those mortals whose psyches were *enslaved* by Dormammu," including Clea.[55] This liberation points once more to Dormammu's position not as a literal being but as a state of mind that has the power to rule over and destroy, one that results from the annihilation of the self. Dr. Strange, through the resolve demonstrated in his trials—along with the assistance of the ultimate, total self in Eternity and the enlightened consciousness of the Ancient One—performs the labor of understanding the power of his own mind in shaping his existence.

As an artifact of mystic liberal ideology, Steve Ditko's Dr. Strange is a significant piece of popular culture that made such thinking available to a broad

Figure 4.8. The final conflict between the oppositional forces of mind and anti-mind, life and anti-life, is symbolically enacted as Dormammu is crushed between dark and light meteors. Dialogue by Dennis O'Neil; Steve Ditko art; Artie Simek letters. "The End—at Last!" *Strange Tales* #146 (July 1966). © Marvel Comics.

audience. Moreover, unlike other major texts, like those by Dale Carnegie or Norman Vincent Peale, Ditko's Dr. Strange comics focus less on the wealth-creating, capitalistic elements of such thinking and more on the self-creating, ethical components and power of the mind. The series also represents a significant moment in Ditko's career, and although he never stopped producing supernatural horror or weird fiction, it is a point when the artist's interest in the philosophic exploration of ethics and self-esteem as they relate to individual existence becomes explicit, even didactic.

While many critics point to Ditko's post-Marvel period, after the final Dr. Strange and Spider-Man stories were turned in, as being the point when his work turned toward philosophic pedantry, what the Dr. Strange stories in *Strange Tales* and his work on *The Amazing Spider-Man* demonstrate is that Ditko was already interested in developing long, allegorical narratives that explored matters of the mind and the creation of the self. Both Dr. Strange and Peter Parker experience a tremendous amount of growth and change throughout the arcs that Ditko plotted out for them. Above all, it was the lived experiences of those characters that shaped them most profoundly, not osmotic events or accidents of nature; it was the lives they lived and their unique experiences as each psychonautically traversed his own cosmic intraspaces. Indubitably, this was more literally true for Dr. Strange than it was for Spider-Man, but even Spidey gets a taste of the mystic inner realms known to Dr. Strange in *Amazing Spider-Man Annual* #2, when the two heroes meet for the first time. But though Spider-Man gets a taste of the mystic realms, Ditko had other plans for the psychological development of the old webhead.

5

GROUNDED IN A MORE CREDIBLE WORLD

Spider-Man, Blue Beetle, the Question, and a More Practical Self-Actualization

For the mystic liberal, cosmic intraspace does not always need to be imagined as a literal cosmos or series of pocket dimensions like those explored and conquered by Dr. Strange, and the power of individual thought need not be explicitly linked to the divine. One of the notable elements of mystic liberalism is that it is so easily secularized and put into the service of neoliberal capitalism, self-esteem, and any number of self-help practices, or, as is often the case, some alchemical mixture of the above. In the social, philosophic, and spiritual production of mystic liberalism, one consistently sees some embrace not just of the wisdom of the past but also of the value of experience: what is felt and observed but may defy quantifiable explanation.

In certain ways, we can understand such encounters with the unexplainable as the sublime. In the mystic liberal imagination, the individual experience of the sublime functions as a passageway to actualizing the power of thought, the power of oneself, and such a passageway can be revealed through art and literature. Introducing readers to mystic and mysterious dark karmic forces and cosmic intraspace throughout his earliest horror and weird fiction stories, Ditko presented his readers with a sense of sublime terror and awe. However, with the later influence of a particular—and peculiar—notion of Romanticism, Ditko provided readers a more grounded, secular version of cosmic intraspace and its potential through his 1960s superhero work on characters like Spider-Man, which he produced concurrently with Dr. Strange, as well as later creations like his updated version of the Blue Beetle and the Question.

In considering this more secular application of mystic liberalism, it is important not to misconstrue an effort for self-actualization with the improvement of one's character. "Character," while certainly important to many mystic liberals, is too slippery a notion and invites a variety of political and moralistic frameworks for defining the term. Indeed, this separation is also part of a move away from "character" in liberal thought that Helena Rosenblatt identifies in *The Lost History of Liberalism*. Further, as political progressivism waned in the New Thought movement through the latter part of the twentieth century, Horowitz notes that New Thoughters "disputed the old-fashioned ethic of self-sacrifice," and popularizers of New Thought, like Helen Wilmans, categorically denied that "the individual is to get rid of his individuality and lose himself in nothingness," believing instead that individuals should cultivate what Horowitz refers to as a "muscular self-directedness."[1] This more muscular, capitalistic, and individualist approach to New Thought mind power layers in comfortably with the thinking presented by Ayn Rand and Nathaniel Branden as they conceptualized the need for, and cultivation of, self-esteem in the creation of fully formed individuals. Rand, in particular, applied this kind of thinking in her philosophy of art and her imagination of Romanticism.

The intellectual and cultural components of mystic liberalism are often looking backward in an effort to revise, recoup, or even reinvent the ideas of the past, and its approach to art was no exception. Traditionally, the Romantic period is understood to have run through the first half of the nineteenth century and operated as a response to Enlightenment rationalism. Tellingly, Romantic art and literature often championed the individual and were deeply invested in recovering and reinventing the past. In fiction of the Romantic era, the protagonist regularly either rejected or was rejected by society, placing the hero at odds not just with his or her peers but also with cultural norms and expectations: an outsider to society simultaneously rejected and needed for its salvation. In American popular culture, these notions were also applied to the mythologizing of historical figures like Daniel Boone and the romanticizing of the conquest of the American West. Individualist fantasies such as these have been further ingrained in the collective psyches of Westerners by countless films, novels, and comic books. In adapting such notions for the superhero comic, Steve Ditko presents a mystic liberal vision that aligns with the work of Ayn Rand and her vision of what constituted Romantic ideals.

Rand outlined her literary philosophy in *The Romantic Manifesto*, and although Ditko previously demonstrated his own well-defined set of ethical and individualistic ideals beginning with *The Amazing Spider-Man*, Rand's Objectivism becomes a more useful—though not the singular—guide to establishing a vocabulary distinct to Ditko and the intellectual framework for his comics. Ditko experimented with articulating his sense of justice and heroism in Objectivist-sounding language, and in defining that sense for Mr. A, Ditko cites Rand, saying, "For Ayn Rand, justice is objectively identifying a thing for what it is and treating it accordingly. . . . The innocent is not penalized; the guilty is not rewarded."[2] It is worth noting that Ditko's qualifying phrase frames these ideas as Rand's, not his own. In applying Randian Romanticism to his superhero comics throughout the 1960s, Ditko created heroes who ranged from the affable, like Spider-Man and Blue Beetle, to the more aloof and bordering on Byronic, such as Dr. Strange, the Question, and Mr. A. Yet *none* of Ditko's heroes would reasonably qualify for the self-destructive tendencies often identified by critics as corresponding to the Byronic hero. If such characteristics are identifiable in Ditko's heroes, it would be through no deliberate act on his part. Rather, Ditko's heroes are Byronic in a way more in line with Rand's definition from *The Romantic Manifesto*: the "'Byronic' view of existence . . . is the belief that man must lead a heroic life and fight for his values even if he is doomed to defeat by a malevolent fate over which he has no control."[3]

In applying his particular worldview to Spider-Man and Blue Beetle, Ditko created a character- and publisher-spanning Romantic epic, perhaps a first in superhero comics. Ditko's epic was an unconventional one; psychological in nature, it mapped the emotional and intellectual growth of Ditko's subject, who begins as a whey-faced pushover and becomes a confident individualist. Further complicating matters is that this psychological journey begins with Peter Parker (Spider-Man) and is then transferred to Ted Kord (Blue Beetle), thus extending the narrative over multiple characters and publishers from Marvel to Charlton after Ditko left the former and began working at the latter. The proximity of Ditko's work on the characters is also notable: the first appearance of Ditko's Blue Beetle occurs in *Captain Atom* #83 (cover dated November 1966), only a few months after Ditko's final issue of *The Amazing Spider-Man* (cover dated July 1966). Ditko had already been working on superhero comics, like *Captain Atom*, for Charlton since 1965, so producing more superheroes for the company would have been an easy maneuver to make. Further, as I discussed earlier, Ditko has been careful to point out that he plotted out his stories well in advance. With that in mind, it stands to reason that Ditko may have, wittingly or unwittingly, carried his plots for Spider-Man into the Blue Beetle's adventures to complete the narrative he began in *Amazing Fantasy* #15.

Ditko, however, never publicly admitted to the carryover between characters. In fact, in the same 2014 letter where I asked Ditko about the issue of race in Dr. Strange, I also asked if this connection between Ted Kord and Peter Parker was intentional, and Ditko's response was "!?" followed by "People's minds can make all kinds of connections, have all kinds of beliefs about what others do, etc. It's engaging in fictions and fantasies." Not the most encouraging response to my reading of his work, but I gladly accept the tension between his sense of authorship and my interpretation of his oeuvre.

Unlike the matter of race in Dr. Strange, where authorial intent is vital to the conversation, an instance such as this is more aptly suited to a mode of analysis that takes authorial intent as a single reading among potential others. What is useful about a response like the one I received is that it demonstrates that Ditko was consistently interested in identifying the deliberate moves he made for his characters, that he envisioned each of his characters as unique entities, and that, at minimum, he admitted to no conscious recollection of continuing the life of Peter Parker through Ted Kord. However, the parallels between the character arcs are so remarkably similar that it is difficult not to see how the two complement each other in philosophically and narratively complex ways. In large part because of the theoretical and philosophic matters at play for both characters, and how they lead into the development of Ditko's later characters, these comics are primed for a kind of critical intervention that looks past authorial intent and toward the preexisting pattern of ideas and narrative maneuvers revealed throughout this book.

The path that Peter and Ted follow matches up with the kinds of narrative arcs that Rand developed for many of her characters, but it also fits neatly with the kind of work done with Dr. Strange, as well as with the motifs found in Ditko's earlier comics. Peter Parker's "muscular self-directedness" occurs as he discovers his inner strength through introspection and eliminates the need to prove himself to others. As Peter develops his sense of self-esteem, he (as Nathaniel Branden calls for) issues a "summons to the hero within."[4] As a part of the same mystic liberal framework, Ditko also provides the foundation for a radical shift in how extreme violence perpetrated by heroes would be perceived in the decades to come, a subject I discuss in the next chapter. Constructing that framework for violent acts places Ditko within a unique historical context that separates him from his peers in a way that goes beyond aesthetics or questions of who created what. Ditko brought to the table both unique artistic sensibilities and a worldview that would inspire him to develop narrative structures and motifs that were all but untapped during the Silver Age of American superhero comics.[5]

While my interest lies in moving away from consternation about creative credit—because Spider-Man has become the global cultural icon that he is, and because my arguments about the character are central to understanding how Ditko blended mystic self-exploration with a relatively more realistic one—it is worthwhile to briefly consider the creative process for *The Amazing Spider-Man*. Very early on, I addressed the issue of Ditko's writing and comics production both before and during his time at Marvel, but Spider-Man is something of a special case. Ditko wrote extensively about his time on *The Amazing Spider-Man*, including a sixteen-part series of essays titled *A Mini-History* for Robin Snyder's long-running newsletter *The Comics*, along with numerous other editorial-style cartoons, essays, and letters to fans. Of particular note for this chapter, Ditko, in *A Mini-History*, addresses his early and consistent role in the plotting and character development for Peter Parker / Spider-Man and the world he inhabits. The third chapter of *A Mini-History*, "*The Amazing Spider-Man* #1," explains that Ditko saw that first issue as "the best time, opportunity, to establish the groundwork, the nature of the teenage hero's story adventure world."[6] Never actually receiving a script from Lee, Ditko took responsibility for the world-building and long-term plotting aspects of *The Amazing Spider-Man*, thus minimizing Lee's plotting and developmental contributions. Information such as this demands that an examination of the series be framed within the philosophic and political ideology Ditko is working out in his comics.

Down to the costuming, Ditko injects a philosophic perspective into nearly every decision he makes for how the character appears and interacts within the fantasy world the artist constructed. However, as with Dr. Strange, one can identify some impurities in how Ditko's ideas were presented to readers early on. For example, although the basic costume design and the element of fear it conveyed remained intact for Spider-Man, this was not true for all of Ditko's initial design. According to the artist, Spider-Man's costume was initially "a warm red orange on the webbing section and a cool blue on the body parts," which Ditko chose with the intent of enhancing "the mystery mood" he wanted for the character and series. As a point of reference, for a "cool blue," he points toward a shade more similar to that of the Fantastic Four's early costumes. Of course, these are not the colors ultimately used for the character, and Ditko characterizes the final color on the body sections of Spider-Man's costume as being "warmer," thus "ruining the better contrast and mood." For Ditko, this kind of editorial interference is an example of how "the integrity of [Spider-Man] was undercut, subordinated" to the tastes and wants of "others, outsiders." This was clearly frustrating for Ditko, who did not believe anyone outside the series should have "had the power to dominate, control the insiders."[7] The struggle for control over the portrayal of the character, the very integrity of Spider-Man's existence, as Ditko conceived it, is an interesting metanarrative for a series like *The Amazing Spider-Man*, as it plays out in a way not dissimilar to Peter Parker's literal struggle for control over his own life, as plotted by Ditko.

Setting aside seemingly minor issues like the coloring of the costume, Ditko had other, more pressing social and intellectual concerns in mind when it came to Spider-Man's design. In the 2008 essay "He Giveth and He Taketh Away," Ditko writes, "My not showing the teen face would allow every reader, viewer, to supply their own desired facial expression under the mask." Decisions like this inform other choices Ditko made in his comics for Marvel, like those regarding race in Dr. Strange. But aside from sociopolitical and, frankly, audience-engagement concerns, Spider-Man's mask has an intellectual component as well. For Ditko, "There is a lot written on the psychology of a mask. . . . A mask can generate anxiety, fear." In fact, a psychology of fear is one of the major stakes for Ditko in *The Amazing Spider-Man*: the fear that the hero creates in his enemies, and the hero's overcoming of his own fears and anxieties. In the visual presentation, "the more sleek the [Spider-Man] costume, the spider-web design, etc., the more a psychological fear and advantage for [Spider-Man]." Experimenting with this kind of fear was a prominent feature of Ditko's career, both in and out of the superhero genre; Ditko claimed this interest in the psychology of fear placed him and Lee at odds during the production of Spider-Man. More than the costuming, Ditko played with physical anatomy to give Spider-Man "spider-like poses and action" as a means of exploiting the fear angle, which "Lee did not want [him] to show in [the] art."[8]

Until *The Amazing Spider-Man* launched as a series in 1963, a large portion of Ditko's output at Marvel consisted of short, one-off suspense and monster stories that appeared in anthology series, like those he had produced at Charlton Comics earlier in his career. By taking on the Spider-Man job, Ditko embarked on his first long tenure on a character during his time at Marvel.[9] Given the common publishing practices of the comics industry in the early 1960s, where superhero adventures were a series of self-contained, individual units limited to a given issue, it is highly unlikely that Marvel intended for Spider-Man's tale to appear as something like the form of an epic. From the series' first issue, Ditko was thinking about how seemingly one-off episodes would play out over the duration of Peter Parker's life, which Ditko conceived as being "grounded . . . in a teenager's credible world." Resulting from this desire for verisimilitude was Ditko's opposition to story ideas from Lee that contravened a more realistic superstructure. For example, the first story from *The Amazing Spider-Man* #1 introduces J. Jonah Jameson's son, John, an astronaut whom Spider-Man rescues from a disabled space capsule. For Ditko, this was an absurd notion, because in the realistic world he pushed for in his plots, such an incident "would become a worldwide news spectacle. It would have all kinds of continuing ramifications for the character's following storyline." Ditko did not think that such a phenomenon could realistically be introduced and then simply evaporate into the ether before the events of the next issue.[10] Such thinking sets Ditko apart from many of his contemporaries—even from much of his previous work, where an episodic method of storytelling was most common—and also invites a particular reading of his superhero work as philosophic bildungsroman.

Although pulp publications had experimented with continuity and shared universes in the past, Ditko's Spider-Man came about in an era where notions of continuity and a shared universe specific to the superhero genre of comic books were in their fledgling stages, piloted by Marvel's publishing and editorial practices.[11] Although Lee shepherded a line-wide decision to have the various characters from the Marvel universe interact with one another, it is clear from Ditko's version of events that Lee was not thinking about the characters he edited and collaborated on as being in long-form stories, and certainly not stories where the actions in one episode would have consequences for later installments. Furthermore, the overwhelming majority of superheroes during this era were in fixed positions: they were adult millionaires, scientists, gods, or aliens, and they could not reasonably grow or change without disorienting the audience.[12] The perceived inability for a character to psychically change in significant ways does not necessarily bar such characters from a Romantic classification, but it does exclude their tales from fitting into the mold of an epic, because they cannot participate in any journey of substantial weight, be it physical or metaphysical. What is at stake is less the characters' elite status than their internal capacity for growth and development in their behavior or sense of identity.

As Umberto Eco suggests, the plot of comic book superheroes, whether in a broad or narrow sense, "must be static and evade any development because [the hero] must make virtue consist of many little activities on a small scale, never achieving total awareness."[13] Eco, of course, is oversimplifying matters, and he is directing his attention specifically toward Superman comics produced in the 1950s and early 1960s and then extrapolating from there. Many a comics critic has, rightly, taken issue with this assertion; however, the comics scholar Marc Singer, in his critical reevaluation of Eco's essay, notes that "Eco's oneiric climate is not a simple state of timelessness so much as it is one for managing a contradiction faced by any character in a popular serial narrative: the contradiction between the stasis characteristic of mythological characters and the open-ended, unpredictable, progressive, but ultimately finite development of the modern novel."[14] In contrast to the kinds of mythological stasis Eco identifies for superheroes, Ditko's characters operate as the clichéd exception that proves the rule by embarking on the more progressive, but finite, path Singer identifies.

On a psychological level, the narrative structure developed by Ditko in *The Amazing Spider-Man* does not demonstrate an adherence to Eco's reasoning; instead, Peter Parker's journey is specifically one of awareness and self-discovery. By allowing Spider-Man and his alter ego, Peter Parker, a wide berth, Ditko is able to develop a character that fits into his thinking before and after his engagement with Randian notions of the hero and its Romantic antecedents. Parker has many adventures, but his epic is ultimately a metaphysical one, as each of his adventures is colored by Byronic secrets, a sense of awe, terror, and the increasing influence of Randian individualism on his mystic sensibilities. As Ditko uses each instance of these elements to influence the character of Peter Parker, Parker then grows and changes. He transitions from the shy bookworm who *desperately* wants to be part of the collective (the in crowd) to one who scoffs at and rejects the collective, thus recognizing the superiority of his own worth over those—like Flash Thompson or J. Jonah Jameson—who cruelly mock him. Yet for some critics of liberalism, like Max Stirner, Peter is still shackled by mysticism and the things Stirner identified as ghosts of the mind: his sense of family through his loyalty to Aunt May, the sense of right and wrong he learned from Uncle Ben, and the weight of guilt from his past mistakes.

Peter Parker and Ted Kord as Heroic Ideals

To illustrate how Peter Parker develops over time into a practicing mystic liberal, consider his behavior in *Amazing Fantasy* #15 compared to his actions in *The Amazing Spider-Man* #31–33. In the former, Parker is a nebbish who is mocked but still desperately reaches out to his assailants in hopes of friendship.[15] In the latter comics, the reader is presented with a Parker who is considered brash and arrogant by his classmates, despite not being so;[16] later, Parker wrenches fair pay for his photographs out of J. Jonah Jameson, who has to beg Parker for the product of his labor.[17] Perhaps without coincidence, the scene with Jameson plays like one between the power-hungry Gail Wynand and Howard Roark in Rand's *The Fountainhead*.[18] Furthermore, like Rand's heroes, Parker's awakening to a more confident, independent self does not render him immune to his peers' ire. As seen in issue #32, Peter is still bullied and referred to as "Puny Parker,"[19] but now the insults also label Peter as arrogant and a "swell-head who thinks he's better'n everyone else."[20] When compared to the Peter Parker of *Amazing Fantasy*, what is important is that Parker's peers cease to influence his sense of self-worth. He no longer cares to be their friend; they have nothing to offer him emotionally or socially. But even at his most individualistic, Parker carries deep, Byronic secrets, such as his web-spinning alter ego and the crushing guilt for his uncle's murder at the hands of a thief whom Parker let escape.

It may seem counterintuitive to link the tenets of Objectivism with Romanticism—a movement rooted in rejecting the seemingly rigid rationality of the Enlightenment—but the psychologically alienated and socially discontented heroes of Lord Byron are appealing for Ayn Rand and her particular notions of Romantic fiction as outlined in *The Romantic Manifesto*. Mystic liberal thought, as an individualistic and decentralized mode of political and social praxis, consistently blurs edges in its attempts to merge seemingly disparate ideas in the service of individual exigencies. Rand folding Romanticism into her own philosophy reflects those exigencies, effectively inviting the kind of open-system thinking that David Kelley called for in his break from more fundamentalist Objectivism in 1990. To that end, in *The Romantic Manifesto*, Rand views herself as "a bridge from the unidentified past to the future."[21] Perhaps this vision of an alleged "unidentified past" is what gave her license to provide a new and particular spin on how the ideals of Romanticism had been conceived historically.

Rand is careful to offer the caveat that she is referring not to concretes but to an experiential "sense of life" that she imagined existed in the West before World War I, and she intends to act as a match to the candle of what she considered rational aesthetics. She goes on to say in her definition of Romanticism that there is "no generally accepted definition of [it] (nor of any key element of art, or art itself)."[22] Her specific definition of the term claims that "Romanticism is a category of art based on the principle that man possesses the faculty of volition,"[23] and "Romanticism is a product of the nineteenth century—a (largely subconscious) result of Aristotelianism . . . and capitalism."[24] Functionally, this is the same approach that occultists apply to their own brands of thinking, insisting that they are simultaneously new and rooted in more earlier modes of thought, be they the more ancient hermetic ideas or the more recent transcendentalist, capitalist, or leftist modes of thought. Rand, like many other mystic liberals, performs an alchemy of convenience—and does so effectively.

Rand also identifies a split in Romantic fiction that separated volition into two categories: existence and consciousness. Volitional existence, she explains, occurs in plot-driven works, and volitional consciousness appears in character- and psychologically driven works. Both have merit, but Rand argues that for a Romantic work to be complete and of the highest standard, it *must* incorporate both elements competently. For Rand, literature that features only the Byronic hero but is not plot driven has value but is incomplete because it represents *only* volitional consciousness.[25] A combination of existence and consciousness, as called for by Rand, is precisely the kind of narrative that Steve Ditko was producing at Marvel in the 1960s and would continue to produce later. Both Dr. Strange and Spider-Man are characters learning to engage in a volitional existence led by a volitional consciousness. In the case of both Rand and Ditko, although neither names it explicitly, these are narrative experiments in mind power, and the ability of one's thoughts to create and re-create their protagonists' individual existences. Obviously, Ditko's characters are not transforming the outside world to meet their own desires; rather, they are recalibrating how they exercise their volition to control how they navigate that world.

Rand's contentious interpretation of the Romantic movement aside, that man is a volitional being overlaps with much of the work of Steve Ditko as it applies to the psychological development of his characters, if in no other way than to demonstrate that anyone can and must motivate oneself,[26] supplementing those motivated thoughts with what Wilmans called "courageous action."[27] In the more metaphysically grounded framework Ditko establishes for Spider-Man, we find plenty of room for a more traditional approach to Romanticism as well. Fear and mystery were key elements Ditko brought to the character, and Romanticism's historical celebration of terror, the sublime, and awe, along with its embrace of exotic worlds and landscapes, makes it an ideal candidate for the medium of comic books. Ditko exploited that potential in the terror he created through characters' visual expressions in his suspense and horror comics, the tangled and disorienting sublimity of the landscapes traversed by Dr. Strange, and the awe-inspiring heroic action of his late Spider-Man stories. If we accept, at least tentatively, the Randian approach as a brand of Romanticism and blend it with those more traditional aesthetic elements, it is easy to see how Steve Ditko was able to adapt this into a psychological journey for his characters, creating a form of a "Romantic epic" that had yet to exist in American superhero comics.

The superhero genre was not Ditko's first foray into Romantic fiction in the service of mystic liberalism. He frequently applied a Romantic approach to the horror and weird suspense tales that make up the largest portion of his nonsuperhero work. In those stories, he masterfully creates a sense of terror, apprehension, and awe—a hallmark of his career. Ditko's mastery of these themes plays a critical role in his superhero work, allowing characters like Peter Parker to relate their deep internal struggles and existential despair to the reader in almost purely visual terms. In the case of Peter Parker, each crisis of conscience he faces leads to a major change in his development. This happens most famously when Peter holds himself responsible for failing to stop Uncle Ben's eventual murderer when he had the chance in *Amazing Fantasy* #15, and again during the events of *The Amazing Spider-Man* #32 and #33. These latter issues, particularly the opening five pages of issue #33, have become iconic moments in the history of contemporary superhero comics.

Recognizing the effective use of despair in Ditko's superhero work is not meant to imply that Ditko would have aligned himself with anything approaching a nihilistic worldview—quite the opposite. In fact, in *Blue Beetle* #5, Ditko has one of his more philosophically contemptuous villains utter, "Man . . . is a helpless, meaningless speck in a never-ending universe."[28] Instead of wallowing in existential despair, Ditko uses moments of turmoil as a literary device through which the Romantic hero proves his or her superiority by using reason and a heroic spirit to triumph. Ditko's heroes do not succumb to what Rand calls "the unhampered sway of . . . unleashed emotions" but instead become masters of their own minds.[29]

It is in the face of a world gone mad or at the hands of external torment that heroes must be willing to overcome the crushing weight of their emotions and defend their values, even if doing so means certain death. To Ditko, this is when the hero must employ the volitional ability that Rand links to Romanticism, as he says, "Emotions are not tools of cognition. . . . Only reason can determine what is right and what man should do."[30] In Randian terms, Ditko gives his characters volition in regard to both consciousness and existence. This allows the characters to work within a highly imaginative narrative framework in which their psychological state is grounded in what Wilmans might refer to as a "realistic idealism."[31] For Rand, this approach is an element of "top rank" Romantic literature that has a "full commitment to the premise of volition."[32] Ditko's Peter Parker seems to offer the clearest example of this "top rank" approach to the Romantic hero. A ringing example of this approach appears in *The Amazing Spider-Man* #32–33 in a scene where Parker faces overwhelming odds while trying to manage his personal life, save Aunt May, and defeat Doctor Octopus. Parker's frustration and the channeling of that frustration into heroic action are observable in different stages of the story arc. In each stage, it is Parker's ability to reason that allows him to triumph.

Although the "Master Planner" story that spans issues #31–33 puts an exclamation point on the kind of long-term character development that Ditko is most interested in, because it is both a pinnacle for mystic liberalism and a transitional moment in American comics, I am tabling a close reading of that story until the book's conclusion. Nonetheless, it is still important to demonstrate just how Peter Parker came to that transformative moment. Examples abound of how Ditko planted sometimes very subtle clues about major plot and character developments (e.g., the identity of the Green Goblin discussed in chapter 1), and one of the most significant shifts in Peter Parker's character occurs in *The Amazing Spider-Man* #18. The events of this issue set into motion a number of plot threads that eventually resolve in the "Master Planner" sequence of issues, including problems with Aunt May's health and Peter's love trouble with Betty Brant, but it is an issue where Peter has an epiphany about himself that leads to the payoff in issue #33.

At the close of *The Amazing Spider-Man* #17, Peter runs away from a fight with the Green Goblin because, in the midst of the action, he learns that Aunt May has suffered another heart attack and has been hospitalized. Of course, no one knows *why* Spider-Man is running away from the fight, and J. Jonah Jameson has a field day with it, taking it as an opportunity to once again drag Spider-Man's name through the mud. Jameson, for what it's worth, succeeds in turning the public against Spider-Man, branding him a coward. On top of that, Peter's relationship with Betty is on the rocks because he has failed to communicate with her, which only compounds the shame he is experiencing at the hands of Jameson and the guilt Peter feels for not being able to do more for May. It's all too much for him, and as he wads up his Spider-Man costume and broods about why things never seem to go right for him, he is plagued by self-doubt, blaming himself—and his secret life as Spider-Man—for the hurt experienced by any person who has come into contact with him and every failure he's had to shoulder.

Throughout most of *The Amazing Spider-Man* #18, Peter frets about how he and Aunt May will be able to pay her medical bills, and he tries to implement a handful of get-rich-quick plans by selling his image to a trading card company and the secret formula for his webbing to an adhesive manufacturer—neither of which work out. In between, he avoids a fight with Sandman, running away again, and anxiously remembers each of the times he nearly lost his life fighting supervillains. When he gets back home after a day of psychological defeat, he finds Aunt May home alone, and racked with guilt and fear about her frail condition, he decides he can no longer be Spider-Man and must devote himself to Aunt May's well-being. May doesn't want to hear any of it and more or less ignores Peter's outward self-pity.

May repeatedly tells Peter not to worry about her and to get out of the house; Peter ignores her and slinks back into the passive version of himself that first appeared in *Amazing Fantasy* #15. One of the ways this reversion is evident is when Peter seemingly seeks approval from the likes of his bully, Flash Thompson, and even brags about not confronting Flash[33] when in just the prior issue he was needling the bully.[34] Peter believes that the best thing for him to do is give up his own life and "be the kind of guy [Aunt May] wants [him] to be,"[35] leaving his life as Spider-Man behind. Peter thinks that "if he were just an ordinary Joe . . . all the other worries [he's] got would just melt away."[36] Peter has not understood what kind of guy May wants him to be, but instead of lecturing Peter about what *he should do*, she lectures him about what *she will do*; and what she claims for herself—as though it were out of the mind power playbook—is "gumption" along with "the will to live" and "to fight."[37] This is an important thematic element, as these traits that May identifies for herself are part and parcel of mystic liberal notions of reason and what Ditko would also call "proper principles."[38] Only by adopting this mode of thought can Peter climb out of the well he has fallen into.

Upon hearing this from Aunt May and seeing that she is on the mend, Peter finally sees the light and recognizes that he has wasted "too much time in self-pity."[39] With that, he determines that "there's nothing to *stop* [him] from being *Spider-Man* again," and he puts on his costume and declares himself to be a new man who will no longer be shackled by self-doubt and will fight as he's never fought before.[40] This rebirth, of course, comes with growing pains, but Peter manages to repair some of his friendships (*The Amazing Spider-Man* #19), get his job at the *Daily Bugle* back while simultaneously sticking it to Jameson (#19), stand up to Flash Thompson (#20), draw attention from girls for his personal accomplishments (#21), and earn more respect from his peers by standing up for himself (#21). Later he later nearly succumbs to psychological tricks that cause him to question his sanity. In issue #24, Mysterio poses as a psychiatrist, believing the way to defeat Spider-Man is to destroy his confidence, and for a moment, the plan nearly works. But despite all the ways Peter grows and is able to put his old anxieties and fears behind him, he still struggles with the solitude brought on by being Spider-Man. While Peter seems at peace with the limitations that his dual life as Spider-Man imposes on him, the toll it takes on his relationship with Betty is difficult for him to bear, and he eventually comes to terms with it—though the outcome is not the one he wanted.

The unprecedented psychological growth and approach to character Ditko applied to mainstream superhero comics of the Silver Age set a new standard for storytelling in American comic books. Concurrent with the dramatic changes taking place with Peter Parker as a character, Ditko also included a series of subplots and seeming background characters that eventually pay off later in the series—the most significant of which was revealing Norman Osborn as the secret identity of the Green Goblin, which Ditko did not even have the opportunity to draw, as he left the company one issue before the reveal in *The Amazing Spider-Man* #39. Ditko's Spider-Man stories offered a radical tonal shift in comparison to comics produced by his contemporaries and colleagues at Marvel. While other revolutionary comics were being created at Marvel by the likes of Jack Kirby, Ditko's Spider-Man work set itself apart by focusing on more than wildly imaginative plots that featured intergalactic threats, magic, or some combination of the two. But similar to the mystical world of Dr. Strange, Ditko's Spider-Man focuses on placing characters' internal struggles at the forefront and allowing those struggles and triumphs to drive the plot.

One way this is exemplified is in the complicated history surrounding Spider-Man's creation and Jack Kirby's involvement with the character. Briefly, Kirby had initially designed the character, and it bore striking—likely not coincidental—similarity to another character Kirby had worked on for Archie Comics called the Fly. Additionally, the alter ego for Kirby's Spider-Man was not merely a teenager but a kid who put on a magic ring that turned him into the adult hero, akin to the magic that turned Billy Batson into Captain Marvel. These examples, along with others not discussed here, assist in demonstrating that before Ditko's involvement, the character was set to fit within the mold that Kirby had employed for several years, both on his own and with his longtime creative partner Joe Simon. Not only did Ditko's approach abandon Kirby's original concepts, but as Sean Howe points out, *The Amazing Spider-Man*'s "moody, almost foreboding style hardly seemed to cry out for teenage superheroics."[41] Ditko's approach to the superhero was a far cry from the bombast of Kirby-drawn works like *Fantastic Four*. The Fantastic Four's Johnny Storm—the Human Torch—had a brash, whimsical energy that matched his superpowers and made him popular with his peers, whereas Ditko's Peter Parker was introspective and unpopular in a way reflective of his fear-inducing costume that hid him away from the world. If Johnny Storm was Elvis Presley, Peter Parker was James Dean.

Especially within the pages of *The Amazing Spider-Man*, Ditko's focus on Peter Parker's internal and interpersonal struggles grounds the series in a way seldom seen in Silver Age superhero comics. It is true that nearly all the Marvel superheroes of the 1960s had some sense of verisimilitude because they were based in New York City as opposed to fictional stand-ins like Gotham or Metropolis, but this was hardly an innovation, and New York City had been continually populated by superheroes since the genre's earliest days. The setting may assist in establishing a certain amount of realness, but *The Amazing Spider-Man* stands apart because its "realness" is a by-product of the characterization and the message it delivers to its readers.

Even if the reader's politics are distant from Ditko's own, by this point in his career, Ditko's intent for his heroes was that they should be "admired for [their] achievements and regarded as an ideal or model."[42] Peter Parker is an example of one of those very models, and just as Peter Parker is able to eliminate his codependence on the collective that mocks him, so too can the reader. In the same way Ditko's choice to completely cover Peter Parker's face with the Spider-Man mask was, in part, designed to allow readers from any background to identify with the character, Peter's internal quest for personal control and integrity could be mapped onto the reader as well. That superheroes represented a moral ideal to one degree or another was anything but a new notion for comic books of the mid-1960s. Instead of Superman selling war bonds or Batman offering ham-fisted life lessons to Robin, what is different in Ditko's configuration is that the hero operated not as a literal but as a philosophic model for how to deal with the very real and complex social and psychological struggles the reader may have faced. The lessons that Ditko's brand of philosophy offered readers demanded scrutiny, reflection, and ongoing personal action to see it through. It is at once the New Thought insistence on personal experience as a marker of efficacy and Rand's insistence that by writing and publishing books like *Atlas Shrugged*, such people can and do exist in the real world.[43]

Superheroes Signifying Something Deeper

Separating himself from Marvel, Steve Ditko left the company and *The Amazing Spider-Man* in 1966 and began producing more superhero work for Charlton Comics. As discussed in chapter 3, after studying under Jerry Robinson, Ditko had cut his teeth on horror comics published by Charlton in the 1950s and never really stopped selling work to the company. Free of Lee's editorial oversight and the impact of those "others" and "outsiders" he believed obfuscated his intent, Ditko took full advantage of the creative freedom afforded by Charlton. Continuing to experiment with more explicitly philosophic explorations,

Ditko returned to Captain Atom with writer Joe Gill and independently created a new version of the Blue Beetle and that version's alter ego, Ted Kord.

The original Blue Beetle—and his alter ego, Dan Garret—was created for Fox Comics in 1939 by Charles Nicholas, and he appeared in comic books, a comic strip, and his own radio serial. Nicholas was a house name employed by Will Eisner and Jerry Iger's studio for the comic book packages they sold to publishers. At the time, house names were a practice carried over from the pulps and were used to indicate that the "package," which included the character and the name of the "creator" sold to the publisher were the intellectual property of the publisher.[44] Charles Nicholas was such a name at Eisner & Iger and indicated the work of Chuck Cuidera, Jack Kirby, and Charles Wojtkoski. All three worked on Blue Beetle at various points, but Wojtkoski is generally regarded as having originated the character. As the character first appeared, Dan Garret was a rookie cop who took "Vitamin 2X," which granted him superhuman abilities, assisted by a pharmacist who kept Garret supplied with enough 2X to continue his war on crime. As the 1940s came to a close, the character appeared only sporadically and was eventually acquired by Charlton Comics, which reintroduced Garret in 1964. In this new version, Garrett (now spelled with two *ts*) was an archaeologist who gained his powers from a magic scarab he found while on a dig in Egypt. Written by Ditko collaborator Joe Gill and drawn by Tony Tallarico, Garrett would say the magic words "Kaji Dha" to transform into his superhero alter ego.

When Ditko took over the character in 1966, he was credited as the artist but billed himself as D. C. Glanzman for the writing credit. Jettisoning most of the continuity of the stories that came before, Ditko completely reimagined the character, making the character a legacy hero, where the mantle would pass on to new generations.[45] In Ditko's version, Ted Kord was a student of Dan Garrett's who took on the responsibility of being the Blue Beetle after Garrett died. Kord, a brilliant inventor and industrialist, devised a number gadgets and a beetle-shaped flying vehicle to assist in his campaign against corruption and supervillainy, forgoing the magic scarab. Ditko's removal of the scarab, at one level, returned the character to the slightly more realistic mode of adventuring found in the Fox stories; however, it also butts up directly against the kind of grounded storytelling that Ditko been developing on Spider-Man at Marvel.

The temporal proximity and the similarity between the characters lend additional weight to the reading that Ted Kord's story served as the logical extension of Peter Parker's life into the adult world and that Ditko picked up right where he left off with *The Amazing Spider-Man*. Kord is affable, brilliant, and at ease taunting supervillains when in combat—just like Peter Parker. These traits, as they apply to Kord, are also worth noting when questions arise about the portrayal of Spider-Man and who was responsible for the playful banter as

Figure 5.1. Peter Parker pawns his personal possessions to collect the money needed to help Curt Connors (the Lizard) develop a serum that will save Aunt May's life. Dialogue edited by Stan Lee; Steve Ditko art; Stan Goldberg colors; Artie Simek letters. "Man on a Rampage!" *The Amazing Spider-Man* #33 (January 1966). © Marvel Comics.

it informed the character's identity. By eschewing the mystical elements associated with the Dan Garrett version of Blue Beetle, Ditko also grounds Ted Kord's adventures in a more metaphysically realistic setting, just as he had intended for Peter Parker. Kord even looks stunningly similar to Parker.

Not only does Parker look like Kord, but his life seems to be Ditko's vision for Parker's future: from brilliant science student to brilliant inventor and industrialist. The two are all but exactly the same character. As I said, Ditko scoffed at me when I asked him about this remarkable coincidence, but the choice to illustrate the characters virtually identically, right down to the facial expressions and hair color, seems to be anything but an accident; Ditko is more than capable of drawing unique characters with distinct physical and facial features.[46] Even a cursory glance at the characters reveals that Ditko makes no clear visual distinction between Kord and the Peter Parker who appears in his later issues of *The Amazing Spider-Man* (figs. 5.1, 5.2).

Figure 5.2. Ted Kord internally struggles with being accused of murdering Dan Garrett (the previous Blue Beetle). Kord bears a striking, more adult, resemblance to Peter Parker as seen in figure 5.1. In its original printing, this story was untitled. In reprint editions, later editors provided the title "The Masked Marauder" for "reader convenience." Dialogue by Gary Friedrich; art by Steve Ditko. ["The Masked Marauder"], *Captain Atom* #86 (June 1967). © DC Comics.

Where this reading runs into trouble, unfortunately, is that Blue Beetle initially appeared as a backup feature in *Captain Atom*, and when the character received his own series, it ran for only five issues. As a result, the number of available stories for comparison is limited. Further, because the early stories are trying to establish Blue Beetle as a character, they are more heavily focused on action. Along with that foregrounding, Ditko deals with the continuity issue of presenting readers with a *new* version of Blue Beetle by inventing a mystery to explain what happened to the previous Blue Beetle, Dan Garrett. In a manner similar to how Ditko structured his Spider-Man stories, this Dan Garrett subplot runs in the background while keeping an invigorating pace, presumably to maintain reader interest. Although the backup features and the first four issues of *Blue Beetle* deal less with the personal struggles and psychic overcoming that Peter Parker faced, there are other similarities between the life of Peter Parker and the life of Ted

Figure 5.3. Peter Parker and Curt Connors bond over a mutual love of science as they work to create a serum that will save the life of Aunt May. Dialogue edited by Stan Lee; Steve Ditko art; Stan Goldberg colors; Artie Simek letters. "Man on a Rampage!" *The Amazing Spider-Man* #33 (January 1966). © Marvel Comics.

Kord, some of which never saw print until nearly forty years after Charlton canceled its superhero line in 1968.

In 2007, DC Comics printed the previously unreleased *Blue Beetle* #6. The story features a few key moments as they relate to the overlaps between Ted Kord and Peter Parker. The first is the way Ted Kord is treated by others because of his status as a "brainy type."[47] The rejection by the in crowd here follows directly on the jeers and bullying that Peter Parker constantly faced, most recently in *The Amazing Spider-Man* #34, where Harry Osborn ridicules Peter for being an "egg-head" and tries to edge Peter out of his social scene.[48] Similarly—though this is true of most of Ditko's heroes—just as Peter Parker consistently found himself smeared in the *Daily Bugle*, so Ted Kord finds himself under fire from the media, which has already tried and convicted him for being involved with a murder he did not commit. Another intriguing commonality occurs in the relationship that Ted Kord strikes up with Professor

Figure 5.4. Just like Peter Parker and Curt Connors, Ted Kord and Tot Rodor bond over their mutual love of science. Also like the Parker-Connors relationship, Kord and Rodor employ their shared interest to solve Kord's problems. Dialogue and art by Steve Ditko (writing as D. C. Glanzman). Originally unpublished story intended for *Blue Beetle* #6. "A Specter Is Haunting Hub City," in *The Action Heroes Archives*, vol. 2 (DC Comics, 2007). © DC Comics.

Aristotle Rodor to solve the murder for which Blue Beetle has unjustly been accused. Professor Rodor is an associate of the Question (but first appeared in the Question backup feature in *Blue Beetle* #1) and is a scientist and inventor who created the special features of the Question's costume. Unlike the relationship between Professor Rodor and the Question, the one between Ted Kord and Rodor has a dynamic similar to the one Ditko established for Peter Parker and Curt Connors in *The Amazing Spider-Man* #32 (figs. 5.3, 5.4).

Along with these strikingly familiar circumstances for both characters, one of the most interesting is Ted Kord's crisis of conscience that, just like Peter Parker's moments of doubt, leads Kord to question whether he should continue on as the Blue Beetle. Unsure of whether he is responsible for a man's death, Tracey—Kord's girlfriend and lab assistant—asks, "Now what happens to you and the Beetle?" Kord replies, "It's too early to say! Even though Fend was a killer, my aim was to catch him, not to be his executioner! Maybe I don't have the legal right to fight crime and no one could legally make me catch a murderer" (fig. 5.5).[49] The key difference between this moment and one of Peter Parker's episodes where he considers his future as a costumed hero is that Kord is much more measured in his response. Whereas Parker is more overcome by the moment, Kord is more contemplative and unwilling to make an immediate decision. To my reading, this is an outcropping of the kind of psychological growth experienced by Peter Parker as he moved from adolescence into adulthood and is evidenced by the changes discussed earlier. Even when Parker considers quitting, after the events of *The Amazing Spider-Man* #18, his struggles with doubt are never about whether he will actually quit being Spider-Man but about how he will cope with the complications such a dual existence begets. Kord deals with those same complications, and just as Peter Parker pledged to face those consequences at the end of *The Amazing Spider-Man* #18, so Kord is also prepared to accept responsibility for his actions—even if accidental.

As Ditko continues the development of the hero from the pages of *The Amazing Spider-Man* into *Blue Beetle*, he still leaves room for psychological development in terms of understanding what it meant and means to be this mystic liberal heroic ideal. Unlike a traditional quest, there is no clear psychological peak or ending that his Romantic hero reaches. This is not to say that Ted Kord / Peter Parker could not reach that level. Instead Ditko takes a cue from Ayn Rand's narrative choices and places Ted Kord / Peter Parker in a role similar to *Atlas Shrugged*'s Hank Rearden, a dynamic common in mystic liberal circles: the master and the apprentice. In Rand's novel, Rearden needs John Galt to serve as the ideal type that represents the kind of man Rearden can be, and in keeping with the Randian model, Ted Kord / Peter Parker requires a similar figure. Both Rand's and Ditko's narratives demand a figure who would validate the psychological trajectory of an emerging hero: a presumed philosophic and moral pinnacle. Of course, neither Ditko nor Rand writes as though their philosophy needs outside validation to determine its truth, but their narratives require a heroic ideal to demonstrate that such a person could exist in the realistic worlds that both authors are attempting to create. In *Atlas Shrugged*, Hank Rearden looks to John Galt as an intellectual and human ideal, and the two become fast friends, building a relationship based on mutual respect. In the pages of *Blue Beetle*, Vic Sage, alias the Question, would serve as Kord's John Galt.

What Makes a Hero?

Before Ted Kord and Vic Sage met, Ditko offered readers an in-depth look at Vic Sage in what ended up being the only issue of *Mysterious Suspense* in October

Figure 5.5. Like the crises of conscience that Peter Parker regularly faced, Ted Kord, too, struggles with whether he should continue on as a costumed hero. Dialogue and art by Steve Ditko (writing as D. C. Glanzman). Originally unpublished story intended for *Blue Beetle* #6. "A Specter Is Haunting Hub City," in *The Action Heroes Archives*, vol. 2 (DC Comics, 2007). © DC Comics.

1968. The comic featured an issue-long story broken up into two distinct episodes, written and drawn by Ditko. What this issue accomplishes is to unambiguously establish the Question as an emblem for the kind of heroism that Peter Parker and Ted Kord are struggling toward. Each chapter in *Mysterious Suspense* is bookended by narration boxes that offer philosophic questions and precepts for which the story provides a kind of praxis. Whereas Parker and Kord must cope with and overcome their internal conflicts, the Question has already determined that, regardless of the consequences, he will conquer any obstacle by way of his integrity and unwavering sense of what is right; his will and thus his mind are his greatest assets. Norman Vincent Peale might add that failure to achieve such ends results from a lack of wholeheartedness. Says Peale, "People are defeated in life not because of lack of ability but for lack of wholeheartedness. . . . Results do not yield themselves to the person who refuses to give himself the desired results."[50] In the opening and closing narration boxes from part 1 of the issue, Ditko echoes Peale's assignment of responsibility, addressing his readers:

What is the greatest battle an individual must fight? Is it against the mystic terrors of unknown dimensions? Is it against the hordes of alien beings from outer space, or against foreign armies or criminal conspiracies? No! The great battle you or any person must *constantly* fight is not any of those! . . .

The greatest battle a person must *constantly* fight is to uphold proper principles, known truths, against everyone he deals with! A truth cannot be defeated! But when a man refuses to know what is right or deliberately accepts, or does, what he knows is wrong . . . he defeats himself! The truth remains unbeaten![51]

In the opening passage, Ditko is neither dismissing nor distancing himself from the battles and action of other superhero comics. Grounding characters—like the Question, Blue Beetle, and Spider-Man—in a credible world in no way implies that other modes of fantasy are necessarily inferior. Instead, what is most at hazard in Ditko's stories are those things that cohabitate in the mind: principles and truth. Unlike Parker and Kord, who are on their search for "proper principles" and "known truths," the Question has completed his quest for those intangibles, and his adventures, like those of Mr. A, are better understood as allegorical intellectual exercises. The Question serves as an avatar who guides the reader through a series of thought experiments where the hero must apply the fantastic courage he displays in fighting crime to his mundane existence. Put differently, *the question* posed by the actions of Vic Sage is: What makes a hero? The power of his fists? Or strength of his integrity?

In addressing that question, Ditko strips away from Vic Sage, and later from Mr. A, much of the depth that he painstakingly developed for characters like Peter Parker, making Vic Sage an avatar—a sort of Platonic ideal.[52] As an ideal form, the Question is then held up as a mirror for supporting characters to be identified as imperfect reflections. In Ditko's Question stories, those imperfect supporting characters then have to choose whether to follow a path toward the ideal or away from it. In another way, the Question is similar to Stirner's true egoist, as described in chapter 3: a frightening ghost who haunts the supporting cast and must be dealt with accordingly. The conflict, or lack thereof, that each of the supporting cast members experiences creates the dramatic tension, as opposed to the actions taken and words spoken by the ideal form, in this case the Question / Vic Sage. The Question, then, is not to be read as a character; he is a fully formed idea—a state of mind—that other characters, and the reader, respond to. It's no wonder, then, that Ditko chose to name the Question's alter ego "Sage." Although Ditko's dialogue and narration boxes make the Question's emblematic position clear, he achieves this effect through visual representation as well. Whether as Vic Sage or the Question, the character is always illustrated with excellent posture, head held high, shoulders set back, his expression content. This element of the Question's character is further emphasized as Ditko frequently illustrates him as being jeered at by a mob of slouching, dumpy, angry, and often pointing figures, demonstrating how the masses respond when presented with the very idea of what Ditko defines as heroism.

The visual and narrative-philosophic tropes Ditko presents in *Mysterious Suspense* are a hallmark of the artist's post-Marvel work as he sharpens his philosophic perspective. For instance, the indictment of the mob that is readily available in *The Amazing Spider-Man* and *Strange Tales*, by this point, has been refined to a distinct kind of staging that appears throughout Ditko's later works: the singular, ideal hero flanked by jeering, angry faces or a confusion of chaotic, formless shapes or both. Moreover, this visual philosophic representation was one that Ditko also mapped onto some of his later work-for-hire art, including a Superman pinup he contributed to the four hundredth issue of *Superman* (fig. 5.6).[53] These visual motifs embody Ditko's answer to what makes a hero; indeed, these elements literalize, in some ways, Ditko's argument that a hero is one "who faces up to the challenges and obstacles of life and acts on them in a manner that does credit to himself and the proper principles that have proven to be true."[54] That Vic Sage, the avatar for this ideal, is a hard-hitting investigative reporter points the reader toward the ongoing thematic in Ditko's work that "truth" is a by-product of a ruthless interrogation of all that exists.

Throughout the story in *Mysterious Suspense*, that ruthless interrogation is a costly practice, and Vic Sage's job at the television station that broadcasts his reports is threatened. Sage refuses to accept tainted money from a corrupt businessman in the form of sponsorship dollars, and this sets into motion the drama of the story as Sage's supporting cast must respond to his unwavering convictions. Most, of course, position themselves against Sage because they hate what he stands for or they fear that he will be rewarded and thus given some kind of interoffice authority over them. This outward resentment toward Sage and the desire for his failure present the reader with the kind of person who "refuses to know what is right or deliberately accepts, or does, what he knows is wrong," and this self-defeating attitude proves to be not the professional but the personal undoing of Sage's enemies at the station. However, characters like Nora, who is part of Sage's staff at the station, and Sage's boss, Mr. Starr, respond to Sage in a very different way, representing a more reasoned approach: neither of them distrusts Sage, but neither is blindly loyal. Both characters parse out the information that Sage gives them, and they ultimately side with him because he has made a convincing case without appeals to popular opinion, money, or neck saving of any kind. And while neither Nora nor Starr faces any kind of social or personal consequences, Sage does. His story is scooped by another reporter who takes credit not just for Sage's reporting but for his convictions, and when Sage passes him in the hall, the other reporter literally breaks into a cold sweat, fearing a confrontation with Ditko's symbol of truth and reason (fig. 5.7).

At the end of the issue, Vic Sage can claim victory, but not publicly, because the scoop robs that particular outcome from him. Instead of being spiteful toward the reporter who stole his story, Sage seems at peace, confident in the karmic retribution that runs throughout Ditko's work, noting that the other reporter "is building his own trap and he'll find himself caught in it!"[55] Implicit here is that the components of that trap are failures of the mind and a negative response to the world as it is and the truth it reveals. The victory, then, that Sage claims is security in the knowledge that what informs character is not public perception but rather an internal sturdiness and a personal

Figure 5.6. Classic Ditko motifs are employed to present Superman as an idealized hero, visualized by the character's posture and positioning on the page as he walks the middle path between violent symbols of anti-life and idealized symbols of life. Art by Steve Ditko; colors by Tom Ziuko. Untitled pinup, *Superman* #400 (December 1984). © DC Comics.

Figure 5.7. As a symbol of truth, reason, and integrity, the mere presence of Vic Sage fills with fear and nervous energy those who lack the drive and convictions Sage represents. Dialogue and art by Steve Ditko (writing as D. C. Glanzman). "What Makes a Hero?" *Mysterious Suspense* #1 (October 1968). © DC Comics.

sense of accomplishment. The story closes with a final narration box, informing the reader that victory comes after one "has honestly applied himself to the task facing him and having overcome it . . . is secure in that knowledge . . . the fruits of that goal belong to him! He will know . . . no one else matters!"[56] It is the power of the mind alone that makes such securities, and operating as a state of mind, Sage provides that security for individuals, like Nora and Starr, who have embraced the precepts he offers. The cost for Sage, if it can be considered as such, is that he must accept his victories without recognition or social acceptance, but this is mitigated by the small social circle he maintains that does recognize what he has done.

In the pages of *Blue Beetle*, Ted Kord joins that social circle as he is also confronted with the ideal form, the Question. Kord first meets Vic Sage in *Blue Beetle* #5 in a story titled "The Destroyer of Heroes" that features a supporting cast seemingly pulled right from *The Fountainhead*, and it is instances such as this that have led many a reader to reduce Ditko's work to a parroting of Objectivism. This is especially true because the story includes an art critic named Boris Ebar, who is an Ellsworth Toohey analogue, and although Vic Sage serves the narrative role of John Galt, he appears more as an artistic representation of Howard Roark, "tall and gaunt"[57] and complete with hair the color of a "ripe orange rind."[58] In Ditko's story, Kord and Sage meet at an art gallery where two rival statues are on display: the first is *Our Man*, a misshapen lump that eschews what Ebar refers to as the "grotesque, heroic pose" and has a hollowed-out place where the figure's heart should be;[59] the second statue is called *The Unconquered* and appears to be a reference to the statue from *The Fountainhead*. Kord refers to the latter as "signif[ying] . . . something deeper. . . . That man is not helpless,"[60] just as Roark explains that the statue he commissioned should represent "the human spirit. The heroic in man."[61]

Sage and Kord bond over their defense of the statue in the face of those who would ostensibly slander it and Romantic notions about man's heroic potential. As the Blue Beetle, Kord visits the gallery to defend *The Unconquered* against those who would deface and destroy it. Eventually he finds himself in a battle against the sculptor of *Our Man*, who has made a suit of armor out of his statue and is on a rampage to destroy all heroic images. Blue Beetle tracks the menace all over Hub City, and throughout the chase and eventual battle, Ditko applies his mystic liberal philosophy, and its incorporation of Objectivist elements, to explain the role of the superhero and what the existence of such a figure *must* mean to have any merit. However, much of this explanation comes by way of presenting counterexamples through Our Man, Boris Ebar, and their ilk. Like Spider-Man and the Question, Blue Beetle is detested by the public, who adores the malformed Our Man and the mindlessness he represents in the story.

Throughout the chase, Blue Beetle is threatened by a mob of unkempt (none of them are wearing shoes) hippies, who call him a brute and pummel him with rocks, to which Blue Beetle responds, "Now there's a frightening example of pure emotionally driven action!" (fig. 5.8).[62] Rather than speaking to the reader, à la the narrator in *Mysterious Suspense*, Blue Beetle distinguishes the violence he is taking part in from those who are hurling rocks at him, the key differential being the lack of controlled thought expressed by the mob of hippies. But Ditko does not just level his cannon at hippies: Boris Ebar is erudite, well-dressed, and speaks eloquently of class and the everyman. Ditko presents Ebar's ideas as calculated but intellectually bankrupt, leading a group to believe that "man can feel better than he can think." The sculptor (and alter ego) of *Our Man* shares this view in his internal dialogue, considering himself as "merely an instrument of some unknown force. I cannot question it. . . . I can only obey its commands."[63] In each instance with the mob, Ebar, and the sculptor, those characters operate both as an antithesis to the kind of heroism Ditko pushes and as a complement to the narrative operations of those found in *Mysterious Suspense*. With the exception of the Blue Beetle, each of the supporting characters in the story—Boris Ebar, Our Man / the sculptor, the mob, and the Question—is an ideal form that Ted Kord must respond to so as to self-actualize. He must determine the kind of person he wants to be: one who rules his mind, or one who is ruled by emotion and unknown forces.

Figure 5.8. Blue Beetle is threatened by a mob of shoeless hippies who, in Ditko's configuration, represent unthinking emotion; they are visceral reactions instead of disciplined, reasoned thoughts. Dialogue and art by Steve Ditko (writing as D. C. Glanzman). "The Destroyer of Heroes," *Blue Beetle* #5 (November 1968). © DC Comics.

While Kord struggles in symbolic battle with the submissive anti-mind of Our Man, Vic Sage stands among a crowd of onlookers, watching the battle. Over a four-panel sequence, someone from the mob of hippies fires a gun at Blue Beetle to protect Our Man. Attacking the would-be assassin, Sage says, "That self-made idiot! He's refused to use his mind for so long he has nothing to check his impulses!" And as Sage kicks and punches the man, he chides him by saying, "Because you deliberately turned yourself into a mental cripple . . . that doesn't excuse your actions!" Then, when the man asks why Sage kicked him, Sage responds, "Since you won't think, I'll tell you! Your feelings don't determine anything! Especially the life of a human being!"[64] It is the very refusal to think and employ the positive, productive energy of one's mind that drives the shoeless hippie's attempt to murder Blue Beetle. A moment like this also offers an example of what Ditko would later refer to as "anti-life": the rejection of reason, principles, and thought in favor of the supposed unreason of emotion leading to an attempted murder. "The Destroyer of Heroes" story, then, is an opening remark to a larger discourse that I explore in the next chapter.

After the eventual defeat of Our Man in combat, the closing panels of the story show Ted Kord—and thus his antecedent in Peter Parker—making his choice for self-actualization. Speaking to his girlfriend and lab partner,

Tracey, Kord says what carried him to victory was the impression in his mind of *The Unconquered*. "I was fighting for everything it stood for," Kord says. He defeated Our Man because he believed in "whatever it took to make [*The Unconquered*] . . . whatever it takes to achieve anything worthwhile! It can only be done by struggling to succeed!"[65] Among the available options, Kord has made his choice, and it is one of wholeheartedness. The final panels of the story first feature the sculptor of *Our Man*, who is, as Peale might describe, "inwardly afraid . . . shrink[ing] from life . . . [and] suffer[ing] from a deep sense of inadequacy and insecurity."[66] Glumly staring at the audience, the sculptor thinks, "We can achieve nothing. We are doomed to failure before we try."[67] But the final panel of the story might be described as more uplifting, as it centers on an unknown student who, just as Ted Kord was inspired by his encounter with Vic Sage and *The Unconquered*, was inspired by what he saw in Blue Beetle to struggle for the improvement of his mind.

Officially, *Blue Beetle* was canceled after issue #5,[68] but it is probably fair to project an imaginary world where Ted Kord continued to grow and develop into the ideal hero, like the one Ditko presents in the Question and the even harder hitting Mr. A. However, what makes the Question and Mr. A so striking is not just their hard-line idealism and iconoclastic nature. Rather, it is their willingness to perform acts of violence seldom seen in post–Comics Code publications. These characters act on what Ditko refers to as "the right to kill," and in *Mr. A* #1, Ditko explains that this right can only be exercised against those who initiate force against others and thereby renounce their right to life.[69] For Ditko, the right to kill comes in response to the symbolic battle between "life" and "anti-life" that sits at the heart of the struggles faced by Spider-Man and the Blue Beetle, and the intellectual rationale that underwrites the confidence the Question has in his interactions with the world. In the fantasy world of Ditko's superheroes, the right to kill, not altruism, is the basic premise that justifies the actions of any vigilante hero against criminals. Working from that premise, Ditko begins to significantly challenge the status quo in superhero comics, starting with his independently produced works and those released through Charlton.

6

THE RIGHT TO KILL

The Question, Mr. A, and Life versus Anti-life

Somewhere in the sewer system of Crown City, there are likely the drowned corpses of two thugs, their waterlogged and rotting flesh gnawed away by rats and other nasty things. And in the world above that reeking sewer? Hard-hitting investigative journalist Vic Sage rests easy in the knowledge that these men have met such a fate. As the Question, he kicked those men into the rushing waters of the sewer, and though the thugs begged him for mercy, the Question ignored their pleas and even assured them they deserved their terrible fate. After all, *they* had attempted to murder *him*. When the thugs screamed for the Question to do his heroic "duty" and spare their lives, he responded, "Duty?—To whom?" (fig. 6.1).[1] In the late summer of 1967, Charlton comics published "Kill Vic Sage!" as a Question backup feature in *Blue Beetle* #4. Ditko's radical approach to presenting violence and philosophy in comics reverberated with contemporaries, angered some fans, and laid the groundwork for the increasingly violent and "relevant" comics of the 1970s and 1980s.

Major contributors to the comics scene of those decades, such as Jim Starlin and Denny O'Neil, have made special note of Ditko's work as being significantly different from other comics being released at the time. Starlin specifically cites the Question scene discussed earlier as one that stuck with him,[2] and O'Neil is quick to point out that whatever philosophic and political differences he and Ditko had, Ditko appeared to be writing for a much older audience than his contemporaries were.[3] Ditko's work seems to demand that readers be able to operate in at least two different registers: a surface level that presents straightforward facts about the characters, and a secondary register at which his stories should also be read for their nonliteral philosophic explorations. These significant differences would prove influential to later artists and writers, and Ditko's approach to violence as a means for exploring

Figure 6.1. The Question looks on as his attackers are dragged into the tangle of the sewer, where they will surely drown. Dialogue by Steve Skeates (as Warren Savin); art by Steve Ditko; Bob Agnew letters. "Kill Vic Sage!" *Blue Beetle* #4 (December 1967). © DC Comics.

philosophic matters marked a major turning point in American comics—a sort of "death of the Silver Age."

Whereas superhero comics today routinely feature violent heroes and amoral antiheroes, Silver Age superhero comics balked at depicting such violence. If villains died, it was through no real fault of the hero, or the circumstances were so mysterious as to make it almost impossible to tell if characters had truly met their demise. Heroes were expected to save the lives of innocents, but they were also expected to *spare* and even *save* the lives of their murderous enemies—even if it meant endangering the hero's own life. Working within a mystic liberal paradigm, along with fine-tuning the dark karmic impulses of his earlier work, Ditko disabused himself of these merciful heroes in the late 1960s, contending through the character of Mr. A that "to have any sympathy for a killer is to insult their victims."[4] In crafting the Question story just mentioned, Ditko does not force his character merely to reject the altruistic code of squeaky-clean Silver Age superheroes; he refuses to even acknowledge the *existence* of mercy in his hero's mind-set. As presented by the Question, what good reason does a hero have to "risk his neck" for the likes of his would-be killers?

First published in the same year as "Kill Vic Sage!," Mr. A also takes a more direct approach when, in *witzend* #3 (published by Wallace Wood), the character allows a crook to plummet to his death (fig. 6.2). The actions of Mr. A and the Question were jaw-dropping for Ditko's contemporaries, and the criticism he received led him to defend the act of outright killing, or indifferently allowing villains to die, as the hero's "right to kill." However, before we get into Ditko's defense of this "right," in defining the intellectual parameters for the right to kill, Ditko attempted to expunge any perceived sense of moral grayness from the violent actions of his characters. Ditko attempted to achieve this through what he identified as "a dramatic presentation revealing [a] character's choices and actions that identify them and lead to a just ending where a hero and a right view of life wins."[5] Of course, that "right view" is one Ditko saw as being wholly rational and measured by clear, noncontradictory standards. Indeed, this dramatization reflects the mind power movement I have associated with mystic liberalism in that Ditko's approach and mind power advocates alike attempt to address the question, as Horowitz notes, of what mental forces exert "an invisible pull on a person's daily life."[6] In examining the right to kill, Ditko identifies those nagging, invisible mental forces as a persistent moral dilemma between right and wrong, and it is only by sorting out this internal mental issue that the hero is afforded the right, gaining access to a higher power, one that offers a "better justice than the prevailing legal moral one."[7]

This extralegal mind power approach to justice is in keeping with Ditko's Romantic vision of nascent heroes, like Spider-Man and the Blue Beetle, progressing on an intellectual journey toward some sort of narrative completion point—the actualization of the self and a higher state of being. To that end, we should not see the actions of Ditko's characters as the result of snap decisions, narrative convenience, or the desire to produce more violent comics; rather, they were the product of Ditko's own sense of moral judgment and sense of reason he drew from his own distinct philosophic outlook. Like many a (liberal) mystic before him, Ditko's approach is autodidactic and rejects the ideas prescribed by authorities in favor of rationalizing a closure between a metaphysical "is" and "ought." In other words, the notion of life is the ultimate end for Ditko's characters when the right to kill is in play, and whatever might put that end at hazard ought to be eliminated. Rather than advocating murder, it is a parabolic exercise where one's own thinking about the preservation of self-esteem, and what informs that esteem, is called into question. Ditko's

Figure 6.2. While explaining that he has no sympathy for those who would initiate force, Mr. A allows a criminal to plummet to his death. Dialogue and art by Steve Ditko; Bill Spicer letters. Untitled story, *witzend* #3 (1967). © Steve Ditko.

right to kill asks: are one's thoughts responsible not just for one's actions but also for one's continued existence?

Few of Ditko's contemporaries parsed the nuances and attempted dialectic found in his early post-Marvel comics. Actions like those of the Question kicking criminals into a sewer ran counter to what was permissible in other Code-approved comics, and the constraints of the Code demanded that Ditko's unambiguous death scene have a tacked-on text pretending that the criminals' fate was somehow mysterious. Dissatisfied with such creative restrictions, Ditko directly responded to the restraints of the Code in *Mr. A* #1 (1973), which featured a story titled ". . . Right to Kill!" This story was introduced by a brief essay on the matter where Ditko says, "How a man will live—if he deserves to live—follows from how he uses his faculty for survival: *reason*." In other words, personhood, the right to life, depends first on one's willingness to reason, to think. In a mystic liberal sense, this notion of Ditko's squares with the New Thought advocate Napoleon Hill's urging to his readers that "[they] will never be greater than the thoughts that dominate [their] mind[s]."[8]

In a Ditkovian sense, if one's mind is cluttered with irrational and contradictory thoughts, then, in a nonliteral sense, one cannot fully achieve personhood, thus relinquishing one's life. However, by engaging with mind power, and not just positive thoughts but reasoned, rational thoughts, then one can (re)gain that life. Only individuals who have rejected reason and positive mind power are likely to initiate force against others, because they lack the ability to attract and create positive outcomes for themselves. The reasonless, in Ditko's view, are still wont to achieve material and emotional gain for themselves, resulting in violence against others. Ditko goes on to clarify that anyone who has initiated force against others thereby renounces reason and forfeits any claim to his life.[9] For Ditko, the hero is not one who initiates force but one who *retaliates* against it. Moreover, the hero is not obligated to save or defend the life of *anyone* who initiates force. Ditko offers a clear example of his polemic in the ". . . Right to Kill!" story that follows.

In this story, a little girl has been kidnapped and is being held for ransom; once the kidnappers receive the ransom money, they decide to kill the girl in an effort to secure their getaway. Mr. A enters and pummels the kidnappers, shooting one in the head. Mr. A then rescues the little girl, leaving her surviving kidnappers to writhe in anguish and presumably die from injuries they inflicted on each other in their attempt to escape. Although *Mr. A* was published independently, as a result of Ditko's general rejection of the undue influence of others and outsiders on the individual mind and what it creates, and thus was not subject to the Code's authority, it is worth noting that Ditko violates four of the Code's provisions on one page alone (fig. 6.3). If Mr. A and the ". . . Right to Kill!" feature were subject to the Comics Code, at minimum the story would have violated the following Code provisions:

- No comics shall explicitly present the unique details and methods of a crime.
- Scenes of excessive violence shall be prohibited. Scenes of brutal torture, excessive and unnecessary knife and gun play, physical agony, gory and gruesome crime shall be eliminated.
- The crime of kidnapping shall never be portrayed in any detail, nor shall any profit accrue to the abductor or kidnapper. The criminal or the kidnapper must be punished in every case.
- All scenes of horror, excessive bloodshed, gory or gruesome crimes, depravity, lust, sadism, masochism, shall not be permitted.

Like the earlier Question story, the villains beg for mercy and accuse Mr. A of being inhuman when he refuses to help them. When the little girl asks Mr. A why he won't save the lives of her suffering kidnappers, he responds that he "treat[s] people the way they act toward human life," and "[he] grant[s] them what their actions *deserve* [and] have *earned*."[10]

Ditko's line of reasoning should have a familiar ring to it: it tracks with the dark karma of his early horror and suspense stories and the reasoning that was injected into the zeitgeist by Blavatsky, and folds in neatly with the writing of Nathaniel Branden and his claims that thoughts create character. Ditko's rationale—along with Branden's, in particular—reflects mystic liberalism's interest in the more mystical side by way of New Thought and the "Law of Attraction," a well-traveled term in mind power philosophy that was given its contemporary usage by Prentice Mulford in *Your Forces, and How to Use Them* (1892). In essence, the Law of Attraction insists that the mind, and

Figure 6.3. In a stunning sequence of violence that moves the reader's eye in a roller-coaster fashion, Mr. A shoots a kidnapper in the head after she threatens to slash the throat of her child victim. Text, art, and letters by Steve Ditko. ". . . Right to Kill!" *Mr. A* #1 (1973). © Steve Ditko.

therefore individuals, exists in an ongoing negotiation with reality where the bargaining chips are one's own thoughts. Whatever circumstances one faces, according to the Law of Attraction, result from the mental state of the individual facing those circumstances. Like Ditko's push to beat back irrationality and wrong thinking, if one is able to maintain appropriate control over one's thoughts, then one will attract good fortune.

However, if people are unable to control their thoughts, giving in to negativity or something branded as immorality or irrationality, then they place their fortunes, their relationships, their lives, at hazard. It is important to note that not all believers and proponents of the Law of Attraction accepted, fully contended with, or even considered this destructive potentiality, but it is certainly present and has routinely been addressed by critics of New Thought. The dark karma of Ditko, as informed by Blavatsky and later buttressed by

Branden, embraces these negative elements and puts them to apparently productive use in the service of mystic liberalism's pursuit of rational justice.

To insist that criminals and villains deserve to die, and then have heroes
purposefully follow through on that insistence, would not be permitted of
Captain America, Batman, or even Ditko's own creations like Spider-Man or
Dr. Strange, but these were the words and actions of what Ditko defined as
a genuine, rational hero—or at least the artistic representation of one. It is
true that superheroes did kill with impunity in the pre–Comics Code era—
Superman threw crooks off of buildings, Batman punched a man into a vat
of acid and shot a sleeping vampire to death, and in Robin's first appearance,
the young boy knocked a crook off a skyscraper with his slingshot—but the
industry had been moving away from such violence years before the Code,
and those killings were largely forgotten or disregarded once the Comics
Code was in place. Such actions by comic book superheroes had become
objects of scorn and were nearly unthinkable, thanks not just to Fredric Wer-
tham but to the long-standing impositions of in-house editorial guidelines
developed at the most powerful comics publishers, like DC Comics.[11]

As a result of the antikilling post-Code attitude, Ditko found himself
defending not only the right for heroes to kill but also fantasy violence in general, claiming that force and the initiation of force "[were] the real issue and
evil." For Ditko, "stopping violence would solve nothing,"[12] since the real problem was volitional and philosophic. In the real world, these matters played
out not just with violent criminals or with government encroaching on individual rights, but with artists whose work was altered by editors,[13] was unduly
resented,[14] or was usurped by others.[15] For Ditko, issues of force are also put
into play when one embraces a nonrational view of the world, where "an honest (even if mistaken) examination" is at the furthest odds with judgments
that suspend one's own mind in favor of opinions delivered "by authorities,
pressures of cliques, groups of belonging."[16] In these latter cases, a literal death
warrant is obviously unjustifiable, and Ditko never advocates one. However,
what each of these instances of force represents in Ditko's philosophy is a way
of thinking that is anti-life, and it is so because each one operates in opposition to the rational, creative forces of the individual mind. These are the
ultimate philosophic stakes for Ditko: life versus anti-life, generative thought
versus the destruction of thought, mind versus anti-mind.

Paradoxically, this Manichaean, good-and-evil paradigm is an ontological claim about being as much as it is a Nietzschean concern with becoming,
where, as opposed to Nietzsche, Ditko's thought-based approach to becoming
produces abstractions with a fixed real-world application. The thought forms of
self-esteem, justice, rationality, and independence produce life, which is made
concrete through personal action. However, in this same sense, reality is a continuum of choices; it hangs on the precipice of chaos and anti-life, maintained

only by the pursuit and protection of life as an ultimate value. Ditko made this need for continual life-affirming thought and deed poignant in an image of Mr. A produced for the cover of *The Collector* #26 in 1972 (fig. 6.4).

Without explicitly stating it, Ditko's thinking about being and object reality falls in line with another philosopher interested in mind power: William James. Of being, James wrote: "How comes the world to be here at all instead of the nonentity which might be imagined in its place?"[17] In the Ditkovian configuration, if those thought forms noted earlier did not produce life, then what did they produce? And what of their opposites? What did they produce? Anti-life. At no point did Ditko indicate in either his comics or essays that he believed this conflict between life and anti-life was a literal battle fought on a tangible plane of existence. Instead it is played out on a metaphysical plane, as allegory in artistic representations, and given weight through the use of fantasy violence.

Admittedly, this metaphorical reading of the right to kill runs counter to long-standing perceptions of Ditko's work, particularly his post-Marvel efforts, as being resistant to figurative readings. Characters like Mr. A, the Question, and later creator-owned characters seem to speak in direct, didactic terms with an outward-facing ideology. However, as discussed in the previous chapter, the more outwardly philosophic and ideological that Ditko's characters are, the less it seems they are to be seen as literal people inhabiting a space than they are ideas to which other characters are responding. These flat characters take on an emblematic narrative function: they are ideas that other characters and the reader must respond to in the way one might respond to other parables. In the example of the Mr. A story from *witzend* #3 discussed earlier, Miss Kinder, the victim, responds to Mr. A not as she would a person but as she would the psychological conflict of dealing with her would-be murderer. Moreover, the murder of those who have initiated force against others is not an imperative in Ditko's comics, as exemplified in the story from the unpublished *Blue Beetle* #6, also discussed in chapter 5. As a more rounded character, who faces psychological challenges, Ted Kord ponders the very problem that characters like Mr. A and the Question present; ultimately, while taking responsibility for his potential actions, Kord clearly regrets that he could have killed another person, saying that he never intended to be another person's executioner.[18] Although he feels no compassion for the dead criminal, it is the act of murder that is in question. Unlike emblematic characters such as the Question and Mr. A, the more developed Ted Kord steers away from actions that lead to the deliberate killing of criminals. This latter story, for what it is worth, would have been published at the end of 1967, in the same series that introduced the Question and in the same year Ditko published "Kill Vic Sage!" and premiered Mr. A.

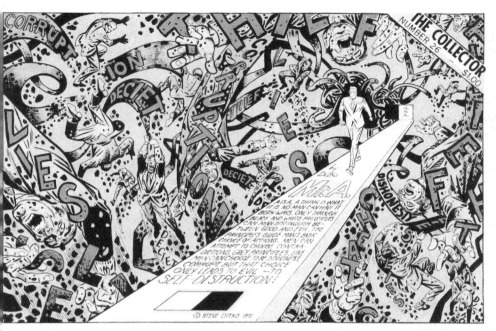

Figure 6.4. Emerging from a darkened opening, Mr. A walks down the narrow path of rationality, flanked on all sides by chaos and disorder in the external world. Text, art, and letters by Steve Ditko. *The Collector* #26 (1972). © Steve Ditko.

However, it is not only studying Ditko's work that reveals a nonliteral reading of the right to kill. Shortly after his death in 2018, a number of letters that Ditko sent to fans were shared with the public through social media platforms, and some of those letters provide insight into the claim I am making here. In a September 2012 letter to the fan Mark Strong, Ditko writes, "All fiction, fantasy from fables to novels offer an imaginative exploration [of] possibilities of 'what if,' 'suppose,' 'imagine,' etc. With *no* '*must*,' '*duty*,' or '*law*' and penalties."[19] For Ditko, there is no imperative to act on any of the ideas presented in his comics, and he is careful to note that his comics, like all other fictional media, are just that: fantasies, thought experiments. In a March 2017 letter, Ditko writes to Scott Mills that "reality, life is a continuum," and then goes on to list several ideas: life and death, rational and irrational, real and false.[20] Each of the oppositional ideas is presented as distant from the others, with a squiggly line keeping them apart, signifying the multitudinous possibilities between either extreme. An acknowledgment that any of these exist on a continuum immediately disrupts the hard, black-and-white view taken by Mr. A in how the character deals with issues and how Ditko presents them visually. This seems clearly to suggest that Ditko is taking Mr. A and the ideology the character represents as a philosophic experiment presented in fictional form, not as a literal set of instructions to his readers about who should live and die. In writing about visual gimmicks in response to the fan Bryan Stroud in 2007, Ditko says, "Drama depends on conflicts, opposites in action. . . . The dual nature of mankind is freedom or slavery. The dual nature of man is life or death."[21] These dual natures, then, inform the kind of fictional drama Ditko presents on the comics page, and staging such problems as distinct opposites, as opposed to the continuum in which they actually exist, is necessary for creating compelling fictional drama. However, it is perhaps a 1994 letter to Daniel Reed where Ditko makes it most clear that life and anti-life are narrative-philosophic functions and not literal reality. He writes:

> There is *no* battle "between life and death" in human terms. They are *not* 2 "living" entities in mortal combat. Anti-life as an entity could *not* exist because if it did, then it would be "alive," have "life" and then it would *first* have to be anti-self, i.e., to act to *destroy itself*, to destroy whatever "life" it had, to seek non-life, non-existence, to be inanimate matter like a stone.
>
> Anti-life in human terms is a default, a not acting to sustain, to protect to preserve the ultimate value of life.
>
> It is the blank-outs, the evasions of not caring to know what is the real, the true, and the good. It results in self blindness and the willingly acting blindly, of not knowing or caring what one is actually doing. The anti-life is the irrational.[22]

So not only is there no literal battle between life and anti-life, as Ditko relates the idea, but the very notion of anti-life itself is a substitute for that which is irrational. This lends significant weight to the notion that Ditko takes the opportunity with his most philosophic, least literal characters to explore these issues in an allegorical, emblematic register. Given these examples, as well as the evidence from the texts considered, I argue that this figurative reading is more sensible than the assumption that Ditko is advocating the literal murder of perceived criminals by vigilante reporters.

Moreover, by couching his sense of justified fantasy violence in choice— the choice one makes to adopt an anti-life mentality—Ditko again aligns himself with the mind power elements of mystic liberalism, where, as New Thought mystics like Warren Felt Evans or later proponents like Neville Goddard would likely argue, thought and imagination create reality. It is not that Evans, Goddard, or most other mind power advocates weaponized thought as a means—even if theoretical—for eliminating violent criminals. But the blending of Blavatsky's sense of karma and her direct influence on New Thought make such justifications available. Furthermore, the Randian ingredients that Ditko adds to this stew work to temper the use of violence by clarifying that the hero did not have a right to initiate force but only had the right to retaliate against it in equal measure. Unfortunately, at the time, the

Comics Code did not share Ditko's nuanced approach and was not equipped to regulate that kind of complexity.

In a 1969 essay titled "Violence the Phoney Issue," Ditko further dismisses criticism of fantasy violence by reiterating his position about retaliation versus initiation and pointing out that violence in the arts is fictitious and done in a "controlled make-believe atmosphere." He also asserts that violence in the arts is not responsible for real-life violence perpetrated by "people who choose to *initiate* force." Furthermore, "Those profiteers of *initiated* force can never be sure of holding onto anything they possess, including their lives."[23] Ditko is not attempting to reduce an acceptance of violent actions to a childish "he started it!" argument. Rather, he is attempting to demonstrate through fiction that, philosophically and morally, individuals have a right to use force against those who would attempt to strip them of their rights, lives, or property. Ditko reinforces this stance, referring to Aristotle, insisting: "Art is philosophically more important than History. History tells how men did act. *Art shows how men could and should act.*"[24] Note that Ditko misquotes Aristotle's *Poetics* in a way similar to how Rand conscripts the philosopher into her notion of Romantic fiction; Ditko drafts Aristotle into his cause to differentiate his own explorations of what might be from what is or was lived reality. Although his interpretation and application of Aristotle here are questionable, for the purposes of my argument, it is more important to note that, for Ditko, "art"—like Aristotle's "poetry"—is more a function of philosophy, a systematic presentation of ideas and not a recounting particular facts.[25]

In other words, verisimilitude in his work is not about historical reality or whether everyday people should be dropping criminals from rooftops. Ditko is instead speaking in the register of philosophic, idealistic truths—ones that are experienced more than they are tangibly measured. Part of the appeal for those philosophic truths depends on a sense of karmic retaliation—as well as villainy being the product of internal, mental corruption. Fictitious representations of violence, then, place the more ethereal notion of dark karma into mundane practicability. Because the machinations of karma and "mental science" are running in the background, the right to retaliatory force is extended beyond personal injury. The result is that the individual characters have a right to use force against *anyone* who initiates force against *anyone* else. Moreover, although Ditko's application of these notions is peculiar to himself, has he not also provided a broad intellectual justification for the actions of all superhero vigilantes?

The Real Horror

That the right to kill is as much about philosophic truth as it is about the literal forfeiture of life by those who "choose" irrationality or evil adds a dimension of cosmic intraspace to the concept. In a symbolic sense, the right to kill is translatable to an internal, intellectual exorcism as well as a social one. For one to gain access to the right, then, one must first expel one's own demons or at least learn to identify and contend with them in a positive, rational way that leads to intellectual clarity. One of the most striking visual representations of the internal fortitude needed to access the right to kill occurs in a double-page spread printed in *Mr. A* #1, which first appeared as the cover to *The Collector* noted earlier.

Although the right is, of course, explored throughout *Mr. A* #1, this spread presents Mr. A walking down an uncluttered path toward the reader, away from Mr. A's signature black-and-white card, and the path appears to originate *inside* the card. As Mr. A marches on, he is surrounded by chaos and despair as those who have chosen irrationality—anti-life—writhe and scream in horrific contorted positions, wrapped in words that reveal the actions resulting from their evil, or even morally gray, thoughts. That their thoughts created this hell for them is made clear by the text that sits just below Mr. A on the path. Dripping with Randian vocabulary and sentiment, these words admonish the reader that "men can choose to be dishonest, corrupt, but that choice only leads to evil—to self-destruction!" In other words, by pursuing such thoughts, practitioners of evil have chosen death, and only by choosing the thoughts that result in consistent, right, rational principles—according to Mr. A—can one choose life.

Unlike the more literal, internal cosmic quests of Dr. Strange, characters like Mr. A fall in line with the ostensibly more realistic world of characters like Spider-Man and the Blue Beetle, where the plumbing of psychic depths is presented by more practically useful, if not still theoretical, means. The visual depiction of Ditko's theoretical rhetoric is dramatic, to say the least. But the stark contrast between right and wrong as he presents it moves the cosmic search for the self—the rational self—away from the fantastic, as presented by the conflict among Dr. Strange, Dormammu, and the Mindless Ones. Mr. A places this conflict between volitional good and volitional evil, as they battle for the intellectually incomplete, the nonhuman, into a more practical frame. Again, the search for truth is less literal than it is theoretical, but the more mundane setting of Mr. A and the more practical terminology of what defines good and evil refine Ditko's dialectical approach, making dark karma more tangible by way of retaliatory violence.

By establishing a difference between retaliatory violence and the initiation of force or violence, Ditko demarcates the actions of his heroes from characters that he sees as less heroic. Ditko contends that even if there was a marked increase in societal violence compared to previous decades, it was not related to violence in the arts; it was a corollary and direct result of individuals *choosing* philosophic and moral incompetence. Moreover, Ditko's philosophic and moral right to retaliation cannot properly be understood or applied through mere imitation of fictional violence; it must be a product of a particular sense of reason and rationality. Instead of real-world violence being a product of the arts, Ditko takes the reverse position and views the artistic "drama[tization] of man's inevitable weakness" as a by-product of the intellectual bankruptcy of embracing the initiation of force Ditko defines. Through the voice of Vic Sage, Ditko denounces those dramatizations of weakness as being "perfect for self-admitted nothings who have nowhere to go in their world of nothing."[26]

One of the more powerful instances of Ditko discovering the consequences for operating on the thoughts of a "self-admitted nothing" occurs in the story "My Brother . . . ," which first appeared in *Murder* #3, from Deni Loubert's Renegade Press in 1986. In brief, the story is about two brothers: Ray, a hardworking defense attorney who works to free those who have been wrongly convicted; and Ben, a petty crook who makes his way through graft, violent robbery, and murder as a hit man. One defends the innocent, and one silences and destroys the innocent. For Ditko, the story plays out another conflict between his metaphysical notions of life and anti-life.

The story parallels the two brothers' lives as each rises through his respective ranks, emphasizing the theme of life versus anti-life. Throughout the story, Ben resents Ray, blaming Ray for his troubles and his life of crime, growing increasingly petulant and vengeful as Ray is championed by the public, so much so that Ben decides Ray needs to suffer for his achievements and happiness. Ben says, pouting, "But it's *Ray's* fault I turned out the way I did! #*@!! He didn't do enough for me. #*@!! Someday I'll show him. I'll make him *pay*!!"[27] As Ben takes on contract hits, he fantasizes about each murder being a stand-in for his brother, until he eventually decides to contract himself for Ray's murder, musing, "Soon, *brother*, we'll see who is the *better* man,"[28] as though Ben's entire existence can only be understood in contrast to and in competition with his brother, and as though such thoughts are reserved only for those who have engaged with an anti-life perspective. Ray—the avatar of life, of course—has no such feelings toward Ben and sees no competition between them, evoking the encounter between Howard Roark and Ellsworth Toohey in *The Fountainhead*, where Toohey asks, "Mr. Roark, we're alone here. Why don't you tell me what you think of me? In any words you wish. No one will hear us." To which Roark responds, "But I don't think of you."[29]

Indeed, Ray has no interest in his brother's choices, other than recognizing them as a clear marker of the difference between them and as an understanding of his brother's extreme sense of resentment. After receiving an anonymous tip, Ray is lured to a dark alley where his brother, Ben, waits, prepared to murder Ray in cold blood for the crimes of "*always* [being] *too good*" and wanting "something *better* . . . but *only* for [him]self."[30] At gunpoint, Ben demands that his brother beg for his life and justify his existence, which Ray flatly refuses before inverting the argument. Steely eyed, Ray stands in the face of his brother and his gun, proclaiming that Ben is "right . . . [he] *should* kill that hateful, disgusting, loathsome creature! You have every right to kill him . . . !"[31]

Of course, Ray means that Ben is that "loathsome creature," urging Ben to turn the gun on himself, demanding that he contend with all the "reasons why [Ben] can no longer let him live."[32] Ray continues his verbal assault: "hate him," "you can no longer let him live," "an insult to life," "obscene, revolting creature," "totally evil," "must be destroyed," "Kill him, Ben! He's unfit to live. Kill that rotten, evil, slimy excuse for a *human being—kill him now!*" Ben then turns the guns on himself and fires. Ray, without emotion, looks on as his brother's body collapses into the cluttered alleyway.[33]

On a surface reading, Ditko *seems* to be arguing that those who don't hold themselves to a very specific moral standard, which Ditko prescribes, should kill themselves. Beneath that, there is something more complex going on, and it begins with the fact that Ray and Ben are brothers who look uncannily similar. This physical similarity is central to a complete reading of the story and its relationship to the philosophic stakes of Ditko's "right to kill." In his 2002 essay "Tools of the Trade," Ditko wrote:

> An artist must show, present a visual concrete, things, objects. His "real" story is external in the actual artwork, picture. . . .
>
> Neither a writer or artist's work can be effective/correct/coherent/have integrity with the arbitrary inclusion or exclusion of certain elements. What is there (added or left out) must be the result of a definite purpose.[34]

As I have throughout this book, I take Ditko seriously on this point—certainly insofar as every element of the stories he writes and draws is designed to elicit some philosophic point. Moreover, accounts by contemporaries, like Gil Kane, suggest that Ditko was not just invested in political theory but deeply passionate about it, both in and outside of his work. In an interview in the *Comics Journal*, Kane suggests that the thrust of Ditko's approach to philosophy was entirely introspective: "I think his ideas could have been almost anything, simply because he self-counseled himself."[35]

For the most part, I think Kane is right, certainly about the stakes of Ditko's more explicitly philosophic comics: they are interested in matters of the interior. What must be "killed" in "My Brother . . ." is not an actual human person, or brother, but those negative thoughts and urges that push one toward what Ditko would conceive of as the unearned and parasitic. This becomes clear through the visual representation of Ben and Ray, as well as their narrative representation as brothers and thus as products of the same root (fig. 6.5). To succeed and operate as a rational, productive individual, one must eliminate thoughts that encourage infringement on the rights and actions of others, especially those in service of quick, unearned success. Put differently, what Ditko argues for in "My Brother . . ." is not the literal murder or suicide of *people* who are unfit for a rational existence but rather the elimination of thoughts and ideas that corrupt an individual's view of themself—which amounts, as Gil Kane suggests, to a sort of self-counseling. This seems to be true throughout Ditko's use of the right to kill: not a destruction of human beings but an elimination of negative, cancerous thoughts. The violence associated with "the right," therefore, is both figurative and in service of self-improvement.

Ditko is unambiguous in his defense of violence in entertainment. After all, violence is a philosophic tool in the artist's toolbox; it should be used whenever appropriate. But appropriate is the operative term for Ditko, and his appreciation of the use of violence is another matter and is limited to violence that is used in the service of reason and justice. For those who perpetuate a sort of "irrational violence" in media, Ditko prefers that their ideas are open to rational criticism and eventually defeated in the marketplace of ideas. In a feature titled "Social Justice," which appears in the same issue of *Murder* as "My Brother . . . ," Ditko went on the attack again against those who would blame their own violent actions or the violent actions of criminals on the influence of popular culture. In this satiric story, Ditko does not let the presence of *mindless* violence on television or its corresponding antiheroes off the hook but makes plain that each individual is responsible for their actions. As such, no depiction of violence should be forbidden in creative pursuits, even if the creator is operating on ethical and philosophic principles counter to Ditko's own.

Ditko sporadically published a number of Mr. A stories, all the way up to his death in 2018, and like those early tales, each one took on philosophic concerns related to the conflict of life and anti-life. In 2016, Ditko and Snyder published *Mr. A* #18, which featured the stories "Mr. A and the Horror" and "Mr. A and the Score." Both stories operate allegorically, where, as Norman Vincent Peale might frame it, "people who are lacking in inner peace are victims of a self-punishment mechanism."[36] Of course, this is the same intellectual framing device used in "My Brother . . . ," but the first story, "Mr. A and the Horror," disrupts readings that imagine Ditko's interest in the conflict between life and anti-life as being necessarily politically reactionary. And "The Score" ultimately questions whether lethal retaliatory violence can serve as an effective tool for enacting justice.

"The Horror" opens with "The *real horror* is *not* the *villain* or his *actions*" and invites the reader to "discover what *it is*."[37] What "it is" is a manifestation of negative thoughts in the form of depression, guilt, addiction, and fear, and their power to silence otherwise good people, even forcing them to lash out against those who would try to help them. The villain of the story is a man who wears a monster costume, the malformed shape of which is evocative

Figure 6.5. Brothers Ben and Ray serve as avatars for competing thought forms, where the "good" rational thought form must urge the evil one to destroy itself. This suicide is presented in dramatic and haunting fashion through the changing panel sizes and the intensity of expression Ditko gives each character until the final dramatic moments in which Ben collapses into the darkness of the alleyway. Dialogue and art by Steve Ditko. "My Brother . . . ," *Murder* #3 (October 1986). © Steve Ditko.

of the kind of monster stories Ditko worked on at Atlas/Marvel in the late 1950s and early 1960s. The man, known as the Horror, torments several people, extorting money from them under the threat of violence, demanding that they quietly pay and that they never, ever discuss his existence. To avoid his violence, they must remain silent. But the silence is punishing, creating tremendous mental anguish for each of his victims. Like Mr. A, the Horror is less a literal person than an avatar, and for each of his victims, he represents something different. In one particular case, the Horror stands in for gendered relationship violence. The principal victim of the story is the singer Lana Lojen, a friend of Rex Graine, alter ego of Mr. A.

After attacking Lana and threatening to pour acid down her throat, the Horror escapes into an alleyway; Lana leaves her apartment afraid and near tears. Recognizing that something is wrong, Rex Graine decides to take up the matter and interviews a number of people who he knows have dealt with the

Horror, but all deny any knowledge of such a figure for fear of what the Horror might do to them if they open themselves up. At the same moment, Lana is in her dressing room when the Horror appears, and as he threatens her, placing his hands around her throat, he insists that he doesn't "mean to cause [her] hardships" and he "admire[s her] talent." "Believe me!" he pleads.[38] Lana decides she has had enough and, believing she has no one to turn to, gets a gun. When the Horror attacks her again after a concert, Rex shows up as Mr. A to put a stop to it. While fighting with the Horror, Mr. A urges Lana to call the police. Instead of firing at the Horror, Lana tries to shoot Mr. A, insisting that she cannot involve the police, going so far as to attack Mr. A, screaming, "You're the enemy! He's not threatening me! . . . [He's] Being generous, will soon stop! You'll make him blame, take it out on, me!"[39]

Mr. A eventually catches up with the Horror and subdues him, tying him up and leaving him in the dark, where he has nightmares about Mr. A showing up and panics about his fate before the police arrive and arrest him. The police remove his costume to reveal an ordinary man who had created so much trouble. In a strange turn of events, nothing actually happens to the man. He receives one of Mr. A's black-and-white cards, and when he touches it, the card turns black, informing him that he is evil. However, because none of his victims are willing to testify against him, the police have to set him free. Other than chasing him down, pummeling and subduing him, Mr. A does not enact any additional violence against the Horror.

Perceptibly, this is a strange case, but it points to the larger stakes of what Ditko is exploring in all his comics, particularly with Mr. A. If we limit Ditko to being nothing more than a mouthpiece for Objectivism, then a story like this can be seen as an exploration of the Randian concept of the "sanction of the victim," which is the notion that good people will position themselves as sacrificial victims to protect something they have been led to believe is the greater good. In Rand's view, for victims to permit or excuse the actions of their oppressors is morally evil. This is a deeply troubling worldview, and in fairness, the Horror does have that bent to him: the reason the Horror threatens his victims—all of whom are great successes—is because he "really need[s]" money, and so they give in. However, reading the story in this way demands that we ignore the violence that Lana faces and how it influences her state of mind and her actions. In fact, as Lana lashes out at Mr. A, she screams in terror that the Horror will take out anything Mr. A does to the Horror on *her*. Her response is not simply the "sanction of the victim" but a response to very real fear caused by the violence she has suffered.

The problem of "the sanction of the victim" being a potential reading is not limited to this late contribution. Early in this chapter, I mentioned Mr. A's first appearance in *witzend* #3 and his killing of a murderer, whom Mr. A allows to drop from a flagpole atop a tall building. In the closing panels of that story,

Mr. A also deals with the killer's last victim, the aptly named Miss Kinder—a name signaling her allegorical function. Miss Kinder tries to show compassion for her attacker, and Mr. A berates her for this apparent transgression. But even so, Mr. A still chooses to save her, and he carries her off in the final scene. If the purpose of the story were to demonstrate that there should be no sympathy for victims who don't employ the "proper principles" laid out in comics like *Mysterious Suspense*, then why not just let Miss Kinder bleed out on the roof? While it seems clear that Ditko is presenting a troubling view that empathy is a major reason why crimes and criminals persist, it is worth noting that Mr. A is not unsympathetic to even supposedly misguided victims. That sympathy, as it applies to both Miss Kinder and Lana, is not necessarily incompatible with the harsh, black-and-white worldview Mr. A is a stand-in for. In fact, it's kind of his thing: in the story from *witzend*, Mr. A tells the victim that he would have let the killer die regardless of whether she was attacked. That victims exist is reason enough for Mr. A to kill initiators of force. In the context of these stories, it is not necessary for victims to take any kind of action at all, and Ditko concerns himself with the psychology of victims only when it serves a narrative or philosophic purpose. In the story from *witzend* #3, that purpose is to lay out the stakes of life and anti-life in a figurative manner, and in *Mr. A* #18, the purpose is to explore the rationale for why some victims cling to their abusers.

Alternatively, this story positions Mr. A as an avatar for how Ditko envisions the difficult, competing thoughts in the mind of a victim. Mr. A as the stand-in for rationality and the Horror as the destructive forces of fear and doubt, and the physical conflict between the two, represent Lana's, and any victim's, struggle to do what is right for herself—even if she is not always able to do so. Admittedly, stripping any kind of emotional, mental turmoil, much less relationship violence, down to an allegory about "choosing" to leave is deeply problematic, but Ditko doesn't offer such a solution. By the end, neither Lana, nor any other victim, has turned on or left the Horror, rendering his and their fates ambiguous—an indication that a clean psychological break from traumatic events, like those Lana experienced, is not always possible.

So in spite of Mr. A's demand's for rationality, the choice is not always so easy. Where Ditko tries to seal matters up is with the man who dresses as the Horror, who, in an ironic twist, is now haunted by Mr. A, the knowledge of his own evil, and the fear that his victims will eventually turn on him. Meanwhile the unhaunted heroes of the story—Rex, a cop, and Rex's editor—vow to eventually "nail him." So in the metaphysical conflict between life and anti-life, there are choices to be made, but even good people can fall prey to anti-life thoughts and tendencies, and it is through vigilant, positive thought and deeds that the tentacles of anti-life can be forced to retreat.

Opening with the suicide of an innocent but troubled man, the second story in *Mr. A* #18 addresses the very real consequences of not being able to exorcise the ghosts of anti-life. As news of the suicide is being reported, Rex Graine is among those covering the case. The man's, Jay's, grief-stricken wife and daughter struggle to understand what happened, as three of Jay's "friends" tell reporters that his suicide was a result of personal weakness and family trouble. Without prompting, they also suspiciously insist that his "death is not related to [their] real estate business." Graine isn't buying any of it and is certain Jay was "*driven* to [suicide] *deliberately* and *cold bloodedly*."[40] It is then revealed that Jay's three friends had been involved in political corruption to aid their real estate endeavors. Jay was ready to blow the whistle, until the others framed him for crimes he didn't commit, and it was that pressure that drove Jay to take his own life. Graine vows to "take care of Jay's unfinished business and the corrupt 'businessmen.'"[41]

As Mr. A, Graine tracks each of the men down, appearing as a ghostly apparition in their homes while they sleep, giving each one the black-and-white card that reveals the true nature of their minds. One of them, Stu, is the particular target of Mr. A's fear tactics; Mr. A visits him multiple times and during one incident fires a gun directly at Stu's face, deliberately missing, after delivering a newspaper that features a headline that pronounces Stu's guilt. Although the events literally happen in the story, Stu at first takes them to be dreams and figments of his imagination, narratively signaling that what frightens Stu most is not Mr. A but the idea of him, the idea of an ethically, morally upright person, of how such a person stands in contrast to Stu's own despicable behavior. Stu, an apparent play on "stew," is overcome with anxiety for the next several days, while the other two plot against him.

After collecting the evidence necessary to convict Stu and his partners, Mr. A shows up at Stu's house one final time. He stokes Stu's anxiety, telling him that it was his partners who hired him to come and scare Stu, and he sets up a meeting between the four of them so that Stu can see just how rotten his cronies are. When Stu shows up to the meeting, he bursts through the door and shoots both of his partners dead. Stu then turns the gun on Mr. A, only to find that Mr. A had loaded the last two bullets as blanks. Mr. A then says to Stu, "I tricked you. They really were innocent, didn't hire me! You killed them. You'll pay for being a *killer!*" In a scene reminiscent of "My Brother . . . ," Mr. A then lays the gun on a table in front of Stu and tells him, "You have one out, *only one.* Think it over, *killer! Killer!*"[42] Mr. A then confidently strides out of the house as a bang goes off in the background.

All the beats of this story fall in with what one would expect from a Mr. A story as it pertains to the character's and series' view of morality, the meting out of justice, and how these are ultimately matters contended within the mind of each individual. But then it takes an interesting turn. As Mr. A walks away, he ponders:

Is the score really even? All those corrupters [the political pawns Stu and company were paying off] seeking the unearned who dealt with those three, should they also pay a price for Jay's death? Is a price their knowing they're dishonest, unworthy human beings, unfit for real human relationships? Can they be proud of themselves? Like themselves? The price—never escaping themselves?[43]

This is a curious moment for Mr. A. Clearly he has no regard for the three men whose deaths he has facilitated, and he even seems to be wondering if he should try to kill everyone who was connected with these crimes. However, because these stories are not so much about the actual deaths of the characters as they are parables about the choice between life and anti-life, as has been discussed throughout, this is not so much what interests me. Rather, what is striking about Mr. A's statement is how it stakes out for the reader precisely that this is a fictitious story, and facilitating murder-suicide is *not* a sensible solution to these problems. Instead Mr. A lays out an ontological approach to being an avatar of "life" by explaining its contrast. To be "anti-life" is to be not just one of the three dead bodies on the floor of that house; it's to be willfully complicit in the crimes that led to that moment. And the karmic retribution for that crime is not a literal death but, instead, the crippling knowledge that they are "unworthy of human relationships" and unworthy of the kind of self-esteem that Nathaniel Branden prescribes. Indeed, to Mr. A, such people, as Peale puts it, expect the worst and will get the worst through the Law of Attraction.[44] Those are the "real" consequences for such people.

The story ends on one other intriguing note. Rex Graine visits Jay's still-grieving family and explains that Jay was "a brave and honest man" and had committed suicide because he believed it was the only way to spare his wife and daughter from suffering through the frame Stu and the others set up for him. In an attempt to be kind and work through the trauma with Jay's family, Rex soliloquizes:

We can all become self-trapped in the *unreal*. It is hard for many, especially for innocent victims, to understand that in the world of objective truth, evil has *no* power of its own. The corrupt, the seekers of the unearned, give evil its *destructive* power. Left on their own, the unreal—lies, evil—will self-destruct. The compromisers, corrupters, gray men, feed, arm, and unleash the destructive evil.[45]

Sharp readers may notice that Graine's words to the grieving widow are cribbed from Galt's Speech in *Atlas Shrugged*, where he describes the sanction of the victim. However, in doing so, Ditko complicates the notion by moving away from condemning sanctioners and, instead, offering empathy and assurance of karmic justice. Although this is certainly an obtuse way to comfort a grieving widow, Graine reframes one of the central arguments of *Mr. A*, and of mystic liberalism, generally: that one's mental attitude determines what kinds of friends and situations one attracts; it is up to the life-affirming innocent to avoid the mental traps that allow negativity to creep in, and to shut out evil so that it withers on its own. In his way, Graine is attempting to be sensitive to the despair Jay felt by being trapped in what he believed to be a world where "truth, justice seemed powerless, the legal, moral authorities indifferent,"[46] a world that acted against him through its apathy. But according to Graine, it's not the world that is unjust; it's the world's self-corrupted, anti-life inhabitants who are, and only through such a recognition can one can navigate existence.

Through the voice of Mr. A, the reader is repeatedly informed that accepting and practicing morally gray principles mean accepting an anti-life frame of mind and a forfeiture of rationality. Ditko challenges the status quo and blind acceptance of what he considered to be popular—but false—ways of thinking that embrace the middle ground and antiheroes; however, the ways in which his sense of rational violence has been co-opted by artists and writers who followed him do not always fit the mold Ditko cast. Indeed, for as much as Ditko's right to kill fits within the mystic liberal collage and all of mystic liberalism's borrowing and reinterpreting, Ditko's attempt at orthodoxy did anything but stick for those who would follow him, and a common response by later creators is to cherry-pick the rational violence of the Question and Mr. A and merge it with their own philosophy and the popular media of their day. In some cases, the end product reads as a criticism of Ditko's work; in others, it represents a sort of evolution of the violent hero. As such, the conjoining of Ditko's "right to kill" with other superheroes has created a paradigm shift in the way superheroes have been approached in more recent decades.

The superhero comics that immediately followed the Question and Mr. A began to take on a more serious tone, dealing with street-level concerns (like drug use) and allowing for increased violence as a narrative tool for both heroes and villains. A fair portion of this shift almost certainly reflects the changing societal norms, expectations about readers, and cultural mood of the late 1960s and early 1970s, and this cultural mood created a number of opportunities for individuals to invest in different means of political thought, borrowing from whatever useful elements were available. The mind power movement that was embraced by liberal-capitalist thought in the mid-twentieth century and its repurposing as self-esteem by Nathaniel Branden and Ayn Rand was appealing. By embracing this kind of revised liberal thinking, Ditko's work blazes a trail in the American superhero comic, and it is his heroes who first *deliberately* kill in this era. It is not clear whether Ditko would have approved of many of the narrative and thematic choices that have since cropped up in comics, and in many cases, it is most likely he would not.

The philosophic and narrative structure that Ditko created for his characters leaves room for complexity of thought and deed, but there is no room for a positive view of the antihero. Ironically, whatever Ditko's intentions were, by arguing for an acceptance of retaliatory violence, he helped create an entry point for the more violent content and antiheroes that began to appear in the superhero comics of the early 1970s—characters like the Punisher come immediately to mind. However, according to the Punisher's cocreator Gerry Conway, the character was based on Don Pendleton's *Executioner* novels, Brian Garfield's *Death Wish* (the 1972 novel, not the film), and the early pulp hero the Shadow.[47] But the Punisher, along with later, more bizarre characters, such Foolkiller[48] and the Scourge of the Underworld,[49] do point to a larger trend in comics after Mr. A.

Although I am confident that there is not sufficient reason to believe that Steve Ditko takes the right to kill as a justification for the literal execution of anyone who violates the rights to life or property of another person, the yields of his figurative explorations of this right trouble many readers, and for good reason. The Punisher, in particular, presents an interesting case. Although I have no reason to believe that Gerry Conway actually entertained any reactionary politics—either now or when he helped develop the Punisher—the Punisher presents an interesting case of the right to kill in action, especially as Conway notes that he was inspired by Brian Garfield's *Death Wish*. Relatedly, I currently have no reason to conjecture that Garfield was at all familiar with Ditko's Mr. A or the Question, but he was active during the same period as Ditko and would have had access to the same zeitgeist as Ditko was drawing from in developing his own philosophy.

Garfield's *Death Wish* is a revenge novel that introduces readers to Paul Benjamin, a left-leaning accountant whose wife and daughter are brutalized by a gang of drug addicts, leading to the death of Paul's wife. Benjamin then takes stock of his life and, resulting from his grief and disillusionment, radically reforms his political views. Adopting a racist, reactionary perspective, Benjamin arms himself and begins murdering drug addicts and criminals in New York City, never actually avenging the crimes committed against his family but managing to murder several African American, Puerto Rican, and white criminals and drug addicts—with the novel making a point to identify Benjamin's racist views of African Americans. In a scene that takes place on the New York subway, Benjamin says to himself, "*I should have been a Nazi.* . . . Human cattle most of them: you could see in their faces and bodies they don't deserve life, they had nothing to contribute except the small unimaginative existences of their wretched carcasses. . . . They whined their way from cradle to grave. . . . Exterminate them."[50] The bold white supremacy of the novel is made even more troubling because it launched the series of films starring Charles Bronson. Further, that this is one of the inspirations for Marvel Comics' the Punisher should unsettle any comics reader partial to the character.

As it relates to the arguments made here, it seems to me that Ditko's exploration of the right to kill, no matter how metaphorical, along with other popular media, contributed to the conditions that made such a character viable in the comics market, not as a villain (as he first appeared) but as an antihero—precisely the kind of character that Ditko railed against in essays and letters until his death. Additionally, it is not as though the consequences of heroes-who-kill, like the Punisher, are limited to a small window in the 1970s. And fans know it. In a 2019 comics essay, the comics artist Nate Powell addresses this very problem, as the Punisher, and his skull logo, have become symbols of the modern white supremacist movement, "normalizing the language of force" and encroaching fascism promoted by other popular media.[51] Powell's argument is an important and compelling one, and as much as I think that a substantial distance exists between Ditko's intellectual exercises and the issues Powell raises, I cannot, in good conscience, completely divorce them. Superficial readings, misreadings, and outright poor readings of Ditko's work encourage the kind of violence and politics Powell associates with "aggrieved, insecure white Americans with an exaggerated sense of sovereignty" who have "declared their existence as above the law."

Of course, Ditko alone would not have influenced these characters and ideas, but Ditko, within the specific medium of comics, had redefined what it meant to be a hero and set a trend that would not just redefine what actions a hero could take but reshape the comics industry. For writers like Alan Moore, it also means applying a "ferocious moral drive and integrity" to characters who most embody a Ditkovian spirit,[52] and we see this spirit in characters like *Watchmen*'s Rorschach, another character often associated with a violent turn in comics. Just as important as that contribution, Moore *reveres* Ditko. Although Moore's political agenda is very different from Ditko's, at least Ditko felt confident in expressing that agenda, and according to Moore, "that in some ways set him above most of his contemporaries."[53]

The changes Ditko helped usher in can also be witnessed in mainstream comics, as well as in the rise of Code-free comic magazines—like those published by Warren and Marvel in their attempt to revive the genres and content found in the comics published by Bill Gaines at EC in the 1950s. The Comics Code even loosened *its* grip during this same period, allowing horror comics to be published more freely. It would be an overstatement to argue that the work of Steve Ditko was directly responsible for those changes; however, the challenges Ditko presented to the superhero status quo and the adoption of his tactics—if not his philosophy—by the creators who followed him appear to be speaking to a paradigm shift in the cultural consciousness. Though most of these changes in comics were gradual, this shift became inescapably clear in the 1980s with Alan Moore and Dave Gibbons's *Watchmen* (1986). Moore created analogues for the characters Ditko had worked on at Charlton and then imposed on them an extreme, almost parodied version of Ditko's notions of violence—particularly with Rorschach, an emotionally troubled and psychopathic version of the Question / Mr. A.

The violence and drama presented in *Watchmen* are certainly a direct product of the comics of Steve Ditko, and this is true on several different levels—particularly the psychological growth and development of characters, and the right of heroes to kill. As such, *Watchmen* has been criticized and praised for being at the forefront of an era of violent, grim, and gritty comics that attempted to present characters in "real" and "relatable" forms. These were characters that would not be able to escape using extreme violence, and they would not be willing to spare the life of every thief, rapist, and murderer that they encountered; they were characters that had cast moral judgments and dealt with the ramifications of their actions.

These "newly realistic" characters began to appear in long character arcs that simultaneously engrossed the reader and brought about significant internal growth and change for the characters on the page. What is often overlooked is that Moore and Gibbons's *Watchmen* did not invent this approach; Moore drew clear inspiration from Ditko's superhero output of the 1960s—at both Marvel and Charlton—not just by reimagining Ditko's characters but also by adopting Ditko's long-form narrative techniques. What Moore and others mimicked did not appear in superhero comics before Ditko came onto the scene, and they did not exist in any significant sense until a post-Ditko generation of artists and writers, many of whom were Ditko readers and fans, began to dominate the comics industry in the 1970s and early 1980s. The work of Frank Miller along with David Mazzucchelli in *Daredevil: Born Again* (1987) and Miller's work with Klaus Janson and Lynn Varley in *The Dark Knight Returns* (1986) are other classic examples of this Ditko-influenced, mystic liberal style that took mainstream comics by storm in the 1980s.

But Ditko wasn't through. In the 1970s and 1980s, he introduced some of his strangest characters yet.

7

THESE MAGAZINES ARE HAUNTED!

Steve Ditko beyond the Silver Age

Aside from the powerful work that Ditko developed for independent publications like *witzend* and at Charlton—works that would directly inform
Alan Moore and Dave Gibbons's *Watchmen*—the next twenty years would
see some of the most innovative and interesting work of Ditko's career. In
that period, Ditko worked with a number of collaborators like Joe Gill, Wallace Wood, Jack C. Harris, Gerry Conway, Archie Goodwin, Dennis O'Neil,
P. Craig Russell, Paul Levitz, J. M. DeMatteis, Otto Binder, Len Wein, Robert
Kanigher, Sheldon Mayer, Bernie Wrightson, and a number of other prominent contributors to the medium during that period. And although Ditko
continued to produce new, intriguing creator-owned work across a variety of
genres, all the way up to his passing in the summer of 2018, the years 1965 to
1986 will be the final period covered in this volume, as it leads into the publication of *Watchmen*—along with other significant works like those produced
by Frank Miller and his creative partners David Mazzucchelli, Lynn Varley,
and Klaus Janson—which ushered in a sea change to mainstream American
comics. These transformative works were by-products of the work of Steve
Ditko and the mystic liberal ideology found within the pages he produced. As
I discuss in chapters 5 and 6, that ideology was becoming ever more explicit
during this period.

What follows here are several brief considerations of comics that are
among Ditko's most interesting work. It is within many of the stories considered here that Ditko offers refined and concise examples of his philosophy in
practice after its development in the earlier works considered in this volume.
I begin the chapter with a short look at the work he produced for Warren
Publications, and then focus primarily on characters and stories either owned
by Ditko or created and written by Ditko for major publishers. Although my

look at this two-decade period is far from comprehensive—the number of examples is limited, and each example is worthy of its own extended study—what each example offers is an insight into the internal consistency of Ditko's philosophic outlook as he presents it across genres and publishers.

In his Spider-Man and Dr. Strange stories, Ditko refined the visual motifs and narrative themes that made his ideological investments in his earliest comics come to the fore. After those refinements at Marvel, these themes persisted through the later stories considered in this chapter. Ditko imbued each one with even more verve and vigor as characters like Shade the Changing Man, Hawk and Dove, Static, the Mocker, and even a proposed return to Blue Beetle worked to make Ditko's philosophic worldview available to readers. Creator-owned characters like the Mocker and Static were even less restrained in their pursuit and presentation of a consistent ideology and reached the comics direct market through the independent publishers Pacific Comics and Eclipse Comics, respectively.

After leaving Marvel, Ditko picked up more work at Charlton Comics, and in his introduction to *Creepy Presents: Steve Ditko*, Mark Evanier notes that, with the exception of adherence to the Comics Code Authority, Charlton was willing to accept stories "as is," a scenario that was extremely attractive to Ditko and his desire to push away from traditional approaches to comics narratives.[1] In addition to his major superhero contributions at Charlton—such as Blue Beetle, the Question, and Captain Atom—during his post-Marvel period, Ditko produced comics for Dell, Tower, ACG, and DC. However, some of Ditko's most visually arresting work during this period was produced at Jim Warren's publishing house, working on *Creepy* and its sister publication, *Eerie*. Ditko's work at Warren was much more collaborative than many of his contributions throughout the 1960s and 1970s, resulting in comics that not only were masterfully illustrated but also demonstrated a tenacious dedication to creating a sense of sublime awe for the impossible terrors contained within the recesses of cosmic intraspace and the madness that awaits those who lack the apparent conviction of reason.

In chapter 1, I briefly discussed one such story, "Deep Ruby!" It was first published in *Creepy* #6 in 1966, and I cited it as one of numerous examples of Ditko's exploration of cosmic intraspace as it relates to the development and projection of the self. It also presents an important complication to typical readings of Ditko's work that are searching for a strictly Objectivist thread, as opposed to a reading that reveals an ideology that is more distinctly Ditkovian than the singular product of someone else's mind. Ditko contributed frequently to Warren Publishing's *Eerie* and *Creepy* in the early days of both magazines, and he worked from a number of Goodwin scripts. Although I would concede that, in many cases, much of the subtlety and nuance in these collaborations starts with Goodwin's authorial and editorial voice, what collaborative efforts like this demonstrate, just as in Ditko's earliest work discussed in chapter 2, is that through his visualization of the narrative, he is able to infuse a fully formed ideological perspective that, in this case, complements the script written by Archie Goodwin.

In the same period that Ditko was collaborating with Goodwin, he also began introducing new superheroes at DC Comics.

The Creeper

In 1968, Ditko began producing work and creating new characters for DC Comics under editor Dick Giordano. Ditko and Giordano had worked together for a number of years at Charlton on series like *Captain Atom* and *Blue Beetle*, so the timing of the pairing seems natural. Early on at DC, Ditko premiered three characters: first, the Creeper with writer Don Segall in *Showcase* #73 (March 1968), and then the Hawk and the Dove in *Showcase* #75 (June 1968), the latter of which was developed with writer Steve Skeates, whom Ditko had also worked with at Charlton on *Blue Beetle* #4 for the "Kill Vic Sage!" story. At the time, *Showcase* served as an anthology series, aiming to either present new characters or spotlight minor and forgotten characters to gauge reader interest. Essentially it was a way for DC to give new series and characters a trial run without taking the risk of producing and marketing a new series cold. Most famously, *Showcase* #4 (October 1956) introduced the revitalized Barry Allen version of the Flash, which for most readers and fans marks the beginning of the so-called Silver Age of Comics, one of the hallmarks of which is a return to prominence for superhero stories in the comics marketplace.

Ditko's offerings were successful, and both the Creeper and Hawk and Dove received their own series in 1968. However, both series were short-lived, as Ditko briefly left comics and returned home to deal with a tuberculosis relapse. *Beware the Creeper* lasted six issues, and Ditko collaborated with writer Denny O'Neil, who at first worked under his pen name, Sergius O'Shaughnessy. When Ditko returned to DC a decade later, he produced a number of other Creeper stories, first for a series called *First Issue Special*, and then a number of backup features for *World's Finest Comics*.

The Creeper is often described as being a strange reading experience,[2] and I assume that the less familiarity a reader has with Ditko's other works, the more this feeling is heightened. In some ways, the Creeper is a fairly standard Ditko character and adopts many of the tropes found in earlier Ditko comics: the superhero's alter ego, Jack Ryder, is a hard-hitting investigative journalist who finds himself at odds with his station manager à la Peter Parker, Vic Sage, Rex Graine, and others; the superhero has an encounter with a wizened scientist type who provides him with the tools and special powers requisite for superheroing; the superhero finds himself misunderstood by and at odds with the authorities; there is a steep learning curve for the hero as he develops over time; and the superhero often finds himself squaring off against all manner of moral and civic corruption. So what is so strange about the Creeper?

Jack Ryder received his powers after investigating the kidnapping of a research scientist named Dr. Yatz. During the rescue, Ryder is stabbed, and fearing that escape and survival are no longer in reach, Yatz injects Ryder with a secret super-soldier serum and stashes a molecular transporter he invented—inside of Ryder's open wound! The combination of the serum and device allows Ryder to gain his superhuman powers and also transition from his street clothes to his costumed identity as the Creeper at the flick of a switch. After stitching Ryder up, Dr. Yatz is shot to death by his kidnappers, leaving Ryder and the reader with lots of questions about how he can take advantage of his new abilities.

Aside from the unusually violent origin story, I am hard-pressed to say that this alone is what readers might have found so strange. Perhaps, then, it's the Creeper's garish, bright yellow, green, and red costume—an outfit Ryder cobbled together as a disguise during his attempt to save Dr. Yatz. But this isn't quite satisfying, either. Of course, the costume is offbeat, but it doesn't strike me as *that* unusual when stacked against Ditko's other innovative and unique costume designs. Rather, a big part of what was so jarring about the Creeper in those early issues is one particular trait: his laugh.

The Creeper bounds around and punches people just like any other superhero, but he does all of this while bellowing out a bizarre cackle that he uses to disorient his foes, especially when he may be physically outmatched or at least outnumbered. This kind of haunted mirthfulness is a great tool in the Creeper's arsenal, driving criminals to the brink of madness just before the Creeper strikes. Ditko would employ a similar trait for later characters like the Mocker and Odd Man, but perhaps because of when and where the Creeper first appeared, this kind of joy is unsettling for readers—particularly those encountering the character ex post facto in a world where ardently serious comic book heroes are the order of the day.

However readers take the Creeper's laugh, I am far less interested in reader response than in thinking through what is at stake for Ditko in choosing this particular character trait. Like the other narrative choices Ditko makes, this one is not without intellectual and philosophic consequence, and what is playing out is a metaphysics of joy that expands on an Objectivist framework where happiness is a conscious state that follows "the achievement of one's values."[3] Neither Ditko nor the writers he worked with early on explicitly link the Creeper's laugh to a particular set of values; however, as we have seen, Ditko's comics are not bound by dialogue or narration to get their point across. The Creeper is no different, and it is through his vigilante actions that he is able to express his values: justice and the pursuit of truth. These are the same values that Jack Ryder does explicitly claim for himself as a journalist, but while Jack Ryder, hard-hitting reporter, might be hamstrung by his station manager or the limits of the law, the Creeper knows no such bounds and is free to pursue these ideals to their furthest end.

In and of itself, this doesn't seem like a great revelation when compared to other superheroes whose alter egos are agents of the press, but again, what sets the Creeper apart in Ditko's intellectual configuration is not simply that there is a joy in pursuing just causes; it's how the pursuit of truth and justice is received by those who oppose it. What makes the Creeper's cackle so unsettling for his enemies is that his joy in doing what is right, by embracing his life, immediately calls into question the values and existence of his enemies. Ditko, in 2008, wrote that the creation of fear by his heroes was a consistent theme throughout his superhero comics, and the Creeper "actively played at scaring criminals." Ditko was able to achieve this by illustrating the character with "bright colors and openly challenging, *laughing at*, [villains'] guns and power."⁴ The Creeper's laugh creates a sense of inner turmoil and dissonance so great that villains are "gripped by the cold clutch of terror [in] a moment of *dread*, *guilt*, and *despair*."⁵ Because of their legally and morally corrupt actions, villains in Ditko's Creeper stories are incapable of anything describable as happiness but instead, as Rand describes, are held captive by a "chronic state of terror."⁶ For both Ditko and Rand, that chronic state of terror is a symptom of a rejection of life, and the embrace of irrational beliefs.

Where Ditko parts ways with Rand and rounds out his metaphysics is through the Creeper's individual actions, which are not metaphorically limited to his singular experience or rational values. He is not acting *only* "in the service of *his* life."⁷ The Creeper is a symbolic agent of the cosmos, one that expresses his internal self through his garish costume, spirited banter, and haunting laugh, and one that acts as a karmic intercessor when *others* have been wronged or made to suffer. This flies in the face of the Objectivist notion that "the universe is neutral"; it is indifferent, and as a result, "pain, suffering, failure do not have a metaphysical significance—they do not reveal the nature of reality."⁸ This theme plays out in at least two interesting ways: as a reporter, Jack Ryder works for an industry that, to the public mind, ought to be objective and neutral in all matters, reporting simply on the facts without interfering for one ideal or another. Ditko clearly rejects this notion on its own as being too limited; as such, all his journalist heroes not only collect and report on objective facts but also act as activists for truth and justice, in stark contrast to caricatures like the Neutralist, discussed in chapter 2, who refuse to choose a side.

Yet, in an important way, Ryder is different. When Ditko returned as the sole writer for the character in 1978, Ryder's place of employment had been firmly established: Cosmic TV. As on the nose as it is, Jack Ryder, the Creeper, is a literal cosmic agent, and this plays out with symbolic consequence throughout his adventures: revealing that the cosmos is *not*, and should not be, neutral in matters of injustice, that there *is* a metaphysical significance to such a state. In the form of the Creeper, Jack Ryder hyperbolically embodies the pleasure in acting on one's virtues, alongside each of his foes, with their distorted features and frail egos, revealing the nature of reality as competing forces of virtue and evil, white and black.

As theoretical as any of his other works, Ditko's Creeper stories, especially those where he is the singular creative force, also reveal an interesting contrast from other comics, like those featuring Dr. Strange, the Question, or Mr. A: they're funny. It's fitting that a series that explores the metaphysics of joy is among Ditko's most whimsical work, but it is also important, as it reveals a complex interweaving of theoretical, metaphysical ideals within stories that were constructed for the kind of mass appeal necessary at a publisher like DC. In fact, it was at DC during this period where Ditko developed some of his most complex and theoretically invested characters since Dr. Strange. Just two months after the Creeper appeared, Ditko introduced two more such heroes: the Hawk and the Dove.

Hawk and Dove

Like *Beware the Creeper*, *The Hawk and the Dove* ran only six issues, but Ditko departed after the second, and including the duo's first appearance in *Showcase*, readers received only three complete Ditko stories for the characters. Although they would appear here and there before being completely revised by Karl and Barbara Kesel in the 1980s, Ditko never returned to Hawk and Dove as he did for the Creeper's later appearances in *World's Finest Comics*. However, in the limited time that he did work on the characters, Ditko presented an interesting set of challenges to those who would try to reduce his comics to Objectivist or right-wing tracts.

Ditko and Skeates's Hawk and Dove set themselves apart from many of Ditko's other characters because they received their initial cues from the vocabulary of the antiwar and youth movements of the 1960s. *Showcase* #75 introduced readers to brothers Don and Hank Hall, high school students attending a demonstration at a local university. Don, who would later become Dove, finds himself on the side of the antiwar and pacifist protesters, while Hank, later Hawk, is firmly and loudly on the side of the pro-war counterprotest. Don and Hank's father, a judge in criminal court, constantly admonishes the boys for their bickering, though he never chooses a side and is more worried about their inability to reason through their arguments.

The boys receive their powers after chasing down a hit man who attempted to assassinate their father. In chasing the man down, the boys are trapped in a room, arguing about the "right" way to go about capturing the hit man and avenging their father. As they squabble, a mysterious disembodied voice fills the cramped space of the room, informing both boys that they will receive powers that reflect their internal states and underdeveloped philosophic stances. Without coincidence, this voice behaves just like H. P. Blavatsky's Mahatmas discussed in chapter 2: an intercessor from parts—nay, dimensions—unknown who arrives to impart special wisdom or abilities and then disappears from the scene. After being granted their powers by this occult agent, Hank and Don escape, and by cooperating they are able to capture the hit man and bring him to justice, only to find out that their father doesn't condone their vigilantism.

Because the characters are initially entrenched in the contemporary debates about war, it would be easy enough to anchor Hawk and Dove to this particular historical moment and conversation, and such an exploration certainly has merit. The trouble with such a reading is that it is far too superficial and lends itself to the interpolation of the readers' own biases as opposed to examining the characters under the themes and circumstances consistent with Ditko's work, principally the exploration of the mind and the complexities of the human experience found in that exploration. Because Ditko was consistently preoccupied with such matters, what I propose is that instead of reading Don, Hank, and their father as literal characters inhabiting the DC Universe (whatever that meant in 1968), let us instead consider them as analogues for competing pressures and principles populating an individual mind. Put differently, as we can with Ditko's other works, let us place Hawk and Dove within the Aristotelian framework that Ditko was so fond of and treat Hank, Don, and their father as the artistic representation of ideas—ideas not necessarily limited to the social conflicts of the late 1960s.

As we have seen throughout Ditko's work presented here, one of the major presuppositions of his approach to the mind is that each person contains an urge for violent, despotic, brute force, and even when it is principled, it must be tempered and ultimately repressed in favor of a more rational approach. As a clear case in point, one need not look much farther than Dormammu: a cruel, monomaniacal authoritarian enemy to human existence, but also one bound by an ethical code (even though skewed) and by his role as a barrier against a mindless mob. A similar scenario arises in *Shade the Changing Man*, as will be seen later, with the character Xexlo. In *The Hawk and the Dove*, Hank Hall serves a dialectical purpose similar to Dormammu and Xexlo, but because of his age, along with his intellectual and emotional immaturity, Hank presents an opportunity for redemption through a reflection on, and refinement of, his principles. One of the ways this occurs is through Hawk's inability to find success as a vigilante hero without being tempered by Dove's pacifism and insistence on nonviolent negotiation. The other emerges through the constant disapproval of Hank and Don's father, who sees Hawk's "vicious and unlawful attack[s]," even on criminals, as irresponsible, dangerous, and a threat to the rule of law.[9]

Given the language and tenor of the dialogue between the Halls, it seems apparent that Ditko was largely responsible for this admonition of Hawk's actions, a position that runs counter to any notion that Ditko's sympathies lay with Hawk. Even *if* Ditko would have sided with Hawk on the Vietnam War debate,[10] it is clear that the war alone is not what is at stake in *The Hawk and the Dove*; rather, the stakes are the soul and state of the youthful mind as it tries to develop its own set of principles through careful reflection. Further, it is hardly the case that Hawk's violence and action-first disposition are presented as unimpeachable. Rather, his actions lack any kind of intellectual grounding or the temperament necessary to allow for nuance. Just as we saw in Ditko's development of the "right to kill," to avoid being classified as anti-mind, and therefore anti-life, one must choose to engage one's capacity to reason, acting not as an aggressor but as a defender. Swinging the pendulum too far away from retaliatory violence, though, is equally problematic in the Ditkovian paradigm.

Don Hall, Dove, represents just such a swing in that direction. Although Steve Skeates indubitably played a major part in the long-term development of Hawk and Dove, Dove's actions are very much in line with the kinds of heroes Ditko had presented in the past. Dove, like Dr. Strange when he engages in combat, first attempts to reason with his adversaries and then takes evasive and defensive maneuvers. However, unlike the more intellectually and psychologically mature Dr. Strange, Dove never fully engages in combat after reason fails; instead he attempts to subdue his opponents as nonviolently as possible by evading them and forcing them to tangle and subdue themselves. These actions are absolutely compatible with how characters like the Question and Mr. A ultimately rely on intellectual and psychological weakness to eventually be the undoing of any number of their rivals and foes.

By and large, this approach proves to be effective for Dove, and while Ditko was working on the characters and plots, Dove is far more effective at capturing criminals than Hawk and his blind rage. Although Dove is often portrayed as petrified and flailing in combat, he gets the job done, unlike Hawk, who even when successful takes beating after beating. The takeaway here seems to be that Dove, under Ditko's hand and plotting, represents an effective means to an end, but like Hawk, Dove's approach and the principles behind it were at best underdeveloped and misguided. The deliberate choice to portray the ideologies of *both* Hawk and Dove as fragments of a whole goes a long way in demonstrating that Ditko's approach is not so simple as taking the then conservative political point of view where Hawk would obviously have been right.

Although it is not a point of view I currently accept, one might be able to make the case that Dove's complexity resulted only from the intervention of Skeates. But this argument would necessarily require jettisoning everything else Ditko had produced in the fifteen years before *The Hawk and the Dove*, along with everything that came after it. It would also necessitate an assumption that Ditko held a purely monolithic political perspective or that his objective was to create didactic tracts that demanded intellectual fealty, as opposed to exploring questions about individual existence and creation. Because Ditko is clearly more interested in the questions than demanding exclusive answers, Dove, like Hawk, is on the hook when it comes to questions about his ideology.

What is primarily called into question for Dove is, first, his subservience to public opinion over his own conscience. Throughout all three of the Hawk and Dove stories that Ditko worked on, this theme is constant and, in almost undeniable ways, is reminiscent of Peter Parker and his desire to be part of the in crowd in Spider-Man's early adventures. Like the nascent Peter Parker, Dove finds himself at the beginning of his own quest for internal growth and development, but unlike Peter, Dove is much more willing to vocalize his position when debating his brother. Dove is also presented as intellectually weak because of his views on personal property when, after a robbery that Hawk fails to stop, he says that none of the victims of the robbery "would have been hurt! The guests would just have lost money that they'd never really miss!" The boys' father quickly admonishes Don/Dove for being "pretty free with other people's property."[11] The point here is not just that property rights are important, but also that Dove's dismissal of property rights or his argument that the wealthy are less victims of crime because of their socioeconomic status is just as unproductive as the violent, brute force Hawk engages in: both are destructive to property; both place the lives and property of others in jeopardy; both, according to Judge Hall, lack a foundation in objective principles.

If Don and Hank operate on the same Aristotelian narrative premise that seems to have guided Ditko's other characters, then the emotional, intellectual, and ethical polarities that Don and Hank represent need to be both balanced and challenged by the one force capable of doing so: the rational, principled human mind. Judge Hall stands in for that force. Of paramount importance to Judge Hall is the rule of law—at least laws that are objectively defined—and while he continually admonishes both of his sons for their underdeveloped ideologies, he does not wholly reject either approach. Instead, just as Hawk and Dove have difficulty succeeding against criminals without each other's willing cooperation, Judge Hall blends the apparent strengths of both Don's and Hank's outlooks. In essence, Judge Hall performs the function of the mind: sorting out competing ideas, accepting and dismissing whatever portions of them he chooses, as his principles allow. For Ditko, as realized through Judge Hall, the chief function of the mind is to take in as many ideas as possible, sift through them, and retain the nuggets of wisdom it finds, regardless of where the idea originated. This imagination of the mind is at once merciless and generous.

For Judge Irwin Hall, "the *only* way to solve problems is through logic," and it is "not enough to repeat slogans"; one has to "have more *reasoning* behind [one's] beliefs."[12] To that end, as a justice in criminal court, Judge Hall is merciless in his sentencing of convicted criminals, less because he wants to do it and more because he seems to believe that he owes it to them to enact the strictest possible sentence, certainly when it comes to serious crimes of graft, assault, murder, and the like—anything that does direct harm to the property or person of another individual.

When one criminal begs for clemency because he "didn't mean to do it," Judge Hall sternly fires back, "Sir, this is a court of law! Law is based on facts, on logic . . . not on emotion! . . . How you feel . . . is irrelevant!" And then, pointing directly at the reader, "You *knowingly* committed a crime. . . . The damage done to the innocent cannot be wiped away by how you feel! You don't deserve favors or special consideration!"[13] In an obvious sense, the judge's harsh words here mirror those of Mr. A when exemplifying the right to kill, and Judge Hall certainly seems to see cold, logical enforcement of the law—insofar as the law is a defense mechanism for protecting the lives and property of others—as a matter of choosing the ingredients of life over death. In fact, he says as much just a page later when discussing the same ruling with his sons: "Courts exist for the *protection* of the *innocent*! To make sure that the guilty pay for violating another man's rights!"[14] And while the judge is presenting a notion of justice particular to Ditko and many other mystic liberals, the larger significance of his words and actions in the courtroom balances the opposing ideological forces presented by Don and Hank. Whereas Hank loudly argues that his father should have invented a stiffer sentence for the convict, and Don argues for one that "would have helped rehabilitate that man," Judge Hall splits the difference between them by arguing not for an extreme solution or even a compromise but for reasoned action based on what is presented as logical clarity.

But it is not just the criminal acts that come before him in court where Judge Hall refuses leniency. When he refuses to support the vigilante actions of Hawk—because he operates outside the law and thus jeopardizes the property and safety of others—Judge Hall is skewered in the media, but he refuses to back down, unaware that Hawk is really his son, Hank. The judge's unwavering conviction takes center stage in *The Hawk and the Dove* #1 when, because of his stance on vigilantism, "he is viciously attacked by those who oppose his views, but gains no support from those that agree. . . . They simply won't get involved."[15] In the panel that contains this quote, Judge Hall stands firm with his arms crossed as he is flanked by the screaming faces of his opponents and the averted, evasive gazes of his silent supporters, and what seems to be at stake in the narration box, as well as the imagery, is the intellectual cowardice of those who know what is "right" but will say or do nothing to defend that position (fig. 7.1). Indeed, as emphasized by the visuals in this image, these are precisely the stakes for much of Ditko's oeuvre and his own relationship to his work; and Ditko makes clear the philosophy behind these images in comics like *Mysterious Suspense*, the Mr. A stories, and other creator-owned works all the way up to his death: one must have the intellectual fortitude to stand by one's own reasoning and principles, regardless of the consequences. In a more oblique, but certainly important, sense, this kind of uncompromising attitude and belief in one's self is also part and parcel of mystic liberalism's insistence on harnessing the power of the mind to create one's own circumstances, regardless of what others may believe or do: a commitment to the self breeds contentment, whereas acquiescing to the whims of others is at best a gamble.

Judge Hall's ruthless commitment to his own sense of logic and reason—his own mind—as a means of judging and reshaping society, of course, is a function of the mystic liberal notion of mind power, but we should not understand Judge Hall's merciless actions as they relate to application of the law as a heartlessness toward humanity or even those who have been ruled guilty of a crime. Ditko, through Judge Hall, goes to significant lengths to demonstrate that, through honest self-examination, *anyone* can reform their self and lead a just, productive life. However, this redemption cannot come from the hand of some external, merciful savior—a supreme forgiver—but is only earned through one's own efforts to change. *The Hawk and the Dove* #2, Ditko's last issue in the series, makes this plain through the actions of an unnamed convict who is wrangled into a prison escape against his will and better judgment.

Titled "Jailbreak!," the issue opens in a prison where Harker, a "maniac" and "sadist," is brutalizing several of his fellow inmates to force them to take part in an escape. Our unnamed exemplar of self-redemption laments to himself that he has no choice but to obey Harker, lest Harker kill him and anyone else who opposes. "I'm paying for my debt, so I can get outta here and lead an honest life! But Harker won't let that be!"[16] This introduction is worth noting for at least two reasons: first, it demonstrates the man's *inner* desire to recognize his failings and willingness to reform, and second, it shows the dangers of outside intrusions and influences on those who might lack the constitution to hold fast to their convictions. In the latter case, it is less that such individuals are necessarily undesirable than that they are susceptible to danger as they travel the inner path to redemption and selfhood. Shortly after the jailbreak happens, the forced-escapee crosses paths with Judge Hall when the convicts attempt to hijack his car.

Figure 7.1. Judge Hall in the Ditko motif of the rational hero flanked on all sides by competing worldviews, emphasized in the expressions on the faces of those holding competing views. Dialogue by Steve Skeates; art by Steve Ditko; Gaspar Saladino letters. "The Dove Is a Very Gentle Bird," *The Hawk and the Dove* #1 (August–September 1968). © DC Comics.

Seeing this as his opportunity to separate himself from the other escaped convicts, the forced-escapee screams that he sees police cars on the horizon and that his fellow convicts should scatter, thus saving Judge Hall, Hank, and the judge's brother from further violence by the convicts. After the others vacate the scene, the forced-escapee surrenders himself to Judge Hall, revealing that there were never any police cars approaching; it was all a diversion to save the judge and his family. The forced-escapee has no idea who Judge Hall is when he enacts his plan, and after he surrenders and explains himself, Judge Hall *offers* to testify on the forced-escapee's behalf. In this moment, the judge is not necessarily demonstrating mercy, especially as he insists that "he can't promise" clemency for the man, but he is showing his commitment to those who commit to integrity and themselves.

Our forced-escapee makes plain his own worthiness when he says to Judge Hall, "I don't *want* any promises! I just want what's *fair*! Nobody owes me anything!"[17] Key to this moment is not that Judge Hall retracts any previously held position (he does not) but that he sees the nuance in human behavior and action, at once recognizing personal responsibility and acknowledging that when one is sucked into a criminal or otherwise deleterious life, it is difficult to escape. In a certain sense, Judge Hall embodies the ancient axiom "God helps those who help themselves," a notion rooted in ancient Greek dramas as well as Aesop's Fables, which has been reapplied across Western religion, is often attributed to Ben Franklin, and is foundational to mystic liberalism when, for instance, Dale Carnegie calls for his followers to "let the other man save his face."[18]

With Judge Hall at the center, maintaining the delicate balance between the competing forces of Hank and Don, Ditko's Hawk and Dove stories are an exercise in demonstrating the necessity of a rational mind in finding success and the self, as well as an opportunity to guide readers through his philosophy without being overly didactic. In a certain way, this is the kind of leading by example that Carnegie calls for in *How to Win Friends and Influence People*, but it is not at all clear that Ditko is making direct reference to Carnegie. Rather, the balance that he strikes in his collaboration with Skeates, along with the balance presented by Judge Hall, offers readers an opportunity to consume his philosophy and methodology for exploring and defining the self, as opposed to ramming a worldview down the reader's throat.

Judge Hall's scolding of his sons for their political opinions is never to say that either one has an exclusive hold on the truth or the "right" way to approach the problems of the world but that both are deficient without introspection and a clear sense of why the boys hold the beliefs that they do. For Ditko, whatever platitudes are espoused by the holder of any one mind are just so much vacuous nonsense without first excavating one's own thoughts and rationalizing a commitment to them. Contra readings that might label Ditko as an archconservative, or those that pin him strictly to Objectivist thought, I have endeavored to establish a more nuanced approach that is willing to embrace a multiplicity of ideals and political positions for Ditko, which are established on his own consistent and reasoned principles.

After Ditko's abrupt departure from *The Hawk and the Dove* in 1968, he never returned to the characters. Although this meant that he was never able to fully realize his vision for Hank and Don alongside Steve Skeates, a little less than a decade later, Ditko offered readers of DC Comics another new character that, like his previous creations, delved into an exploration of the mind. But this time, instead of presenting an earthbound praxeology of mental clarity, Ditko took his ideas off-world into universes secreted away by a nearly impenetrable barrier of chaos and confusion.

Shade the Changing Man

In the summer of 1977, DC Comics was priming for what is commonly known in fan circles as the DC Explosion, which began the following summer in 1978. The publisher had released several new titles, featuring newer characters like Black Lightning, Firestorm, and Isis. The Explosion was set to introduce fans to several new or rebooted titles, and house ads boasted more pages and stories, which often meant backup or cofeatures. Those extra pages and backups also meant higher cover prices. The campaign for the Explosion lasted about three months before what came to be known as the DC Implosion, when over thirty titles were canceled as a result of market overreach.[19] Of those, twenty were abruptly canceled, and issues that had completed pencils, inks, and lettering were published in two issues of in-house-only comics called *Cancelled Comic Cavalcade*. Only thirty-five copies of each of those two issues were printed in black and white, and the stories were never made available to the public by DC until some stories were reprinted in character- and artist-specific collections in the late 2000s and 2010s. Among the victims of the Implosion was one of Steve Ditko's creations: Shade the Changing Man.

Ditko conceived and plotted the entirety of Shade's eight-issue run (the ninth issue was printed in *Cancelled Comic Cavalcade*), and the veteran writer and comics historian Michael Fleisher was credited as the writer, likely working from Ditko's rough panel script. Different from any other superhero comics being published by DC at the time, the basic premise is that Rac Shade possesses the mysterious M-Vest, which allows him to project a distorted appearance so as to intimidate and terrify his enemies. But although the vest provides a force field for Shade, the projected version of himself that Shade's enemies see is largely a product of their own (mis)perceptions. Ditko complicates this ability in places when the projection of the vest also matches Shade's own emotional state, but in either case, the image that the M-Vest casts is not a literal, physical form but the product of some internal state.

As the series opens, Shade is an Earth expert and security agent who had recently been wrongly convicted of treason on his home world of Meta, a zone outside of Earth on the other side of a chaotic realm known as the Zero Zone. During a prison break, Shade escapes with several other convicts, retrieves the M-Vest, and vows to clear his name, all the while being hunted by his fiancée and fellow security agent, Mellu. While the people of Earth are unaware of Meta's existence—the Zero Zone prevents Earth from detecting Meta—the people of Meta are absolutely aware of Earth and have stationed a base of operations there called the Occult Research Center (ORC), in a building that looks suspiciously like Dr. Strange's Sanctum Sanctorum and even has the same distinctive windows. The reasons for Meta's interest in Earth are never made explicit (perhaps because the series was canceled before Ditko could get to it), but it is clear that the villainous criminal element of Meta wants to conquer and rule over Earth so that they can, in turn, gain control over Meta.

Although the characters, especially Mellu, have an opportunity to breathe and develop over time, the final fates of Shade, Mellu, Earth, Meta, the ORC, and the rest are never fully resolved because of the series' short life, and the comic ends with Shade lunging into the Zero Zone through a demonic-looking gateway similar to those rendered in Dr. Strange, stories like "Deep Ruby!," or any number of weird fiction stories Ditko produced. In the long-unpublished ninth issue, Shade explores the Zero Zone and encounters characters, forces, and ideas (usually all three at once) similar to those found in Dr. Strange that ask philosophical questions and challenge Shade with ideological difference in his effort to restore order to the ironically named internal Meta Zone. Limited though the series was, Ditko included within those nine short issues a complex view of human relationships and returned to themes of psychological perception and projection, all set against a backdrop that explored the connection between the mind and the body, as symbolized by the disconnected realms of Meta and Earth, respectively.

When we first encounter Rac Shade, he is more or less a fully realized character in the Ditkovian sense, capturing the sense of life that Ditko's heroes often possessed in their first appearances, like the Question and Mr. A; or were in search of, like Spider-Man; or even those who were somewhere in between, like Dr. Strange and Blue Beetle. Although Rac Shade faces many challenges, like being wrongly accused of treason, his philosophic-ethical compass is set and unwavering. And he respects this uncompromising attitude in others, as he does with the combative and morally suspect Xexlo in the Zero Zone; Shade disapproves of Xexlo's methods and motives, respects his conviction, and is disappointed that Xexlo brutishly and unthinkingly forced his hand in combat, lamenting, "We could have parted as friends or allies instead of enemies! But if *death* is all that will satisfy you—."[20] Of course, linking intellectual and ideological weakness to death is not new for Ditko—to be anti-mind is to be anti-life—but as Ditko demonstrates throughout *Shade the Changing Man*, confusion or errors in judgment are not necessarily the same as being anti-mind (fig. 7.2). Through Mellu, and her estrangement from Shade, Ditko offers a meditation on the challenges of human relationships, especially those that arise from

Figure 7.2. Shade and Xexlo personify the intellectual, often internal, battle between competing ideas and world-views. Dialogue by Michael Fleisher; art by Steve Ditko; Ben Oda letters. Originally unpublished story intended for *Shade the Changing Man* #9. "The Deadly Ally," in *The Steve Ditko Archive*, vol. 1 (DC Comics, 2011). © DC Comics.

misunderstandings, those caused by emotional impediments, and those where one's experiences do not fit within the narrative issued by authorities.

When the series opens, Shade has escaped, and Mellu is assigned to (and even argues for her right to) hunt him down and assassinate him for his crimes of treason. Mellu is eager to take on this task because she believes Shade to be responsible for crippling her parents, high-ranking Metan officials. Distraught over the state of two of the people she cared for the most, Mellu's judgment is clouded, and she accepts the conspiracy against Shade as fact—as does nearly everyone else on Meta. Throughout their estrangement, Shade remains committed to Mellu and trusts what he knows of her inner strength and convictions, believing that, given time, the cloud of negative emotion will be lifted, revealing the truth to her. Without question, Mellu is a heroic character, and at the end of issue #8, she and Shade are finally reunited after she, on her own, comes to realize Shade's innocence. While Mellu's narrative role certainly demonstrates the dangers of being overly emotional about any decision, her greater functions are, first, to demonstrate the ability for one to make an honest mistake that can be exacerbated by conviction and, second, to show how commitment to one's ideals can be manipulated or even weaponized by others. The only way to defeat such external pressures is through deep reflection.

To put a finer, more mystic liberal point on it: even though Mellu hunts and tries to kill Shade, that Shade still believes in her inherent goodness and justness, is attracted to her, and wants to repair his relationship with her reveals what Nathaniel Branden would say is a *"trust in our process*—and, as a consequence, *a disposition to expect success for our efforts."*[21] Norman Vincent Peale's *The Power of Positive Thinking* offers an earlier, identical approach: "Formulate and stamp indelibly on your mind a mental picture of yourself as succeeding." That "process," in Branden's formulation one of reason, mutual respect, and a particular view of self-esteem, plays out for Mellu through each of the interactions she has with Shade throughout the series and her earlier, happier memories and experiences with him. In doing so, she does as Branden would later prescribe: she confronts her destructive voices and "engage[s] them in inner dialogue,"[22] ultimately cleansing herself of earlier doubt.

Just as Mellu experiences cognitive dissonance about her feelings for Shade, with that dissonance manifesting in her behavior, so Shade's presence offers readers a similar kind of psychological insight into the workings of his mind. Shade's actions are direct and confident, his posture almost always perfectly erect—all indications of the clarity of mind that Shade has. But it is not Shade's demeanor alone that projects his inner self; the mysterious M-Vest, too, offers such a projection. While the primary, practical function of the vest is to exploit the psycho-ethical weaknesses of his enemies, Ditko also uses the vest to provide visual cues for Shade's immediate emotional state—most often expressing frustration, resolve, or a kind of manic glee when squaring off against his enemies.

Whatever the case may be for the M-Vest's projections, they are a clear indicator of Ditko's long-standing interest—and the interest of mystic liberalism—in the outward manifestation of the inner self. However, as the origins of the M-Vest are revealed, readers also learn that the vest was created to allow its wearer to penetrate the "force barriers of varying strength and intensity" that encapsulate the Meta Zone and prevent Earth's knowledge of this separate plane of existence. The vest was initially designed for *mining* the Zero Zone and protecting the wearer from the potentially harmful effects of that chaotic space.[23] This rationale for the vest's initial invention, for excavation and insulation, gives further evidence for the vest's symbolic role in Ditko's ongoing concern with allegorizing the search and development of the self through an inward process. Shade—and any other wearer of the vest—embarks on this search for and development of the self as he moves outward from Meta to the Zero Zone and eventually to Earth, further underscoring the vest's symbolic value as it demonstrates Meta's role as the plane of the mind and its efforts to project its values and sense of being to the outer world, the body, as represented by Earth.

Unsurprisingly, the relationship (or lack thereof) between Meta and Earth is one of the major background elements of *Shade the Changing Man*, and Earth is often made susceptible to the more chaotic, despotic, and formless beings from Meta who seek control over Earth. Similar to the dynamic in Dr. Strange, the rational, good people of Meta (the mind) have pledged themselves to stand as protectors against those corrupting elements that would try to rule Earth (the body). Shade, of course, is not the lone avatar for Ditko's and mystic liberalism's man-at-his-best ideology. Already established on Earth is a Metan agency to simultaneously protect and study Earth, by vainly revealing the hidden truths of the mind to Earth's unbelieving, sense-denying inhabitants.

That agency is the less-than-fortuitously named Occult Research Center, led by the equally less-than-fortuitously named Wizor, and it serves an ironic but important purpose. Just as occult knowledge is obscured by the mundane world, research into the occult is meant to reveal those secret truths, if only one is willing to trust in the observations and experiences of one's own mind. The purpose of the ORC, as Wizor tells Mellu, is that "whenever evidence of Meta's existence is accidentally *exposed*, we can make people *disbelieve* it by insisting on the *truth* of it!" Wizor also says, "When we insist on the truth of it, [the people of Earth] refuse to credit even their own *senses* and disbelieve all the stronger!"[24] But as the work of Ditko and other mystic liberals would suggest, a conscious awareness of the activity of the mind, no matter how much it tries to reveal its truth, does not prevent the mind from affecting the external world. For immediate evidence of this, one need only consider the Law of Attraction, as first proposed by H. P. Blavatsky, then accepted and modified by New Thought and its progeny, along with the acceptance of that law by supposedly materialist Objectivists like Nathaniel Branden. Further, although superficial, Wizor's attempts to shield Earthlings from full knowledge of Meta might seem to conflict with Ditko's otherwise consistent presentation of the mind, but Wizor's actions still exemplify a persistence of the mind to make itself known through the body.

At no point does Wizor ever deny the truth of Metan involvement on Earth; it is Earthlings who are unable to recognize that the events on their planet are a consequence of actions begun on a separate, internalized plane—in this case, zone—of existence. Rather, Wizor exploits Earthlings' unwillingness to be reflective and accept the truth, so that they can protect themselves from what they are not willing to accept. In a certain sense, this recalls Matthew 11:15's call for those who have ears to hear, and although Ditko was an atheist (at least opposed to the three major Western religions), this kind of thinking is a particularity of Christian-based occult thought, like that found in New Thought.

In the end, *Shade the Changing Man* was one of the most interesting products of Ditko's work-for-hire efforts during this period. *Shade* offered distinct and profound challenges to its readers that resonated for decades to come as the characters and their worlds were reimagined by different creative teams. Perhaps most prominent was the series from DC's Vertigo imprint in the 1990s by writer Peter Milligan and several artists, with the bulk of the series illustrated by Chris Bachalo. Although Milligan and company completely disrupted and reimagined much of what made Ditko's character fit within a particular ideological construct, a core theme of the series was the issue of identity, and Shade, who in this version is trapped in the body of a convicted serial killer, remained a sort of avatar of the mind as he had in the Ditko series.

The Milligan series, also like Ditko's, explored the complexity of human interactions, presented through the relationship between Shade and a woman whose parents were murdered by Shade's host body. This kind of change and reinvention for corporately owned characters is anything but surprising, and for Ditko to maintain the long-term integrity of his characters and the philosophy that propelled their narratives forward, he had to independently publish these stories, retaining ownership of the characters. Of course, Ditko had done this before with Mr. A, but with the changes that came to the comics publishing landscape resulting from the rise of the direct market and the black-and-white alternative comics boom of the 1980s, new opportunities were arising for unique ideas.

Static

In keeping with his previous emphasis on master-and-apprentice relationships in characters like Blue Beetle, Dr. Strange, and others, *Static* introduced readers to Stac Rae, a research assistant to scientist Dr. Ed Serch in the Quest Research Lab, where they have developed "an experimental space-environmental suit" that is, tellingly, designed to protect wearers from the extremes of the outside world and allow them to work in the harshest, most unforgiving conditions.[25] After an attack on Stac and Dr. Serch resulting from industrial espionage, Stac discovers that his mind has bonded with the suit, unlocking even greater potential.

The series portrays a complex set of relationships between Stac, Dr. Serch, and the doctor's daughter, Fera, who cares deeply about Stac. The primary conflict in the relationship between these three, and throughout the series, centers on the suit and Stac's use of it to act, as the story puts it early on, as an independent "agent of justice."[26] Fera opposes Stac's use of the suit for anything other than its intended, lab-based function and believes that any illegal activity they encounter should be left to the police. Stac, of course, argues for his continued use of the suit, which provides him with the ability to defend both himself and the innocent, and to operate as an agent of justice, even if outside the law.

Dr. Serch sympathizes with Stac but often finds himself pondering the wisdom of that decision. The immediate surface argument that exists among the characters focuses on the ethics of Stac's use of the suit and operating outside the law, but just beneath that are the themes that should be more than familiar by this point: Stac's exercising of his mind to control the suit/body that contains him, using his mind to manipulate the world around him, and, second, the ability of the suit to insulate and protect the mind from extreme conditions, which is to say the suit allows the mind to function freely, exploring and discovering. While the series is unquestionably interested in wading through the ethical waters also considered in *The Hawk and the Dove*, its primary investment seems to be in the power of the mind in the service of those ethical questions.

With several starts and stops, *Static* was published throughout the 1980s during a period many consider to be one of the creative peaks of comics history. During this time, fans were exposed to many titles considered to be among the best the industry has to offer: Frank Miller and company's *Daredevil* and *The Dark Knight Returns*; Alan Moore, Stephen Bissette, John Totleben, and Rick Veitch's *Swamp Thing*; Moore and Dave Gibbons's *Watchmen*; Chris Claremont and John Byrne's *Uncanny X-Men*; and Marv Wolfman and George Pérez's *New Teen Titans* all shared shelf space with independent, self-published, and creator-owned works like Dave Sim's *Cerebus*, the Hernandez Brothers' *Love and Rockets*, Matt Wagner's *Mage*, and Kevin Eastman and Peter Laird's *Teenage Mutant Ninja Turtles*—and these are just the tip of the iceberg. It was an incredible time for comics, with an explosion of creativity that would help shape the industry for the next few decades. Tucked inside this moment, Steve Ditko brought his new creator-owned character Static to independent publisher Eclipse Comics.

A part of the independent and alternative comics boom of the 1980s, often referred to as "the black-and-white boom," Eclipse was a company that worked to champion creators' rights. Over the course of its existence, Eclipse published innovative new comics like Scott McCloud's *Zot!*, Alan Moore's *Miracleman*, and Dave Stevens's *Rocketeer*. Among the company's titles was *Eclipse Monthly*, a throwback to the anthology series of the late 1940s and early 1950s that published the ongoing adventures of several characters. Among those characters was Ditko's Static. After appearing in the first three issues of *Eclipse Monthly*, Static performed the then-unusual feat of bouncing around between several different publishers, including Charlton in its waning days and then Renegade Press, before being collected in a two-volume set at the end of the 1980s by Robin Snyder, with new and reprinted material. The version of the comic that I discuss here is the final version, published by Robin Snyder and Steve Ditko, that collects all the Static stories into a single reprint volume. Some of the later reprints by Snyder and Ditko contain notable differences between Ditko's final version of the story and how it was originally printed. Static is such a case. I am electing to use the later printing, as it is the (for lack of a better term) Ditko-approved version, and it seems most prudent to examine this version of the story. Although I have noted earlier in this book that Ditko updated and revised his essays to clarify his meaning, the key difference between the kinds of revisions that Ditko made for reprints of comics like *Static* is that Ditko saw these reprints as corrections and restorations of his original intent without the perceptible interference of "others and outsiders."

Blake Bell discusses the publication history of *Static* in his Ditko biography, *Strange and Stranger*, and notes that amid the frustration Ditko had with editorial requests and fan responses, one change he did approve of was the name of the main character. As it was originally published in *Eclipse Monthly*, Static's alter ego was "Mac Ray," but in the final Ditko version, the character's name was restored to "Stac Rae." According to Bell's book, Ditko okayed this change, which appeased editor Dean Mullaney, who wanted the character to have a more relatable name. Perhaps tellingly, it also helped avoid potential confusion with Rac Shade from *Shade the Changing Man.*[27]

In 2019, Ken Parille, a comics scholar and columnist at the *Comics Journal*, wrote a detailed and persuasive comparison of a *Static* story called "The Exploder," considering Ditko's final version of the story and the one that appeared in *Eclipse Monthly*. Parille addresses how many of the changes implemented at Eclipse overwrote Ditko's design preferences, and observed that some of those preferences involved differences not just in approaches to the comics page but in meaning. For example, Parille draws attention to the changes in the lettering and script that did more than just regularize Ditko's distinct prose. Parille writes:

> Another form of editorial intervention through lettering affects the artist's use of symbols to suggest profanity: while Ditko's upright heroes never swear, his villains do, a lot. Conventional "censor lettering" follows a basic pattern: e.g., four symbols represent a four-letter swear. But in "The Exploder" and elsewhere, Ditko's defies regularity. He creates interpretive ambiguity by using one, two, or three symbols, which, rather than represent letters (is there a one- or two-word swear?), can represent a word, an "obscene" sound, and/or a disturbed mental or emotional state. While [the Eclipse version] generally employs standard typographical symbols, [Ditko's version] mixes familiar forms with

Ditko's inventions, which morph as inspiration and spacing requires. Such a freewheeling approach seemingly didn't align with Eclipse's practices.[28]

As Parille reads Ditko's distinctive dialogue and lettering style, each element that Ditko includes on a page is a deliberate action intended to convey meaning to the reader—not to avoid ambiguity or interpretation but to foster it. This runs counter to how many readers approach Ditko's comics from this period as being too wordy or featuring unnatural dialogue, as readers who wrote to *Eclipse Monthly* complained.

Parille notes that Ditko's seemingly unusual "syntax, with sentence fragments, strings of nouns or adjectives connected by commas, repeated words, and philosophical terms . . . are as *essential* to his work as his characters' famous hand gestures—and to change them would be to go beyond house-style edits and significantly rewrite the script, making Ditko's dialogue less rhythmic and far more prosaic."[29] At minimum, it would seem that Ditko had a similar view of the situation, and *Static* was removed from the anthology going forward because, according to Mullaney, Ditko refused to let Mullaney edit any of his scripts. It seems clear, however, that the disagreements that arose between Ditko and Mullaney were not at all about ideology and instead about aesthetics.[30] However, for Ditko, the aesthetic choices he makes are delivery mechanisms for ideology, and changes to them compromise his artistic and intellection vision.

The complicated publication history of *Static* is worth noting because it is an indicator of the importance of complete creator control over characters and series Ditko owned, including the right of the creator to determine what material is published how and by whom. The publication history also places Ditko as part of a particular moment in comics history, when the pendulum had started to swing toward creators' rights and away from the notion that corporate-owned comics—the relinquishing of one's ideas to the likes of Marvel, DC, Archie, or Dell—were the *only* way to succeed in the industry.

Of course, it's not that Ditko had not produced creator-owned works free from editorial oversight before. Mr. A is a prime example and represents another case where, like Static, the character floated between publishers and publications. The difference is that, unlike the late 1960s and early 1970s, independent creators no longer had to depend on the network that supported underground comix; instead, by working with an independent or alternative comics press—such as Eclipse, Fantagraphics, Renegade, Pacific Comics, Comico, and the like—creators could retain control over their intellectual property *and* access the comics direct market through the distribution network that delivered to comic book retailers across the country. For Ditko, who was still doing work-for-hire projects throughout the 1980s and 1990s, this scenario would have been ideal. He could strike a balance that allowed for the continued production of creator-owned comics that could be viable for a wider audience. He could do so without the burden of being asked to compromise his creations through the involvement of editors and collaborators who might not share his precise vision. And just as Ditko seemed to have found a balance here, so Static, too, took on the search for personal, internal balance in the face of external demands.

Static ran for fourteen installments over its roughly seven-year publication history, and Ditko immediately laid out the philosophic stakes for the series in the first chapter. Initially, this happens with the introduction of the space-environmental suit, but the stakes are made even more explicit when Dr. Serch meets with several other scientists who want to purchase one of Serch's inventions, or at least partner with him. Serch, of course, turns them down, and the conversation takes a turn when one of his colleagues announces that Serch "believes that science is *not* free of value judgements" after Serch, almost unprompted, declares that humanity "can and [does] act on unreal ideas. But reality will not let them get away with errors in identity and causality . . . in its laws."[31] What Serch—and, by extension, Ditko—is getting at is an application of the Aristotelian notion of the "Law of Identity," which, in the Randian and thus mystic liberal configuration, insists that "the contradictory is impossible."[32] The implication is that truth and values can be derived from that basic premise and, further, that this law was applicable not just to metaphysics and ethics but to scientific consideration as a means of discerning an observable reality.[33] And, as Nathaniel Branden argues, the ability to process that reality, to reason about and gain a "sense of control over reality," depends on the power of the mind.[34]

Stac Rae has just such a "sense of control over reality" as a result of the power of his mind, as he quickly finds out from both his conscious and subconscious will what is needed for his success. First, Stac learns that he can will the space-environmental suit on and off, and shortly thereafter, while in pursuit of violent criminals, he learns that his subconscious affects reality as well when he realizes he needs to tether himself to the fleeing criminals' vehicle and "an energy line" materializes from his hands, attaching him to the escaping van.[35] To put, perhaps, a finer point on what Ditko is demonstrating to his readers, through the words of Dr. Serch and the actions of Stac, readers see that reality is necessarily discernible by and susceptible to control from the power of the human mind. This power comes with the caveat that such a mind is accountable to the intangible laws of causality and identity that govern such a reality. Moreover, that Stac can will the suit on and off speaks to the ability one has to interact with the outside world on its own terms. By turning off the suit, Stac submits himself to the outside world, dealing with that world on its own terms; and by willing the suit on, he deliberately insulates himself from that corrupted existence, manipulating and correcting it through the power of his mind.

It is that corrective, avenging action that fuels the ethical debate among Stac, Dr. Serch, and Fera, as Stac and Dr. Serch continue to learn about the suit's power and use it in the service of defending rationality and the mind. As a research scientist, Stac sees himself, Dr. Serch, and Fera in a role similar to the one Ditko defined for his journalist heroes. In Stac's mind, the role of the hero-scientist is not to be a neutral observer but to "investigat[e] to find the truth. Even if it is unpopular or risky."[36] Those truths, then, include the full potential of the suit when commanded by a mind like Stac's, as well as harnessing the power of the suit to investigate criminal activity that affects the researchers at Quest Labs. But Fera doesn't buy it, and committed to her own values and principles, she argues that "investigating crimes is not the business of science" and asks Stac and Dr. Serch, "Are we really scientists or vigilantes?" Aside from her concerns about Stac's safety or the legality of his actions, what is really at stake in Fera's reasoning is that "scientific truths are only testable—not provable, not absolutes. And [Stac is] going where [he] can't go—from *facts* to *values*, to *moral truths*, to *unscientific truths*."[37] In other words, for Fera, a demonstrable, concrete reality is not and, indeed, cannot be discerned by the theoretical, by philosophy, only by the testable hypotheses of science, and even what can be determined is provisional and "not absolute." It is this point that Stac takes the greatest issue with, and we briefly return to the moment cited in chapter 2 as a defining element of mystic liberalism: Stac sees "no dichotomy between is and ought" (fig. 7.3).[38]

While Fera wants Stac to "forget theory and be realistic," Stac snaps back, "A true theory is realistic," and the source of truth is the reasoning mind. Moreover, the source of all "creation [is] a reasoning mind," according to Stac. What Stac is laying out for readers is less a defense of vigilantism (an issue addressed earlier in other series like *The Hawk and the Dove*) and more a defense of the mind, its creative powers, and the ability of the mind to create not just material objects but *life* itself. Stac's rationale for performing aveng-ing vigilante acts is because he understands "justice, the life-serving, injustice, [and] the anti-life," and it is his choice, not his duty, to act on that knowledge to defend life, and therefore the mind, by whatever means are available to him. Throughout the series, this conflict between, principally, Fera and Stac is never resolved and finally results in Stac and Fera parting ways. This split is ostensibly for good because what the presence of the suit and the ensuing argument revealed to Stac was that he and Fera were intellectually too far apart. Stac tells Fera that because he knows she is a good person, he over-looked their underlying differences, but because he can't accept her premises and she can't accept his, they can no longer be together.

As Stac leaves, there is some light at the end of the tunnel for him and Fera as she comes to accept that she may have been mistaken in her views, and Stac, surprised by her sudden awakening, encourages her, saying that if

Figure 7.3. Ditko stresses the importance of Stac's argument by first shifting the perspective to Stac's face and then angling the camera inward and upward toward Stac's face, so that by the third panel, the reader is focused on the intensity of Stac's glare, and the reader's gaze is drawn upward by the placement and increasing size of the bottom word balloons. Art, story, and letters by Steve Ditko. "The Exploder," revised and restored version, in *Steve Ditko's Static* (2000). © Steve Ditko.

she follows through on her self-examination, she will "drive away every dark cloud[, and] the sun will forever be inside [her]." Dr. Serch then chimes in, "The glory of life is not living in security, but in doing justice to one's self and to the life—to live one's truth and to earn our worthy desires and dreams." After leaving Fera with this quintessential positive-thinking, mind power axiom, Stac does his Shane impression and rides off into the sunset, and Dr. Serch ends the series by identifying Stac as moving on to continue his own quest to "honor life's potentials" as he seeks new and unknown challenges.[39]

Having advanced far enough in his quest as an apprentice to the aptly named Dr. Serch, Stac is able to move on and continue on his own to experience the world and his life on his own terms, a completion of the quest that was not available to Blue Beetle or Dr. Strange because of practical publishing limitations. But far more important than the master-apprentice cycle that Ditko was finally able to complete is Ditko's effort to explicitly link the *mind* to *life*, and the idea that the former is a prerequisite, a creator of the latter. Presenting his readers with a sense of the mind as a causative force, of course, aligns Ditko with the mind power elements of mystic liberalism. Through *Static*, Ditko seems to have aligned himself with the kind of thinking promoted by more individualist mental science and New Thought practitioners like Helen Wilmans, publisher of the newspaper the *Woman's World* and books like *The Conquest of Poverty*, and founder of the University of Psychical Research. Wilmans, as Mitch Horowitz has pointed out, "believed in muscular self-directedness and personal action,"[40] which she called "realistic idealism," or the practical execution of truths made known to the realistic idealist, by trusting one's thoughts as a means of accessing those truths.[41] Indeed, Stac Rae puts that realistic idealism into practice through the "muscular self-directedness" of his vigilante actions as the practical execution of what truths his mind has made available to him.

Of course, it was not within the unique world of *Static* alone where Ditko explored muscular self-directedness. During this same time period, Ditko also produced work for Pacific Comics where he introduced readers to the Mocker.

The Mocker

Pacific Comics was the publishing arm of a San Diego comics retailer of the same name. The retailer was an early member of the comic book direct market—the system by which comics publishers could sell their products to comic book specialty shops through dedicated distribution channels. Founded by brothers Bill and Steve Schanes in 1981, Pacific, along with similar publishers like First, Comico, and Eclipse, worked to take advantage of the emerging direct market and made their product lines appealing to readers and retailers by reaching out to major creative voices with the opportunity to develop creator-owned content. The most prominent among those voices was the Fantastic Four creator Jack Kirby, who brought Pacific *Captain Victory and the Galactic Rangers* and *Silver Star*. Aside from its creative content and embrace of the new comics distribution model, Pacific also offered readers comics produced on better-quality paper with better production values in its printing and coloring, practices later adopted by DC and Marvel. The company was also the first to publish Dave Stevens's *The Rocketeer* before he moved the character to Eclipse and then Comico, and Pacific was also the first to publish Sergio Aragonés and Mark Evanier's *Groo the Wanderer* before it also traveled to other publishers. Along with the other established creative minds who joined ranks at Pacific was, of course, Steve Ditko. At Pacific, Ditko offered readers their first taste of his character the Missing Man as a backup feature in *Captain Victory* #6, and in *Silver Star* #2 (1983), he introduced readers to the Mocker as another cofeature.

However, while this issue was where *The Mocker* first appeared, its publication was a surprise, if not a disappointment, to Ditko. The first Mocker story was originally intended for a larger, magazine-sized publication called *Adventure Illustrated* from a company called New Media Publishing. When

New Media folded in 1982, unbeknownst to Ditko, the Mocker story was then sold to Pacific, which had the original black-and-white work colored and published in *Silver Star* #2, sized in the same manner as other American comic books of the era. According to Ditko, "The Mocker was intended for a magazine size so [the Pacific version's] proportions didn't fit the comics-size page. There was a lot of wasted space. Worse, The Mocker was never intended for color." Eventually the art was returned to Ditko, and after deciding to scrap plans for *Static*'s continuation, Ditko concluded the series and set his sights on returning to *The Mocker* in 1987 and completing it for publication in 1989.[42] One of the most significant takeaways from this somewhat tangled publication history is that it demonstrates Ditko's commitment to his artistic vision for his creations and shows that each element he places on the page comes after some deliberation that is distinct to his artistic voice.

It is not that Ditko was unaware of the often-collaborative nature of comics or that some editors may have heavier or more careless hands than others; he certainly was aware of those circumstances. Ditko's bristling at the production choices at the creator-friendly Pacific seems more related to his having no notion that the story was being printed and that he was apparently not consulted. More important, this episode provides further evidence that, for Ditko, whatever message is being delivered by his work is largely done visually—including choices in the lettering and word balloons[43]—and any compromise of his vision distorts the work's ability to deliver that message, reemphasizing the value of taking his art itself as the delivery mechanism of both narrative and philosophic content.

The form that *The Mocker* takes is stunning, as the majority of pages feature as many as twenty or more panels per page, an artistic choice perhaps suited for *The Mocker*'s originally intended magazine size and unheard of in traditionally sized comic books. The philosophic exploration that happens within the dense pages of *The Mocker* is, unsurprisingly, in harmony with Ditko's previous works, and much of the series focuses on themes of self-esteem and redemption. The series features hard-nosed former district attorney Tyler Rayne as the titular vigilante hero, the Mocker, and like Rac Shade in *Shade the Changing Man*, Rayne has been framed for crimes of political corruption. Before his imprisonment, Rayne had been investigating the corrupt Senator Durn, who, in a twist of fate again reminiscent of *Shade*, is the father of Rayne's girlfriend Ella. Caught in a delicate balancing act of trying to survive prison while maintaining his integrity and innocence, Rayne finds favor with fellow inmate Ziger, a mob boss who both respects and wants to control Rayne.

After Rayne is released from prison, Ziger offers him information and connections that would help Rayne prove his innocence along with his case against Senator Durn, while in return Ziger gains information that assists his outfit. Rayne takes the offer. That Rayne chooses to be even distantly associated with Ziger might seem incongruous with Ditko's other works, as his heroes rarely acknowledge, much less agree to cooperate with, the morally and ethically suspect, but such a reading would neglect the roles that characters like Xexlo and Dormammu played in Ditko's previous stories. Further, Ditko is not attempting a rehabilitation of a mob boss; it is Tyler Rayne who is being put through his paces as he attempts to exonerate himself and rebuild his life.

Rayne is facing the grim realities of the world just outside his door: political corruption, graft, greed, and an aversion to the truth inform the circumstances that put him in prison, literally and figuratively. To redeem himself and create a new life, Rayne has to navigate and expose the gray and tangled world that put him in prison in the first place. As the Mocker, Rayne's identity is concealed by impossibly squiggly, knotty, and confused lines that cover his entire body. On a symbolic level, Rayne's appearance simultaneously mocks and replicates the discordant world he must interact with for his own restoration, and it does so, in part, by rendering him invisible as he moves through the shadows, tracking criminals and building his case against Senator Durn. And when Rayne comes into physical contact with his prey, the kinked and snarled mass that shields Rayne's identity can spread over criminals, terrifying them into confessing what they have done or revealing the information Rayne seeks.

Rayne's path toward justice and his own restoration, of course, is not as simple as becoming the Mocker and forcing those who conspired against him to admit what they have done. Other characters in *The Mocker* also have to excavate themselves in an effort to better understand who they are and what their relationship to the world, to life, is. Ziger is willing to accept who his choices have led him to become, and even seems to relish it, and he struggles to understand why Tyler Rayne doesn't seek power for himself, leveraging what he knows about Senator Durn for his own personal, political, or financial gain.

While Ziger's perspective offers something of a meditation on power, Rayne's former girlfriend, Ella Durn, has her own complex feelings to work through after being caught in the middle of the conflict between Rayne and her father. Ella embarks on her own—perhaps more obviously internal—quest, and her mental changes eventually result in her reembrace of Rayne after she is willing to admit the truth of her experiences. We also meet Bram, a well-meaning, tough-as-nails cop who is at first unwilling to accept that redemption is possible for criminals or that the justice system is flawed in such a way as to convict the innocent, thus betraying not just the victim but the law itself. Bram, too, is forced to confront his own philosophic shortcomings through his relationship with Rayne, and Bram revises his views. It is telling that only Ziger, who unapologetically embraces his lust for power, is the only one of these three characters who is not changed or redeemed by the end of the series. It is not just those who desire change who are capable of it; one must first be willing to operate from a set of rational, nonconflicting principles to begin on the path to redemption, which Ziger, in the Ditkovian sense, is not.

But just because Ziger is not being redeemed does not mean that the series has written off the character, and rather than being a stagnant figure, Ziger is one of the most important characters in the pages of *The Mocker*. Until the end of the series, readers never actually see Ziger. There are moments where they read Ziger's words, maybe catching a glimpse of his silhouette or a point-ing hand, even his dreams, but otherwise he always operates from the noirish lighting of his prison cell. From that place, he manipulates the outside world through a shadowy network of enforcers and informants, including some within the justice system. As such, Ziger serves an important symbolic func-tion in *The Mocker*, and like the reckless forces of Hawk and Xexlo, the paci-fistic Dove, or the principled evil of Dormammu, Ziger stands in for another kind of internal struggle distinct to Ditko's worldview: the gray area.

How can one interact with corrupt people or ideas and maintain one's integrity? Put differently, how can Tyler Rayne get himself out of the soup? As a district attorney, his conviction for political corruption demonstrates not his guilt but his implication in a corrupt system of justice. To restore himself, he negotiates with an avatar of that corrupt system in Ziger. The point being made does not contradict Ditko's commitment to the morality he had made plain in earlier works; instead, like the other examples noted earlier, he is providing another instance where the path to redemption and a clear mental state involves confronting one's own internal conflicts and contradictions.

When Ziger does finally physically appear at the end of the series, the showdown between him and Tyler Rayne begins when Ziger tries to congrat-ulate Rayne after all their mutual enemies are captured or killed. But Rayne isn't having any of it: "Crime never wins," Rayne says, "it's allowed to sur-vive,"[44] indicating that these kinds of internal pressures and temptations never really go away for any individual mind; they can only be suppressed after acknowledging and confronting them. Ziger tries tempting Rayne further by insisting that he helped Rayne clear his name, and Rayne fires back that Ziger held back on the information to keep Rayne tied to him.

As the argument escalates, with Rayne dressed in a white suit and Ziger in black, Ditko uses the lighting to emphasize the contrast in drapery, particu-larly Rayne's, as he moves in and out of shadow and light. After things finally boil over to a physical confrontation, Rayne removes his jacket to use as a weapon, rendering his figure completely white. Rayne deflects a knife attack from Ziger, disarming him, and then throws the knife back at Ziger, lodg-ing it in his throat. As Ziger gurgles his last words about never going back to

Figure 7.4. The final showdown between Tyler Rayne and Ziger, where Rayne draws a philosophic distinction between himself and Ziger, a distinction made visually and through dialogue: Ziger has been trapped inside a prison created by his own negative thoughts. Art, story, and letters by Steve Ditko. "The Mocker and the Wind-Up," in *The Mocker* (1990). © Steve Ditko.

prison, Rayne, standing over him, says, "All your life, you kept yourself in a worse prison, Zige."[45] That prison is Ziger's own mind and his compromised existence (fig. 7.4).

After Ziger and his cabal of criminals are either eliminated or arrested, and an investigation into Senator Durn's crimes begins, Tyler Rayne reunites with Ella Durn. Rayne and Ella are now free to live their lives as they see fit, but investigators inform Rayne that he can never be fully cleared of the crimes that sent him to jail. Rayne takes this information in stride and is at relative ease. No longer interested in what others have to say or think about him, he turns to Ella, saying that "the right people know the truth, believe it. Others don't matter."[46] Thus he makes clear that it is not how the justice system or anyone else sees Rayne; it only matters what Rayne thinks of himself, finally basing his sense of self-esteem on his own mind rather than on the judgments of others. *The Mocker* ends with Tyler and Ella getting on a plane as Tyler asks Ella if she has any regrets. She has none and is ready to build a new life on what they have together,[47] completing the rebirth for both Tyler and Ella. This rebirth is only made possible by their willingness to face their own internal struggles and revise in favor of knowing the truth, as Rayne might put it.

The Mocker, like each of the series briefly considered in this chapter, is remarkably consistent in presenting Ditko's ideological perspective through his art and narrative choices, but as Bram puts it when referring to Tyler Rayne, "He never fits in [Bram's] neat patterns."[48] What is at stake in such a comment from one of Ditko's characters is not that he doesn't have a sense of his own ideological consistency, even as it has evolved over time, or that no one ever changes their positions. The point is that no matter how virtuous Bram or anyone else is, or how much Bram respects Tyler Rayne, Bram's own imagination of who Tyler Rayne is or should be has nothing to do with who Rayne actually is and chooses to be. Although it is a small moment in the grander scheme of *The Mocker*, and even smaller when set against the volume of Ditko's career, it speaks to the problem of misunderstanding and misinterpretation that Ditko's work faced during the middle and late 1980s and for much of the decades to come.

8

"IF I LIKE IT, I HOPE SOMEBODY ELSE LIKES IT, TOO"

Mystic Liberalism Confronted in Real and Imagined Worlds

Early on, I noted that one of the challenges inherent to a study like this is that Steve Ditko never, and never could have, identified himself as a mystic liberal. However, that does not preclude his implication and position in a broad set of cultural and political circumstances—circumstances not restrained by the ideological approach of any one mind. To that end, Ditko never identified himself as anything other than the producer of his work. He insisted that he was not "a spokesman" for any particular worldview and that "[he] alone [is] responsible for the views" expressed through his work and in his essays.[1] In a house interview DC Comics conducted to promote *The Creeper*, Ditko famously said, "I never talk about myself. My work is me. I do my best, and if I like it, I hope somebody else likes it, too."[2] That was the extent of Ditko's quoted material in the brief interview. Ditko's tone is gentle and endearing about whatever enjoyment he and his readers get from his work. He speaks with a genuine kindness that offsets, if not belies, the curmudgeonly demeanor often ascribed to Ditko by fans and readers.

There is also something to be said about Ditko's sincerely held belief that his work speaks for itself, needing no additional explanation from him about its intent. While I accept that Ditko need not explain his work to anyone, interpretation and contextualization by readers who want to understand his work's value and sociohistorical context are critical—particularly by those who may not share Ditko's worldview. I include myself in that number. Of course, this is obvious to critics and those familiar with literary, art, and film criticism, but it is not just comic book critics and scholars that took Ditko's art seriously and reinterpreted it for a mass audience.

In the 1980s, a number of comic book series at DC Comics took on the task of both reimagining and critiquing Ditko's work, particularly the characters DC had acquired from Charlton Comics in 1983: the Question, Blue Beetle, and Captain Atom. According to Ditko and Robin Snyder, DC asked Ditko to submit a proposal for Blue Beetle, which was ultimately rejected.[3] Instead DC went with an approach to the character that fit within the current superhero standard, using the creative team of Len Wein, Paris Cullins, and Bruce Patterson. Captain Atom received his own series as well, by Cary Bates and Pat Broderick. While it might be difficult to read an explicit criticism of Ditko into the early Blue Beetle and Captain Atom issues from DC, Dennis O'Neil and Denys Cowan's reimagined version of the Question is more easily read as a critique of Ditko's worldview. O'Neil and Cowan's *The Question* seemed to adopt an interpretation of Ditko's work as strictly materialist and Objectivist and presented a challenge to that perceived set of politics by introducing a Westernized sense of Zen philosophy into Vic Sage's story. (In a certain way, this is unintentionally evocative of the operations of mystic liberalism as it appropriates Eastern mysticism in the service of Western values.) However, the most well-known comic to respond to Ditko's work is Alan Moore, Dave Gibbons, and colorist John Higgins's *Watchmen*.

Production on *Watchmen* began in 1984 with writer Alan Moore, and the series was initially released in twelve issues during 1986 and 1987. Set outside the traditional DC Comics universe, the comic posits an alternate, dystopian 1985 where superheroes exist in a more realistic world than that of Superman or Batman, with the historical divergence having occurred in 1938 with the release of *Action Comics* #1. It was those first Superman comics that inspired seemingly ordinary people to don garish costumes and fight crime. In the upside-down world of *Watchmen*, the United States won the Vietnam War, the Watergate burglary by members of the Committee to Re-elect the President was never exposed, Richard Nixon retained a stranglehold on the presidency through 1985, and the Soviet invasion of Afghanistan put the world on the precipice of a nuclear holocaust. Meanwhile, superhero vigilantism is outlawed with the exception of those who are in the employ of the US government.

The typical understanding of the series notes that *Watchmen* deconstructs and satirizes the notion of the superhero and does so by orchestrating a history of superheroes through several layers of metatext, but primarily through text excerpts from *Under the Hood*—the fictional biography by Hollis Mason, a former superhero in the *Watchmen* universe. The series also features a number of flashbacks that have historical markers that pair with the ebbs and flows of the production history of superhero comics in the real world. Along with the narrative exploration of psychology and traumas that make up its vigilante superheroes, *Watchmen* invents the psychiatric evaluations of characters, media coverage of the cultural backlash against superheroes, promotional materials for marketing superhero toys, and a number of personal correspondences among other pseudo-artifacts. Each element critiques some aspect of the real-world superhero industry and its relationship to liberal capitalism.[4]

In conceiving the series, Moore initially intended for it to be populated by the Charlton Comics superheroes acquired by DC Comics. But largely because the DC editorial team had other plans for folding those characters into the company's regular lineup after 1985's event series *Crisis on Infinite Earths*, Ditko's Blue Beetle, the Question, and Captain Atom were transformed into Nite Owl, Rorschach, and Dr. Manhattan, respectively. And it is through the character of Rorschach that readers have most commonly observed a reflection and critique of the politics presented in Ditko's comics. Before changing the character name and design to Rorschach, Moore wrote in his character notes for Dave Gibbons:

> I suppose what I want to do with the character is to keep him as true as possible to the quintessential Steve Ditko character and philosophy. Now, while I've always found Steve Ditko's expressed political opinions to be strange and possibly dangerous, I have a huge amount of admiration for anybody who is prepared to take an unpopular position simply because they happen to believe it's morally right. . . . On top of this, I have the greatest possible regard for Steve Ditko as an artist and creator and wouldn't want to portray his characters falsely.[5]

Given this information, it seems that Moore's intent is less an inversion of Ditko's characters and politics, as is now commonplace for other superheroes in works like *Supreme, Superman: Red Son, The Authority,* and others.[6] Rather, Moore is taking Ditko seriously in his interpretation of the characters, reflecting a version of Ditko's politics that is as close as Moore thinks he can approximate for the world of *Watchmen*. As such, this presentation contains an inherent critique, as evidenced by the dystopian world created by the ideological perspective championed by Ditko and others. Recognizing the pervasive nature of such an ideology, as well as contemporary challenges to it, Moore also writes of the Question / Rorschach that the character is likely understood by readers as "either one incorruptible force at large in a world of eroded morals and values or he is a dangerous and near-psychotic sociopath who kills without compassion or regard for legal niceties."[7] This assumed either/or reaction to the character, in a certain way, reflects Ditko's own set of standards about ethical behavior but also calls them into question by taking what Ditko sees as moral absolutes and then insisting that, in the real world, they are anything but.

While undoubtedly conscious of the ideological framework Ditko presented with the Question, Mr. A, and in a number of other comics, Moore and Gibbons's choice to make abstract principles literal is an interesting one and remains one of the key features of the series. For Ditko, the principles held up by Mr. A and the Question as they drop criminals off buildings or kick them into improbably deep and dangerous sewers are less about advocating the literal taking of a life to rid a city of its corrupt elements and more about the philosophic, internal struggle *for* life—a life lived on one's own terms. The consequences of moving what Moore categorizes as "possibly dangerous" from the abstract to the ostensibly concrete are a significant element throughout *Watchmen*, signaled not just by the challenges leveled directly at Ditko through the character of Rorschach but by the first wave of superheroes in the comic whose vigilantism was inspired by the Superman comics they read. According to *Watchmen*, in other words, some things may better be left to the imagination. The fantasies and philosophic explorations played out on the comic book page, therefore, are potential invitations to disaster.

Of course, one might apply Moore and Gibbons's critique across other media as well, and this is the kind of criticism Ditko had responded to in the past, first with the essay "Violence the Phoney Issue" and later with the short comic "Social Justice," both discussed in chapter 6. However, it is not just the ideological interpretation and challenges that are worth noting in *Watchmen*'s dependence on the work of Steve Ditko. The pseudohistory presented in *Watchmen*, too, depends on the markers that Ditko laid down. Within the context of the story, superheroes were outlawed in 1977, largely as a result of the actions of Rorschach, whom the public saw as a violent loose cannon who openly and brutally murdered criminals.

Beyond linking the violent acts perpetrated by Rorschach to those of Ditko's Question and Mr. A, the historical and character markers the series laid out are loaded with reference. In a vaguer sense, the transition away from the more sanitized, Comics Code–approved Question into the more unfiltered Mr. A is highlighted in *Watchmen* as Rorschach becomes increasingly violent, until in 1975 the character snaps after discovering the mutilated body of a six-year-old girl. The fictional events presented here mirror the horrors inflicted on another little girl in the 1973 Mr. A story ". . . the Right to Kill" (figs. 8.1, 6.3). Moore and Gibbons use this moment to highlight another key change in Rorschach's behavior that also represents a shift in Ditko's work. This time it comes through the seemingly unusual staccato dialogue given to Rorschach. Punctuated with ellipses and stripped down to only the most essential words to get his point across, Rorschach rarely speaks in sentences of more than five or six words. This element of his character is also linked to Rorschach's discovery of the kidnapped little girl, but just as importantly, it reflects the kind of essentialized dialogue found in many, if not the majority of, independent comics produced by Steve Ditko.

Figure 8.1. With a deliberate parallel drawn between this moment and moments found in Mr. A, Rorschach sets fire to a man responsible for murdering a child. Written by Alan Moore; art and letters by Dave Gibbons; colors by John Higgins. "The Abyss Gazes Also," *Watchmen* #6 (February 1987). © DC Comics.

As readers of Ditko's work, Moore and Gibbons would certainly have identified this unusual pattern of speech Ditko gave to his heroes and then transferred it to Rorschach as a gesture toward Ditko and the changes in his characters from the cleaned-up, corporately produced comics of the 1960s to his grittier underground and independent work of the 1970s and beyond. Moreover, this creative nod toward Steve Ditko is also positioned as a transformative moment in the history of the superhero, where the apologetics applied to the violence and ugliness of such characters were pushed aside in favor of something more tangible and brutal, forcing readers—in *Watchmen*, the public—to acknowledge that, as Rorschach might put it, instead of facing the truth, they had "made a face that [they] could bear to look at in the mirror."[8]

Watchmen offers a fairly obvious critique of contemporary liberalism, and that it does so principally by using the comics and characters created by Steve Ditko is significant both for understanding *Watchmen* and for plotting out the trajectory of the comics that followed and responded to *Watchmen*. That Moore had initially chosen characters created specifically by Ditko is not inconsequential, because if he had only wanted to reevaluate the role of the superhero in the American consciousness, he could have selected any number of other properties DC had acquired, or he could have done as Mark Gruenwald and company had with *The Squadron Supreme* years earlier at Marvel, by creating analogues for some of the most well-known DC Comics heroes. Or he could simply have created entirely new characters that essentialized the issues he wanted to address. Moore and Gibbons were forced to merge these latter two options when DC would not let them have the Charlton characters. That Moore and Gibbons took on Ditko specifically means that their interpretation and the trials they put his *ideas* through put their imitators, albeit obliquely, in conversation with Ditko, too.

By placing much of the post-*Watchmen* output of the 1980s and 1990s in relationship to the work of Steve Ditko, it is worth noting that the criticism presented by *Watchmen* should not be misunderstood as being necessarily harshly adversarial toward Steve Ditko's work; rather, it can be understood as conversational and curious. There is no reason to assume that Ditko himself approved of war or interpersonal violence as a means of solving the world's problems,[9] and he undoubtedly would not have approved of the antiheroes that populated *Watchmen* (which is not to say that Moore, Gibbons, and Higgins did). Further, Moore's presumption that the imaginary violent acts of Ditko's characters should be construed as a call for actual violence is a fundamental misunderstanding of the philosophic mechanics of Ditko's work. This is not to demean the artistic achievement and historical significance of *Watchmen*, but it does shed light on the misperceptions many fans and readers held about Ditko's work at the time—even still today. And although the concern and critique are obvious, they, too, should not be misunderstood as contemptuous on the part of Moore and Gibbons. In numerous interviews, both Moore and Gibbons have expressed a sincere reverence for Ditko, his work, and the innovations he brought to comics.[10] Instead, the challenge of *Watchmen* is more about a broadly accepted ideological and philosophical framework of which Ditko's comics and characters were representative.

Although most readings of Ditko—this study included—focus on the work he did at Marvel, Ditko was producing new comics all the way up to his death in the summer of 2018, with several posthumous works released and in production. Many of these comics and essays directly address Ditko's recollection of comics history and his time at Marvel, including his reasons for abruptly leaving the company in 1966, as well as essays on creator rights, the creation of Spider-Man and Dr. Strange, violence in the media, and a number of essays and comics about his view of the comics press and fandom. Although he did not and would not have used the specific term "toxic" to describe many comic book fans (CBFs, to Ditko), toxic is precisely how he presented them, and perhaps not unjustifiably so.

In spite of what he saw as misunderstandings and misrepresentations of his work, Ditko did not see it as his obligation to make recommendations "for other minds, interests,"[11] or even to provide ostensibly definitive readings of his own work. Rather, like the ancient masters that informed Blavatsky and those that followed her, or like Nietzsche's Zarathustra, Ditko's work seems bent on disrupting mores and providing emblematic narratives of self-cultivation and redemption. It was up to readers to make those connections on their own and to apply those ideas as they saw fit. While the effort to present readers with a distinct, complex ideological perspective is clear, Ditko held that readers should not obey his commands or share his sense of ideological purity. A commitment to earnestly held principles seems to have outweighed a difference in philosophic ideals for Ditko, as evidenced by his maintaining warm and long friendships with people, like fellow comics artist and some-time collaborator Wallace Wood, whose political outlook was diametrically opposed to Ditko's own.

On the other hand, once Ditko began to explicitly experiment with Objectivism, it is easy to understand why many readers and critics would have difficulty in looking past Rand, Objectivism, and their troubling legacies. Even setting the differences of economic worldview aside, Rand wrote privately about her admiration of the serial killer William Hickman,[12] and she publicly espoused white-supremacist views about Indigenous peoples, insisting that "any white person who brought the element of civilization had the right to take over this continent."[13] These are deeply troubling words and ideas, and they certainly contravene the social and political values Ditko outlined in his comics and essays.

It is not clear exactly *why* Ditko chose to cleave himself from Objectivism as the *singular* force in his thought, but Rand's troubling contradictions in claimed ideals—the admiration of a murderer and explicit racism—are clear points of separation between Ditko and Rand. This is perhaps made most obvious in the difference between Ditko's words in the introduction to "Violence the Phoney Issue" as it appeared in *Guts* #5 (1969) and subsequent printings of the same cartoon and essay, where the original essay claims Objectivism as a base for Ditko's philosophy, and later printings remove any reference to it.[14] Further evidence of this appears throughout chapter 7.

Ditko most certainly took Objectivism as a legitimate mode of inquiry about the world, but as I have emphasized, there is a messiness that disallows reading Ditko's work only in Objectivist terms or ways that are slavishly devoted to Rand. Ditko would most certainly have held his philosophy as complex and distinctly his own, but even so, that does not excuse his work from being implicated in broader political and philosophic conversations. And he was not alone in this kind of pick-and-choose liberalism that took on a number of seemingly disparate ideas, funneling them into a set of consequential, even if peculiar, ideological principles. In the service of a categorical and conceptual framework, I have identified that approach as mystic liberalism, and like any politically motivated labeling, it implies a viscosity where practitioners do not make up a monolithic group, but a squishy one that finds itself sticking to both benign and malignant actors. In spite of positioning himself as intellectually independent, evidence from Ditko's work places him firmly in the mystic liberal camp, and his experimentation with such ideas continued into the comics he produced until the end of his life.

Still Conjuring Fantasees

Among a number of new characters Ditko developed during the last twenty-eight years of his life were mysterious hero characters, like the Cape, who provide a distinct sense of cosmic intraspace and what happens when individuals are forced to confront the contents of their own conscious and subconscious minds. In a 2015 story appearing in *The 32-Page Series*,[15] the Cape—a sentient, bodiless cape that looks similar to the one worn by Dr. Strange—encounters a member of a group of nameless crooks. The story contains no description of the crooks or the nature of their crimes, but Ditko's art and narrative style make the characters' criminality plain. After the crooks go their separate ways, the Cape descends on one of them, opening itself wide to reveal a blackened inner lining and then enveloping the crook. The crook is sucked into a disorienting and confused intraspace, where he is faced with his own sense of greed, what Ditko would consider the unearned, and after chasing after a giant pile of money, the crook is brutalized by two ethereal figures that represent the crook's partners (fig. 8.2). Exiting the cape, paranoid that his partners are about to do him in, the crook shambles down the street, where he is immediately bludgeoned from behind and bleeds out on the street. A witness who sees the crime notifies the police, who arrest the murderer, who is revealed as one of the crook's partners. It is also revealed that the arrested hood had also murdered the third partner.

The story has a limited amount of dialogue, and Ditko conveys much of the narrative visually, perfectly in line with the aesthetic he had cultivated over the previous decades. Also in line with the work he had produced since the 1950s is the sense of dark karma and cosmic intraspace that populates the story. The crook is pulled into the cosmic intraspace held within the Cape, a being that consciously seeks out ne'er-do-wells, where he faces his own ethical

Figure 8.2. The Cape swallows a nameless crook into the cosmic intraspace the Cape contains within itself. Art, story, and letters by Steve Ditko. "The Cape," *The 32-Page Series: #20ww30ww* #23 (2015). © Steve Ditko.

failings, and both the crook and his cronies face the dark karmic punishments for whatever crimes they have committed. In the ten short pages of the story, Ditko provides a distinct sense of how dark karma and cosmic intraspace work in tandem with each other. This pairing exemplifies how the Law of Attraction invites and begets violent ends for those who would impose themselves on the rights and property of others, and how a presumably rational justice system is invoked as a retaliatory force against evil. The desire for the unearned—an internal disposition—led the criminals to their crimes; their crimes, then, operate as a physical manifestation of a diseased mind; the deaths and arrests of the criminals are the cosmic corrective. Unsurprisingly, these kinds of mystic and cosmological correctives appear throughout Ditko's late-period stories, and so do more direct references to the occult as a means of accessing these intangible forces.

In a 2018 issue of *The 32-Page Series*, Ditko enlists an occult apparatus for a vignette called "A Fantasee." In the first panel of this story, a crystal ball sits under a dangling overhead light on a small round table, with the crystal ball recessed in a small room with a doorway framed by drawn curtains. Although there is no narration or signage to explicitly say so, the scene has all the trappings of the dens inhabited by psychic mediums and fortune-tellers found in popular culture. Over the next seven panels on the nine-panel page, a mysterious creature emerges from the crystal ball, first appearing as an enormous eye (giving the story its name) and then as a pained face that is pushing its way out of the confines of the orb containing it. Once the phantasmagoric creature emerges, it rushes out the door to a scene where a man is holding a woman at gunpoint and then shoots her dead. Immediately after the shot is fired, the phantasm enters the scene, and the man begins firing his gun, to no effect. The phantasm envelops and disarms the man, apparently killing him

Figure 8.3. A mysterious phantasm emerges from the mystic interior space of a crystal ball to punish a man who murders a woman. Art, story, and letters by Steve Ditko. "A Fantasee," *The 32-Page Series* #26 (2018). © Steve Ditko.

and leaving the man's corpse on the floor, atrophied with fear. The phantasm then returns to the crystal ball, ending the story. All of this occurs over two pages and eighteen panels (fig. 8.3).

The remarkable economy of Ditko's story is evident in the action on the page and the way the story distills the themes that drove Ditko's output since

1953. The story features occult, mystic elements as a source knowledge that informs a rational sense of justice, the dark karmic force of retaliatory violence, and the cosmic intraspace—this time the interior of a crystal ball that houses it all. Of further significance, the story is almost entirely wordless, except for a single panel where the man threatens the woman, shouting, "No one says 'no' to me!"[16] Embedded in this single phrase from a single panel is another constant in Ditko's work: the evil of imposition by the second-hander, believing one is owed dominance over another.

It is not just the initiation of violence that must be dealt with by the mysterious phantasm, but the anti-mind, anti-life premises that invited the violence to begin with. Moreover, the comic's dependence on the page layout and the contents of the panels to drive the narrative and deliver its symbolism again emphasizes the primacy of reading the visuals in any analysis of Ditko's work. While this story was far from the last new work that Ditko would publish with Robin Snyder, it gives us a fitting, aphoristic coda for all that he had achieved up to this point and a marker of the consistency of his philosophy across nearly seven decades of work.

Mysterious Strangers in American Political Discourse

Although my aim in this study is not to make Ditko the spokesman for mystic liberalism, Ditko's work dependably reflects a distinct set of political and ideological precepts found not just in the popular texts by Nathaniel Branden, Ayn Rand, or Norman Vincent Peale but in the words and actions of Ronald Reagan and other contemporary neoliberal politicians.

Recognizing Ditko's work as being in line with mystic liberalism is less intended to brand Ditko with such a label than it is to present Ditko's work as a clear lens for identifying mystic liberalism in popular and political discourse. The coherence that Ditko brings to seemingly incongruous ideas enables a broad application of his philosophy to a range of texts, phenomena, and political actions. Without the advantage of having Ditko specifically name his approach, my coining of the term "mystic liberalism," as explicated in this study, and its observability outside of Ditko's oeuvre, seems appropriate for making plain a complex worldview that is not easily placed within a preexisting category.

But it is not lexical expedience alone that makes mystic liberalism a useful framework. In an April 2010 guest column for the *Washington Post*'s "Political Bookworm," Mitch Horowitz does a bit of occult forensic work, identifying the source of a peculiar speech delivered by Ronald Reagan in 1957 at Eureka College, a speech that was later carted out again for a piece Reagan wrote for *Parade* magazine in 1981 called "What the Fourth of July Means to Me." In the essay, Reagan tells readers "a legend about the day of our nation's birth," where a mysterious stranger rose and spoke to the squabbling Founders as they debated the contents of the Declaration of Independence. The stranger's impassioned plea that they answer the call of destiny and sign that immortal document at once confounded and convinced the delegates to the Second Continental Congress to, as Reagan put it, rush forward and sign the Declaration "to be as immortal as a work of man can be." After the frenzy to sign the Declaration, the delegates turned to see that the mysterious stranger had disappeared from the room, in spite of the locked and guarded doors.[17] On its own, Reagan's story might come across as the kind of nationalist boosterism expected on the Fourth of July, but Horowitz provides a revised context that places Reagan, and his story, within the mystic liberal frame.

What Horowitz recognized in the story was "the unmistakable mark of a little-known but widely influential scholar of occult philosophy, Manly P. Hall."[18] Hall had written a number of texts and lectured on the occult throughout the middle years of the twentieth century, but it was *The Secret Destiny of America* (1944) that seems to have grabbed Reagan's attention, as it was there, among evidence for America's place in the "Great Plan," where the story of the mysterious stranger appeared. Reagan never publicly named his source, either in 1957 or in 1981, but the similarity between Reagan's language and Hall's is clear, and Horowitz makes a compelling case. Horowitz cites, in comparison to Reagan's version of the legend, Hall's *Secret Destiny*: "When they turned to thank him for his timely oratory, he was not to be found, nor could any be found who knew who he was or how he had come in or gone out through the locked and guarded doors."[19] Although the story had been in circulation for some time, it is not clear whether Hall was familiar with the earliest known version of the story as it appeared in George Lippard's *Washington and His Generals*, a collection of legends about the events of 1776 published in 1847; but as Horowitz notes, the story seems to have been delivered to Hall by a secretary of the Theosophical Society,[20] repacking the mystic baggage for the story.

What is significant for my purposes here is not just that Ronald Reagan cribbed a story from an occult author but that both Hall and Reagan entangle mid-twentieth-century liberal politics with the occult, and Ronald Reagan, specifically, made those entanglements accessible to a mass audience, encouraging them to link their political worldview and affection for their country's ideals with what Hall pondered was "one of the agents of the Secret Order."[21] While the comic books and essays of Steve Ditko provide a clear and reliable insight into mystic liberalism, the result of this confluence of ideas presented by Hall and Reagan is to demonstrate the practical operations of mystic liberalism in American political discourse.

It's all well and good to take a revised view of Steve Ditko's work and apply it to the ongoing conversations in comics studies, particularly discussions about major contributions to the medium, like *Watchmen*. However, because

Ditko's work provides insight into a peculiar phenomenon in twentieth-century American politics, we can use the ideology presented in his comics as a means for at once understanding that phenomenon, demonstrating its availability to audiences through popular media, and extrapolating from there how it manifested across different media platforms over time. Even within the microcosm of the Reagan example, the language and practices of mystic liberalism identified here can then be used to complicate and revise the historical and cultural interpretation of a broad spectrum of practical political activity.

Facing Up to the Unknown

This book has sought to revise popular perception of the work of Steve Ditko as well as to reposition the role of comics studies in cultural and academic conversations. As grandiose as the latter may seem to some readers, identifying a significant strand of unusual political thought as it appeared in American comic books demonstrates that comics studies should be doing more than reporting back recent discoveries or performing historical recontextualization of exclusive interest to the field's constituents or comics fans. Rather, comics studies should be playing detective in the ongoing investigations conducted by the humanities, offering new insights procured from the comics that have spawned global multimedia empires.

Indeed, an increasing number of studies are attempting just such a feat, and I have cited many of those studies throughout this book. Recent works like Qiana Whitted's *EC Comics: Race, Shock, and Social Protest*, Deborah Elizabeth Whaley's *Black Women in Sequence: Re-inking Comics, Graphic Novels, and Anime*, Rebecca Wanzo's *The Content of Our Caricature*, and Kate Polak's *Ethics in the Gutter: Empathy and Historical Fiction in Comics* make important interventions for the field and employ comics as useful means of exploring significant cultural and intersectional issues. Books like Marc Singer's *Breaking the Frames: Populism and Prestige in Comics Studies* provide significant critical evaluations of the field as it comes into its own as a discipline that unapologetically engages in critical discourse with all due rigor and enthusiasm. But to keep the momentum going, comics studies itself must continue to identify the key contributors and contributions that helped produce potent political and theoretical insights. As the creator and cocreator of some of the most widely recognized cultural icons in the world, Steve Ditko is one of those productive minds that demand attention and scrutiny.

The apex of Ditko's contributions to multimedia empires and their role in shaping cultural consciousness came through his work on *The Amazing Spider-Man*. Those comics offered readers a unique long-form psychodrama about the internal search for the self, a hero with the capacity for reflection and growth. Ditko structured this narrative for more than three years in *The*

Amazing Spider-Man, but he was able to distill that message into four powerful pages of issue #33. These pages are among the most defining moments of the American superhero genre. Although the phrase "With great power comes great responsibility" has become an indelible part of Western cultural vocabulary, these four pages defined the superhero as a person, any person, who, no matter how many times they get knocked down, *always* gets back up. It is an affective trope that has been mimicked and attributed to characters across Marvel's transmedia universe, but it begins with Ditko and the lifting sequence in a story titled "The Final Chapter!" This was the culminating issue of a three-part arc in Ditko's major push to shift Peter Parker into a character who could accept who he was, independent of what his peers thought and said about him—a shift that was the result of the mystic introspection and bildungsroman discussed in chapter 5.

Leading up to issue #33, Aunt May had been struck with a mysterious terminal illness. After he combined mental forces with Dr. Curt Connors (whom Peter also knew as the villainous Lizard) to find a cure, the exhaustion and frustration Peter experienced in trying to save May had pushed him to an emotional breaking point. To make matters worse, Dr. Octopus had stolen the only vial of an experimental serum that Peter and Dr. Connors needed to save May's life. As the mystery of who stole the serum unfolds, Peter, as Spider-Man, finds himself face-to-face with Dr. Octopus, and the discovery that it was he who stole the serum sends Spider-Man into a blind rage. In his mindless anger, Spider-Man accidentally causes the collapse of Octopus's underwater hideout, literally bringing the building down on himself, pinning the webslinger beneath an immeasurable weight as water rushes in all around him.

After a brief recap on the first page, issue #33 opens with Spider-Man trapped under the collapsed building. Symbolically, Spider-Man is entombed in a cosmic intraspace fashioned from his own actions, as well as his own internal turmoil and psychic grief. He is buried by the weight of the past, the weight of his own shortcomings, the weight of guilt. By freeing himself from this collective weight, he reconciles his own inner struggles and those thoughts and emotions that restrict his self-esteem and, therefore, his agency. Over the next four pages, Ditko presents that very moment of overcoming, and he does so in a way that stands as a towering achievement of form and genre.

Page 2 of the story is a seven-panel grid. The first two tiers contain three panels each; the panels are narrow and tightly compressed, and the interiors enhance the sense of claustrophobia with cluttering bits of debris surrounding the trapped Spider-Man as he struggles to find the resolve to survive. But he is reminded of the dying Aunt May, who appears apparitionally in panel 5; in panel 6, the long-deceased Uncle Ben joins her. Products of Spider-Man's mind, brought forth for the reader to see as Spider-Man imagines them, Ben and May are symbols of failure and grief because he could not help them when they needed him most, Spider-Man's anguished mask buried in his hands.

Then something astonishing happens on the page and inside Spider-Man's head. The seventh panel is wide and open. Spider-Man is still trapped, centered in the panel, while May and Ben are pushed out to the left and right, and much of the debris is cleared. Spider-Man has a moment of recognition that May's illness and Ben's death are not reasons to despair but to fight for the people he loves and the principles that matter to him, declaring that he will "no longer be haunted by the memory—of Uncle Ben!"[22] The buildup of the compressed, claustrophobic panels into the open, breathable seventh panel heightens the drama and carries the necessary symbolic weight for Spider-Man's internal journey in finding himself. But internal strength alone is not enough. Action is also necessary, and Spider-Man is not free from all the things that bind him just yet (fig. 8.4).

The third page contains three tiers of panels, with two panels per tier. In the first tier, the short panels intensify the immense, nearly impossible, psychic and literal weight as it presses down on Spider-Man. The panels in the second tier grow slightly in height as Spider-Man begins to find the wherewithal to force the weight upward, locking his arms in place, shifting power to his upper body. The third tier grows taller still as his head spins and the resistance almost becomes unbearable, and just as the page allows some sense of relief, the fourth page torques the narrative back in the other direction with a tier of three tight, narrow panels at the top of the page that jarringly shift from aspect to aspect in a quick cut between the crumbling roof that holds back the rushing waters and the struggling Spider-Man, whose head hangs in anguish. But in the third panel, Spider-Man lifts his head and *decides* he will escape and save May. Just beneath that tier is a large panel that takes up two-thirds of the page where Spider-Man has gotten just beneath the wreckage, with a deliberately placed page turn, and the fifth page is a splash panel where Spider-Man shrugs off the enormous burden and has connected the strength of his mind and his convictions with the strength of his body.[23] This is the culminating moment of the epic that Ditko set Spider-Man on in *Amazing Fantasy* #15, and although Spider-Man's personal struggles do not stop here, that is hardly the point (fig. 8.5).

In terms of form, the lifting sequence is precisely the kind of rhythmically arranged iconostasis that Andre Molotiu describes for Ditko's work, where the layout of each page is a unified composition.[24] The elegance of Ditko's approach to using the icon of the comic book panel as the driving force of visual narrative, as opposed to relying solely on the contents of the panel or the dialogue, is a significant achievement on its own. However, his approach to visual narrative in these pages serves another purpose: it redefines the superhero. In these four, brief pages, the masked Spider-Man, whom

Figure 8.4. Peter Parker faces his greatest struggle: his own self-doubt. To overcome it, he must put the past behind him, as symbolized by Uncle Ben. Dialogue edited by Stan Lee; Steve Ditko art; Stan Goldberg colors; Sam Rosen letters. "The Final Chapter!" *The Amazing Spider-Man* #33 (February 1966). © Marvel Comics.

Ditko designed so that *any* reader could identify with the character, gives the sequence further emotional weight. As Spider-Man struggles to free himself, the reader learns that Spider-Man is a different kind of superhero—one who is not defined by a cape or a cowl. One not defined by gadgets, or infinite wealth, or popularity. One who, in spite of Peter Parker's appearance, need not be white. In these four pages, the reader learns that Spider-Man is not a hero because of any of those conventional means. He is a hero because of his heart, and the reader can be, too.

In a certain way, this is also a moment to consider Ditko's assertion that he is his work. One always wants to keep a minimum safe distance from claims about interchangeability between authors and their creations, but it is difficult to overlook the psychological epic and search for self that Ditko set Peter Parker and Spider-Man on as it compares to his own intellectual journey and quest for concretes in a world of abstractions. From the ethereal and mystical answers provided by dark karma in his earliest weird horror and suspense tales, to the personal cosmic intraspace explored in Dr. Strange, and then on to the concretes of the Question and Mr. A, Ditko's work, like Spider-Man's life, has been emblematic of that very search for self he pondered for thirty-eight issues of *The Amazing Spider-Man*, a series and character that have guideposted this study as well. And it is not through Spider-Man alone where Ditko reveals the importance of the *search* for truth as being every bit as important as the truth itself.

In the closing moments of *Static*, Fera surprises Stac and Dr. Serch by proclaiming that, like Stac, she is going to strike out on her own to find new quests and means of knowing herself. Realizing that she was not acting in

Figure 8.5. In one of the most iconic moments in American superhero comics, Peter Parker finds the inner strength to free himself from the weight of guilt, self-doubt, and blind emotion. Dialogue edited by Stan Lee; Steve Ditko art; Stan Goldberg colors; Sam Rosen letters. "The Final Chapter!" *The Amazing Spider-Man* #33 (February 1966). © Marvel Comics.

accord with her own previously held beliefs, Fera says that she has woken from her self-imposed slumber and is "beginning to see the naked, unpleasant truth about [herself]," and she will be leaving "to do some studying, experiencing—learning to face up to the unknown." After all, what does she "really have to fear from life?"[25] In spite of the creeping terrors and horrors of cosmic intraspace that populated so much of Ditko's output, the final say that Ditko offers is not to fear those internal terrors but to acknowledge them, embrace them, and replace them with a life-affirming willingness to charge headlong into the unknown, to be the Nietzschean child.

The restless excavation of the interior in search of the self, and the ethereal battles of mind and anti-mind, life and anti-life, presented through the tension of stark blacks against the white of the blank page often set Ditko at odds with his readers, but in between, anchoring those tensions was this: we become what we think and believe about ourselves. What Ditko, and all his mysterious travelers, seemed to think most about was the search for a better version.

ACKNOWLEDGMENTS

In a certain way, I've been working on this book since I was in the fifth grade, reading and rereading, thinking and rethinking about Steve Ditko's work, and it would be impossible for me to remember everyone I encountered along the way or who listened as I exuberantly went on and on about Static or Dr. Strange or Shade the Changing Man. I've been very lucky to know so many people with so much patience. However, finishing this book would not have been possible without Gary Hoppenstand, Scott Michaelsen, Carol Tilley, Stephen Arch, and David Stowe, whose care and guidance helped me to shape the ideas presented here.

Gary believed in me when I needed someone to, and he was willing to let me explore the ideas here with the zeal and openness they needed. Scott's contagious enthusiasm and endless passion for the practice of thought consistently inspired and challenged me. Carol's warm demeanor and her deep passion for, and knowledge of, comics studies are a model not just for me but for the field. Steve's steady hand and thoughtful critiques reminded me of the truth that we all stand on the shoulders of giants, and that listening can be more persuasive than telling. David's generosity taught me that a human response is often the most effective one. I am humbled by each of them, and I hope to live up to the individual standards they set as scholars and mentors.

I am also grateful to Tom Inge and Vijay Shah, who generously provided me this opportunity, as well as Katie Keene and the hard work of the editors and reviewers at the University Press of Mississippi. I am also indebted to the comics studies journals that first agreed to publish the articles I have revised for this book. An early version of chapter 3 appeared in *Inks: The Journal of the Comics Studies Society* in 2017, and portions of chapters 5 and 6 originally appeared in *Studies in Comics* in 2014. I thank the editors and reviewers of those publications for shepherding those individual projects, as they have served this larger whole.

I am also incredibly grateful for those who read and contributed their thoughts to the development of this manuscript and its ideas. Diana Schutz taught me the value of being a thorough editor, and her passion for and contributions to the medium of comics cannot be overstated. I admire her greatly. The careful eyes and editorial acumen of Sean Guynes, Christine Peffer, Ronny Ford, and Bill Henry helped me whip my prose into shape. Lance Conley, Kylene Cave, Mitch Ploskonka, Justin Wigard, and Amrutha Kunapulli all responded critically and helped me simplify my often-winding way of sharing new ideas. Mark Ditko, Robert Hafferman, Will Pfeifer, and Ben Tiede kindly offered their time and effort to thinking about how these ideas might be received by comics readers at large. Bill Zanowitz assisted with tracking down comics that I didn't own or have quick access to, and Cameron Merkler and Andy Tom were the first two people to say, "So, when are you going to write a book about Ditko?" (So, really, if anyone deserves blame for this, it's Cameron and Andy.) Christina and Cameron Merkler, too, were there with me at the beginning as these ideas started to form and carried on the work I began at their store, Discount Comic Book Service, making Ditko's work available to a wide audience through DCBS's global network of customers. And in the world of Ditko fandom and knowledge, I have to acknowledge the value of the work done by Rob Imes, Bob Heer, and others in their contributions to knowledge about Ditko's career: Rob with his continuation of *Ditkomania* and Bob's bibliographic work. And, of course, Robin Snyder has been an indispensable resource as a correspondent, Ditko's copublisher, and the publisher of *The Comics*. The comics scholars Qiana Whitted, Brannon Costello, Andy Kunka, Julian Chambliss, Marc Singer, John Jennings, Stacey Robinson, Dan Yezbick, and Charles Hatfield generously shared their time and feedback with me and set an intellectual standard that I aspire to. I am lucky to know them.

Early in my career, Troy Bassett, Debrah Huffman, Lewis Roberts, Rachel Hile, Jennifer Stewart, Michael Kaufmann, and Andrew Kopec all helped me build the scholarly skill set I needed to even begin thinking about this project, and they set ablaze my passion for the work. Friends like Vince Bonavoglia, David Price, Jason Wood, and Christopher Neeseman provided me a public platform on *11 O'Clock Comics*, where I first started to share gestational versions of the ideas presented in this book. Ryan Claytor has been pillar of kindness who gave me opportunities with the Michigan State University Comics Forum that kept cynicism from creeping in.

Finally, not one jot or tittle of this book would have been written if not for Brenna Kruse, Aleesa Kruse, Delaney Kruse, and Maggie Kruse. I read, write, think, and critique because I am passionate about the work. I live and breathe because these four incredible women have made every one of my days better.

NOTES

1. "From Out of the Depths!"

1. Steve Ditko and Stan Lee, "The Incredible Hulk!" *Tales to Astonish*, no. 60 (October 1964).

2. I refer to Captain Atom as an original cocreation here because it is not clear that he is a revised version of the Captain Atom who appeared at Australia's Atlas Publishing from 1948 to 1954 or the Captain Atom who appeared at the publishing house Nation-wide from 1950 to 1951. However, I do concede that the number of characters with the same name over such a short span of time is curious, if not understandable. The Australian publisher Atlas has no known connection to the American comics publisher Martin Goodman's Atlas Comics line, although both were active during the same period. The Australian Atlas should also not be confused with the revived American Atlas Comics line of the 1970s, where Ditko worked on comics like *The Destructor*, but I digress. If Joe Gill and Steve Ditko's Captain Atom has a direct antecedent, a sensible choice might be Spark Comics' Atoman, who first appeared in 1946. Atoman was cocreated by Jerry Robinson and Mort Meskin; Ditko studied under Robinson and also worked with and greatly admired Meskin. The original design of the Gill and Ditko Captain Atom is an unmistakable nod to Meskin and Robinson's much earlier Atoman.

3. In his dissertation project "Four-Color Political Visions," the political scientist Joshua Plencner comments that totalizing views of Ditko's work as reflecting his politics—still accepting and identifying those politics as Objectivist—are problematic, as such views imagine "the comic book page as a transposition of artist ideology rather than as a vector of relation." Plencner argues that comic art should not be regarded as a "predictable mechanism of meaning-making" as opposed to a component of "an emergent social process." I agree with Plencner that the politics of a piece of comic art do not end with the last bits of ink placed on a page and that they are instead implicated in a social process of meaning making. Indeed, this book is largely predicated on a similar line of reasoning: a body of work has a politics, and those politics have a complicated relationship with a variety of publics and counterpublics. However, the notion that Ditko's comics can or should be entirely untethered from his politics and philosophy is an equally problematic way of considering the work of an artist who, as I discuss throughout this book, endeavors to link his own philosophy—which he treats as largely unique to himself—to the comics he produced throughout his career. This is the case not just for his independent work but for the corporate comics that featured characters Ditko wrote, like Shade the Changing Man, Dr. Strange, Spider-Man, the Hawk and the Dove, and others. So it's both: Ditko's work must be treated as a reliable vessel for his ideology that is also part of a complex network of cultural conversations. "Four-Color Political Visions: Origin, Affect, and Assemblage in American Superhero Comic Books" (PhD diss., University of Oregon, Eugene, January 14,

2015), 89–90n105, accessed March 7, 2019, https://scholarsbank.uoregon.edu/xmlui /handle/1794/18748.

4. Blake Bell, *Strange and Stranger: The World of Steve Ditko* (Seattle, WA: Fantagraphics Books, 2008), 95.

5. Robert Beerbohm, "Goodman vs Ditko & Kirby," *Kirby Museum* (blog), February 11, 2012, https://kirbymuseum.org/blogs/dynamics/2012/02/11/goodman-vs-ditko-kirby-by-robert -beerbohm.

6. "And Ditko said the same thing to me in 1970 that he said to Bob Beerbohm." Mark Evanier, Facebook, September 9, 2019, https://www.facebook.com/stephen.bissette.7/posts /10159059148538289.

7. Steve Ditko, "Why I Quit S-M, Marvel," *Four Page Series*, no. 9 (September 2015). It is also worth noting that the comics writer and historian Mark Evanier has claimed that, based on personal conversations with Ditko in 1970, there may have been more to the situation than Ditko lets on in his 2015 essay. Responding to a Facebook discussion started by a post from the comics artist Stephen Bissette, Evanier believes that Ditko thought "Marvel would come after him and give him everything he wanted." Evanier's claim is plausible and merits some histori- cal consideration. Evanier is also clear to point out that Ditko *never* specifically said this; it was the impression Evanier received from the conversation. Evanier also claims that Jack Kirby and Marvel office manager Sol Brodsky had similar impressions. Speculative as it is, I take Evanier's impression to be an honest one and worth noting at least because of the complications it presents to thinking about Ditko's working relationship with Marvel and a potential desire for more favorable terms as the company moved to license many of its characters, including Spi- der-Man. However, Ditko never publicly substantiated such an assertion, and if true, it would seem to be a significant omission from his several essays about his history at Marvel. The claim has also not yet been substantiated by other sources close to Ditko in the immediate days and years after his departure from Marvel. Evanier's comment begins: "This is an interesting dis- cussion and I'm too busy today to plunge into it but let me throw in a fact that some folks have missed . . ." Mark Evanier, Facebook, September 8, 2019, https://www.facebook.com/stephen .bissette.7/posts/10159059148538289.

8. Douglas Wolk, *Reading Comics: How Graphic Novels Work and What They Mean* (Cam- bridge, MA: Da Capo, 2008), 156–65.

9. For readers unfamiliar with Ditko's writing style, I have endeavored to make it plainer; however, there are some instances where doing so would mean making substantial alterations to the text. In those instances, I have elected to leave the text as is to avoid any unintentional alteration of meaning or intent. Among other distinctive syntactic elements, Ditko often runs together near synonyms, presumably to clarify his intent. Additionally, when he writes about the characters he developed at Marvel, he almost never refers to those characters by their full names. Rather, he uses S-M, GG, JJJ, and DS to indicate the characters Spider-Man, Green Goblin, J. Jonah Jameson, and Doctor Strange, respectively.

10. Steve Ditko, "The Ever Unwilling," *The Comics*, March 2009.

11. While this is a common perception, in a 2015 Twitter microessay, Jeet Heer, without sub- stantive support, claimed that "Randian pseudo-logic" will cost Steve Ditko "$50 to $100 mil- lion." In fairness to Heer, he does rightly acknowledge the role that Ditko had in the creation and development of characters like Spider-Man, but like many of the other scholars discussed in this book, Heer defaults to Objectivism as a shorthand to explain apparent perplexities about Ditko's actions and output. Moreover, he refers to Ditko's post-Marvel work as being split between "commercial hack work" and "Randian tracts," again neglecting some of Ditko's most significant contributions in favor of a reductive shorthand.

12. Claudia Franziska Brühwiler, "'A Is A': Spider-Man, Ayn Rand, and What Man Ought to Be," *PS: Political Science and Politics* 47, no. 1 (2014): 91.

13. Antonio Pineda and Jesús Jiménez-Varea, "Popular Culture, Ideology, and the Comics Industry: Steve Ditko's Objectivist Spider-Man," *Journal of Popular Culture* 46, no. 6 (2013): 1161.

14. Pineda and Jiménez-Varea, "Popular Culture," 1162.

15. Pineda and Jiménez-Varea, "Popular Culture," 1164.

16. Pineda and Jiménez-Varea, "Popular Culture," 1171.

17. Andrew Hultkrans, "Steve Ditko's Hands," in *Give Our Regards to the Atomsmashers! Writers on Comics*, ed. Sean Howe (New York: Pantheon Books, 2004), 209.

18. Hultkrans, "Steve Ditko's Hands," 222.

19. Hultkrans, "Steve Ditko's Hands," 222.

20. Chris Sciabarra, "The Illustrated Rand," *Journal of Ayn Rand Studies* 6, no. 1 (2004): 2.

21. Sciabarra, "The Illustrated Rand," 11.

22. Jennifer Grossman, "Steve Ditko's Indelible Legacy," editorial, *Atlas Society*, last modified July 9, 2018, https://atlassociety.org/commentary/commentary-blog/6231-steve-ditko-s-indelible-legacy.

23. "Sorry to hear of Steve Ditko's passing. Steve loved John Severin's work and would pore over his pages when Steve visited our offices." Mort Todd, Facebook, July 6, 2018, https://www.facebook.com/groups/131715966970482/permalink/1114350858706983.

24. Steve Ditko, "Anti-Ditko 'Fans,'" *Four-Page Series*, June 2013, 7 (italics mine).

25. Andrei Molotiu, "Abstract Form: Sequential Dynamism and Iconostasis in Abstract Comics and Steve Ditko's *Amazing Spider-Man*," in *Critical Approaches to Comics: Theories and Methods*, ed. Matthew J. Smith and Randy Duncan (New York: Routledge, 2012), 89.

26. Molotiu, "Abstract Form," 89.

27. Molotiu, "Abstract Form," 91.

28. Molotiu, "Abstract Form," 94.

29. Paul Karasik and Mark Newgarden, *How to Read Nancy: The Elements of Comics in Three Easy Panels* (Seattle, WA: Fantagraphics Books, 2017), 23.

30. Pascal Lefèvre, "Mise en Scène and Framing: Visual Storytelling in *Lone Wolf and Cub*," in *Critical Approaches to Comics: Theories and Methods*, ed. Randy Duncan and Matthew J. Smith (New York: Routledge, 2012), 71.

31. Steve Ditko, "At Some Point," in *Avenging World* (Bellingham, WA: Robin Snyder and Steve Ditko, 2002), 36.

32. Steve Ditko, "ART!?" in *Avenging World* (Bellingham, WA: Robin Snyder and Steve Ditko, 2002), 143–54.

33. Ditko, "ART!?" 146.

34. Ditko, "ART!?" 146.

35. Ditko, "ART!?" 147 (italics mine).

36. Stan Lee, "Superheroes with Super Problems," interview by Nat Freedland, *New York Herald Tribune*, January 9, 1966.

37. Rand, specifically, has been compared to and explicitly called a cult leader by Michael Shermer in *Why People Believe Weird Things* (1997) and Jeff Walker in *The Ayn Rand Cult* (1999).

38. The popular historian Mitch Horowitz uncovered this specific relationship for the *Washington Post*'s blog *Political Bookworm* in a piece called "Reagan and the Occult," published in April 2010. The article makes a direct connection between Manly P. Hall's tale of the mysterious, unknown speaker at the signing of the Declaration of Independence, published in Hall's 1944 book *The Secret Destiny of America* and Reagan's 1957 commencement address at Eureka College in 1957, as well as an essay the president wrote for *Parade* in July 1981.

39. Gwenda Blair's books *The Trumps: Three Generations of Builders and a Presidential Candidate* (2015) and *Donald Trump: The Candidate* (2015), along with Gary Lachman's *Dark Star Rising: Magick and Power in the Age of Trump* (2018), have considered the connection between Trump and Peale. The key difference between the authors is that Blair's books are developing a historical look at the Trumps and their ascendancy to power, and Lachman is situating the presidency of Donald Trump and the rise of the alt-right within conversations about the occult and mystic thought in the twentieth century.

40. Steve Ditko, "Philosophy vs. No- or Anti-Philosophy," editorial, *Out of This World*, no. 25 (Fall 2016) (italics in the original).

41. Steve Ditko, *Avenging World*, ed. Robin Snyder (Bellingham, WA: R. Snyder and S. Ditko, 2002), 3.

42. Helena Rosenblatt, *The Lost History of Liberalism: From Ancient Rome to the Twenty-First Century* (Princeton, NJ: Princeton University Press, 2018), 3.

43. Rosenblatt, *The Lost History of Liberalism*, 2.

44. Rosenblatt, *The Lost History of Liberalism*, 142.

45. Alexis de Tocqueville, *Recollections: The French Revolution of 1848* (New York: Routledge, 2017), chap. 3, n.p., Google Books.

46. Rosenblatt, *The Lost History of Liberalism*, 26.

47. C. B. Macpherson, *The Political Theory of Possessive Individualism: Hobbes to Locke* (Oxford: Oxford University Press, 1962), 262.

48. Ayn Rand et al., *Capitalism: The Unknown Ideal*, centennial ed. (New York: Signet, 2008), 136.

49. Arthur Versluis, *Magic and Mysticism: An Introduction to Western Esotericism* (Lanham, MD: Rowman & Littlefield, 2007), 2 (italics mine).

50. John S. Haller, *The History of New Thought: From Mind Cure to Positive Thinking and the Prosperity Gospel* (West Chester, PA: Swedenborg Foundation Press, 2012), 2.

51. Haller, *The History of New Thought*, 217.

52. Haller, *The History of New Thought*, 217.

53. Gita Mehta, *Karma Cola: Marketing the Mystic East* (New York: Vintage Books, 1994), 100.

54. Horowitz, *Occult America*, 49.

55. Horowitz, *Occult America*, 49 (italics in original).

56. Blavatsky, *Isis Unveiled*, 87.

57. Blavatsky, *Isis Unveiled*, 199.

58. Blavatsky, *Isis Unveiled*, 133.

59. Steve Ditko, ". . . Right to Kill!" *Mr. A*, no. 1 (1973): 14.

60. Ditko, ". . . Right to Kill!" 25.

61. In the wake of public outcry against the violence inflicted by superheroes, many of these impositions, reportedly, came directly from onetime National/DC Comics editor Whitney Ellsworth, after collaborating with DC Comics copublisher Jack Liebowitz on the development of in-house guidelines for content (See Jones, *Men of Tomorrow*, 165; Brooker, *Batman Unmasked*, 60).

62. Archie Goodwin and Steve Ditko, "Deep Ruby!" in *Eerie Archives*, vol. 2, by Steve Ditko and Archie Goodwin, ed. Shawna Gore (Milwaukie, OR: Dark Horse Books, 2009), 23.

63. This story may have been produced with the writer Joe Gill, who was a frequent collaborator with Ditko at Charlton. Although no evidence currently confirms that this was the case, I do take this as being a serious possibility, and it would seem to be supported by the circumstances.

64. Steve Ditko, "From Out of the Depths," in *Impossible Tales: The Steve Ditko Archives*, vol. 4, comp. Blake Bell (Seattle, WA: Fantagraphics Books, 2013), 145.

65. Ditko, "From Out of the Depths," 148.

66. Ditko, "From Out of the Depths," 146.

67. Ditko, "From Out of the Depths," 147.

68. Gerry Conway and Archie Goodwin, "Doomsday—Minus One," *The Destructor*, no. 4 (August 1975): 9 (italics in the original).

2. Beyond What We Are Told Is Fact

1. Steve Ditko, "The Exploder," *Charlton Action: Featuring Static*, no. 12 (December 1985): 5 (italics in the original).

2. John S. Haller, *The History of New Thought: From Mind Cure to Positive Thinking and the Prosperity Gospel* (West Chester, PA: Swedenborg Foundation Press, 2012), 16.

3. Mitch Horowitz, *One Simple Idea: How the Lessons of Positive Thinking Can Transform Your Life* (New York: Skyhorse Publishing, 2016), 213. See also Ronald Reagan, "Ronald Reagan's Announcement for Presidential Candidacy," November 13, 1979, accessed February 10, 2019, https://www.reaganlibrary.gov/11-13-79.

4. Norman Vincent Peale, *The Power of Positive Thinking* (New York: Touchstone / Simon & Schuster, 2015), 32.

5. Reagan, "Ronald Reagan's Announcement for Presidential Candidacy," November 13, 1979.

6. Bill Morrison, "An Idea in Any Form," foreword to *witzend*, collected ed., vol. 1 (Seattle, WA: Fantagraphics Books, 2014), vii.

7. Bill Pearson, ed., *witzend*, no. 3 (New York: Wallace Wood, 1967).

8. Pearson, *witzend*, no. 3, inside front cover.

9. Steve Ditko, "The Avenging World: Part 1," in *witzend*, no. 6, ed. Bill Pearson (New York: Wallace Wood, 1969), 31.

10. Ditko, "The Avenging World: Part 1," 35.

11. Ditko, "The Avenging World: Part 1," 39.

12. Lysander Spooner, *The Constitution of No Authority*, vol. 4, *No Tyranny* (Boston: Lysander Spooner, 1870), 13 (italics in the original).

13. Steve Ditko, "The Avenging World: Part 2," in *witzend*, no. 7, ed. Bill Pearson (New York: Wallace Wood, 1970), 21 (italics mine).

14. Steve Ditko, *Avenging World*, ed. Robin Snyder (Bellingham, WA: R. Snyder and S. Ditko, 2002), 2.

15. Ewa Morawska, *For Bread with Butter* (New York: Cambridge University Press, 1985), 3.

16. Morawska, *For Bread with Butter*, 3.

17. Morawska, *For Bread with Butter*, 111.

18. Morawska, *For Bread with Butter*, 101, 267.

19. Morawska, *For Bread with Butter*, 268.

20. Morawska, *For Bread with Butter*, 269–71.

21. Morawska explains that many Slovaks who arrived in Johnstown were members of the German-American alliance, were often referred to as "German Slovaks," and gave the impression to many of their country-people of believing they were better than other immigrants. Speculatively, this impression had to do with the good relationships and solid connections many Slovaks, who were able to speak fluent German, had with German mill workers at Cambria, thus leading to better-paying jobs for these "German Slovaks" at Cambria. Many of these connections were also religiously linked through immigrant-founded churches, particularly Lutheran parishes (109). Although what I write next is highly speculative, this wrinkle in the story of Johnstown immigrants is worth noting because of the Slovak background that the Ditkos claim: the elder Stephen Ditko's job as a master carpenter, and the younger Steve Ditko's distinct references to German thinkers and writers in the story "My Brother . . ." from 1986. The connections are too tenuous to claim that the Ditkos were specifically part of this community,

especially as Steve Ditko's parents are buried in a Byzantine Catholic cemetery, but even this would not eliminate the artist's paternal lineage from being part of a Lutheran German Slovak community. So while I am not comfortable making any assertions about the Ditkos' association with such cultural subsets, the superficial connections are difficult to dismiss.

22. Morawska, *For Bread with Butter*, 103–4.

23. Morawska, *For Bread with Butter*, 85–89.

24. Werner Sollors's *Beyond Ethnicity* (New York: Oxford University Press, 1986), released in the year after Morawska's ethnography of Johnstown, makes a different case insofar as Sollors is interested not in the "raw data of the so-called ethnic experience, but in the mental formations and cultural constructions (the codes, beliefs, rites, and rituals which were developed in America to make sense of ethnicity and immigration in a melting pot culture" (9). One of the means by which sense is made is the production of art, and in Sollors's particular case, literature.

25. Morawska, *For Bread with Butter*, 112.

26. Morawska, *For Bread with Butter*, 117, 132.

27. Related to note 7, Steve Ditko quotes Goethe in "My Brother . . ."

28. Pierre Teilhard de Chardin (1881–1955) was a French idealist philosopher and Jesuit priest. A vitalist, de Chardin is perhaps most famous for his conception of the Omega Point, which is the belief that all life is moving toward a divine unification point, which is to say all will become one with God. This unification will be achieved through ever-accumulating spiritual, psychic energy—which he refers to as Radial Energy—and this energy is beyond what can presently be measured by physical means.

29. Haller, *The History of New Thought*, 9.

30. Haller, *The History of New Thought*, 91.

31. Haller, *The History of New Thought*, 191–92.

32. Haller, *The History of New Thought*, 33.

33. John Locke, *Locke: Two Treatises of Government, Student Edition* (Cambridge: Cambridge University Press, 1988), 357.

34. Locke, *Two Treatises*, 350.

35. Locke, *Two Treatises*, 296.

36. Locke, *Two Treatises*, 287–88 (italics in the original).

37. Locke, *Two Treatises*, 358 (italics mine).

38. Morawska, *For Bread with Butter*, 160, 194, 196, 202.

39. Coined in the late nineteenth century, the term "praxeology" was made popular by the Austrian economist Ludwig von Mises in texts like *Human Action*. Broadly, praxeology is the scientific study of human action, from which von Mises gains the title of his book. However, the term is not necessarily applied to random acts performed by human beings but describes *purposeful* actions performed by individuals in the service of achieving specific values. For further explication of praxeology, at least as it has been applied by thinkers concerned with liberal political and economic policy, see von Mises's *Human Action*, as well as Murray Rothbard's "Praxeology: A Reply to Mr. Schuller," *American Economic Review*, December 1951.

40. For further exploration of this perspective, in addition to the works of Ayn Rand cited here, I refer the reader to monographs more sensibly engaged with economic theory. From the Chicago school of economics, consider Milton Friedman's *Capitalism and Freedom* (2002 ed.), and from a revised Austrian perspective, consider Murray Rothbard's *Anatomy of the State* (1974) and *Man, Economy, and State with Power and Market* (2009).

41. See Mitch Horowitz, *Occult America* (New York: Bantam, 2009), 11–41. Horowitz traces a history that begins with the Shakers and literal, fundamentalist readings of Christian scripture by the Millerites as it moves past Miller's failed apocalyptic prophecies into increasingly mystical and magical approaches to Christianity, Swedenborgians like the man-cum-tall-tale

John Chapman (Johnny Appleseed), to mesmerism and Andrew Jackson Davis, to Henry Steel Olcott—a history of American mystics that opens in the rural American Northeast and spreads its way westward throughout the eighteenth and nineteenth centuries.

42. Nicholas Goodrick-Clarke, *The Occult Roots of Nazism* (New York: New York University Press, 1992), 1.

43. James Webb, *The Occult Establishment* (LaSalle, IL: Open Court, 1976), 13.

44. Webb, *The Occult Establishment*, 14.

45. One of the specific challenges made is to the connection between the Theosophy of Madame Blavatsky and Nazism. Both Lachman and Horowitz do acknowledge that Nazis did appropriate many occult symbols and adopted what Lachman calls a traditionalist mode of esoteric and occult thought; however, both are also strongly opposed to the notion that Blavatsky would have aligned herself with any substantive element of Nazi ideology, such as racism, anti-Semitism, or the notion of a one-world regime.

46. See Paula Rabinowitz's *American Pulp: How Paperbacks Brought Modernism to Main Street* (2016), in which she makes a thorough and compelling case for how increasingly mobile postwar Americans were exposed to challenging new ideas and reflections through mass-produced, inexpensive pulp paperbacks marketed to an increasingly literate population.

47. I am invoking the language of the Italian Marxist philosopher Antonio Gramsci offered in his prison writings during his captivity by Mussolini's fascist regime. Given the propensity for capitalism and an application of neoliberal and libertarian politics by the mystic liberals I describe in this book, it is extremely unlikely that any such person would *deliberately* invoke or cite a Marxist theorist. However, Gramsci's language is particularly useful, as it describes a group of intellectuals who are not credentialed by the ruling classes and instead articulate the experiences of the masses—a certain kind of common sense. Indeed, mystic liberals frequently rely on such messaging, distancing themselves from what they imagine to be the hegemony of academic and political elites, identifying themselves as an excluded minority. In *Capitalism: The Unknown Ideal*, Rand invokes this kind of language when she writes that "the smallest minority on earth is the individual" at the end of her essay "America's Persecuted Minority: Big Business." Furthermore, it is worth noting that many of the American mystics identified by Horowitz, Lachman, and others were, in fact, leftists, Marxists, and communists, like the Christian Socialist Wallace Wattles; Lachman and Horowitz often apply the term "liberal" here, but it is not in the same register in which I am using the term. So it is with intentional nuance and advisedness that I refer to Gramscian language and believe it to be the most appropriate for the purposes of this study. For convenient reference, the reader might consult Gramsci's *Selections from the Prison Notebooks* (2014), edited by Quintin Hoare and Geoffrey Nowell Smith.

48. Horowitz, *Occult America*, 46–47 (italics mine).

49. Mitch Horowitz, "Mitch Horowitz: HP Blavatsky versus Darth Vader," Theosophical Society, YouTube, July 18, 2016, https://youtu.be/dKdaoWOrAnQ.

50. Lippard's story was later appropriated by Theosophists and then passed along to Manly P. Hall, who repeated the story as a matter of Theosophic truth in *The Secret History of America* (1944). The story was then repeated numerous times by Ronald Reagan as part of his speeches, and Reagan published his version of the story, complete with Hall's Theosophic context, as an essay for *Parade* magazine in July 1981.

51. Blavatsky, *The Key to Theosophy*, 131–32 (italics in the original).

52. Mitch Horowitz's *Occult America* and John S. Haller's *The History of New Thought* (Swedenborg Foundation Publishers, 2012) are useful starting points for disentangling this history. Horowitz's *One Simple Idea* (Skyhorse Publishing, 2016) also presents a focused look at the movement and its contemporary implications.

53. Horowitz, *Occult America*, 83.

54. For example, in the chapter titled "Aristotle's Logic," in *A History of Western Philosophy* (2005 ed.), Bertrand Russell provides a thorough analysis of the categorical problems not addressed by Aristotelian logic, particularly arguing that notions like Aristotle's law of identity (A is A, for Rand and Ditko) fall apart once a predicate is deployed as part of a syllogism. For Russell, engaging with an Aristotelian system is "wasting [one's] time." However, he notes the staying power of Aristotle in Western thought up to the contemporary moment, lamenting that "throughout modern times, practically every advance in science, in logic, or in philosophy has had to be made in the teeth of the opposition from Aristotle's disciples."

55. This was true even in libertarian and anarchistic intellectual circles of the mid-twentieth century. For further examination of this criticism of Rand from her would-be audience, see Brian Doherty, *Radicals for Capitalism* (New York: PublicAffairs, 2008).

56. Ayn Rand, *Atlas Shrugged* (New York: Plume, 1999), 1170–71.

57. See the previously noted *Radicals for Capitalism*, as well as Jeff Walker, *The Ayn Rand Cult* (New York: Open Court, 1998); Adam Weiner, *How Bad Writing Destroyed the World* (New York: Bloomsbury, 2016); Jennifer Burns, *Goddess of the Market: Ayn Rand and the American Right* (New York: Oxford University Press, 2011); Anne Conover Heller, *Ayn Rand and the World She Made* (New York: Anchor, 2010); Douglas J. Den Uyl and Douglas B. Rasmussen, eds., *The Philosophic Thought of Ayn Rand* (Champaign: University of Illinois Press, 1987); David Kelley, *The Contested Legacy of Ayn Rand* (New Brunswick, NJ: Transaction Publishers, 2000); Lisa Duggan, *Mean Girl: Ayn Rand and the Culture of Greed* (Oakland: University of California Press, 2019); and Michael Shermer, "The Unlikeliest Cult," in *Why People Believe Weird Things* (New York: Holt, 2002).

58. Many of these works are self-published and range from the interesting, like Peter Saint-Andre's *The Tao of Roark* (Parker, CO: Monadnock Valley Press, 2013), to more obtuse and strained works like Morgan Rosenberg's *Dark Buddhism* (CreateSpace, 2011).

59. Rachel Weiner, "Paul Ryan and Ayn Rand," *Washington Post*, August 13, 2012, https://www.washingtonpost.com/blogs/the-fix/post/what-ayn-rand-says-about-paul-ryan/2012/08/13/fd40d574-e56d-11e1-8741-940e3f6dbf48_blog.html?utm_term=.bd6c335ef96b.

60. Nemo, "Satanism and Objectivism," Church of Satan, accessed April 8, 2018, https://www.churchofsatan.com/satanism-and-objectivism.php.

61. William Thomas, "What Is the Objectivist View of Reality (Metaphysics)?" Atlas Society, accessed April 8, 2018, https://atlassociety.org/objectivism/atlas-university/what-is-objectivism/objectivism-101-blog/5485-what-is-the-objectivist-view-of-reality-metaphysics.

62. The origins and nature of Smith's "invisible hand" are contested among scholars; however, Peter Harrison has made a compelling case for the religious origins of the term and asserts that Smith's earliest readers would have understood the term in that spiritual context. Harrison, "Adam Smith and the History of the Invisible Hand," *Journal of the History of Ideas* 72, no. 1 (2011): 29–49.

63. Wattles was a prominent New Thought writer and minister who wrote a trilogy of books titled *The Science of Getting Rich* (1910), *The Science of Being Great* (1910), and *The Science of Being Well* (1910), along with other titles like *How to Get What You Want* (1907) and *How to Promote Yourself* (1915). Wattles, however, was a Christian Socialist and believed that harnessing the power of the mind could and should be used to wipe away the robber barons of industry, creating a more egalitarian society.

64. Horowitz, *Occult America*, 81.

65. See Stirner's *The Ego and His Own*.

66. According to the *Ayn Rand Lexicon*, "a 'whim' is a desire experienced by a person who does not know and does not care to know its cause." http://aynrandlexicon.com/lexicon/whims-whim-worship.html. Further discussion of "whims" can be found in work such as

Rand's "The Objectivist Ethics," in *The Virtue of Selfishness*, 14; "Philosophic Detection," in *Philosophy: Who Needs It?* 19; and "Galt's Speech," in *For the New Intellectual*, 149. The relation of this usage to Stirner, as of this writing, remains somewhat oblique to me, and I'm not certain of its merit or if it has any at all.

67. See Nathaniel Branden's 1962 essay "Counterfeit Individualism," in Rand, *The Virtue of Selfishness*, 158–61. Rand herself never directly engages with Stirner, and this is the only time Stirner is specifically referenced in nonfiction books produced by the Ayn Rand Institute. Many of these books, like the ones referenced here, are collections of essays that originally appeared in the *Objectivist*, Rand's newsletter.

68. One might also be tempted to invoke Jung's mining of the unconscious, which may also have some interesting results for thinking about someone like Steve Ditko, rendering him as a kind of ghost hunter, searching for the self. However, given Ditko's apparent interest in German thinkers, egoism, and Stirner's invocation by Nathaniel Branden in "Counterfeit Individualists," Stirner's "ghosts" seem, at least for this particular question, to be a more prudent example for considering Ditko's work. And, for what it may be worth, Stirner's ghosts position Ditko as a kind of ghost hunter as well.

69. Stirner, *The Ego and His Own*, 96 (italics in the original).

70. Branden, in Rand, *The Virtue of Selfishness*, 158.

71. It is also worth briefly mentioning that post-9/11 Objectivists sought to merge Rand's philosophy with Eastern mysticism and philosophy, producing bizarre texts like Mark Rosenberg's *Dark Buddhism* and the more interesting, if not compelling, *Tao of Roark*, by Peter Saint-Andre. The occult historian Mitch Horowitz also counts himself as an admirer of both Rand and Ditko and frequently uses his Twitter account to extol the virtues of New Age thought and both the Randian and Ditkovian brands of Objectivism.

72. *Ayn Rand Lexicon*, s.v. "Mysticism," http://aynrandlexicon.com/lexicon/mysticism.html.

73. See Rand, "The Objectivist Ethics," in *The Virtue of Selfishness* (New York: Signet, 1964), 13.

74. Rand, "The Objectivist Ethics," 14.

75. Rand, "The Objectivist Ethics," 14.

76. Horatio Dresser, *A History of the New Thought Movement* (McAllister Editions, 2015), 4.

77. Dresser, *New Thought Movement*, 4.

78. Dresser, *New Thought Movement*, 3.

79. Dresser, *New Thought Movement*, 3.

80. Dresser, *New Thought Movement*, 68.

81. Dresser, *New Thought Movement*, 68.

82. Ditko, *Avenging World*, 1.

83. Dresser, *New Thought Movement*, 67.

84. Rand, *The Virtue of Selfishness*, 23 (italics in the original).

85. This is also precisely the kind of reasoning that placed *The Secret* (another book deeply indebted to New Thought) under attack, and with good reason.

86. Begrudging Rand biographer Jeff Walker compares NBI to Bhagwan Rajneesh's cult. See Walker, *The Ayn Rand Cult*, 141–76.

87. Walker, *The Ayn Rand Cult*, 144.

88. Walker, *The Ayn Rand Cult*, 153–54.

89. Walker, *The Ayn Rand Cult*, 160–64.

90. Walker, *The Ayn Rand Cult*, 164.

91. See Mitch Horowitz, *Occult America*.

92. In the "About the Author" appendix to *Atlas Shrugged*, Rand went so far as to claim that she had no philosophic influences or antecedents aside from Aristotle, with whom she was quick to point out she did not always agree.

93. It is worth noting that Lisa Duggan, in *Mean Girl* (2019), her study of Rand's cultural impact, argues that this interpretation of Rand's intellectual approach is limiting, if not wholly inaccurate. Duggan notes Rand's aversion to Judaism beginning as early as thirteen and observes that Rand's earliest writings sculpt heroes "who were radically unlike those around her." Duggan further notes that Rand's "ambivalence [to Judaism] shaped her views in myriad ways," and therefore it is "not fair or accurate to say that Rand's politics were somehow Jewish." Lisa Duggan, *Mean Girl: Ayn Rand and the Culture of Greed* (Oakland: University of California Press, 2019), 15–16.

94. Webb, *The Occult Establishment*, 16.

95. For further consideration of the evolution of neoliberalism as an intellectual matter, see David Kotz, *The Rise and Fall of Neoliberal Capitalism* (Cambridge, MA: Harvard University Press, 2015). Some of the most significant criticism of neoliberalism, thus leading to the expanded use of the term, comes from the work of Michel Foucault; see Foucault, *The Birth of Biopolitics: Lectures at the Collège de France, 1978–1979* (Picador, 2010), 217–19.

96. *Oxford English Dictionary*, s.v. "Individualism," accessed March 2, 2019, https://www.oed.com.

97. "Google Books Ngram Viewer: Individualism," chart, in *Google Ngrams*, accessed March 2, 2019, https://books.google.com/ngrams/graph?content=individualism&year_start=1800&year_end=2000&corpus=15&smoothing=3&share=&direct_url=t1%3B%2Cindividualism%3B%2Cco#t1%3B%2Cindividualism%3B%2Cco.

98. Alexis de Tocqueville, *Democracy in America and Two Essays on America* (New York: Penguin, 2003).

99. John Stuart Mill, *On Liberty, Utilitarianism and Other Essays* (New York: Oxford University Press, 2015).

100. C. B. Macpherson, *The Political Theory of Possessive Individualism* (London: Oxford University Press, 1962).

101. Macpherson, *Political Theory of Possessive Individualism*, 263.

102. Macpherson's seven propositions for possessive individualism are as follows (263–64):

> I. What makes a man human is freedom from dependence on the wills of others.
>
> II. Freedom from dependence on others means freedom from any relations with others except those whose relations which the individual enters voluntarily with a view of his own interest.
>
> III. The individual is essentially the proprietor of his own person and capacities, for which he owes nothing to society.
>
> IV. Although the individual cannot alienate the whole of his property in his own person, he may alienate his capacity to labor.
>
> V. Human society consists of a series of market relations.
>
> VI. Since Freedom from the wills of others is what makes a man human, each individual's freedom can rightfully be limited only by such obligations and rules as are necessary to secure the same freedom for others.
>
> VII. Political society is a human contrivance for the protection of the individual's property in his person and goods, and (therefore) for the maintenance of orderly relations of exchange between individuals regarded as proprietors of themselves.

103. Steve Ditko, *Avenging World*, ed. Robin Snyder (Bellingham, WA: R. Snyder and S. Ditko, 2002), 3 (italics in the original).

104. Arthur Versluis, *Magic and Mysticism: An Introduction to Western Esotericism* (Lanham, MD: Rowman & Littlefield, 2007), 2.

105. In a personal letter to me, dated March 13, 2018, in response to a question about whether he read occult works—specifically Theosophy, New Thought, and a few others—Ditko

refused to say whether or not he had read any such works. However, in the same letter, he was careful to acknowledge that artists must do research to present items and ideas as accurately as possible, seeming to suggest, albeit obliquely, that he had done just such research.

106. Russ Mahares, "Steve Ditko: Inside His Studio Sanctum Sanctorum," *Pop Culture Squad* (blog), March 16, 2019, accessed March 19, 2019, https://popculturesquad.com/2019/03/16/steve -ditko-inside-his-studio-sanatorium.

107. Bell, *Strange and Stranger*, 86.

108. Steve Ditko and Robin Snyder, *Down Memory Lane*, ed. Robin Snyder (Bellingham, WA: Robin Snyder and Steve Ditko, 2019), 14.

109. Ditko and Snyder, *Down Memory Lane*, 28.

110. For further exploration of this subject, see Peter Saint-Andre, "Our Man in Greece: On the Use and Abuse of Aristotle in the Works of Ayn Rand," *StPeter* (blog), entry posted 2009, accessed July 30, 2019, https://stpeter.im/writings/rand/aristotle-rand.html. Peter Saint-Andre, a self-identified philosopher, is, at the time of this writing, the principal engineer at Mozilla, a nonprofit tech firm responsible for the Firefox web browser. Saint-Andre has a decided inter- est in Objectivism and wrote a book significant to my earliest thinking for this study, *The Tao of Roark* (2013). While Saint-Andre does have an appreciation for Rand, I am not sure it is reasonable to lump him in with the supposedly "strict" Objectivists, like those at the Ayn Rand Institute. As such, Saint-Andre is also interesting as someone, like Ditko, who has a fondness for many of Rand's ideas but cannot be sensibly understood as a disciple. Instead, Saint-Andre frequently lenses Randian ideas through a more mystical glass.

3. Overwhelmed by a Cloak of Darkness

1. The Grand Comics Database (GCD) is an excellent resource for tracking down the names of writers and artists who worked on comics in an era before proper credit was the industry standard. While I hold the GCD in the highest regard, it is, understandably, an incomplete record. I trust GCD's attributions, even if I harbor a small amount of skepticism that it can be perfect in its accuracy at all times. As it relates to this chapter, I am convinced that Carl Memling is correctly credited as the writer of "Day of Reckoning"; and substantive efforts have been made by Martin O'Hearn on his blog *Who Created the Comic Books* to identify Memling's work, pinpointing stylistic flourishes common to Memling's writing. What I am leery about is crediting any other unidentified writers who worked with Ditko during this period, without some thorough vetting for those attributions. Because my aim is to scrutinize Ditko's specific contributions, I have not engaged in such a thorough vetting for other potential writers on the series. However, I checked in with Robin Snyder, Ditko's longtime publisher and comics historian, to see if he had any information regarding writers Ditko may have worked with in his earliest days. Snyder assured me that neither he nor Ditko had any clear recollection or knowledge (some sixty-plus years later) of what writers would have contributed the scripts for Ditko's earliest comics. This lack of recollection, of course, does not mean that Ditko did not speak with, know, or otherwise explicitly collaborate with writers about how a particular script should be illustrated, but there is simply no reliable information to suggest one way or the other. The result of this ambiguity, for the purposes of this book, is that I rely on the visual cues that Ditko provides as markers of consistency throughout his career—regardless of who his collaborators or editors were.

2. Of particular note should be the clear artistic influence of the comics artist Mort Meskin on Ditko's early work. Meskin and Ditko were mates at Joe Simon and Jack Kirby's S&K Studio in Ditko's early years, and Ditko was a great admirer of Meskin's work, adopting much from his

approach to layout and character design. In fact, when Ditko did the design work for writer Joe Gill's Captain Atom, he plainly swiped Meskin's design for Atoman, whom Meskin had created for Spark Publications in 1946. For further reading on Meskin, see Steven Brower, *From Shadow to Light: The Life and Art of Mort Meskin* (Seattle, WA: Fantagraphics, 2010).

3. The literature scholar James Machin further considers the VanderMeers' definition of weird fiction and the implication of its usage in his 2017 article "Weird Fiction and the Virtues of Obscurity: Machen, Stenbock, and the Weird Connoisseurs." Machin suggests that definitions of the weird, particularly as they eschew other popular elements of horror fiction (e.g., werewolves, zombies, etc.), are made in the service of claiming "cultural value above that normally afforded 'genre' fiction." This distinction, Machin argues, gives weird fiction some sort of cachet for a "more educated, cultural elite" to draw from in designating a particular kind of horror and speculative fiction as being a more "nuanced, literary writing." Put differently, identifying a text as "weird" lends a sense of authenticity to both the text and the reader. This is an interesting critique of the emergence of the weird as it has gained popularity in scholarly circles, and it seems to run parallel to the kind of tension that Marc Singer considers in his 2019 book on the ongoing concerns in comics studies, *Breaking the Frames: Populism and Prestige in Comics Studies*. As a brief example, Singer notes the anxiety among academics concerning what to call comics: Comics? Graphic novels? Graphic narrative? In both cases, it appears that the primary concern is staking out some kind of respectability for the reader-scholar's selected texts. Although I don't think my writing here is afflicted with the kind of anxiety identified by either Machin or Singer, I take their points. However, in terms of the weird and how it is being used in this chapter, I am less inclined to apply Machin's reading here for at least the reason that the comics Ditko was working on (along with numerous other titles at other publishers and any number of pulp magazines) were identified by the publishers and authors as "weird" in an attempt to differentiate themselves in terms of content more than literary value. In some cases, not even a content differentiation was at hazard as much as a means of diversifying a product line, even if superficially.

4. Ann and Jeff VanderMeer, "The Weird: An Introduction," *Weird Fiction Review* 6 (May 2012), http://weirdfictionreview.com/2012/05/the-weird-an-introduction.

5. See Steve Ditko, *Mr. A*, no. 1 (1973): 25–33.

6. See Mitch Horowitz, *Occult America: White House Seances, Oujia Circles, Masons, and the Secret Mystic History of Our Nation* (New York: Bantam, 2010), 45–50, 146, 164–65, 186–91, 194.

7. Horowitz, *Occult America*, 49 (italics in the original).

8. See Brian Doherty, *Radicals for Capitalism: A Freewheeling History of the Modern American Libertarian Movement* (New York: PublicAffairs, 2007).

9. For further exploration of Ditko's introduction of the "right to kill," see Zack Kruse, "Steve Ditko: Violence and Romanticism in the Silver Age," *Studies in Comics* 5, no. 2 (2014): 344–52.

10. Steve Ditko, "Steve Ditko: A Portrait of the Master," interview by Larry Herndon, *Ditkomania*, no. 24 (June–July 1988): 1–6.

11. Fully recognizing that "Golden Age" is a contested term with a long history of scholarly and fan debate, I believe it to be appropriate in this specific context, as it is a term Ditko himself uses in the interview cited. Further, it is clear from his references that Ditko means this term to be applied to comics produced before the implementation of the Comics Code.

12. For a more detailed examination of this history and the history of the Comics Code, see Amy Kiste Nyberg, *Seal of Approval: The History of the Comics Code* (Jackson: University Press of Mississippi, 1998); Mike Benton, *Crime Comics: The Illustrated History* (Houston, TX: Taylor, 1993); and David Hajdu, *The Ten Cent Plague* (New York: Farrar, Straus and Giroux, 2008).

13. Mike Benton, *Horror Comics: The Illustrated History* (Dallas, TX: Taylor, 1991), 25.

14. For further discussion of Charlton and its history, see Jon B. Cooke, "The Action Hero Man: The Great Giordano Talks Candidly about Charlton," *Comic Book Artist* 9 (2000): 30–51, 109; and Randy Duncan and Michael Smith, "The Charlton Comics Story," *Power of Comics*, http://www.powerofcomics.com/the-charlton-comics-story.

15. Quoted in Steve Ditko, "Introduction," in *Strange Suspense*, by Steve Ditko, ed. Blake Bell, vol. 1 of *The Steve Ditko Archives* (Seattle, WA: Fantagraphics, 2009), 7.

16. For a detailed scholarly look at EC's sociopolitical messaging, particularly as it relates to race, see Qiana Whitted, *EC Comics: Race, Shock, and Social Protest* (New Brunswick, NJ: Rutgers University Press, 2019). The book provides a convincing analysis of the EC stories known as "preachies," which appeared in the series *Shock SuspenStories*. While the preachies took on a variety of sociopolitical issues, the thrust of Whitted's analysis—which includes the reaction of readers—is how the stories addressed the problems of racism and anti-Semitism in 1950s America. Although this chapter is not substantially engaged with EC enough to warrant a full examination of its line, Whitted's book provides important insight into considerations of race in comics and provides important insight for the opening section of chapter 4.

17. Ditko, *Strange Suspense*, 46, 63, 142, 171.

18. Mike Benton also notes Dr. Strange's link to "theosophy" in his 1991 book *The Illustrated History of Superhero Comics: The Silver Age*. However, I will make a few important distinctions. First, Benton links "theosophy" and Eastern mysticism to the dialogue edited by Stan Lee, giving Lee primary consideration in the matter. This is problematic, as it does not account for Ditko being responsible for plotting Dr. Strange, along with the panel scripts he wrote independent of Lee's influence. Even if one wanted to look at later stories where Lee's editorial demands (discussed in chap. 4) made their way into the plots, the character was wholly conceived—and the first two stories were written—by Ditko. Additionally, Benton is using "theosophy" in an entirely different register from the way I am using it throughout this study. Benton's use of "theosophy" implies a wide range of vaguely Christian beliefs that typically involve a knowledge of God achieved through spiritual ecstasy. Capital-*T* Theosophy, as I use the term, refers exclusively to the religious movement founded by H. P. Blavatsky and Henry Steel Olcott and explicated in texts like *The Key to Theosophy* and *Isis Unveiled*. Mike Benton, *Superhero Comics of the Silver Age: The Illustrated History* (Dallas, TX: Taylor, 1991), 62–63.

19. See H. P. Blavatsky, *The Key to Theosophy* (Kshetra Books, 2016); H. P. Blavatsky, *Isis Unveiled* (Wheaton, IL: Quest Books, 1997); H. P. Blavatsky, *The Secret Doctrine* (New York: Jeremy P. Tarcher, 2009); Mitch Horowitz, *Occult America*; and K. Paul Johnson, *The Masters Revealed: Madame Blavatsky and the Myth of the Great White Lodge* (Albany: State University of New York Press, 1994).

20. Blavatsky, *The Key to Theosophy*, 131–32 (italics in the original).

21. Blavatsky, *The Key to Theosophy*, 133.

22. Blavatsky, *The Key to Theosophy*, 149.

23. Carl Memling and Steve Ditko, "Doom in the Air," in *Strange Suspense*, by Steve Ditko, ed. Blake Bell, vol. 1 of *The Steve Ditko Archives* (Seattle, WA: Fantagraphics, 2009), 158–65.

24. Blavatsky, *The Key to Theosophy*, 203.

25. Carl Memling and Steve Ditko, "Day of Reckoning," in *Strange Suspense*, vol. 1 of *The Steve Ditko Archives*, ed. Blake Bell (Seattle, WA: Fantagraphics, 2009), 178–83.

26. Memling and Ditko, "Day of Reckoning," 178.

27. This motif may be most recognizable in the adversarial relationship that Peter Parker has with the grotesquely rendered J. Jonah Jameson in *The Amazing Spider-Man*. Greed and cheapness always signify moral corruptness in Ditko's oeuvre. One may be tempted to apply a Marxist critique of capital and labor here, but such a reading would be significantly

complicated by the recurrence of this motif in Ditko's later work, which is deeply invested in a liberal imagination of capitalism in the late twentieth century.

28. Memling and Ditko, "Day of Reckoning," 178.

29. I consider this issue and its historical impact more extensively in an earlier work on Ditko's contributions to the superhero genre, later in this book, and in my youthfully composed article for *Studies in Comics*, "Steve Ditko: Violence and Romanticism in the Silver Age."

30. Steve Ditko and Steve Skeates, "Kill Vic Sage!" in *Action Heroes*, vol. 2, DC Archive Editions (New York: DC Comics, 2007), 269–76.

31. Steve Ditko, "Library of Horror," in *Strange Suspense*, by Steve Ditko, ed. Blake Bell, vol. 1 of *The Steve Ditko Archives* (Seattle, WA: Fantagraphics, 2009), 64–70.

32. Ditko, "Library of Horror," 64.

33. Ditko, "Library of Horror," 65.

34. Ditko, "Library of Horror," 65 (italics mine).

35. Current records do not identify a potential writer for the story.

36. Ditko, "Library of Horror," 66.

37. Steve Ditko, "Inheritance," in *Strange Suspense*, by Steve Ditko, ed. Blake Bell, vol. 1 of *The Steve Ditko Archives* (Seattle, WA: Fantagraphics, 2009), 166–70.

38. Ditko, "Library of Horror," 70.

39. For a thorough and engaging examination of the comics work of Jack Kirby, see Charles Hatfield, *Hand of Fire: The Comics Art of Jack Kirby* (Jackson: University Press of Mississippi, 2012).

40. Steve Ditko and Stan Lee, *Essential Doctor Strange*, direct ed. (New York: Marvel Comics, 2001).

41. Steve Ditko and Stan Lee, *The Amazing Spider-Man*, Marvel Omnibus (New York: Marvel Comics, 2007).

42. Steve Ditko, "Die Laughing," in *Strange Suspense*, by Steve Ditko, ed. Blake Bell, vol. 1 of *The Steve Ditko Archives* (Seattle, WA: Fantagraphics, 2009, 71–77).

43. Ditko, "Die Laughing," 75.

44. Ditko, "Die Laughing," 77 (italics mine).

45. For a more detailed reading of the presentation of violence in Ditko's work, see Kruse, "Steve Ditko: Violence and Romanticism."

4. "'Twas Steve's Idea"

1. The religious studies scholar Paul G. Hackett comments on the casting of Tilda Swinton in the Dr. Strange film and notes that the casting of Swinton is "*not* an instance of 'whitewashing' because it entails the specific erasure of Tibet and Tibetans as a distinct people and unique culture both by omission and by lumping them into the amorphous category of 'Asians' as if all members of that group were somehow interchangeable." Hackett also notes the complicated politics of the casting, citing screenwriters who "explicitly acknowledged that the erasure of Tibet was a political move premeditated and designed specifically to avoid the inevitable, theatrically hypersensitive response of the [People's Republic of China's] government concerning any and all things Tibetan" so as to avoid negatively impacting the box office success of the film. However, although Hackett is focusing specifically on the racial problematics of the 2016 film, he does take time to consider the earliest comics produced by Ditko, but he either does not recognize or take into account the depicted racial identity of Dr. Strange and instead relies on the assumption of the character's Western identity. Paul Hackett, "From the Razor's Edge to the Scalpel's Blade: Larry Darrell, Doctor Strange, and the Trope of the Rehabilitated Western

Man as Yogi," in *The Assimilation of Yogic Religions through Pop Culture*, ed. Paul G. Hackett (Lanham, MD: Lexington Books, 2017), 64–65 (italics in the original).

2. Qiana J. Whitted, *EC Comics: Race, Shock, and Social Protest* (New Brunswick, NJ: Rutgers University Press, 2019), 64.

3. W. J. T. Mitchell, *Picture Theory: Essays on Visual and Verbal Representation* (Chicago: University of Chicago Press, 1995), 162–63; see also Whitted, *EC Comics*, 64.

4. Whitted, *EC Comics*, 64–65.

5. See, e.g., Frances K. Gateward and John Jennings, eds., *The Blacker the Ink: Constructions of Black Identity in Comics and Sequential Art* (New Brunswick, NJ: Rutgers University Press, 2015); Sheena C. Howard and Ronald L. Jackson, eds., *Black Comics: Politics of Race and Representation*, repr. ed. (London: Bloomsbury Academic, 2014); Adilifu Nama, *Super Black: American Pop Culture and Black Superheroes* (Austin: University of Texas Press, 2011); and Deborah Elizabeth Whaley, *Black Women in Sequence: Re-inking Comics, Graphic Novels, and Anime* (Seattle: University of Washington Press, 2016).

6. Although East Asian characters had long existed in other comics formats—like Alex Raymond's newspaper strip *Flash Gordon*—Stuff is one of the earliest East Asian heroes to appear in the comic book format. It is worth noting that Stuff first appeared in 1942 in *Action Comics* #45 in a story that was written by Mort Weisinger and drawn by Mort Meskin. The reader will observe that in note 2 of chapter 3, Meskin was linked to Ditko as being a source of inspiration for Ditko and his developing visual style, and the two worked together at Joe Simon and Jack Kirby's S&K Studio in Ditko's earliest years. Absent from Ditko's Doctor Strange are the overtly racist character renderings of the evil Chinese gangsters in Meskin's Vigilante story from 1945, and also absent are the racist dialogue affectations of Weisinger's script. However, that Ditko was exposed early on to an artist—an artist whom Ditko greatly admired—whose collaborations produced one of the earliest superheroes or sidekicks of clear East Asian descent is significant. Moreover, despite the troubling dialogue affectations and the visual depictions of Chinese gangsters, the way in which Meskin renders Stuff strikes me as unoffensive, particularly when compared to other East Asian sidekicks from the 1940s, like Chop-Chop. Chop-Chop, at best, was a horrifically racist cartoon caricature in a world populated by more photorealistic white characters. Although Ditko's admiration for Meskin is no secret, for further reading about Ditko's thoughts on Meskin's work, see Steven Brower, *From Shadow to Light: The Life and Art of Mort Meskin* (Seattle, WA: Fantagraphics, 2010), 122–23.

7. Steve Ditko and Robin Snyder, *Down Memory Lane*, ed. Robin Snyder (Bellingham, WA: Robin Snyder and Steve Ditko, 2019), 18.

8. Coincidentally, the Nick Fury and SHIELD series appeared in *Strange Tales* alongside Dr. Strange, but Woo did not appear alongside Fury until 1967, after Ditko left Dr. Strange.

9. Dr. Droom quickly faded into obscurity and was eventually revived at Marvel under the name Dr. Druid in a reprint of *Amazing Adventures* #1 in *Weird Wonder Tales* #19 (1976). Obviously, the name was changed to avoid confusion with the Fantastic Four villain Dr. Doom.

10. Imes makes clear that Lee also explicitly stated this view. Rob Imes, "DitkoFAQ—Who Created Dr. Strange?" Official Website of the United Fanzine Organization, last modified January 15, 2018, http://unitedfanzineorganization.weebly.com/ditkofaq.html#006.

11. The religious studies scholar Anya Foxen briefly considers Dr. Strange and Dr. Droom in "Supermen, Mystical Women, and Oriental Others," and she correctly identifies the East Asian features given to Dr. Strange, as well as the convergences and divergences with Dr. Droom. She also correctly identifies the transition of Strange into a more distinctly Western character a few issues after his first appearance in *Strange Tales*. However, I differ with Foxen's categorization of Dr. Strange's earliest appearance in a few key areas. She identifies the character as being

in yellow face, and while I agree that there are troubling Orientalist perspectives on display throughout Dr. Strange's stories, it is my presumption that Ditko is not attempting to re-create a white actor playing an Asian character but rather presents a distinctly Asian character. Where I also differ with her reading of the character is in her reliance on sources that prioritize Stan Lee's hand in the initial creation of the character. However, her assessments of later stories, ones without Ditko's involvement, are productive. Anya P. Foxen, "Supermen, Mystical Women, and Oriental Others: Dynamics of Race and Gender in Pop-Cultural Yogis and the Universal Superhuman," in *The Assimilation of Yogic Religions through Pop Culture*, ed. Paul G. Hackett (Lanham, MD: Lexington Books, 2017), 47–50.

12. Roussos, it is worth noting, worked on some of EC Comics' "preachies," which were the social protest stories that the company regularly inserted into its publication *Shock SuspenStories*. However, similarly messaged stories appeared in other publications, and one such example is "Slave Ship," which appeared in *Weird Fantasy* #8 (1951). The story was written by Al Feldstein (who had written nearly all of EC's other preachies) and featured pencils and inks by George Roussos. Whitted notes that this story "reckons with the brutal legacy of white hegemony through otherworldly vengeance of the weird." Incidents like this are significant, at least in reference to Roussos, because he was sure to have encountered issues with race and representation in his earlier works, so one can safely assume that the issues of race in Dr. Strange would not be entirely lost on him when he accepted the assignment. Whitted, *EC Comics*, 112.

13. Steve Ditko, "He Giveth and He Taketh Away," in *The Avenging Mind* (2008), 19.

14. Ditko, "He Giveth," 19.

15. In a 1963 letter to Jerry Bails, Stan Lee infamously wrote, "Well, we have a new character in the works for *Strange Tales*, just a 5-page filler named Dr. Strange. Steve Ditko is gonna draw him. It has sort of a black magic theme. The first story is nothing great, but perhaps we can make something of him. *'Twas Steve's idea*. I figured we'd give it a chance, although again, we had to rush the first one too much" (italics mine). The letter was later reproduced in the fanzine the *Comic Reader*, which Bails also published. The clear indication of the letter is, first, that it supports Ditko's version of events, and, second, that Lee initially distanced himself from the character before Dr. Strange became a hit with readers.

16. Steve Ditko, "Toyland: Martin Goodman / Stan Lee," in *The Avenging Mind* (2008).

17. Mr. Crime first appeared in *Crime Does Not Pay* #24 (1942), but even his introduction was not a wholly original innovation. Mr. Crime, as created by Charles Biro, is likely based on a cartoon mascot, Mr. Coffee Nerves. Mr. Coffee Nerves was designed by Milt Caniff and Noel Sickles and appeared in a series of advertisements for Postum, a caffeine-free coffee alternative developed by the Post Cereal Company. However, it was after the introduction of Mr. Crime and the success of *Crime Does Not Pay* that the horror host became a staple of the horror, crime, and suspense stories of the 1940s, 1950s, and beyond, perhaps the best known of which being the Crypt Keeper from EC Comics' *Tales from the Crypt*. The trope was so well-known and popular that it was eventually adopted by local television stations as a part of their horror and monster movie programming, beginning with Vampira in 1954, with the tradition continuing into the present day with hosts like Elvira and Svengoolie. Even the Crypt Keeper transitioned into television horror host for HBO's *Tales from the Crypt* anthology series.

18. According to Robin Snyder, while Snyder was at Western Publishing in the early 1980s, he had intended to pair Ditko with Al McWilliams and writer Robert Kanigher on a Flash Gordon comic, as Western held the license at the time. The opening page of a Ditko Flash Gordon story, written by George Kashdan, appeared in the 2015 Snyder-Ditko publication *Out of This World* #17 as the story "Web of Treachery." See Bob Heer and Robin Snyder, "Oh, boy. Web of Treachery brings up so, so many good memories of the way it was at Western. If only management had left us alone, it was our intention to give Flash to RK and Ditko and McWilliams,"

Facebook, October 23, 2018, https://www.facebook.com/groups/robinsnyder/permalink
/1105406142955049.

19. Steve Ditko, "A Mini-History: *The Amazing Spider-Man #1,*" *The Comics*, November 2001, 1.

20. Ditko, "He Giveth," 20.

21. The comment about the character leading a title is important when historicizing the continual publication of characters of color. A significant example of this is the character Chop-Chop, a racist Chinese caricature who appeared as a sidekick to the character Blackhawk. Chop-Chop first appeared at Quality Comics in 1941, and the character then remained in publication when Blackhawk was purchased by DC Comics, and his publication continued there from 1957 to 1968. The Blackhawk series appeared sporadically until 1990. That Chop-Chop has a longer publication history than Dr. Strange is indisputable, but the distinction I am making here is whether or not the character is the lead heroic figure in the title. Although the character evolved over time in an attempt to shed his racist past, Chop-Chop was not the lead character that Dr. Strange was.

22. Jeffrey Kripal's *Mutants and Mystics* spends little time exploring Theosophy and Western esotericism in Dr. Strange's stories. Kripal does explicitly link Dr. Strange's journey into Tibet in search of ancient knowledge to Theosophy, but he then immediately moves on and does not explore the issue or Ditko's interest in occult knowledge. Instead he defers to other considerations of Dr. Strange that describe Ditko's work in comparison with Salvador Dalí and its supposed references to Beat culture. In so doing, Kripal, like Mike Benton and others, also accepts the mistaken notion that Stan Lee was responsible for Dr. Strange's links to the occult. Jeffrey J. Kripal, *Mutants and Mystics: Science Fiction, Superhero Comics, and the Paranormal* (Chicago: University of Chicago Press, 2015), 133–34.

23. Blavatsky, *The Key to Theosophy*, 41, 59.

24. Stirner, "Second Part: The Owner: 3—My Self Enjoyment," in *The Ego and His Own*.

25. *Strange Tales* #110, in *Dr. Strange Omnibus* (Marvel, 2016), 1.

26. Charles W. Leadbeater, *The Astral Plane: Its Scenery, Inhabitants and Phenomena* (CreateSpace, 2016).

27. This is according to ACE Comics publisher Ron Frantz. See *Ditkomania*, no. 90 (March 2013); and Rob Imes, "Ditko FAQ," United Fanzine Organization: Ditkomania, accessed June 14, 2018, http://unitedfanzineorganization.weebly.com/ditkofaq.html.

28. Nathaniel Branden, *The Six Pillars of Self Esteem* (Bantam, 1994), 3–4.

29. Branden, *The Six Pillars of Self Esteem*, 5–6 (italics mine).

30. This is also precisely the kind of reasoning that placed *The Secret* (another book deeply indebted to New Thought) under attack, and with good reason.

31. Branden, *The Six Pillars of Self-Esteem*, 18 (italics in the original).

32. *Strange Tales* #110, 5.

33. *Strange Tales* #126, in *Dr. Strange Omnibus* (Marvel, 2016), 2–3.

34. *Strange Tales* #126, 3–4 (italics in the original).

35. *Strange Tales* #126, 2 (italics in the original).

36. *Strange Tales* #126, 6.

37. In the early Dr. Strange comics, editor and dialogue embellisher Stan Lee did not have either a clear recollection or a grasp of the centrality of the amulet Strange wore. As a result, Lee frequently inserted different language for the amulet, sometimes referring to it as only an "enchanted amulet," as he does in this particular story (*Strange Tales* #126). The object more commonly known as the Eye of Agamotto does not appear until the end of this two-part arc in *Strange Tales* #127, and even after that point, Lee has difficulty in keeping the name straight. Regardless of what language Lee inserts for either object, it is the visual and symbolic importance that is paramount.

38. Ella Wheeler Wilcox, *The Heart of New Thought* (London: Psychic Research Company), 17.

39. *Strange Tales* #126, 8.

40. *Strange Tales* #126, 9.

41. *Strange Tales* #127, in *Dr. Strange Omnibus* (Marvel, 2016), 3 (italics in the original).

42. Ayn Rand, *The Romantic Manifesto: A Philosophy of Literature*, 2nd ed. (New York: Signet, 1975), 76 (italics in the original).

43. *Strange Tales* #127, 7.

44. *Strange Tales* #127, 10.

45. Steve Ditko and Stan Lee, "What Lurks beneath the Mask," *Strange Tales* #136.

46. Rand, "The Nature of the Second-Hander," in *For the New Intellectual*, 70.

47. Rand, "The Nature of the Second-Hander," 69 (italics mine).

48. Rand uses this precise terminology in her conception of the second-hander, but it is also significant when discussing the work of Steve Ditko because of the obvious connection this kind of phrasing and thinking have to the character of Spider-Man and that series' most well-known theme: "With great power comes great responsibility."

49. Rand, *For the New Intellectual*, 83.

50. *Strange Tales* #136, in *Dr. Strange Omnibus* (Marvel, 2016), 8.

51. *Strange Tales* #137, in *Dr. Strange Omnibus* (Marvel, 2016), 7.

52. Ernest Holmes, *The Science of the Mind* (Dodd, Mead, 1953), 44.

53. Charles Haanel, *The Master Key System* (Murine Press, 1912), 101.

54. *Strange Tales* #146, in *Dr. Strange Omnibus* (Marvel, 2016), 2.

55. *Strange Tales* #146, in *Dr. Strange Omnibus* (Marvel, 2016), 9.

5. Grounded in a More Credible World

1. Horowitz, *One Simple Idea*, 91, 97.

2. Steve Ditko, in *The Masters of Comic Book Art*, directed by Ken Viola (Rhino Home Video, 1987).

3. Ayn Rand, *The Romantic Manifesto: A Philosophy of Literature*, 2nd ed. (New York: Signet, 1975), 109.

4. Branden, *The Six Pillars of Self-Esteem*, 42.

5. I am using "Silver Age" as a historical denotation that identifies a thematic and artistic shift in the production of superhero comics that begins with the release of DC Comics' *Showcase* #4 in 1956. Comics historians and scholars debate the precise closing date for the Silver Age; however, the consensus is that the era closes in the early 1970s, and the comics scholar Peter Coogan argues that 1970 marks the end of the era in his book *Superhero: The Secret Origin of a Genre*. Scholars such as Geoff Klock push the end of the Silver Age to as late as 1986. However, as we will see, the major shifts that build toward some of the publications of the mid-1980s (*Watchmen*, *Daredevil: Born Again*, *The Dark Knight Returns*) have their narrative roots in the superhero comics that Steve Ditko produced from 1962 to 1972. Finally, it is worth noting that Benjamin Woo argues effectively in "An Age-Old Problem: Problematics of Comics Historiography" that comics ages are almost always unstable, even if they are occasionally useful. Further, such ages are bound to a historical narrative about comics that focuses entirely on the superhero genre, neglecting the myriad other genres that regularly outsold superhero comics at various historical moments.

6. Steve Ditko, "A Mini-History: *The Amazing Spider-Man* #1," *The Comics*, November 2001, 1.

7. Ditko, "A Mini-History: *The Amazing Spider-Man*," 1.

8. Steve Ditko, "He Giveth and He Taketh Away," in *The Avenging Mind* (2008), 19.

9. Indeed, when Ditko first took the Spider-Man job, it was uncertain that the character would endure beyond *Amazing Fantasy* #15, but the popularity of the character allowed him to continue beyond *Amazing Fantasy* and into *The Amazing Spider-Man*. Ditko began working on Spider-Man in 1962 and created Dr. Strange in 1963, the only other character for whom Ditko had a sustained run at Marvel.

10. Ditko, "A Mini-History: *The Amazing Spider-Man*," 1.

11. Another potential criticism of Ditko employing the "epic" form is the role that seriality plays in the publication of the story. However, where Ditko's work is set apart is that during his tenure on *The Amazing Spider-Man*, Ditko—even though he was producing panel scripts with dialogue—was not necessarily in complete control of the final content of word balloons or narration boxes as edited by Stan Lee; but Ditko was in control over the visual narrative, which allowed him to put Peter Parker through his paces. Additionally, as Ditko gained more accurate, if not complete, credit and creative control for plotting, the serialized elements are pushed farther back as the narrative becomes a more unified voice and vision. The character begins to work within arcs instead of simply "one and done" stories. Moreover, once Ditko left Marvel to produce superhero comics at Charlton, he gained almost total control over the narrative and character arcs (aside from the Comics Code), again disrupting the notion that serialization would necessarily be problematic. What is key here is that the framework that Ditko was working within was not necessarily coequal with the types of narratives of contemporary works or even the kinds of presuperhero stories Ditko had produced at Marvel. His work on Spider-Man, Blue Beetle, the Question, and Mr. A fits within a context unique for the 1960s and early 1970s. While one could certainly not make a one-to-one comparison, one might consider serialization of these specific works by Ditko in the same way that one would consider the serialization of modern comics stories that are long-form tales but broken into installments.

12. Umberto Eco's article "The Myth of Superman" offers a counterpoint to this perspective where Eco briefly suggests that the reader *can* self-identify with the character of Superman though the character's alter ego, Clark Kent. This is not the focus of Eco's article, but it does force the question of whether Spider-Man *really* was different from other heroes of the era. Even if the reader is able to identify with Superman through his alter ego, Kent, in the case of Peter Parker, we find no clear distinction between the identity of Peter Parker and the identity of Spider-Man, only the costume. The character of Superman plays a convincing Clark Kent and vice versa; but Spider-Man is not playing Peter Parker—he *is* Peter Parker.

13. Umberto Eco, "The Myth of Superman," *Diacritics* 2, no. 1 (1972): 22.

14. Marc Singer, *Breaking the Frames: Populism and Prestige in Comics Studies* (Austin: University of Texas Press, 2019), 40.

15. Steve Ditko and Stan Lee, *The Amazing Spider-Man Omnibus* (New York: Marvel, 2016), 10.

16. Ditko and Lee, *The Amazing Spider-Man Omnibus*, 890–98.

17. Ditko and Lee, *The Amazing Spider-Man Omnibus*, 945–47. Another—I think viable—way to read the interactions Peter has at the *Daily Bugle* offices is to put them in the context of Ditko's own working conditions at Marvel and the relationships he had there. As an exceedingly brief example, in *Amazing Spider-Man* #25, Peter attempts to sell some photographs of Spider-Man assisting the police in thwarting some car thieves. Jameson doesn't want the pictures because they don't actually show Spider-Man but rather show his Spider-Signal guiding the cops toward the criminals. Peter then explains why the shots are valuable to Jameson: they actually make Spider-Man look bad because he couldn't stop a couple of hoods on his own. Jameson realizes that's a great angle for his purposes and immediately takes credit for the idea in a way all too similar to Stan Lee to be overlooked. In fact, Jameson's complaints about Spider-Man not actually being photographed in action are similar to the perceptibly sarcastic narration boxes Lee wrote for *Amazing Spider-Man* #18, an issue that featured no

combat with a foe but was instead about Peter dealing with his personal life and a grave illness for Aunt May. This relationship between freelancer and editor seems to parallel the interplay between Ditko and Lee, at least as Ditko and others have described their working relationship with Lee. We see another interesting case in the ups and downs of Peter's romantic relationship with Betty Brant. As the office secretary at the *Daily Bugle*, Betty seems to be a stand-in for Flo Steinberg, the secretary at the Marvel office and a pivotal figure in the company's early days (for an extended look at Steinberg's contributions, see *Alter Ego*, no. 153 [July 2018]). Photographs of Steinberg from the period bear an uncanny resemblance to Ditko's rendering of Betty Brant, and Steinberg, along with Sol Brodsky, would have been Ditko's main point of contact in the Marvel offices—especially after Ditko and Lee stopped speaking to each other. Even more intriguingly, in the September 2019 issue of *Alter Ego*, Bernie Bubnis writes of his time with Ditko in the 1960s, and he recounts an anecdote about Ditko asking Steinberg to lunch, which she rejected. Bubnis then says that, years later, he asked Steinberg whether or not Ditko had asked her on other dates, to which she said, "Probably, but times were different then. You didn't date fellow employees," and, according to Bubnis, Steinberg then went on to say that she probably would not have gone out with him anyway. Bernie Bubnis, "A Life Lived on His Own Terms," *Alter Ego*, no. 160 (September 2019): 40. This is an intriguing bit of information, as it seems to inform the relationship between Peter and Betty at the *Daily Bugle*, along with Peter's eventual heartbreaking acceptance, in *Amazing Spider-Man* #30, that as much as he cared about Betty, there was just not a future for them together. I feel compelled to acknowledge how speculative these connections are, and that, along with a reticence about relying on anecdotal evidence from second and third parties, led me to move these connections to a note. However, I believe that the coincidences are too profound to not at least mention.

18. Gail Wynand is a particularly apt comparison in this case, and the similarities he shares with J. Jonah Jameson are compelling (but not as compelling as comparisons to Stan Lee, as in the previous note). Jameson is a powerful newspaper-tabloid publisher who opposes everything that Peter Parker stands for and the acts he performs as Spider-Man. In *The Fountainhead*, Wynand is a powerful tabloid publisher who opposes the moral values that Howard Roark claims for himself. In addition, both the characters of Jameson and Wynand are conflicted—or, as Rand and Ditko might say, of mixed premises—and both characters are strong-willed and refuse to bend to the whims of others, until their backs are against the wall. Where the two diverge is that Jameson's *Daily Bugle* seems to be an extension of his very being, whereas Wynand's publication, the *Banner*, does not reflect Wynand's privately held beliefs.

19. Ditko and Lee, *The Amazing Spider-Man Omnibus*, 890.

20. Ditko and Lee, *The Amazing Spider-Man Omnibus*, 892.

21. Rand, *The Romantic Manifesto*, vi.

22. Rand, *The Romantic Manifesto*, 103.

23. Rand, *The Romantic Manifesto*, 99.

24. Rand, *The Romantic Manifesto*, 103.

25. Rand, *The Romantic Manifesto*, 107–9.

26. Ditko makes this point explicit through the voice of Ted Kord, the Blue Beetle, in *Blue Beetle* #5.

27. Quoted in Horowitz, *One Simple Idea*, 97.

28. Steve Ditko, "The Destroyer of Heroes!" *Blue Beetle*, no. 5 (November 1968): 4.

29. Ayn Rand, *The Virtue of Selfishness* (New York: Signet, 2014), 128.

30. Steve Ditko, "Violence the Phoney Issue," *Guts*, no. 5 (1969): 26.

31. Quoted in Horowitz, *One Simple Idea*, 97.

32. Rand, *The Romantic Manifesto*, 106.

33. Ditko and Lee, *The Amazing Spider-Man Omnibus*, 564.

34. Ditko and Lee, *The Amazing Spider-Man Omnibus*, 537.

35. Ditko and Lee, *The Amazing Spider-Man Omnibus*, 564.

36. Ditko and Lee, *The Amazing Spider-Man Omnibus*, 565.

37. Ditko and Lee, *The Amazing Spider-Man Omnibus*, 566.

38. Ditko, *Mysterious Suspense*, no. 1 (October 1968): 2.

39. Ditko and Lee, *The Amazing Spider-Man Omnibus*, 566.

40. Ditko and Lee, *The Amazing Spider-Man Omnibus*, 577 (italics in the original).

41. Sean Howe, *Marvel Comics: The Untold Story* (New York: HarperCollins, 2013), 41.

42. Ditko, *Masters of Comic Book Art*.

43. In the dedication for *Atlas Shrugged*, Rand writes: "*The Fountainhead* was only an over-ture to *Atlas Shrugged*. I trust that no one will tell me that men such as I write about don't exist. That this book has been written—and published—is my proof that they do."

44. Will Eisner and Chuck Cuidera, "Point of View: The Blackhawk Panel Part 1," interview by Mark Evanier, *News from Me* (blog), https://www.newsfromme.com/pov/col305.

45. When Alan Moore and Dave Gibbons revised the Charlton superheroes, they were careful to keep intact the legacy element as a crucial plot element for *Watchmen* in the mid-1980s, with the character Nite Owl operating as an avatar of Blue Beetle. I address the relation-ship between Ditko's superhero comics and *Watchmen* further in later chapters.

46. Ditko was notoriously silent when it came to entertaining the comics press, and with the exception of participating in a few house interviews, his last published interview was in 1968. Even in Ditko's revealing essays and critiques on the history of comics and the creation of certain characters, he rarely reveals substantial information about his (nonphilosophic) narrative intent or the kind of structural strategies he has employed, preferring that his art speak for itself. This places the critic in the difficult position of gleaning Ditko's narrative intent from direct textual evidence and melding it with what is demonstrable about his artistic and literary influences, as well as relevant historical circumstances. Untangling this web is no small task, and it makes anecdotal and peripheral pieces of evidence tempting. For example, in Jonathan Ross's *In Search of Steve Ditko*, Alan Moore offers an oft-repeated anecdote about an incident where Ditko was asked what he thought about Moore's character Rorschach in *Watchmen*. Reportedly, Ditko said he knew the character and that "he's like Mr. A, except insane." Two distinct layers to this story are significant for my analysis. The first is that Moore's story itself tacitly acknowledges that Mr. A and the Question are effectively interchangeable, demonstrating that Ditko was in the habit of repeating and extending the narratives of characters across publications, as has been noted by professional peers. Second, *if true*, this anecdote is an instance of Ditko openly conflating the two characters, and Ditko seems to assume that it was the latter version or that there is no signif-icant feature that distinguishes one from the other. Even if Ditko is *not* acknowledging that these characters are effectively the same, that the two are so easily conflated by both Moore and Ditko would still demonstrate that he carries his narratives between characters. Of course, the largest problem is assuming that the anecdote is true at all. Perhaps it is, perhaps it is only partially true, or perhaps it is like so many stories about Ditko: an invention based on what someone *assumed* about Ditko. Because of this problem, I can't cite it as evidence for my interpretation, but because it is a story that exists as part of the Ditko mythos, I believe it is at least worth acknowledging.

47. Steve Ditko, *The Action Heroes*, vol. 2, DC Archives (New York: DC Comics, 2007), 335.

48. Ditko and Lee, *The Amazing Spider-Man Omnibus*, 957.

49. Ditko, *The Action Heroes*, 2:347.

50. Peale, *The Power of Positive Thinking*, 87.

51. Ditko, *Mysterious Suspense*, 2, 9 (italics mine).

52. I recognize the perceptible incongruity of associating Ditko with Platonic thought, given his substantial interest in Aristotelianism, but this strikes me as the most apt philosophic

comparison. Further, there is no reason to believe that Ditko would not be interested in, or familiar with, the metaphysical aspects of idealism that insist reality, lived experience, is a mental construction—a notion that Ditko plays with throughout his works.

53. Steve Ditko, untitled pinup, *Superman* 1, no. 400 (October 1984): 41.

54. Ditko, *Mysterious Suspense*, 10.

55. Ditko, *Mysterious Suspense*, 26.

56. Ditko, *Mysterious Suspense*, 26.

57. Ayn Rand, *The Fountainhead* (New York: Plume, 2002), 529.

58. Rand, *The Fountainhead*, 3.

59. Ditko, "The Destroyer," 4.

60. Ditko, "The Destroyer," 2.

61. Rand, *The Fountainhead*, 341.

62. Ditko, "The Destroyer," 8–9.

63. Ditko, "The Destroyer," 9–10.

64. Ditko, "The Destroyer," 17.

65. Ditko, "The Destroyer," 18.

66. Peale, *The Power of Positive Thinking*, 8.

67. Ditko, "The Destroyer," 18.

68. An unpublished sixth issue was printed in *The Action Heroes*, vol. 2, DC Archives (New York: DC Comics, 2007), 2.

69. Steve Ditko, ". . . Right to Kill!" *Mr. A*, no. 1 (1973): 25.

6. The Right to Kill

1. Steve Ditko, *The Action Heroes*, vol. 2, DC Archives (New York: DC Comics, 2007), 276.

2. Blake Bell, *Strange and Stranger: The World of Steve Ditko* (Seattle, WA: Fantagraphics Books, 2008), 112.

3. Bell, *Strange and Stranger*, 118.

4. Bell, *Strange and Stranger*, 113.

5. Ditko, *Mr. A*, no. 21 (2017): 2.

6. Horowitz, *One Simple Idea*, 5.

7. Ditko, *Mr. A*, no. 21, 2.

8. Napoleon Hill, *Napoleon Hill's Positive Action Plan: 365 Meditations for Making Each Day a Success* (Plume, 1997), 52.

9. Steve Ditko, ". . . Right to Kill!' *Mr. A*, no. 1 (1973): 25.

10. Ditko, ". . . Right to Kill!" 33.

11. There are notable exceptions to this, particularly with a publisher like Dell, who had the market power to skirt the Comics Code without jeopardizing its access to distribution. The comics scholar Andrew Kunka has produced convincing research about Dell's publishing practices after the implementation of the Comics Code, noting that not only did Dell not submit its comics to the Code offices, but it continued publishing crime and horror comics, genres gutted and all but abandoned after the implementation of the Code. Kunka further notes that Dell, particularly in its comics featuring licensed properties—such as now forgotten TV series like *The 87th Precinct*—provided detailed descriptions of drug use, which were explicitly forbidden by the Code. Kunka's point is not that Dell flouted rules it never agreed to but that "Code violations" were not the exclusive domain of independent and underground comics. Nor were such violations inaccessible to a wide readership. However, Kunka is also careful to note that Dell's "Code violations" likely fell under the radar not because of Dell's power as a publisher but

because "their tepidly transgressive content was not enough to warrant attention from readers, cultural guardians, and future fans and scholars." To this last point, Ditko is relevant, as his transgressions both were aggressive and caught the immediate attention of fans and readers. Andrew Kunka, "Dell Comics and the Comics Code: The Case of *The 87th Precinct*," address transcript, 2017 International Comic Arts Forum, Seattle, WA, November 3, 2017.

12. Steve Ditko, "Violence the Phoney Issue," *Guts*, no. 5 (1969): 24.

13. Steve Ditko, "A Mini-History: *The Amazing Spider-Man #1*," *The Comics*, November 2001, 1.

14. Steve Ditko, *Steve Ditko's 32-Page Package: Tsk! Tsk!* (Bellingham, WA: Robin Snyder and Steve Ditko, 2000), 26.

15. Ditko, *Steve Ditko's 32-Page Package*, 30.

16. Ditko, *Steve Ditko's 32-Page Package*, 20.

17. William James, *Some Problems of Philosophy: A Beginning of an Introduction to Philosophy* (Lincoln: University of Nebraska Press, 1996), 38. See also James's discussion of the "religion of healthy-mindedness" in *The Varieties of Religious Experience: A Study in Human Nature* (New York: Penguin Books, 2015).

18. Ditko, *The Action Heroes*, 2:347.

19. Steve Ditko, "Letter to Mark Strong 9/2/12," Facebook: Steve Ditko Letters, August 28, 2018, https://www.facebook.com/photo.php?fbid=10156587645639770&set=g.279226006163749&type=1&theater&ifg=1 (italics in the original).

20. Steve Ditko, "Letter to Scott Mills 3/14/17," Facebook: Steve Ditko Letters, July 28, 2018, https://www.facebook.com/photo.php?fbid=10156631226879388&set=g.279226006163749&type=1&theater&ifg=1.

21. Steve Ditko, "Letter to Bryan Stroud 10/13/07," Facebook: Steve Ditko Letters, July 9, 2018, https://www.facebook.com/photo.php?fbid=10157612281125760&set=g.279226006163749&type=1&theater&ifg=1.

22. Steve Ditko, "Letter to Daniel Reed 6/13/94," Facebook: Steve Ditko Letters, July 8, 2018, https://www.facebook.com/photo.php?fbid=786185485104304&set=g.279226006163749&type=1&theater&ifg=1 (italics in the original).

23. Ditko, "Violence the Phoney Issue," 24–25.

24. Ditko, *Mr. A*, no. 21, 2 (capitalization in the original; italics mine).

25. A more detailed examination of how Objectivists and libertarians have abused Aristotle to buttress their own imaginations of aesthetics, politics, and ethics likely begins with the work of the early libertarian thinker Albert Jay Nock in his 1943 book *Memoirs of a Superfluous Man*. For further reading on this matter, I again refer the reader to Peter Saint-Andre, "Our Man in Greece: On the Use and Abuse of Aristotle in the Works of Ayn Rand," *StPeter* (blog), entry posted 2009, accessed July 30, 2019, https://stpeter.im/writings/rand/aristotle-rand.html; and Jennifer Burns, *Goddess of the Market: Ayn Rand and the American Right* (New York: Oxford University Press, 2011). The Saint-Andre essay, as discussed earlier, is a useful consideration, and he depends on Burns's book for tracing the history of how Rand and the libertarians came to their interpolations in Aristotle.

26. Steve Ditko, "The Destroyer of Heroes!" *Blue Beetle*, no. 5 (November 1968): 2.

27. Steve Ditko, "My Brother," *Murder*, no. 3 (October 1986): 4.

28. Ditko, "My Brother," 5.

29. Ayn Rand, *The Fountainhead* (New York: Plume, 2002), 413.

30. Ditko, "My Brother," 6.

31. Ditko, "My Brother," 7.

32. Ditko, "My Brother," 8.

33. Ditko, "My Brother," 8.

34. Ditko, *Avenging World*, 49–50.

35. From issue #186, reproduced in Steve Ditko, *Steve Ditko's Strange Avenging Tales* (Fantagraphics, 1997), 23.

36. Norman Vincent Peale, *The Power of Positive Thinking* (New York: Touchstone / Simon & Schuster, 2015), 25.

37. Steve Ditko, *Mr. A*, no. 18 (Bellingham, WA: Robin Snyder and Steve Ditko, 2016), 1 (italics in the original).

38. Ditko, *Mr. A*, no. 18, 5.

39. Ditko, *Mr. A*, no. 18, 8.

40. Ditko, *Mr. A*, no. 18, 14 (italics in the original).

41. Ditko, *Mr. A*, no. 18, 16.

42. Ditko, *Mr. A*, no. 18, 29 (italics in the original).

43. Ditko, *Mr. A*, no. 18, 29.

44. Peale, *The Power of Positive Thinking*, 83–84.

45. Ditko, *Mr. A*, no. 18, 30 (italics in the original).

46. Ditko, *Mr. A*, no. 18, 30.

47. "Pendleton was an influence, so was 'Death Wish' (the book, not the movie) and, of course, the original pulp avenger, The Shadow." Gerry Conway, @gerryconway, Twitter, December 29, 2016, 11:51 a.m., https://twitter.com/gerryconway/status/814514108947001344.

48. Foolkiller is a character created by Steve Gerber and Val Mayerik, and he first appeared in Gerber and Mayerik's *Howard the Duck*. Sadly, Gerber passed away in 2008, long before this project was under way, and I never had the occasion to meet Gerber and ask him about his creations. However, I was able to contact Val Mayerik in 2018, and to his recollection, Gerber made no reference to Ditko, Mr. A, or the Question when discussing Foolkiller and his roots with Gerber. However, with the exception of their collaboration on *Void Indigo*, Mayerik and Gerber rarely discussed Gerber's ideas in depth, and Mayerik was quick to point out that "Steve [Gerber] was well read and a bright guy and would have brought all his knowledge about the world to bear in his writing."

49. Admittedly, Scourge was created more as a plot device to thin out Marvel Comics' cast of villains, and numerous characters have donned the costume and taken up the moniker. However, in appearance and deed, the influence of Ditko and Mr. A seems apparent, as he was a character whose sole purpose was to kill supervillains in the name of justice, and he appears to have the strongest visual reference to Mr. A, with his all-white costume.

50. Brian Garfield, *Death Wish* (New York: Overlook Duckworth, 2013), 77 (italics in the original).

51. Nate Powell, "About Face: Death and Surrender to Power in the Clothing of Men," *Popula*, February 24, 2019, accessed August 8, 2019, https://popula.com/2019/02/24/about-face.

52. *In Search of Steve Ditko*, BBC Four, September 16, 2007.

53. Bell, *Strange and Stranger*, 112.

7. These Magazines Are Haunted!

1. Mark Evanier, foreword to *Creepy Presents Steve Ditko: The Definitive Collection of Steve Ditko's Stories from Creepy and Eerie*, by Steve Ditko and Archie Goodwin (Milwaukie, OR: Dark Horse, 2013), 7.

2. The comics writer Steve Niles makes precisely this case in his introduction to DC's 2010 collection of Ditko Creeper stories. Niles marks himself as a fan of the character and wrote a Creeper miniseries for DC in 2007.

3. Ayn Rand, *The Virtue of Selfishness* (New York: Signet, 2014), 27.

4. Steve Ditko, "He Giveth and He Taketh Away," in *The Avenging Mind* (2008), 21 (italics mine).

5. Steve Ditko and Sergius O'Shaughnessy, "The Isle of Fear," *Beware the Creeper*, no. 3 (September–October 1968): 1 (italics mine).

6. Rand, *The Virtue of Selfishness*, 27.

7. Rand, *The Virtue of Selfishness*, 27 (italics mine).

8. Ayn Rand, *Return of the Primitive: The Anti-industrial Revolution* (New York: Meridian, 1999), 122.

9. Steve Ditko and Steve Skeates, "The Dove Is a Very Gentle Bird," *The Hawk and the Dove*, no. 1 (1968): 7.

10. In a 1999 interview with *Comic Book Artist Magazine*, Skeates recalled: "It was strange. A lot of changes would happen after I turned in a script. Quite often, my idea of what to do with the Dove was [to] have him do brave stuff—and then it would be changed by either Dick [Giordano, the editor] or Steve into the Hawk doing that stuff. They'd say it was out of character for the Dove. They seemed to be equating Dove with wimp, wuss, coward or whatever. And I don't really think it was because they were more hawkish. I just don't think that they knew what a dove was." This is an interesting and important interpretation of events as it relates to how Ditko's Hawk and Dove stories should be understood. In the first case, it is yet another indication that Ditko consistently, when he felt it necessary, took a heavy hand in the plotting and characterization, regardless of the script he received, and any changes were delivered not just visually but as part of the overarching narrative. It is also telling because Skeates did not see Ditko as necessarily being more "hawkish" or conservative but rather observed that a communication breakdown occurred between the collaborators about how the characters were being presented—though perhaps not so much a breakdown as a case of Ditko deliberately developing Don/Dove in a way more consistent with his other characters as opposed to compromising with Skeates's vision. Rather than robbing Dove of his bravery, as Skeates sees it, it seems that Ditko offered a different kind of bravery: the courage of his convictions, even if those convictions are at times unsatisfying or intellectually incomplete. See Steve Skeates, interview, *Comic Book Artist Magazine*, no. 5 (1999).

11. Ditko and Skeates, "The Dove Is a Very Gentle Bird," *The Hawk and the Dove*, no. 1 (1968): 7.

12. Steve Ditko and Steve Skeates, ". . . In the Beginning," *Showcase*, no. 75 (1968): 4 (italics in the original).

13. "Jailbreak!" *The Hawk and the Dove*, no. 2 (1968): 4 (italics in the original).

14. "Jailbreak!" 5.

15. "The Dove Is a Very Gentle Bird," 14.

16. "Jailbreak!" 4.

17. "Jailbreak!" 9.

18. Dale Carnegie, *How to Win Friends and Influence People* (New York: Simon & Schuster, 1964), 183–85.

19. The DC Comics Explosion and Implosion are a fascinating moment in the history of American superhero comics, and although the scope of this book does not warrant a detailed exploration of that moment here, I strongly recommend that readers interested in the material circumstances of how comics are produced and distributed to the public should pursue this topic. Of particular note is Keith Dallas and John Wells, *Comic Book Implosion: An Oral History of DC Comics circa 1978* (Raleigh, NC: TwoMorrows Publishing, 2018), which provides valuable insight from a number of industry insiders regarding one of the several times that comics were thought to be on the brink of collapse because of shifting market forces.

20. Steve Ditko and Michael Fleisher, *The Steve Ditko Omnibus*, vol. 1 (New York: DC Comics, 2011), 174 (italics in the original).

21. Branden, *The Six Pillars of Self-Esteem*, 34 (italics in the original).

22. Branden, *The Six Pillars of Self-Esteem*, 11.

23. *Shade the Changing Man*, no. 7 (June–July 1978): 5.

24. *Shade the Changing Man*, no. 1 (June–July 1977): 17 (italics in the original).

25. Steve Ditko, "The Armed Man!" in *Steve Ditko's Static* (Bellingham, WA: Robin Snyder and Steve Ditko, 2000), 2.

26. "The Exploder," in *Steve Ditko's Static* (Bellingham, WA: Robin Snyder and Steve Ditko, 2000), 18.

27. Blake Bell, *Strange and Stranger: The World of Steve Ditko* (Seattle, WA: Fantagraphics Books, 2008), 148.

28. Ken Parille, "Steve Ditko and the Comic-Book People," Grid, *Comics Journal*, June 27, 2019, accessed June 30, 2019, http://www.tcj.com/steve-ditko-and-the-comic-book-people.

29. Parille, "Steve Ditko."

30. See *Eclipse Monthly*, no. 4 (January 1984). In the letters page of this issue, Dean Mullaney runs three fan letters that complain about Ditko's dialogue—both in form and in length—and Mullaney lays out his own problems with Ditko's "excessive" dialogue, as well as his explanation of why *Static* would be discontinued at Eclipse.

31. "The Armed Man!" in *Steve Ditko's Static* (Bellingham, WA: Robin Snyder and Steve Ditko, 2000), 5 (italics mine).

32. Ayn Rand, "The 'Conflicts' of Men's Interests," in *The Virtue of Selfishness* (New York: Signet, 1964), 58.

33. It is worth noting that Rand specifically positions the Law of Identity as a challenge to what she considers mysticism and subjectivism, by which she means "all those who regard faith, feelings, or desires as man's standards of value." This is all well and good for the parameters that Rand wants to establish for her explanation of Objectivist philosophy, but this line of reasoning does not necessarily contravene the views of mystics like Nathaniel Branden or more explicit practitioners of New Thought who are interested in an observable reality as it relates to the projection of one's own thoughts or the power of the mind. Branden, in his essay "Mental Health versus Mysticism and Self Sacrifice," writes that "the sense of control over reality" is directly related to self-esteem, which, as he argues, "is a *metaphysical* estimate," which is to say a question about the nature of the mind. Ultimately, Rand and Branden define mysticism as a reliance on faith over reason, but as I have shown, not only do practicing mystics call on their own sense of reason, but Branden himself frequently appropriates the language of mystics, specifically that of New Thought. Ultimately, the takeaway here is not that Rand deliberately obfuscated her relationship to practicing contemporary mystics. Rather, it is that her definition of mysticism, while useful for her specific argument, is, in the most generous sense, incomplete when placed within the context of a broader cultural conversation. That broader context demonstrates clear overlap between the ideologies—an overlap that Branden capitalized on through the production of his series of self-help books on self-esteem.

34. Nathaniel Branden, "Mental Health versus Mysticism and Self Sacrifice," in *The Virtue of Selfishness* (New York: Signet, 1964), 41.

35. Although Stac says that he "thought of catching on" just before the energy line appears, there is no indication that he has any conscious notion of achieving such a feat, only that he *wants* it, and he is not fully aware of how his mind is influencing the actions taken by his body through the suit. See "The Armed Man!" in *Steve Ditko's Static* (Bellingham, WA: Robin Snyder and Steve Ditko, 2000), 6–7.

36. "The Exploder," in *Steve Ditko's Static* (Bellingham, WA: Robin Snyder and Steve Ditko, 2000), 16.

37. "The Exploder," 16 (italics in the original).

38. "The Exploder," 16.

39. "Dangerous Moves," in *Steve Ditko's Static* (Bellingham, WA: Robin Snyder and Steve Ditko, 2000), 146–47.

40. Mitch Horowitz, *One Simple Idea* (New York: Skyhorse, 2016), 97.

41. Helen Wilmans, *The Conquest of Poverty* (Sea Breeze, FL: International Scientific Association, 1900), 62.

42. Steve Ditko, "History of the Mocker," in *The Mocker* (Bellingham, WA: Robin Snyder and Steve Ditko, 1990), 103.

43. Ditko addresses this point directly in "ART!?" in *Avenging World* (Bellingham, WA: Robin Snyder and Steve Ditko, 2002), 143–54.

44. "The Mocker and the Wind-Up," in *The Mocker* (Bellingham, WA: Robin Snyder and Steve Ditko, 1990), 96.

45. "The Mocker and the Wind-Up," 97.

46. "The Mocker and the Wind-Up," 102.

47. "The Mocker and the Wind-Up," 102.

48. "The Mocker and the Wind-Up," 98.

8. "If I Like It, I Hope Somebody Else Likes It, Too"

1. Steve Ditko, "Violence the Phoney Issue," *Guts*, no. 5 (1969): 23. It is worth noting that in the opening of this essay where the cited quote appears, Ditko also writes: "While accepting Objectivism as my philosophical base: I am not a spokesman for Objectivism and I alone am responsible for the views expressed here!" This text is the closest Ditko ever came to saying he was an Objectivist, and even setting aside the important bit of hedging he does here, it is worth noting that this phrasing was removed in later reproductions of the essay, beginning in *The Ditko Collection*, vol. 1, in 1985. Thus Ditko specifically removed any verbiage, even if accidentally or inappropriately, that would tie him to being a strict adherent of Objectivism.

2. Quoted in Murray Boltinoff, "Meet the Men behind the Creeper," editorial, *Showcase*, no. 73 (March–April 1968): 25.

3. In the spring of 2018, Robin Snyder and Steve Ditko shared their version of events regarding Ditko's proposal for a new Blue Beetle series. According to their recollections, they turned the proposal in, but the work was never paid for, and neither Snyder nor Ditko ever heard from then DC editor Dick Giordano, whom both had worked with previously. After they confronted Giordano about the lack of payment, Giordano "grudgingly delivered up a check and in handing it over, threatened that Snyder was no longer welcome at DC." No reason was given, in this accounting, for Snyder's expulsion, and nothing ever came of the proposal. Along with the history, Snyder and Ditko reproduced the original proposal, some visual mock-ups of the characters' personal entanglements, and some character sketches. Briefly, the plot picked up with a young Ted Kord, "a dedicated young research scientist who, fresh from college, made an error of judgement in working for his uncle Jarvis, the consequences of which set in motion a monstrous juggernaut of evil." Kord has to reconcile with his complicity and stop the Jarvis Nation, "not from guilt but a cold appraisal that he is responsible for these events." The familiar themes of rational self-reflection and reconciliation appear to run throughout this story, as they did through nearly all of Ditko's work. See Robin Snyder, "The Legend of the Blue Beetle," *Hero Comics*, no. 26 (Spring 2018): 2–13.

4. The irony of the endless perpetuation of *Watchmen* through multimedia licenses, toys, toasters, and other tchotchkes is likely not lost on Moore and Gibbons. For further reading on the politics of *Watchmen*'s content as well as its status as a cultural artifact and keystone for

issues regarding issues surround intellectual property, see Andrew Hoeberek's 2014 study *Considering Watchmen: Poetics, Property, Politics.*

5. Alan Moore, Dave Gibbons, and John Higgins, *Watchmen*, Absolute Ed. (New York: DC Comics, 2005), 431.

6. *Supreme*, as conceived by creator Rob Liefeld, imagines an egotistical and ultraviolent Superman archetype and was later revamped by Alan Moore to operate as a tribute to the Silver Age Superman, in a manner not dissimilar to Moore's classic Superman story *Whatever Happened to the Man from Tomorrow? Supreme* is an interesting case at least because it represents an inversion of the Superman archetype, which is inverted again to act as a kind of tribute to the character and the sincerity the initial version of Supreme rejected. *Superman: Red Son* imagines a world where Superman was raised in the Soviet Union, and *The Authority* is a series that introduced analogues for Superman and Batman (Apollo and Midnighter) who engage in lethal force and are a romantic couple.

7. Moore, Gibbons, and Higgins, *Watchmen*, Absolute Ed., 431.

8. Alan Moore, Dave Gibbons, and John Higgins, "The Abyss Gazes Also," *Watchmen* no. 6 (1987): 10.

9. In an April 2017 letter to the fan Erich Mees, posted to a Facebook group dedicated to Ditko's letters, Ditko writes: "We have people, globally willing to throw away their lives on all kinds of causes, wars. Comic book companies, buyers, readers continue to support ANTI-heroes (anti-mind and life)." The connection Ditko draws between real-world violence and what he sees as the perpetuation of antiheroes is clear. It is not that the media responsible for producing antiheroes are to blame; rather, it is the underlying anti-mind and anti-life world-view that makes both war and antiheroes at once possible and popular. What is necessary is a shift in individual minds and how they see themselves as part of the world. Ditko closes the letter by saying, "One just has to try to do the best one can with no guarantees." See Steve Ditko, Facebook: Steve Ditko Letters update, August 15, 2018, https://www.facebook.com/photo.php?fbid=10215989307501263&set=pcb.317124379040578&type=3&theater&ifg=1.

10. Although there are a number of ex post facto incidents of this, perhaps the most salient example is the paratext included with reprint editions of *Watchmen*, like the one cited in endnote 5.

11. Steve Ditko to Zack Kruse, March 13, 2018.

12. Johann Hari, "How Ayn Rand Became an American Icon," *Slate*, November 2, 2009, accessed January 28, 2019, https://slate.com/culture/2009/11/two-biographies-of-ayn-rand.html.

13. Ayn Rand, "Talk Given at the United States Military Academy at West Point, NY, March 6, 1974," audio file, accessed January 28, 2019, https://ari-cdn.s3.amazonaws.com/audio/ar_library/ar_pwni/ar_pwni_qa.mp3, 00:21:31. See also "Ayn Rand: Talk," Wikiquote, accessed January 28, 2019, https://en.wikiquote.org/wiki/Talk:Ayn_Rand#Native_American_Quote.

14. See note 1.

15. Steve Ditko, "The Cape," *The 32-Page Series: #20ww30ww*, no. 23 (2015): 9–19.

16. Steve Ditko, "A Fantasee," *The 32-Page Series*, no. 26 (2018): 11.

17. Ronald Reagan, "Message on the Observance of Independence Day, 1981," July 3, 1981, accessed January 24, 2019, https://www.reaganlibrary.gov/research/speeches/70381a.

18. Mitch Horowitz, "Reagan and the Occult," *Political Bookworm* (blog), April 10, 2010, http://voices.washingtonpost.com/political-bookworm/2010/04/reagan_and_the_occult.html.

19. Horowitz, "Reagan and the Occult"; Manly P. Hall, *The Secret Destiny of America* (New York: J. P. Tarcher / Penguin, 2008), 118–23.

20. Horowitz, "Reagan and the Occult."

21. Hall, *The Secret Destiny of America*, 122.

22. Steve Ditko and Stan Lee, "The Final Chapter!" *The Amazing Spider-Man*, no. 33 (February 1966): 2.

23. Ditko and Lee, "The Final Chapter!" 3–5.

24. Andrei Molotiu, "Abstract Form: Sequential Dynamism and Iconostasis in Abstract Comics and Steve Ditko's Amazing Spider-Man," in *Critical Approaches to Comics: Theories and Methods*, ed. Matthew J. Smith and Randy Duncan (New York: Routledge, 2012), 89–91.

25. "Dangerous Moves," in *Steve Ditko's Static* (Bellingham, WA: Robin Snyder and Steve Ditko, 2000), 146–47.

BIBLIOGRAPHY

Alter Ego, no. 153 (July 2018).

"Ayn Rand: Talk." Wikiquote. Accessed January 28, 2019. https://en.wikiquote.org/wiki/Talk:Ayn _Rand#Native_American_Quote.

Beerbohm, Robert. "Goodman vs Ditko & Kirby." *Kirby Museum* (blog), February 11, 2012. https://kirbymuseum.org/blogs/dynamics/2012/02/11/goodman-vs-ditko-kirby-by-robert -beerbohm.

Bell, Blake. *Strange and Stranger: The World of Steve Ditko*. Seattle, WA: Fantagraphics Books, 2008.

Benton, Mike. *Horror Comics: The Illustrated History*. Dallas, TX: Taylor, 1991.

Benton, Mike. *Superhero Comics of the Silver Age: The Illustrated History*. Dallas, TX: Taylor, 1991.

Blair, Gwenda. *Donald Trump: The Candidate*. New York: Simon & Schuster Paperbacks, 2015.

Blair, Gwenda. *The Trumps: Three Generations of Builders and a Presidential Candidate*. New York: Simon & Schuster Paperbacks, 2015.

Blavatsky, H. P. *Isis Unveiled: Secrets of the Ancient Wisdom Tradition; Madame Blavatsky's First Work*. Wheaton, IL: Quest Books / Theosophical Publishing House, 2013.

Blavatsky, H. P. *The Secret Doctrine*. New York: Jeremy P. Tarcher / Penguin, 2009.

Blavatsky, Helena Petrovna. *The Key to Theosophy*. Kshetra Books, 2016.

Boltinoff, Murray. "Meet the Men behind the Creeper." Editorial. *Showcase*, no. 73 (March–April 1968).

Branden, Nathaniel. *The Six Pillars of Self-Esteem*. New York: Bantam, 2004.

Brooker, Will. *Batman Unmasked: Analyzing a Cultural Icon*. New York: Continuum, 2001.

Brower, Steven. *From Shadow to Light: The Life and Art of Mort Meskin*. Seattle, WA: Fantagraphics, 2010.

Brühwiler, Claudia Franziska. "'A Is A': Spider-Man, Ayn Rand, and What Man Ought to Be." *PS: Political Science and Politics* 47, no. 1 (2014): 90–93.

Bubnis, Bernie. "'A Life Lived on His Own Terms.'" *Alter Ego*, no. 160 (September 2019): 37–44.

Burns, Jennifer. *Goddess of the Market: Ayn Rand and the American Right*. New York: Oxford University Press, 2011.

Cavendish, Richard. *The Black Arts*. New York: TarcherPerigee, 2017.

"Comic Book Code of 1954." Wikisource. Last modified November 28, 2010. http://en.wikisource .org/w/index.php?title=Comic_book_code_of_1954& oldid=2214276.

Conway, Gerry. "I did like working with Ditko, but our interactions were limited because he drew from full scripts and we met only once (when I hired him to draw Man-Bat)." Twitter, February 21, 2018, 5:10 p.m. EST. https://twitter.com/gerryconway/status/966434879805177856.

Conway, Gerry. "Probably. Ditko Is an Ayn Rand absolutist. I'm a squishy libtard." Twitter, February 21, 2018, 5:03 p.m. EST. https://twitter.com/gerryconway/status/966433152779497472.

Conway, Gerry, Archie Goodwin, and Steve Ditko. "Doomsday—Minus One." *The Destructor*, no. 4 (August 1975).

Cronin, Brian. "Comic Book Urban Legends Revealed #17!" *Comic Book Resources* (blog). Accessed September 22, 2005. https://www.cbr.com/comic-book-urban-legends-revealed-17.

Dallas, Keith, and John Wells. *Comic Book Implosion: An Oral History of DC Comics circa 1978*. Raleigh, NC: TwoMorrows Publishing, 2018.

Ditko, Steve. *The Action Heroes*. Vol. 1. DC Archives. New York: DC Comics, 2004.

Ditko, Steve. *The Action Heroes*. Vol. 2. DC Archives. New York: DC Comics, 2007.

Ditko, Steve. "Anti-Ditko 'Fans.'" *Four-Page Series*, June 2013, 7–8.

Ditko, Steve. "ART!?" In *Avenging World*, 143–54. Bellingham, WA: Robin Snyder and Steve Ditko, 2002.

Ditko, Steve. *The Art of Ditko*. Compiled by Craig Yoe. San Diego, CA: IDW Publishing, 2013.

Ditko, Steve. "At Some Point." In *Avenging World*, 36. Bellingham, WA: Robin Snyder and Steve Ditko, 2002.

Ditko, Steve. *Avenging World*. Edited by Robin Snyder. Bellingham, WA: R. Snyder and S. Ditko, 2002.

Ditko, Steve. "The Avenging World: Part 1." In *witzend*, no. 6, edited by Bill Pearson. New York: Wallace Wood, 1969.

Ditko, Steve. "The Avenging World: Part 2." In *witzend*, no. 7, edited by Bill Pearson. New York: Wallace Wood, 1970.

Ditko, Steve. *The Creativity of Ditko*. Compiled by Craig Yoe. New York: Yoe Books, 2012.

Ditko, Steve. "The Destroyer of Heroes!" *Blue Beetle*, no. 5 (November 1968): 1–18.

Ditko, Steve. *Ditko Package*. Bellingham, WA: R. Snyder and S. Ditko, 1989.

Ditko, Steve. *The Ditko Public Service Package*. Edited by Robin Snyder. Bellingham, WA: R. Snyder and S. Ditko, 1991.

Ditko, Steve. *Ditko's Shorts*. Compiled by Craig Yoe. San Diego, CA: IDW Publishing, 2014.

Ditko, Steve. *Ditko Unleashed! An American Hero*. San Diego, CA: IDW, 2016.

Ditko, Steve. *Dripping with Fear*. Compiled by Blake Bell. Seattle, WA: Fantagraphics Books, 2015.

Ditko, Steve. "Either/Or." *Four Page Series*, June 2015, 12.

Ditko, Steve. "The End Is the Beginning!" *Blue Beetle*, no. 2 (August 1967).

Ditko, Steve. "The Ever Unwilling." *The Comics*, March 2009.

Ditko, Steve. "The Exploder." *Charlton Action: Featuring Static*, no. 12 (December 1985).

Ditko, Steve. "From Out of the Depths." In *Impossible Tales: The Steve Ditko Archives*, compiled by Blake Bell, vol. 4, 145–49. Seattle, WA: Fantagraphics Books, 2013.

Ditko, Steve. "He Giveth and He Taketh Away." In *The Avenging Mind*, 17–21. Bellingham, WA: R. Snyder and S. Ditko, 2008.

Ditko, Steve. *Impossible Tales: The Steve Ditko Archives*. Compiled by Blake Bell. Vol. 4. Seattle, WA: Fantagraphics Books, 2013.

Ditko, Steve. Interview by Bob Greene. *Rapport*, no. 2 (1966). Accessed September 2, 2018. https://ditkocultist.wordpress.com/2012/02/01/steve-ditko-interview-rapport-2-1966.

Ditko, Steve. "An Interview with the Man of Mystery. . . ." Interview by Mike Howell. "Who Is the Question?" Vicsage.com. Accessed August 26, 2019. http://www.vicsage.com/wp/interviews/interview-with-ditko-from-marvel-main-4.

Ditko, Steve. "Letter to Bryan Stroud 10/13/07." Facebook: Steve Ditko Letters, July 9, 2018. https://www.facebook.com/photo.php?fbid=10157612281125760&set=g.279226006163749&type=1&theater&ifg=1.

Ditko, Steve. "Letter to Daniel Reed 6/13/94." Facebook: Steve Ditko Letters, July 8, 2018. https://www.facebook.com/photo.php?fbid=786185485104304&set=g.279226006163749&type=1&theater&ifg=1.

Ditko, Steve. "Letter to Erich Mees 4/16/17." Facebook: Steve Ditko Letters, August 15, 2018. https://www.facebook.com/photo.php?fbid=10215989307501263&set=pcb.317124379040578&type=3&theater&ifg=1.

Ditko, Steve. "Letter to Mark Strong 9/2/12." Facebook: Steve Ditko Letters, August 28, 2018. https://www.facebook.com/photo.php?fbid=10156587645639770&set=g.279226006163749&type=1&theater&ifg=1.

Ditko, Steve. "Letter to Scott Mills 3/14/17." Facebook: Steve Ditko Letters, July 9, 2018. https://www.facebook.com/photo.php?fbid=10156631226879388&set=g.279226006163749&type=1&theater&ifg=1.

Ditko, Steve. Letter to Zack Kruse, January 25, 2015.

Ditko, Steve. Letter to Zack Kruse, March 13, 2018.

Ditko, Steve. *Masters of Comic Book Art*. Directed by Ken Viola. Rhino Home Video, 1987.

Ditko, Steve. "A Mini-History: *The Amazing Spider-Man #1*." *The Comics*, November 2001, 1–4.

Ditko, Steve. *The Mocker*. Bellingham, WA: Robin Snyder and Steve Ditko, 2000.

Ditko, Steve. *Mr. A*, no. 18. Bellingham, WA: Robin Snyder and Steve Ditko, 2016.

Ditko, Steve. *Mr. A*, no. 21. Bellingham, WA: Robin Snyder and Steve Ditko, 2017.

Ditko, Steve. "My Brother." *Murder*, no. 3 (October 1986): 1–8.

Ditko, Steve. *Mysterious Traveler: The Steve Ditko Archives*. Compiled by Blake Bell. Vol. 3. Seattle, WA: Fantagraphics, 2012.

Ditko, Steve. *Out of This World*, no. 25 (Fall 2016).

Ditko, Steve. *Outer Limits: The Steve Ditko Archives*. Compiled by Blake Bell. Vol. 6. Seattle, WA: Fantagraphics Books, 2009.

Ditko, Steve. "Philosophy vs. No- or Anti-philosophy." Editorial. *Out of This World*, no. 25 (Fall 2016).

Ditko, Steve. ". . . Right to Kill!" *Mr. A*, no. 1 (1973).

Ditko, Steve. "Social Justice." *Murder*, October 1986.

Ditko, Steve. *The Steve Ditko Omnibus: Starring Shade, the Changing Man*. Vol. 1. New York: DC Comics, 2011.

Ditko, Steve. *The Steve Ditko Omnibus: Starring the Hawk and the Dove*. Vol. 2. New York: DC Comics, 2011.

Ditko, Steve. *Steve Ditko's 32-Page Package: Tsk! Tsk!* Bellingham, WA: Robin Snyder and Steve Ditko, 2000.

Ditko, Steve. *Steve Ditko's 80-Page Package*. Vol. 2. Bellingham, WA: R. Snyder and S. Ditko, 1999.

Ditko, Steve. *Steve Ditko's 160-Page Package*. Edited by Robin Snyder. Vol. 1. Bellingham, WA: R. Snyder and S. Ditko, 1999.

Ditko, Steve. *Steve Ditko's Static*. Bellingham, WA: R. Snyder and S. Ditko, 2000.

Ditko, Steve. *Strange Suspense: The Steve Ditko Archives*. Compiled by Blake Bell. Vol. 1. Seattle, WA: Fantagraphics Books, 2009.

Ditko, Steve. *The 32-Page Series: #20ww30ww*, no. 23. Bellingham, WA: Robin Snyder and Steve Ditko, 2015.

Ditko, Steve. *The 32-Page Series*, no. 26. Bellingham, WA: Robin Snyder and Steve Ditko, 2018.

Ditko, Steve. *Unexplored Worlds: The Steve Ditko Archives*. Compiled by Blake Bell. Vol. 2. Seattle, WA: Fantagraphics Books, 2009.

Ditko, Steve. *Unknown Anti-war Comics!* Compiled by Craig Yoe. San Diego, CA: IDW, 2018.

Ditko, Steve. Untitled pinup. *Superman* 1, no. 400 (October 1984): 41.

Ditko, Steve. "Violence the Phoney Issue." 2002. In *Avenging World*, 203–7. Bellingham, WA: Robin Snyder and Steve Ditko, 2002.

Ditko, Steve. "Violence the Phoney Issue." *Guts*, no. 5 (1969).

Ditko, Steve. "Why I Quit S-M, Marvel." *Four Page Series*, no. 9 (September 2015): 1–2.

Ditko, Steve, and Michael Fleisher. "The Color Coma!" *Shade the Changing Man*, no. 7 (June–July 1978).

Ditko, Steve, and Michael Fleisher. "Escape to Battleground Earth!" *Shade the Changing Man*, no. 1 (June–July 1977).

Ditko, Steve, and Archie Goodwin. *Creepy Presents Steve Ditko: The Definitive Collection of Steve Ditko's Stories from Creepy and Eerie*. Milwaukie, OR: Dark Horse Comics, 2013.

Ditko, Steve, and Stan Lee. *The Amazing Spider-Man Omnibus*. New York: Marvel, 2016.

Ditko, Steve, and Stan Lee. "The Final Chapter!" *The Amazing Spider-Man*, no. 33 (February 1966).

Ditko, Steve, and Stan Lee. "The Incredible Hulk!" *Tales to Astonish*, no. 60 (October 1964).

Ditko, Steve, and Stan Lee. "Man on a Rampage!" *The Amazing Spider-Man*, no. 32 (January 1966).

Ditko, Steve, and Stan Lee. "Spider-Man!" *Amazing Fantasy*, no. 15 (August–September 1962).

Ditko, Steve, Stan Lee, Don Rico, and Roy Thomas. *Doctor Strange Omnibus*. New York: Marvel, 2016.

Ditko, Steve, and Dennis O'Neil. *The Creeper*. New York: DC Comics, 2010.

Ditko, Steve, and Sergius O'Shaughnessy. "The Isle of Fear." *Beware the Creeper*, no. 3 (September–October 1968).

Ditko, Steve, and Don Segall. "The Coming of the Creeper!" *Showcase*, no. 73 (March–April 1968).

Ditko, Steve, and Steve Skeates. "The Dove Is a Very Gentle Bird." *The Hawk and the Dove*, no. 1 (August–September 1968).

Ditko, Steve, and Steve Skeates. "In the Beginning . . ." *Showcase*, no. 75 (June 1968).

Ditko, Steve, and Steve Skeates. "Jailbreak!" *The Hawk and the Dove*, no. 2 (October–November 1968).

Ditko, Steve, and Steve Skeates. "Kill Vic Sage!" *Blue Beetle*, no. 4 (December 1967).

Ditko, Steve, and Robin Snyder. *Down Memory Lane*. Edited by Robin Snyder. Bellingham, WA: Robin Snyder and Steve Ditko, 2019.

Ditko, Steve, and Robin Snyder. *Steve Ditko's 160-Page Package*. Vol. 3. Bellingham, WA: R. Snyder and S. Ditko, 1999.

Doherty, Brian. *Radicals for Capitalism: A Freewheeling History of the Modern American Libertarian Movement*. New York: PublicAffairs, 2007.

Duggan, Lisa. *Mean Girl: Ayn Rand and the Culture of Greed*. Oakland: University of California Press, 2019.

Eclipse Monthly, no. 4 (January 1984).

Eco, Umberto. "The Myth of Superman." *Diacritics* 2, no. 1 (1972): 14–22.

Eisner, Will, and Chuck Cuidera. "Point of View: The Blackhawk Panel Part 1." Interview by Mark Evanier. *News from Me* (blog). https://www.newsfromme.com/pov/col305.

Evanier, Mark. "And Ditko said the same thing to me in 1970 that he said to Bob Beerbohm." Facebook, September 9, 2019. https://www.facebook.com/stephen.bissette.7/posts/10159059148538289.

Evanier, Mark. "This is an interesting discussion and I'm too busy today to plunge into it but let me throw in a fact that some folks have missed . . ." Facebook, September 8, 2019. https://www.facebook.com/stephen.bissette.7/posts/10159059148538289.

Foucault, Michel. *The Birth of Biopolitics: Lectures at the Collège de France, 1978–1979*. New York: Picador, 2010.

Foxen, Anya P. "Supermen, Mystical Women, and Oriental Others: Dynamics of Race and Gender in Pop-Cultural Yogis and the Universal Superhuman." In *The Assimilation of Yogic*

Religions through Pop Culture, edited by Paul G. Hackett, 35–58. Lanham, MD: Lexington Books, 2017.

Friedman, Milton. *Capitalism and Freedom*. 40th ed. Chicago: University of Chicago Press, 2002.

Garfield, Brian. *Death Wish*. New York: Overlook Duckworth, 2013.

Gateward, Frances K., and John Jennings, eds. *The Blacker the Ink: Constructions of Black Identity in Comics and Sequential Art*. New Brunswick, NJ: Rutgers University Press, 2015.

Gill, Joe, and Steve Ditko. *Ditko Monsters: Gorgo!* Compiled by Craig Yoe. San Diego, CA: IDW, 2013.

Gill, Joe, and Steve Ditko. *Konga!* Compiled by Craig Yoe. San Diego, CA: Yoe, 2013.

Goodrick-Clarke, Nicholas. *Black Sun: Aryan Cults, Esoteric Nazism, and the Politics of Identity*. New York: New York University Press, 2003.

Goodrick-Clarke, Nicholas. *The Occult Roots of Nazism: Secret Aryan Cults and Their Influence on Nazi Ideology*. New York: New York University Press, 2004.

Goodwin, Archie. "Archie Goodwin." Interview by Dwight Zimmerman. *Comics Interview*, no. 36 (June 1986): 24–39.

Goodwin, Archie, and Steve Ditko. "Collector's Edition." *Creepy*, no. 10 (October 1966).

Goodwin, Archie, and Steve Ditko. "Deep Ruby!" *Eerie*, no. 6 (November 1966).

Goodwin, Archie, and Steve Ditko. "Deep Ruby!" In *Eerie Archives*, by Steve Ditko and Archie Goodwin, 23–28. Edited by Shawna Gore. Vol. 2. Milwaukie, OR: Dark Horse Books, 2009.

"Google Books Ngram Viewer: Individualism." Chart. In *Google Ngrams*. Accessed March 2, 2019. https://books.google.com/ngrams/graph?content=individualism&year_start=1800 &year_end=2000&corpus=15&smoothing=3&share=&direct_url=t1%3B%2Cindividualism %3B%2Cc0#t1%3B%2Cindividualism%3B%2Cc0.

Gore, Shawna, ed. *Eerie Archives*. Vol. 2. Milwaukie, OR: Dark Horse Books, 2009.

Gramsci, Antonio. *Selections from the Prison Notebooks of Antonio Gramsci*. Edited by Quintin Hoare and Geoffrey Nowell-Smith. New York: International Publishers, 2014.

Groensteen, Thierry. *The System of Comics*. Jackson: University Press of Mississippi, 2018.

Grossman, Jennifer. "Steve Ditko's Indelible Legacy." Editorial. Atlas Society. Last modified July 9, 2018. https://atlassociety.org/commentary/commentary-blog/6231-steve-ditko-s-indelible -legacy.

Hackett, Paul. "From the Razor's Edge to the Scalpel's Blade: Larry Darrell, Doctor Strange, and the Trope of the Rehabilitated Western Man as Yogi." In *The Assimilation of Yogic Religions through Pop Culture*, edited by Paul G. Hackett, 59–82. Lanham, MD: Lexington Books, 2017.

Hall, Manly P. *The Secret Destiny of America*. New York: J. P. Tarcher / Penguin, 2008.

Haller, John S. *The History of New Thought: From Mind Cure to Positive Thinking and the Prosperity Gospel*. West Chester, PA: Swedenborg Foundation Press, 2012.

Hari, Johann. "How Ayn Rand Became an American Icon." *Slate*, November 2, 2009. Accessed January 28, 2019. https://slate.com/culture/2009/11/two-biographies-of-ayn-rand.html.

Harrison, Peter. "Adam Smith and the History of the Invisible Hand." *Journal of the History of Ideas* 72, no. 1 (2011): 29–49.

Hatfield, Charles. *Hand of Fire: The Comics Art of Jack Kirby*. Jackson: University Press of Mississippi, 2012.

Heer, Bob. "The Curious Incident of the Cut Artwork." *Four Realities* (blog), August 10, 2008. http://fourrealities.blogspot.com/2008/08/curious-incident-of-cut-artwork.html.

Heer, Bob, and Robin Snyder. "Oh, boy. Web of Treachery brings up so, so many good memories of the way it was at Western. If only management had left us alone, it was our intention to give Flash to RK and Ditko and McWilliams." Facebook, October 23, 2018. https://www .facebook.com/groups/robinsnyder/permalink/1105406142955049.

Hill, Napoleon. *Napoleon Hill's Positive Action Plan: 365 Meditations for Making Each Day a Success*. New York: TarcherPerigee, 1997.

Hoberek, Andrew. *Considering Watchmen: Poetics, Property, Politics*. New Brunswick, NJ: Rutgers University Press, 2014.

Horowitz, Mitch. *Occult America: The Secret History of How Mysticism Shaped Our Nation*. New York: Bantam Books, 2009.

Horowitz, Mitch. *One Simple Idea: How the Lessons of Positive Thinking Can Transform Your Life*. New York: Skyhorse Publishing, 2016.

Horowitz, Mitch. "Reagan and the Occult." *Political Bookworm* (blog), April 10, 2010. http://voices.washingtonpost.com/political-bookworm/2010/04/reagan_and_the_occult.html.

Howard, Sheena C., and Ronald L. Jackson, eds. *Black Comics: Politics of Race and Representation*. Repr. ed. London: Bloomsbury Academic, 2014.

Howe, Sean. *Marvel Comics: The Untold Story*. New York: HarperCollins, 2013.

Hultkrans, Andrew. "Steve Ditko's Hands." In *Give Our Regards to the Atomsmashers! Writers on Comics*, edited by Sean Howe, 209–25. New York: Pantheon Books, 2004.

Imes, Rob. "DitkoFAQ—Who Created Dr. Strange?" Official Website of the United Fanzine Organization. Last modified January 15, 2018. http://unitedfanzineorganization.weebly.com/ditkofaq.html#006.

In Search of Steve Ditko. BBC Four. September 16, 2007.

James, William. *Some Problems of Philosophy: A Beginning of an Introduction to Philosophy*. Lincoln: University of Nebraska Press, 1996.

James, William. *The Varieties of Religious Experience: A Study in Human Nature*. New York: Penguin Books, 2015.

Johnson, K. Paul. *The Masters Revealed: Madame Blavatsky and the Myth of the Great White Lodge*. Albany: State University of New York Press, 1994.

Jones, Gerard. *Men of Tomorrow: Geeks, Gangsters, and the Birth of the Comic Book*. New York: Basic Books, 2005.

Jung, Carl Gustav. *The Undiscovered Self*. New York: Signet, 2006.

Karasik, Paul, and Mark Newgarden. *How to Read Nancy: The Elements of Comics in Three Easy Panels*. Seattle, WA: Fantagraphics Books, 2017.

Kelley, David. *The Contested Legacy of Ayn Rand: Truth and Toleration in Objectivism*. Poughkeepsie, NY: Objectivist Center, 2000.

Kirby, Jack, and Steve Ditko. *Machine Man: The Complete Collection*. New York: Marvel Worldwide, 2016.

Kirby, Jack, Stan Lee, and Steve Ditko. "I Am Dr. Druid!" *Weird Wonder Tales*, no. 19 (December 1976).

Kirby, Jack, Stan Lee, and Steve Ditko. "I Am the Fantastic Dr. Droom!" *Amazing Adventures*, no. 1 (June 1961).

Kotz, David M. *The Rise and Fall of Neoliberal Capitalism*. Cambridge, MA: Harvard University Press, 2017.

Kripal, Jeffrey J. *Mutants and Mystics: Science Fiction, Superhero Comics, and the Paranormal*. Paperback ed. Chicago: University of Chicago Press, 2015.

Kruse, Zack. "Doctor Strange and the Racial History of a Marvel Icon." *PopMatters*, March 19, 2019. Accessed August 27, 2019. https://www.popmatters.com/doctor-strange-and-race-2631242477.html.

Kruse, Zack. "Steve Ditko: Violence and Romanticism in the Silver Age." *Studies in Comics* 5, no. 2 (2014): 337–54.

Kunka, Andrew. "Dell Comics and the Comics Code: The Case of *The 87th Precinct*." Address transcript, 2017 International Comic Arts Forum, Seattle, WA, November 3, 2017.

Lachman, Gary. *Dark Star Rising: Magick and Power in the Age of Trump*. New York: TarcherPerigee, 2018.

Lachman, Gary. *Politics and the Occult: The Left, the Right, and the Radically Unseen*. Wheaton, IL: Quest Books / Theosophical Publishing House, 2008.

Leadbeater, Charles W. *The Astral Plane: Its Scenery, Inhabitants and Phenomena*. CreateSpace, 2016.

Lee, Stan. Letter to Jerry Bails, January 9, 1963. Accessed November 25, 2018. http://themarvelage ofcomics.tumblr.com/post/16306907460/a-letter-written-by-stan-lee-to-super-fan-dr.

Lee, Stan. "Superheroes with Super Problems." Interview by Nat Freedland. *New York Herald Tribune*, January 9, 1966.

Lefèvre, Pascal. "Mise en Scène and Framing: Visual Storytelling in *Lone Wolf and Cub*." In *Critical Approaches to Comics: Theories and Methods*, edited by Randy Duncan and Matthew J. Smith, 71–83. New York: Routledge, 2012.

Locke, John. *Locke: Two Treatises of Government, Student Edition*. Cambridge: Cambridge University Press, 1988.

Ma, Jerry, ed. *Shattered: The Asian American Comics Anthology: A Secret Identities Book*. New York: New Press, 2012.

Macpherson, C. B. *The Political Theory of Possessive Individualism: Hobbes to Locke*. Oxford: Oxford University Press, 1962.

Mahares, Russ. "Steve Ditko: Inside His Studio Sanctum Sanctorum." *Pop Culture Squad* (blog), March 16, 2019. Accessed March 19, 2019. https://popculturesquad.com/2019/03/16/steve-ditko-inside-his-studio-sanatorium.

McCloud, Scott. *The Invisible Art: Understanding Comics*. New York: HarperCollins, 1994.

Mehta, Gita. *Karma Cola: Marketing the Mystic East*. New York: Vintage Books, 1994.

Memling, Carl, and John Belfi. "A Grave Situation." *The Thing*, April 1953, 8–14.

Memling, Carl, and Bob Forgione. "A Grave Situation." *The Thing*, April 1953, 24–31.

Mill, John Stuart. *On Liberty, Utilitarianism, and Other Essays*. Oxford: Oxford University Press, 2015.

Mitchell, W. J. T. *Picture Theory: Essays on Visual and Verbal Representation*. Chicago: University of Chicago Press, 1995.

Molotiu, Andrei. "Abstract Form: Sequential Dynamism and Iconostasis in Abstract Comics and Steve Ditko's Amazing Spider-Man." In *Critical Approaches to Comics: Theories and Methods*, edited by Matthew J. Smith and Randy Duncan, 84–100. New York: Routledge, 2012.

Moore, Alan, Dave Gibbons, and John Higgins. "'The Abyss Gazes Also.'" *Watchmen*, no. 6 (February 1987).

Moore, Alan, Dave Gibbons, and John Higgins. *Watchmen*. Absolute ed. New York: DC Comics, 2005.

Morawska, Ewa T. *For Bread with Butter: The Life-Worlds of East Central Europeans in Johnstown, Pennsylvania, 1890–1940*. Cambridge: Cambridge University Press, 1985.

Morrison, Bill. "An Idea in Any Form." Foreword to *witzend*, vii–xiii. Collected ed. Vol. 1. Seattle, WA: Fantagraphics Books, 2014.

Mysterious Suspense, no. 1 (October 1968).

"Mysticism." In *Ayn Rand Lexicon*. Ayn Rand Institute. Accessed October 3, 2018. http://aynrand lexicon.com/lexicon/whims-whim-worship.html.

Nama, Adilifu. *Super Black: American Pop Culture and Black Superheroes*. Austin: University of Texas Press, 2011.

Nemo. "Satanism and Objectivism." In *The Church of Satan*. Previously published in *The Black Flame* 6, nos. 1–2 (1997). Accessed April 8, 2018. https://www.churchofsatan.com/satanism -and-objectivism.php.

Nietzsche, Friedrich Wilhelm. *Spoke Zarathustra: A Book for Everyone and No One Thus.* Translated by R. J. Hollingdale. London: Penguin Books, 1969.

Nock, Albert Jay. *Memoirs of a Superfluous Man.* New York: Harper and Brothers, 1943.

Nyberg, Amy Kiste. *Seal of Approval: The History of the Comics Code.* Jackson: University Press of Mississippi, 1998.

O'Hearn, Martin. *Who Created the Comic Books* (blog). Accessed August 7, 2019. http://martin ohearn.blogspot.com/search/label/Memling%20scripts.

Parille, Ken. "Steve Ditko and the Comic-Book People." Grid. *Comics Journal,* June 27, 2019. Accessed June 30, 2019. http://www.tcj.com/steve-ditko-and-the-comic-book-people.

Peale, Norman Vincent. *The Power of Positive Thinking.* New York: Touchstone / Simon & Schuster, 2015.

Pearson, Bill, ed. *witzend,* no. 3. New York: Wallace Wood, 1967.

Phillips, Nickie D., and Staci Strobl. *Comic Book Crime: Truth, Justice, and the American Way.* New York: New York University Press, 2013.

Pineda, Antonio, and Jesús Jiménez-Varea. "Popular Culture, Ideology, and the Comics Industry: Steve Ditko's Objectivist Spider-Man." *Journal of Popular Culture* 46, no. 6 (2013): 1156–76.

Plencner, Joshua. "Four-Color Political Visions: Origin, Affect, and Assemblage in American Superhero Comic Books." PhD diss., University of Oregon, Eugene, January 14, 2015. Accessed March 7, 2019. https://scholarsbank.uoregon.edu/xmlui/handle/1794/18748.

Polak, Kate. *Ethics in the Gutter: Empathy and Historical Fiction in Comics.* Columbus: Ohio State University Press, 2017.

Postema, Barbara. *Narrative Structure in Comics: Making Sense of Fragments.* Rochester, NY: RIT Press, 2013.

Powell, Nate. "About Face: Death and Surrender to Power in the Clothing of Men." *Popula,* February 24, 2019. Accessed August 8, 2019. https://popula.com/2019/02/24/about-face.

Price, Robert M. "Replies to Chris Matthew Sciabarra's Fall 2002 Article: Fancy Meeting Rand Here." *Journal of Ayn Rand Studies* 5, no. 1 (2003): 215–18.

Rabinowitz, Paula. *American Pulp: How Paperbacks Brought Modernism to Main Street.* Princeton, NJ: Princeton University Press, 2016.

Rand, Ayn. *Atlas Shrugged.* New York: Plume, 1992.

Rand, Ayn. *For the New Intellectual: The Philosophy of Ayn Rand (50th Anniversary Edition).* New York: Signet, 2014.

Rand, Ayn. *The Fountainhead.* New York: Plume, 2002.

Rand, Ayn. *Return of the Primitive: The Anti-industrial Revolution.* New York: Meridian, 1999.

Rand, Ayn. *The Romantic Manifesto: A Philosophy of Literature.* 2nd ed. New York: Signet, 1975.

Rand, Ayn. "Talk Given at the United States Military Academy at West Point, NY, March 6, 1974." Audio file. Accessed January 28, 2019. https://ari-cdn.s3.amazonaws.com/audio/ar _library/ar_pwni/ar_pwni_qa.mp3.

Rand, Ayn. *The Virtue of Selfishness.* New York: Signet, 2014.

Rand, Ayn, Nathaniel Branden, Alan Greenspan, and Robert Hessen. *Capitalism: The Unknown Ideal.* Centennial ed. New York: Signet, 2008.

Reagan, Ronald. "Message on the Observance of Independence Day, 1981." July 3, 1981. Accessed January 24, 2019. https://www.reaganlibrary.gov/research/speeches/70381a.

Reagan, Ronald. "Ronald Reagan's Announcement for Presidential Candidacy." November 13, 1979. Accessed February 10, 2019. https://www.reaganlibrary.gov/11-13-79.

Roach, David, and Jon B. Cooke, eds. *The Warren Companion: The Definitive Compendium to the Great Comics of Warren Publishing.* Raleigh, NC: TwoMorrows Publishing, 2001.

Rosenberg, Morgan D. *Dark Buddhism: Integrating Zen Buddhism and Objectivism.* CreateSpace, 2011.

Rosenblatt, Helena. *The Lost History of Liberalism: From Ancient Rome to the Twenty-First Century.* Princeton, NJ: Princeton University Press, 2018.

Rothbard, Murray N. *Anatomy of the State.* Auburn, AL: Ludwig von Mises Institute, 1974.

Rothbard, Murray N. *Man, Economy, and State with Power and Market.* 2nd ed. Auburn, AL: Ludwig von Mises Institute, 2009.

Rothbard, Murray N. "Praxeology: Reply to Mr. Schuller." *American Economic Review,* December 1951, 943–46.

Russell, Bertrand. *A History of Western Philosophy.* 60th ed. New York: Simon & Schuster, 2005.

Saint-Andre, Peter. "Our Man in Greece: On the Use and Abuse of Aristotle in the Works of Ayn Rand." *StPeter* (blog), 2009. Accessed July 30, 2019. https://stpeter.im/writings/rand /aristotle-rand.html.

Saint-Andre, Peter. *The Tao of Roark: Variations on a Theme from Ayn Rand.* Parker, CO: Monadnock Valley Press, 2013.

Sciabarra, Chris Matthew. "The Illustrated Rand." *Journal of Ayn Rand Studies* 6, no. 1 (2004): 1–20.

Shermer, Michael. *Why People Believe Weird Things: Pseudoscience, Superstition, and Other Confusions of Our Time.* New York: W. H. Freeman, 2001.

Singer, Marc. *Breaking the Frames: Populism and Prestige in Comics Studies.* Austin: University of Texas Press, 2019.

Skeates, Steve. Interview. "DC Comics: 1967–74." Special issue, *Comic Book Artist,* no. 5 (Summer 1999).

Snyder, Robin. "The Legend of the Blue Beetle." *Hero Comics,* no. 26 (Spring 2018): 2–13.

Sollors, Werner. *Beyond Ethnicity: Consent and Descent in American Culture.* New York: Oxford University Press, 1986.

Spooner, Lysander. *The Constitution of No Authority.* Vol. 4 of *No Tyranny.* Boston: Lysander Spooner, 1870.

Stirner, Max. *The Ego and His Own: The Case of the Individual against Authority.* Edited by James Joseph Martin. Translated by Steven Byington. Mineola, NY: Dover Publications, 2005.

Thomas, William. "What Is the Objectivist View of Reality (Metaphysics)?" Atlas Society. Last modified April 5, 2011. Accessed April 8, 2018. https://atlassociety.org/objectivism/atlas -university/what-is-objectivism/objectivism-101-blog/5485-what-is-the-objectivist-view-of -reality-metaphysics.

Tocqueville, Alexis de. *Democracy in America and Two Essays on America.* New ed. London: Penguin, 2003.

Tocqueville, Alexis de. *Recollections: The French Revolution of 1848.* New York: Routledge, 2017. Google Books.

Todd, Mort. "Sorry to hear of Steve Ditko's passing. Steve loved John Severin's work and would pore over his pages when Steve visited our offices." Facebook, July 6, 2018. https://www .facebook.com/groups/131715966970482/permalink/1114350858706983.

Versluis, Arthur. *Magic and Mysticism: An Introduction to Western Esotericism.* Lanham, MD: Rowman & Littlefield, 2007.

Von Mises, Ludwig. *Human Action: A Treatise on Economics.* Scholar's ed. Auburn, AL: Ludwig von Mises Institute, 2008.

Walker, Jeff. *The Ayn Rand Cult.* Chicago: Open Court, 1999.

Webb, James. *The Occult Establishment.* LaSalle, IL: Open Court, 1976.

Weiner, Rachel. "Paul Ryan and Ayn Rand." *Washington Post*, August 13, 2012. https://www
.washingtonpost.com/blogs/the-fix/post/what-ayn-rand-says-about-paul-ryan/2012/08/13
/fd40d574-e56d-11e1-8741-940e3f6dbf48_blog.html?utm_term=.bd6c335ef96b.

Weisinger, Mort, and Mort Meskin. "The Vigilante." *Action Comics*, no. 45 (February 1942):
16–28.

Whaley, Deborah Elizabeth. *Black Women in Sequence: Re-inking Comics, Graphic Novels, and
Anime*. Seattle: University of Washington Press, 2016.

"Whim." In *Ayn Rand Lexicon*. Ayn Rand Institute. Accessed October 3, 2018. http://aynrand
lexicon.com/lexicon/whims-whim-worship.html.

Whitted, Qiana J. *EC Comics: Race, Shock, and Social Protest*. New Brunswick, NJ: Rutgers
University Press, 2019.

Wilcox, Ella Wheeler. *The Heart of the New Thought*. London: Psychic Research Company,
1903.

Wilmans, Helen. *The Conquest of Poverty*. Sea Breeze, FL: International Scientific Association,
1900.

Wolk, Douglas. *Reading Comics: How Graphic Novels Work and What They Mean*. Cambridge,
MA: Da Capo, 2008.

Woo, Benjamin. "An Age-Old Problem: Problematics of Comic Book Historiography." *International Journal of Comic Art* 10, no. 1 (2008): 268–79.

Wright, Bradford W. *Comic Book Nation: The Transformation of Youth Culture in America*.
Baltimore, MD: Johns Hopkins University Press, 2003.

Yang, Gene Luen. *American Born Chinese*. New York: Square Fish, 2009.

Yang, Jeff, ed. *Secret Identities: The Asian American Superhero Anthology*. New York: New Press,
2009.

INDEX

References for illustrations appear in **bold**.

ABOUT THE AUTHOR

Credit: Jen Gusey Photography

Zack Kruse is a comics, film, and American literature scholar. His essays have been published in *Inks: The Journal of the Comics Studies Society*, *Studies in Comics*, and *Critique: Studies in Contemporary Fiction*. His comic strip, *Mystery Solved!*, appeared in *Skeptical Inquirer*, and he is a regular contributor to a number of comic book podcasts.

CPSIA information can be obtained
at www.ICGtesting.com
Printed in the USA
JSHW041553050622
26280JS00001B/65